HOW TO RAISE A
Healthy Child

HOW TO RAISE A

Healthy Child

MEDICAL & NUTRITIONAL ADVICE
FROM AMERICA'S BEST-LOVED PEDIATRICIAN

Lendon H. Smith, M.D.

M. EVANS AND COMPANY, INC.
NEW YORK

M. Evans and Company, Inc.
216 East 49th Street
New York, NY 10017

Library of Congress Cataloging-in-Publication Data

Smith, Lendon H., 1921-
    How to raise a healthy child / Lendon Smith.
        p.   cm.
    ISBN 0-87131-798-2
    1. Children—Health and hygiene. 2. Child rearing. I. Title.
    RJ61.S6625 1996
    649'.4—dc20   95-48019
                                                                          CIP

Text Design by Dutton & Sherman Design
Typeset by Dutton & Sherman Design
Manufactured in the United States of America

9 8 7 6 5 4 3 2 1

Contents

Acknowledgments

Dick Thom, D.D.S., N.D., is in practice in Beaverton, Oregon, and is teaching part-time at the National College of Naturopathic Medicine in Portland, Oregon. He has provided me with some insights and methods of treatment scattered throughout this book. His book, *Surviving the Nineties: Coping with Food Intolerances,* is a basic primer in the identification and control of various sensitivities to which we are all exposed. Published by JELD Publications, Portland, Oregon, 1995.

Belinda Chambers has corresponded with me for some years. She has four bright and talented children, so I knew that she must be the one to go over the manuscript and provide some insights and tell me when I was too far off base.

Lauri Aesoph, N.D., helped me with the sections on preconception, pregnancy, and birthing choices. She has her practice in Sioux Falls, South Dakota.

Nora Tallman, N.D., has been very helpful in indicating that most women can deliver their children with less medical intervention. She works at the Natural Childbirth and Family Clinic here in Portland, Oregon.

Justine Dobson, D.C., L.M.T., of Eugene, Oregon, has been helpful with the Delivery section.

Shirley Lorenzani Sperry is an old friend who has helped hundreds of people with her knowledge of health matters. We almost wrote a book on preconception and pregnancy together. She now lives in Boulder City, Nevada.

Victoria Arcadi, D.C., of Winnetka, California, helped me understand the problems of newborn babies.

Beth Schwartz-Stein, a certified lactation consultant, helped get me started on the right road to information about breast-feeding.

Karen Gromada has been with the La Leche League for a couple of decades and knows the hang-ups and frustrations of mothers who want to breast-feed but cannot seem to get started. Judy Torgus of the LLLI helped me also about breast-feeding.

Jerry Warner of Baton Rouge, Louisiana, has sent me much good and reliable information about the needless circumcisions that are a surgical habit in our country.

Dr. Phillip Incao of Ghent, New York, has been supportive of my position on the vaccines.

Svea Gold is a font of knowledge and helped me to see other methods of treating children rather than "It's a phase; he'll outgrow it." She has been able to show me the validity and science behind neuronal therapy. Her comments are scattered throughout the book. She lives in Eugene, Oregon. Her book, *When Children Invite Child Abuse,* was first published in 1986, by Fern Ridge Press of Eugene, Oregon.

Kathi Williams, director of the National Vaccine Information Center, was very careful to get important information to me so that I could be knowledgeable before I wrote about the vaccines. See Appendix B for their address. They will send information to you.

Dr. Michael Ziff puts out the *Bio-Probe Newsletter.* He has given me great help with the section on mercury fillings. This is a well written and researched newsletter about what we are doing to our teeth (5508 Edgewater Dr., Orlando, Florida 32810; 407/290-9670).

Dr. John Yiamouyiannis is the acknowledged world expert on the history and problems with fluoridation of our water supplies. He has helped me bring that section up to present thinking. He lives in Delaware, Ohio.

Dr. Douglas Dvorak of Cedar Rapids, Iowa, has helped orient and improve my thinking about chiropractic treatments. He is a good, intelligent friend.

Steven Davis, D.C., has his practice and a radio show in Anderson, California. He has shown me the wisdom of chiropractic adjustments for many conditions.

Dr. Roger Tabb is a developmental optometrist here in the Portland area. He has found there is more to the eyes than just seeing. He has helped me understand some hyper kids and what his therapy can do for them.

Florence Scott, R.N., Woodburn, Oregon, is the country's pioneer in helping brain injured and hyperactive children regain their lost nerve connections. Her Northwest Neurodevelopmetal Training Center in Woodburn, Oregon, is able to rescue some of these "throwaway" children (503/981-0635).

Renate Lewin is another intelligent friend who knows about writing and communicating. She has helped remove some non sequiturs and redundancies.

Tracy Smith of Portland, Oregon, is a well-known writer and editor. She is largely responsible for the readability and linearity of this manuscript.

I provided the ambiance.

Preface

I wrote the *Encyclopedia of Baby and Child Care* in 1972. At that time I was in the middle of building my practice, and trying to follow the dictates of standard allopathic care I'd learned in medical school and internship. This was followed by two years as an Army psychiatrist, followed by two years of pediatric residency training. I had the notion that if parents used my book as a reference, they would not need to call me with questions about routine care. The book did save some phone-call time, but people wanted more specifics. "What caused this rash?" "Why does she act so mean?" "Why does he get sick all the time?" I began to wonder myself, "Why do children—or adults—get sick at all?" Do they *have* to get sick? What is the meaning of disease? Is there some sort of lesson here?

I have since studied with chiropractors, naturopathic physicians, and medical doctors who use innovative, natural therapies. They are usually more empathetic toward their patients who have vague complaints and are willing to listen and find connections between diet, pollution, stressors, and symptoms. Diet changes and the use of supplements make big differences in behavior and the incidence of sickness. Really sick people need drugs and skilled surgeons, but at the present time—for me, at least—those methods are further down the list of things to try.

This book is not a comprehensive encyclopedia. Since mine came out in 1972, many others have become available. I have purposely left out many rare and exotic conditions. My emphasis in this book is on those more common conditions I feel need more attention. I hope it will allow parents and child-care specialists to take a new look at what we are doing with, and for, our children.

Rapid growth and development make fetuses, infants, and children more vulnerable to toxins in our air and food than adults. This, plus the damage due to nutrient deficiencies, explains the increased numbers of immunologically and neurologically damaged children doctors are trying to "fix" with drugs today. We need to orient our health and education systems to address the root causes of these disorders. We must salvage our children; they are our hope for the future.

Parents must be in the decision-making loop concerning their children's health. I have also discovered if a mother brings a child in to see me, and I am not sure of the diagnosis or what to do, I will ask her what she thinks is wrong. After all, that child was once a part of her. She knows him/her best. If the mother is intelligent, so much the better.

It is my hope that this book will encourage parents to become more educated, and to be the owners of their own health and that of their children. No single type of healing can solve every problem. Question everything. Get another opinion. Try some of the references in Appendix B. The medical doctor should act only as the lifeguard who comes to the rescue if a life-threatening disease or condition is in progress.

And make sure that your doctor is honoring the Hippocratic oath he/she made at graduation: "First, do no harm."

Introduction

The care and feeding of children has developed as a separate study in medical schools because doctors, researchers, and professors have found that children are different from adults. (Surprise!) Children are more fragile in some regards, and yet tougher and more resilient in other ways than adults. I have devoted my professional life to those differences and what can be done to enhance children's immunity to disease, improve their ability to handle stress, and help them achieve their physical and mental potential. As a pediatrician, I want children to develop a good self-image, look on life as a fun adventure, love other people, live a long, disease-free, nonneurotic life, and die peacefully in their sleep after age ninety or so.

Investigations have shown that if a child is carried, cuddled, and loved, the child will feel good about himself or herself. Never smiling at a baby and simply throwing a bottle at the kid every once in a while is not the way to rear a happy, nonneurotic person. An infant must feel loved, appreciated, and accepted. These feelings become incorporated into the child's concept of his or her place in the family and the community, so that the child can say, "I belong." It is also necessary for the development of a sense of humor and a feeling of security.

There are a few things that can get in the way of this normal progress toward security and feelings of belonging. If the parents are afraid of spoiling the baby, they may be reluctant to hold and cuddle the poor little thing. The baby feels cheated—even angry. Some babies are colicky, feisty, wakeful, and unhappy because they are physically miserable. A food sensitivity, a tight anal ring, a subluxation of a cervical vertebra, or a vitamin or mineral deficiency might be the culprit. Some babies do not like to be held and will stiff-arm their parents as if to say, "You are too close." A reasonable parent might say, "Okay, you don't want me around right now. I'll leave, but I'll be back with some magnesium." This sensitive baby just may be deficient in that mineral.

The premise of this book is to show parents that it is possible to have healthy children who are fun—most of the time—to raise. We all want to be surrounded by healthy, upbeat, vibrant people. We especially want—really need—to live with healthy children who rarely get sick, who willingly go to bed when asked, who sleep through the night, who awaken cheerfully in the morning, who eat what is set before them, and who laugh more than they cry.

It's never too late to make the next generation as resilient as chrome-steel. We don't need any more wimps, losers, greedy jerks, or surly jocks. If we give the childbearing-age adults a good diet and a good self-image, they will be able to pass positive attributes on to the next generation.

I hope this book will give you some choices in childrearing. See if you can find your child in this book. This book provides clues to indicate that some deviation from health is on its way. Health should be a vibrancy—a vitality—not just the absence of a disease with a name. And it is the birthright of *all*.

See if this book shows you some answers or therapies that you have not tried. Love and limits are good rules in bringing up children, but we need some science and common sense also. Be reasonable—do it my way.

HOW TO USE THIS BOOK

If you are looking for a specific disease or problem, look it up in the Index or the Table of Contents. I've left out many conditions that are uncommon.

If your child has already been born, you might want to skip the preconception and pregnancy sections, and read about your child in the appropriate chapters.

I started out wanting to give parents some choices about childrearing and treatment decisions, but the evidence regarding the risks of antibiotic use, immunizations, fluoride, circumcisions, aspartame, and mercury in dental fillings is so overwhelming, I now wonder if I should allow you any choices—at least about those items. Forewarned is forearmed. I hope this book will help you become more involved with the decisions that affect your child. You should be able to raise a healthy, happy child who will bring you joy because you know you had a hand in his/her march to maturity.

Max Planck tells us: "Science progresses not by convincing the adherents of old theories that they are wrong, but by allowing enough time to pass so that a new generation can arise unencumbered by the old errors."

CHAPTER 1

Preconception, Pregnancy, and Delivery

Or What to Do Next Time

If you want to raise a healthy child, you must think ahead. Everything starts somewhere. Human beings start when the sperm meets the egg. A life begins. A healthy human being needs a healthy ovum fertilized by a healthy spermatozoan. The male and female carriers of this human beginning should be as healthy and optimally fed as possible. Like an athlete preparing for an event, some training and preparation will assure a salubrious start. I don't mean training for the sex act itself, but preparing the male and female bodies with the proper nutrients that provide a healthy start to the fetus.

PRECONCEPTION

Raising a healthy child requires **preconception** planning at least for a few months, but better for the lifetime of both prospective parents. Choosing perfect grandparents is difficult, but given less than perfect genes, nutrition can improve a meager hereditary endowment. In general, healthy families have healthy children. Most nutrition-oriented writers point out that major dietetic changes have occurred in this century, prompted by the "need" to extend the shelflife of foods. Mineral- and vitamin-free simple sugar has replaced complex starches. This causes abnormal carbohydrate metabolism, which leads to a lowered resistance to disease, both acute infectious and chronic degenerative.[1] Dr. Jay Rommer put it succinctly: "Since nothing can come out of a human being except from what goes into him, one must assume a close correlation between food and fertility. In general, the more generous the diet, the higher the fertility."[2]

Animal breeders know this. "Humans tend to breed at random. By contrast, stock breeders take every precaution to make sure both bull and cow are healthy. The first time a human usually thinks about health is when the woman is three months pregnant. By that time the organ systems are fully formed, which is too late to do anything."[3]

Nutrition, including vitamins and minerals, are all important to the sperm and ovum at the time when they meet. If the woman becomes pregnant within three months after taking the oral contraceptive pill, the baby may be saddled with congenital anomalies. If the fetus does not get enough zinc during the pregnancy, he may suffer immunologic impairments. This cannot be corrected by the administration of zinc after birth. We take better care of our livestock than we do of ourselves!

The male half of the equation, however, cannot be let off the hook, although his contribution seems minimal compared to the mother's nine-month commitment. He should not be drunk when he impregnates his partner; alcohol is a toxin to the sperm. Vitamin B_{12} deficiency leads to infertility. More than half the infertile men studied by Kumamoto responded to daily injections of B_{12}.[4] If he is deficient in zinc and vitamin C, his sperm may not be as robust as necessary for the fertilization itself. Ascorbic acid protects DNA in human sperm from damage that could affect sperm quality and increase the risk of birth defects. Several hundred milligrams of vitamin C might reduce the risk of birth defects.[5] L-arginine in large doses may be helpful.

The semen of all fathers of babies with congenital anomalies showed a high degree of abnormality (malformed sperm, low count, and poor motility).[6] Iodine metabolism and thyroid function were root causes of malformations as well as miscarriages. Much blame for inability to conceive can be placed squarely on the male and the poor quality and quantity of his spermatozoa. One in twelve modern marriages are barren.

The father's supplements should include zinc, fifteen to thirty milligrams (should be balanced with some copper), one thousand milligrams of vitamin C, plus the B complex vitamins all at about the fifty milligram level daily. (Folic acid is at .4 milligrams, and B_{12} is at the one-milligram level.) Taking a multiple vitamin and mineral capsule including all these and the other known supplements would be wise. The quality and the bioavailability of the supplements are important; ask at the health food store or your naturopathic physician for the best one to take. Ideally the father's age should be between twenty and forty years.

The mother-to-be must get herself in the best possible condition because she is the physical and psychological hostess for the very important first nine months, after which she must hang on to her health and sanity for the next eighteen years of her child's dependency and the PTA. Even before the expected impregnation, she would be smart to eat well. (Forgo the wedding cake and the champagne.) She should also prepare herself emotionally for this great biological fulfillment. The prudent couple planning to conceive a baby should avoid any food that is not whole, and take supplements that will help their bodies detoxify harmful substances they are unknowingly eating and breathing.

The incidence of major birth defects in infants born to women younger than thirty-five years was fifteen in one thousand. From thirty-five to thirty-nine the incidence was seventeen in one thousand. In the forty- to forty-four-year age group, the incidence was thirty-one in one thousand, while for those women over forty-five years, the incidence was seventy-six defective children in one thousand. Women who are twenty to thirty-eight years old at the time of their pregnancies have fewer complications than those younger or older.[7]

One's predisposition to disease is determined by the genes one carries. If, when, and how seriously is up to that person's lifestyle. Genes never act alone; they are influenced by the environment. The environment is a modulator and not the primary determinant. "Genes are the loaded gun, but environmental factors pull the trigger. Eating is one way our environment gains access to our genes."[8] Research indicates that allergies can be controlled if people will eat whole foods, as those foods usually have their full complement of vitamins and minerals. Controlling allergies in a pregnant woman seems to cut down on the chance of allergies in her child.

The Food and Drug Administration (FDA) is reluctant to advise vitamin and mineral supplementation for individuals, even though much evidence indicates we could all be healthier if we took some supplements in amounts greater than the recommended daily allowances. After twenty years of research the FDA has finally admitted that folic acid supplementation does reduce the incidence of neural tube defects. Some women have a genetic susceptibility to produce offspring with neural tube deformities (spina bifida, anencephaly). The Centers for Disease Control now recommends that women of childbearing age take prophylactic doses of folic acid daily.[9] That means up to a milligram of folic acid daily, as the damage may be done before the woman knows she is pregnant. Another study suggests that low folate levels during the pregnancy might cause fetal growth retardation.[10]

A researcher placed 454 women who had previously delivered children with neural tube defects (NTD) on folic acid. The women in the control group (519) received no such supplement. In the supplemented group the incidence of NTD was but 0.7 percent, while in the unsupplemented group the incidence was about seven times greater at 4.7 percent. The results were so dramatic and so obvious that Dr. Smithells, the researcher, stopped the study so that no more children would be born with this defect. His conclusion: Some women are prone to deliver NTD babies, and if they receive the appropriate amounts of certain vitamins, this susceptibility is suppressed.[11] Women who seem to have trouble metabolizing homocysteine (from methionine, abundant in red meat and milk) may be at risk to deliver babies with NTD. Adequate levels of B_6, folate, and B_{12} will convert homocysteine to the harmless cystathionine.[12]

In 1989 a similar study conducted by the Centers for Disease Control followed the pregnancies of over three thousand women. Those who took multivitamins before and during their first trimester had fewer NTD. Not much doubt anymore.

Lancet reported in the August 12, 1995, issue that if a woman takes supplements with folic acid during the pregnancy, her child is less likely to have a cleft lip or palate.

In a study of eighty-five women who had previously delivered children with cleft lips or palates who subsequently took vitamins A, C, D, B_1, B_2, B_3, B_6, folate, iron, and calcium for a new pregnancy, only one woman delivered a child with an anomaly, while in the 219 unsupplemented women, there were 15 recurrences of a cleft lip or palate.[13]

"One of the ironies of medical science is the persistent report of superior health among isolated primitive peoples obtained without benefit of our vast medical knowledge." Cheraskin quoted Kemp, who found that the incidence of stillbirth among the Indians of British Columbia from 1925 to 1929 was about half the rate of the rest of Canada. This low incidence occurred despite the fact that the great majority of these Indian women delivered themselves unaided by medical assistance. The food of these Indians was almost entirely salmon, salmon eggs, and seaweed.[14]

Okay. Now you know.

Here's another one: Mexican immigrants have lower rates of low birth-weight, intrauterine growth retardation, and infant mortality—this despite less prenatal care than white or Mexican Americans. Their cultural orientation includes protective behaviors: less alcohol, drugs, and cigarettes, plus a traditional diet high in vitamins A, C, folic acid, protein, calcium, and iron. They also rely on kinship networks for emotional support.[15]

THE PREGNANCY: A GOOD AND NECESSARY BEGINNING

Once the pregnancy has been confirmed, a birth plan should be agreed upon. With the knowledge, consent, and advice of the accoucheur (birth-assisting professional), decisions should be made early and the wishes of the parents should be made known: hospital, home birth, birthing center? Drug use, yes or no? Cesarean section only if what? Electronic fetal monitor? If the baby is a boy, need he be circumcised? Does the baby have to have the hepatitis B shot? If a pregnant woman is not comfortable with her obstetrician or midwife, she should search for another. She should feel safe and empathetic with her accoucheur. It is a stressful time; she should have as few stressors as possible. What is to be done about pain management during labor? You might ask the accoucheur about the Lamaze, Dick-Read, and Bradley methods. Are hot packs and massage permitted? Is the episiotomy necessary? One Canadian study suggested that there is "no evidence that liberal or routine use of episiotomy prevents perineal trauma or pelvic floor relaxation."[16] Episiotomies are one of the most common surgical procedures in North America, but the study indicated they may not be necessary. How safe or necessary are some of the tests done on the pregnant woman? Ultrasound, amniocentesis, AFP? Don't be afraid to ask. Will your birth-assisting professional let you deliver in the squatting position? (Being more upright helps delivery.)

Ultrasound screening may be unsafe, and is often unnecessary. An Australian study suggested a link between frequent scanning and low-birth-weight babies.[17] Ultrasound exposure in utero has been related to delayed speech.[18] Don't accept "routine testing" unless there is a valid reason.

Prenatal care is a must.

Diet and Weight Gain. A well-rounded diet is obviously important, but no food is so important that it should be eaten every day. Obstetricians seem to insist on a "quart of milk a day to get your calcium." Other foods are rich in calcium also. The rotation diet—which means not eating the same food more frequently than every four days—may keep the fetus from developing food sensitivities. Cow milk and cow-dairy foods are at the top of the sensitizing list. A total weight gain of twenty-five to thirty-five pounds for the nine months is a reasonable, acceptable goal, no matter what the preconception weight is. Dieting to lose weight during the pregnancy is dangerous to both mother and fetus. The total weight gain during the pregnancy is related to the birth weight of the baby. A healthy diet is the cornerstone of both baby's and mother's health.

Sickness, depression, heartburn, constipation, sleeplessness, hemorrhoids, varicosities, indigestion, backache, runny nose, edema, and high or low blood pressure are clues that some physical or nutritional slip has occurred and needs immediate investigation. Usually a nutritional remedy will control these problems safely, as drugs could endanger the fetus. If possible, antibiotic use should be limited, as they will allow for the candida yeast overgrowth, a potential threat to mother and baby.

The woman's mental state must be supported. She should be treated like a queen. Don't believe everything you hear: "Don't eat strawberries; you'll mark the baby." "Don't raise your hands over your head; your uterus will drop."

Exercise. How much for each trimester? Your obstetrician should encourage you with this and tell you how much is appropriate. Exercise enhances the health of mother and baby, makes labor easier, decreases healing time after delivery (even if a C-section is necessary), helps offset unnecessary weight gain and makes it easier to lose weight after birth, offsets fatigue, constipation, and edema. Stretching exercises diminish back pain. Ask your birth coach about the Kegel exercise.

Avoiding Toxins. "Differences in toxicity between children and adults are usually less than a factor of approximately tenfold."[19] All the research indicates that the fetus is more at risk for damage from chemicals, pesticides, and heavy metals than children, and that children are more susceptible than adults. Before World War II the production of synthetic organic chemicals was less than one billion pounds each year. In 1976 the production of these toxins had risen to 163 billion pounds annually. It is still increasing. Some authorities are convinced that there is an association between these released toxins absorbed by the fetus and the increased incidence of hyperactivity, chronic fatigue syndrome, and even cancer later in life.

Clearly what the mother ingests during the pregnancy will affect the baby. Some of the most dangerous agents she should avoid are anticonvulsants (if possible), anticancer drugs, steroids, estrogens, lead (ink, pipes, old paint, autos, dumps),[20, 21, 22] mercury (dental fillings, some types of fish, latex paint),[23] and X-radiation. The adverse effects of prenatal exposure to mercury vapor are increasingly well documented. The mother should not have these amalgam fillings either put in nor removed during her pregnancy. The baby will get some of that mercury.

An irreducible minimum of congenital abnormalities ranges at about 3 to 5 percent. That is, three to five babies per hundred births are born with some obvious problem: congenital heart defect, cystic kidneys, extra fingers and toes, inborn errors of metabolism, Down syndrome, absent parts. A few years ago Surgeon General Koop said that birth defects are present in 7 percent of all births, and in 60 to 70 percent of those births, there is no clue as to the cause. Toxin ingestion and faulty nutrition explain some of these unknowns. Other researchers report different percentages of infants with defects (see page 3).

We all carry some morbid genes around with us, but the incidence of structural and metabolic problems can be reduced with optimal nutrition.

Previously, medical authorities assumed that these birth defects represented chance, or "a roll of the dice." Now we are wondering if a large number of them are due to nutrient deficiencies and unavoidable toxins in our environment. The thalidomide tragedy thirty years ago illustrates this. Pregnant women took the drug to help them sleep. When taken during the first few weeks of the pregnancy, it interfered with the proper formation of their babies' arms. Not every baby of a mother who took thalidomide had that defect, however. (Susceptibility + toxin - proper nutrition = defects.)

If women smoke during the pregnancy, they are more likely to deliver a small baby before term. Examination of the placentae in these cases reveals necrotic (dead tissue) areas responsible for reduced blood flow from the mother. It is called underperfusion. A pathologist in Hershey, Pennsylvania, reported a study of 227 women who smoked in one pregnancy but not in subsequent ones. "The mothers who smoked during one pregnancy and not in another had smaller babies in the smoking pregnancy, irrespective of birth order and many other factors that might affect fetal growth." In his cases it was the smoking itself that determined the difference and not some other constitutional factor of the women.[24]

"Cigarette smoking may have a direct toxic effect on the nervous system, possibly leading to a variety of neurodevelopmental abnormalities, including strabismus (crossed eyes)."[25] Four hundred families were evaluated in Olds's study, which reported: Three- and four-year-old children, whose mothers smoked ten or more cigarettes daily during their pregnancies, had 4.35 lower points on the Stanford-Binet IQ test than other children.[26] Dr. Alexander Schauss has warned us that if a mother smokes during the pregnancy, the fetus may not get enough zinc, as the cadmium in the cigarettes prevents zinc absorption. The baby might be smaller and have a smaller brain. There is cadmium in some coffee beans, also.

Scholl evaluated 818 pregnant women; those with low zinc intake had about twice the risk of having low-birth-weight infants.[27] Low zinc early in the pregnancy was associated with more than a threefold increased risk. In a study by Kisters, et al, serum zinc levels were significantly lower in women with preeclampsia compared to healthy pregnant females.[28] (See page 12 and Zinc, Chapter 3).

The term fetal alcohol syndrome (FAS) was coined in the 1970s when it became obvious that women who drank alcohol during pregnancy frequently produced a child with the following features: growth deficiencies prenatally and postnatally, delay in gross and fine motor development, mental retardation, craniofacial anomalies (small head, small eyes, cleft palate, and small jaw), restricted joint motion, rib anomalies, heart anomalies, neural tube defects, liver dysfunction—just about every tissue showed some anomalous structure. At the University of Washington in Seattle in 1973, fifteen hundred educated middle-class mothers were studied. It revealed that even moderate drinking (less than two cocktails or glasses of wine or beer a day) had palpable effects—both physical and psychological—on their children. The effects of the alcohol were especially damaging if consumed during the first trimester, when the tissues are rapidly forming, usually before a woman knows she is pregnant. Babies of heavy drinkers are more likely to have tremors, keep their eyes open, and turn their heads to the left (a sign of neuronal damage). If a mother smoked heavily along with her drinking, her baby was more likely to yawn, sneeze, and have "dazed-looking" eyes. As they grew it was noted that these babies were slow learners. The damage occurred in the first month or two of the pregnancy. This FAS can be helped with neuronal therapy (see Chapters 8 and 9).

Supplements. Taking supplements to counteract the alcohol and tobacco damage is usually fruitless, but a clean pregnancy plus excellent nutrition will reduce prematurity by at least 50 percent, and virtually abolish such complications as toxemia and eclampsia (high blood pressure and convulsions).[29] It was formerly believed that the mother's body is so large relative to the small size of the embryo that all the building blocks will be provided. Not so. If the proper amounts of protein, minerals, vitamins, and essential fatty acids are not present in the bloodstream of the mother—and thus the placenta at critical times—the baby will not get them. *Bioavailability* is the key word. A deficiency of some nutrient could produce a life-threatening structural defect or a child with a serious mental impairment.

The pioneering work of Dr. Weston Price, catalogued in his book, gives abundant evidence for the nutritional method of avoiding structural and mental damage, and achieving full genetic potential.[30] Dr. Francis Pottenger, in his book, shows that abnormalities that have been considered genetic could be reversed by improved nutrition in the same or in subsequent generations.[31] When the mother eats a diet consisting of depleted food, the result is poorly functioning enzyme systems for her and her children. If the mother is well nourished with plenty of the vitamins and minerals naturally occurring in fresh, raw foods, she is far less apt to suffer from postpartum depression, tooth degeneration, unreliable vision, and other assorted symptoms that have been ascribed to psychological problems.

Our ancestors ate whatever was available before they were eaten by carnivorous predators. Our bodies have not yet evolved to be able to digest and metabolize our modern processed foods. Farmers and veterinarians know what animals can and cannot eat. What is the matter with us that we cannot adopt a healthier diet for ourselves and our children? Until we figure out how to eat more healthily, we must compensate for our impoverished foods by supplementing our diets with raw food concentrates, minerals, and vitamins.

Intelligence and individuality of character are powerfully affected by nutrition, especially during the last three months of prenatal development when brain growth is limited by the availability of nutrients, hormones, and oxygen. Poor women in New York were given a supplement of nothing but vitamin B_1 (thiamine) during pregnancy, and their children later had IQs fifteen points higher than a comparison group. United Nations studies in Latin America showed that a simple supplement of cereal with milk and vitamins during pregnancy and nursing increased the children's brain size and their intelligence, compared with children from nearby villages who were unsupplemented.[32] "Progesterone improved delivery of nutrients like glucose and oxygen to the brain of the fetus and increased its growth and intelligence."[33]

Essential fatty acids (EFAs) are crucial for the integrity of the brain. There is no way to make a superior brain if one misses the opportunity during those early weeks of development, since 70 percent of the total maximum number of brain cells one ever possesses develops during fetal life. The EFA for neural integrity should be at the critical ratio of 1:1 of the omega-3s and omega-6s. Don't give up fat for weight control, but do make sure that you are getting the 3s and the 6s.[34] Dr. William Connor of the Oregon Health Sciences University School of Medicine, Portland, Oregon, says, "Nutrition can affect brain composition and perhaps even brain function." When fish oil is added to the diet, brain cells change their fatty acid content for the better. Pregnant and lactating women especially should eat foods containing omega-3 fatty acids." Eat green vegetables, beans, soy oil, seeds, nuts, and fish. Connor recommends substituting four to five ounces of fish for meat products several times a week.

Here are some general and specific suggestions for the newly pregnant woman:

Weight Gain: About one hundred years ago medical wisdom pronounced that since the baby weighed about six pounds and the placenta about four, the ideal weight gain for the whole nine months of the pregnancy should be limited to ten pounds (probably thought up by a man). That weight allowance became twenty pounds in the 1940s, and some doctors even fined women ten dollars for every extra pound over that. Sensible research indicated that the ideal weight gain should be close to thirty pounds, plus or minus a few depending upon preconception weight and nutrition. Fat deposits around the hips and thighs are a normal part of the pregnant condition. If a woman gains twenty-seven pounds in the nine months, this is how it is all divided up: seven pounds for the baby; three pounds for the increased weight of breasts and uterus; nine pounds for the placenta, amniotic fluid, extra blood volume, and other fluids. The other eight pounds is fat that acts as a reserve for the anticipated breast-feeding.

Dr. Roy Pitkin, professor of obstetrics at the University of Iowa College of Medicine, feels that assaying the pregnant woman's weight gain throughout the pregnancy is more important than the total amount for the nine months. Most of the weight gain in the second trimester is maternal, as the blood volume expands by 50 percent, along with much fat storage. In the last three months most of the accumulation occurs in the fetus.

Robert Zimmerman, Psychology Department of the University of Michigan, says, "At age twelve or more years, the effects of low birth weight were still apparent. Intelligence was down, and emotional disturbances and educational difficulties were present." The subcortical structures were hurt, as indicated by emotional responses to strange stimuli and hyperactivity to adverse stimuli, typical of some hurt to the limbic system (see The Nervous System, Chapter 8). He cannot be attentive and flexible. He cannot deal with stimuli in an efficient manner. He is at a disadvantage in the modern world.

Wrong: The fetus gets all its needs from the mother's tissues. If the nutrients are not floating about in the mother's blood and thence into the placenta, the baby will not get them. The need for iron triples, the need for folic acid doubles, and the need for calcium increases by 50 percent. "Significant differences were noted in the frequency distribution of intelligence quotients between placebo- and vitamin-treated pregnancies."[35] The need for calories only increases by 150 to 350 additional calories per day.

Wrong: If you are overweight, you shouldn't gain weight during the pregnancy. Infants born to obese women who gained little weight during the pregnancy had a high death rate. It would be wise to lose before starting (but not during) the pregnancy. Obese women have a higher rate of diabetes, hypertension, toxemia, and need for a cesarean section than women of normal weight.

Maybe: Salt should be restricted during the pregnancy. The only restriction for salt is if the woman has hypertension and the sodium level in her blood is above 143 milliequivalents per deciliter. (Normal range is between 135 and 143.) Pregnancy causes the body to lose more salt than normally.

Wrong: Food cravings have no special meaning. The body is asking for some nutrient. Women who crave starch, plaster, or clay are usually looking for calcium and magnesium. Eating dirt or ice cubes suggest anemia; a blood test might determine the missing element. Chocolate lovers are looking for magnesium. At six months into the pregnancy many women love ice cream, but need pickles to go with it. Explanation: the baby needs calcium, but the mother somehow knows that it will not be absorbed without some acidic component like acetic acid. During stressful times, people crave the very foods they need; their bodies are trying to tell them which foods to eat.

According to Janie and Kevin Metcalf-Kelly, a healthy diet during pregnancy requires that the mother must eat 25 percent more calories than what she consumed prepregnancy. But the quality is more important than the quantity. Meat and milk are recommended by many authorities, but many people are sensitive to dairy products unless the milk is modified in some way. Many women choose to be vegetarians. One must remember that the pregnancy requires twice as much protein. It is now well established that the edema that precedes eclampsia is due to a low-protein diet. Fluid leaks out of the capillaries because of the lack of osmotic pressure to hold the fluid in the vessels.

True: Protein is very important. Protein deprivation during the pregnancy and the first six months after birth will prevent the formation of important brain cells—the resultant brain has fewer cells than a normal brain, leading to irreversible impairment. This can *never* be made up later. If, however, protein is restricted following the first six months of life (post-delivery), after the brain cells have been formed, the defect can be made up with a good diet later; therefore, the problem is reversible. Nutritional deprivation during the pregnancy may affect the child's cerebral and endocrine functions in adulthood as the brain influences the endocrine system.[36]

THE HEALTH OF THE MOTHER DURING THE PREGNANCY

Fifteen years ago, physicians at the National Institute of Neurological Diseases and Blindness studied fifty thousand mothers and their pregnancies. The director of the NINDB, Dr. Richard Masland, felt we should be less concerned about delivery complications and focus on the health of the mother during the pregnancy. Nineteen mothers on protein-deficient diets during pregnancy had children whose IQs at the age of four were sixteen points below the average of children born to women on more normal diets. Most neurological problems were due to increased prematurity, and infants surviving a lack of oxygen at delivery had only minor neurological defects. If a mother suffered from hypertension, the child's IQ was, on the average, about seven points below the control group's. Children of diabetic mothers had IQs about six points below the control group's. Spastic diplegia (stiff, uncontrolled gait) was noted in 22 percent of premature children. Avoiding premature delivery could save a lifetime of physical, intellectual, and psychological problems.

Preeclampsia (late-pregnancy edema, fatigue, headache, and other distressing symptoms) associated with hypertension occurs in 5 percent of pregnancies. It can usually be controlled with a high-protein diet and rest. "Malnutrition, especially protein-calorie deficiencies, can lead to hypoalbuminemia [low protein in the blood], hypovolemia [low blood volume], hemoconcentration, and a pathological type of generalized edema—which also must not be blindly treated with low-calorie, low-salt diets and salt diuretics."[37] Supplementation with calcium and magnesium might help reverse the tendency to preeclampsia.[38]

The incidence of toxemia among women can be reduced if they are treated with progesterone injections or progesterone suppositories.

Dr. Myron Winick, a professor of nutrition and director of the Institute of Human Nutrition, Columbia University College of Physicians and Surgeons, New York, suggests 1.3 grams of protein per kilogram weight per day.[39] Thus a 120-pound woman should get about eighty grams of good-quality protein daily. He also suggests thirty to fifty milligrams of iron (not iron sulfate; iron citrate or fumarate are safer and better absorbed) daily to eliminate the iron-deficiency anemia that plagues the pregnant woman. Many women need iron but suffer from the side effects of its ingestion: nausea, heartburn, diarrhea, or constipation. If iron is taken with food or vitamin C, it is absorbed more readily and she would need less. Iron-bearing foods include: liver, red meat, egg yolks, dried fruit, prunes, apple juice, beans, lentils, almonds, and walnuts. In a study involving West Java women who were anemic, if iron was given with vitamin A, 97 percent returned to normal hemoglobin levels more rapidly than with the iron alone.[40] But we should not allow pregnant women to take iron without a blood examination to see if it is necessary. (Serum ferritin or serum iron would be more accurate than the hemoglobin test. Excess iron damages the liver, and can interfere with the immune system.)

Those who claim that IQ results are based on genetics alone are wrong. Poverty and accompanying poor nutrition seems to be the cause of many diseases we had thought were due solely to heredity. Work in this area has been carefully excluded from textbooks because it contradicted the dominant belief that intelligence was genetically determined. Mental inferiority is caused in large part by malnutrition and can be remedied by diet, but the remedy must be applied during the pregnancy.

Eating a wide variety of foods in as raw a state as possible is one way of pushing us a little closer to our genetic potential in body structure and mental vigor. Eating impoverished foods will not let us achieve what our genes have promised. So we take extra vitamins and minerals, hoping that our educated guesswork will allow us a semblance of health and an above average IQ. We assume that by doing this we will overcome the twin problems of eating impoverished foods and making those nutrients bioavailable, or at least absorbable.

Although some feel that some extra animal protein—or at least some fish, eggs, dairy, and fowl—are necessary or vital during the pregnancy with its increased need for protein, vegetarians feel that food combined

with grains and legumes, along with some greens, nuts, and seeds, is sufficient. Michael Klaper, M.D., is convinced that a healthy vegan diet (no
meat, no milk) during the pregnancy is compatible with a full-term, normal-
weight infant.[41] (The lactovegetarians will allow themselves some dairy
products.) If the woman decides to be strict, she should at least see that her
blood tests for protein and albumin are in the normal range.

Nikki Goldbeck suggests seventy-five to one hundred grams of protein
a day is optimal.[42] Fifteen grams of protein are supplied by three medium-
size eggs; or two ounces of meat, fish, or poultry; or a half cup of cottage
cheese; or one cup of cooked beans.

Wrong: Vomiting during pregnancy is the symbolic rejection of the
unwanted child. Although if you are curled up around the toilet bowl for three
hours every morning, you begin to wonder. (Some doctors still believe this.)
Now we know that "morning sickness" is physiological. Nausea and vomiting
in the first trimester of the pregnancy is associated with low levels of pyridoxine (B_6) in 50 percent of the mothers. (Low B_6 levels in the body are usually
accompanied by dandruff and poor dream recall.) Eight years ago Tim Bird-
sall, N.D., wrote in the *Townsend Letter for Doctors and Nurses* that the best
treatment protocol is the following: fifty milligrams of B_6 one to three times a
day. (New studies indicate that even thirty milligrams a day will help.) If the
nausea is still present after forty-eight hours, add fifteen milligrams of zinc one
to three times a day. If there is still no relief in forty-eight hours, add one hundred micrograms of vitamin K one to three times a day. Some sufferers get
immediate relief with ginger root (available in capsules). One of my consultants had twenty-four-hour nausea with each of her four pregnancies from
about four weeks along until four months along! She finally got acupuncture
with baby number four and it worked instantly and permanently! Others find
that nibbling on some nourishing food every two to three hours is the best for
them, even setting the alarm for 4:00 A.M. so they can grab a bite of food from
the bedside stand to keep the blood sugar from falling too low. (This is hypoglycemia. It must be the reason why women faint in the old movies or
romance novels.) The metabolism of the pregnant woman is so great that if
she does not eat for eight hours, she has used up her glycogen stores and she
starts to burn fat for fuel, which leads to acidosis. (Fatty acids metabolize to
acetone and acetoacetic acid, which cause nausea.) To counter the acidosis, the
body vomits stomach acid to balance the acid/alkaline status.

Dr. John Ellis uses B_6 to treat edema, eclampsia, cramps, and convulsions, along with the nausea and vomiting.

A lack of vitamin C and magnesium can cause the nausea of early pregnancy. If a woman is not getting enough of the B vitamins in that first trimester, her baby may not get the right building blocks to make a well-developed dental arch and palate. Stop the vomiting so the baby gets the nutrients.

Usually safe, homeopathic remedies: anacardium, cocculus, colchicum, pulsatilla, sepia, ipecac, ignatia, nux vomica.[43]

The nausea and vomiting are partly due to the huge amounts of hormones secreted to keep the fetus in the uterus. The liver must be able to detoxify these hormones and the debris that comes from the implantation of the fertilized egg in the endometrium. It can be alleviated by spinal adjustment, especially of T4 to T8, and the liver-sparing diet. Half a lemon in a glass of water morning and evening will help the liver.[44]

The late gestational tendency to diabetes is associated with a B_6 deficiency. One hundred milligrams of B_6 daily will improve the glucose tolerance.[45] There is danger from megadoses of B_6; one should take no more than 300 milligrams or so daily, and it should be the pyridoxal-5-phosphate form, Dr. Dick Thom reminds us.

OTHER NUTRITIONAL AIDS DURING PREGNANCY

"Nutrients furnish energy and the raw materials for building the metabolic machinery in all living cells, which makes it possible for them to do their specialized work. Many nutrients enter into the makeup of enzymes which catalyze most of the chemical reactions taking place in the body. Digestion, absorption, assimilation, and exercise are all essential parts of nutrition. Nutrients work together as a team and always have constructive uses. Drugs, on the other hand, work alone, usually by interfering with certain aspects of metabolism in such a way as to banish unfavorable symptoms, and thus to appear to confer benefit." Dr. Roger Williams suggests that courses in medical schools should include "genetically oriented nutrition, or nutritionally oriented genetics."[46]

Dr. Abram Hoffer gives some important guidelines about the ideal diet: Try to eat like the Stone Age person.[47] Eat:

1. Whole foods
2. No additives, like MSG, artificial colorings or preservatives
3. Fresh foods
4. Locally grown foods
5. Small amounts frequently

6. A variety of foods; do not eat the same food more frequently than every four days
7. Fish or add omega-3 fatty acids

Calcium intake should be about twelve hundred milligrams per day, depending on how absorbable it is. Many doctors feel that if the pregnant woman drinks about a quart of milk a day, she will get enough calcium to fulfill her needs. That recommendation is difficult if one cannot eat dairy products, and could also be a danger to the baby as daily cow milk intake can make the unborn baby allergic to it before it is born. Salmon, sardines, almonds, and soybeans contain calcium. Rotating with soy milk, goat milk, and rice milk might prevent this sensitization. The following items are known to withdraw calcium from the bones and teeth: coffee, salt, sugar, phosphates in many soft drinks, smoking, and lack of exercise.

Adele Davis suggested that the pregnant woman take calcium, one thousand milligrams, and magnesium, five hundred milligrams, daily during the nine months, but it was especially important during the last few months of the pregnancy. She found that five tablets of dolomite at the onset of labor would take the edge off the pain but not slow the delivery. Calcium and magnesium citramate are safer and more easily absorbed by the body. Babies born to mothers who took bone meal during the pregnancy appeared to have unusually long nails and silky hair. Bone meal also appeared to reduce the incidence of dental caries in the mothers during pregnancy, compared with that of mothers taking dicalcium phosphate.[48]

Magnesium at about 500 milligrams daily is optimal. In a study one group of pregnant women took magnesium as a supplement. A control group received none. The magnesium-treated women had a 30 percent reduction in the risk of being hospitalized for pregnancy-related complications. Hemorrhage and preterm labor were less frequent and the gestation length was greater in the magnesium group. Fewer of their babies needed intensive care.[49] Magnesium deficiency is common in pregnant women.

Zinc intake of thirty milligrams should be accompanied by two milligrams of copper. Zinc deficiency is associated with prolonged and difficult labor. A copper deficiency is associated with stillbirth and fetal resorption. Most diets during pregnancy fall short of zinc and copper unless a woman is on supplements.[50] (The proper ratio is thirty milligrams of zinc to two milligrams of copper, otherwise the metabolism will be distorted.) Dr. Lucille Hurley of the University of California at Davis has recently found in animal studies that zinc deficiency in the mother during pregnancy can result in increased fetal abnormalities.

Vitamin A, ten thousand units. (Larger amounts can possibly lead to birth defects.)

Vitamin D, four hundred units.

Vitamin E, four hundred units. (Fathers who took this had babies with fewer defects.)

Vitamin C, four to ten grams daily. Dr. Frederick Klenner investigated over three hundred pregnancies and felt that pregnancy was stress enough to push the needs of vitamin C up to fifteen grams a day. "The human fetus is a parasite draining available C from the mother."[51] He advocates four grams (four thousand milligrams) daily in the first trimester; six grams daily in the second trimester; eight to ten grams in the third trimester. He obtained excellent results with these large doses of C in women who had been habitual aborters. Hemoglobin was easier to maintain, leg cramps were less as the C enhances the iron, calcium, and magnesium absorption. Stretch marks were seldom encountered. Labor was shorter. No postpartum hemorrhage. Fifty milligrams of C was given to the baby on the second day and was gradually increased. Most people taking large doses of C will adjust the dose to bowel tolerance—that is, up to the amount that just softens up the bowel movements.

Essential fatty acids. These are provided by flaxseed oil, one to two tablespoons. (Udo Erasmus has formulated a mixture of omega-3 and omega-6 fatty acids, called Udo's Choice and available in health food stores; it has the proper proportions of these two essential fatty acids.) Studies by William Connor, M.D., find "the most critical periods of life for providing adequate omega-3 fatty acids would be during pregnancy, with placental transfer of these fatty acids to the fetus, in infancy when there continues to be considerable accumulation of these fatty acids in the brain and retina, and during lactation to supply these fatty acids postnatally."[52]

Vitamin B complex, with fifty milligrams of each of B_1, B_2, B_3, B_6. B_{12}, fifty micrograms.

Folic acid, one to four milligrams.

Iron, thirty to sixty milligrams.

Manganese, iodide, boron, selenium, and other trace minerals are needed.

Other helpful things to try:

The interval between pregnancies, rather than the total number of previous pregnancies, plays the more important role in the cause of intrauterine growth retardation. Ideally the pregnancies should be separated by at least two to three years. Insufficient intrauterine growth may lead to insufficient glycogen stores and resultant hypoglycemia. If the baby is small for its age or premature and susceptible to asphyxia, the baby can rapidly go into metabolic acidosis with respiratory distress syndrome (fluid in the lungs).[53]

Primitive people have long known the dangers of pregnancies too close together. (In some tribes, if a mother conceives a child in less than eighteen months or two years from the birth of the previous child, the members of the tribe will cut up the father in significant ways [!]) Continuous breast-feeding will suppress ovulation, but as a contraceptive method, it is not completely reliable. In the United States, where women tend to eliminate nighttime feedings as soon as possible, ovulation tends to resume sooner.

In many primitive tribes the relatives are willing participants in the pregnancy. When a young girl becomes a woman and may soon become pregnant, the relatives feed her with the best foods they can find. When she becomes pregnant, they will wander far afield to get her a variety of foods. If they are mountain people, they will get fish and kelp from the seashore. If they are people from the plains, they will climb the mountains to get the different foods and animals available there.

Herbal remedies that midwives have been using for centuries:

Blue cohosh will help promote strong, regular labor contractions.

Comfrey root in tea bags, applied topically, assists in the healing of perineal tears.

Dandelion tea and extract can be used as a liver tonic.

Echinacea stimulates the body's immune system to help fight infections.

Goldenseal can be used as an antiseptic and antibacterial. It is best taken by the breast-feeding mother to treat her infant who might have colds, flu, fevers, and infections. It may stimulate uterine contractions, so is not to be taken during the pregnancy.

Ginger as a tea or extract is the time-honored remedy for morning sickness and dyspepsia.

Ginseng is an energy builder and mild stimulant to be used after childbirth.

Red raspberry leaves used as a tea or extract is a pregnancy tonic. It may prevent a miscarriage, and reduce morning sickness. It supports the tone of the uterus.[54]

Not all herbs are safe; Richard Scalzo lists herbs that should not be used during the pregnancy.[55] According to Timothy Herron, however, the following are useful during pregnancy: black haw, dandelion, hawthorn, nettles, red raspberry, skullcap, squaw vine and wild yam. But these should be avoided: barberry, cayenne, ephedra, fennel, goldenseal, juniper, licorice, mistletoe, passion flower, rhubarb, sage, thyme, wild cherry, yarrow, and others.[56]

Chiropractors provide spinal adjustments for the pregnant woman. "During pregnancy the pelvic joints and ligaments are relaxed and capable of more extensive movements. This change allows alterations in the diameter of the pelvis at childbirth. The strain of weight-bearing falls on the ligaments, leading to frequent occurrence of sacro-iliac strain."[57] Dr. Joan Fallon says, "Subluxation is an inherent part of pregnancy and thus the chiropractor's role is defined."[58] Chiropractic care can reduce labor time also. The pregnancy throws off a woman's center of gravity because of the anterior protrusion of the abdomen. A chiropractor can determine if the pelvis and vertebrae are properly balanced. Spinal nerve stress may upset bodily functions and cause disease.[59] "Chiropractors are trained to evaluate functional spinal relationships and can correct them relatively easily, providing comfort for the patient as she progresses with her pregnancy. Women who have had multiple pregnancies noted that the pregnancies under chiropractic care were much easier and the recovery was quicker."[60] Chiropractors can do their work without the use of drugs that could damage the fetus, and they can offer dietary and exercise suggestions as well.

Suggestion for husbands: If your pregnant wife sends you out for ice cream in her sixth month, don't forget to bring back some pickles also. Acidifying the calcium will make it more bioavailable to the mother and the baby. You will have a calmer baby.

A word to the wise: If you do not eat and live correctly, nature will cull you and your posterity out of the picture.

THE DELIVERY

Birth should be as nontraumatic and as natural as possible. In many parts of the world, birth is considered an everyday occurrence requiring only the attendance of older, experienced women. Trusting and obeying the midwife or obstetrician is the best assurance of a normal delivery. The pregnant woman does have several choices.

At one extreme of the American birth spectrum is high tech: high cost, complete with electronic fetal monitoring, fetal surgery, obstetrical anesthesia, and a high percent of cesarean deliveries. Home birth, the other extreme, is high touch: low cost, emphasizing the healthy, family-centered aspects of reproduction. In between these extremes are hospital birthing suites—with homelike decor, staffed by nurses with doctors nearby—and freestanding birth centers, staffed by midwives or naturopathic physicians. There is great variety within this home-to-hospital spectrum. Some birthing centers even offer hot-tub deliveries, which may be a very relaxing environment for a laboring woman.

It wasn't so long ago that giving birth at home was the norm, but both in the United States and around the world, varying events and perhaps cultural attitudes propelled obstetric practices onto different paths in Europe and North America. About one hundred years ago, most European physicians were more than happy to hand over the task of childbirth to midwives. But in North America birthing was moved from a home-based, female-assisted event to one that occurred in the hospital under the control of male doctors.[61] The mother is subjected to medical scrutiny as if something is wrong with her condition.

Just a few decades ago, nearly 100 percent of urban births took place in hospital delivery rooms. Anesthesia during birth was rarely questioned and the doctor was the boss. But the anesthesia slows the birthing events and often requires the use of forceps or vacuum suction. Fathers were not allowed even a supporting role. In 1974 only 10 percent of 180 hospitals in the Los Angeles area allowed fathers to enter the delivery room.

Today Dad has been encouraged to enter that sacrosanct arena of birth. Comfortable birthing suites have appeared in many hospitals. Since labor and delivery take place in the same birthing suite, there is much less disruption of the process. A couch is often available so the father can stay in the same room with his wife.

Rooming-in is now available in most hospitals. This has been most supportive for the breast-feeding mother who is able to nurse on demand, which may be every hour or two in those first few days. Bonding is facilitated. If all goes well, mother and infant are often able to get home just a few hours after the birth.

A birthing center is often located in a refurbished home within a few blocks of a hospital that cooperates with the center in emergencies. The care is given by naturopathic doctors with extra obstetrical training, or by licensed midwives who are registered nurses and have completed an extensive course of accredited study and then have passed a rigorous exam given by the American College of Nurse-Midwives.

The birthing centers usually offer an orientation program for clients.

There is a physical exam, taking of a medical history, and the routine lab tests. Questions are encouraged, and family members are invited to attend. The pregnancy is considered a normal process, not a medical problem. Education of the client is central to the program, so childbirth education classes are routine.

The birth is attended by the midwife or naturopathic physician. Husband/coach, siblings, and/or close friends can be in attendance. The laboring mother is encouraged to move about and experiment with different positions. If the labor does not proceed normally, she will be transferred to a nearby, cooperative hospital.

When the baby is born at the center, the infant is placed in the arms of the mother immediately after the birth. Bonding is not interrupted by weighing, bathing, or examining. After things quiet down the baby is checked for anomalies, and if all is well, the family is on its way home in just two to four hours after the delivery. A postpartum check is usually done within twenty-four hours to watch for problems and support breast-feeding. In a month the mother and baby return to the center for a weigh-in, a pelvic exam, and a question-and-answer session.

These centers are defined as alternative natal care for healthy women. If the pregnant woman is carrying twins, or a breech baby, or has chronic health problems such as hypertension or diabetes, she is referred to an M.D. obstetrician. It is interesting to note that only 3 to 7 percent of the birthing center pregnancies need a C-section delivery, while the national hospital average is close to 25 percent.

A home delivery may be ideal when the pregnancy has been uneventful, the pelvic measurements are adequate, the baby is full-term, and help is available if an emergency arises. Most women choose home delivery if they are not at risk for a difficult delivery, a premature baby, diabetes, or placenta previa. With proper screening and a cooperative, well-trained accoucheur, a home birth can be both safe and very rewarding. A woman can be with her family and friends, and the hospital routine will not distract her from breast-feeding. Home delivery teaches the siblings where babies come from. (The mother has choices. Some want all the children there; some don't.) Dr. Robert S. Mendelsohn says, "Home birth eliminates all the risks of a hospital stay and allows you to spend the time immediately following your family's addition enjoying yourself rather than defending yourself against the intrusions of the hospital staff."[62] The male baby delivered at home is free from the risk of the "routine" circumcision also.

Ultimately a woman must rely on herself to birth her own baby. If she needs support, the father is often best suited to supply it. If he needs to move around, he can boil some water, make coffee, gather newspapers, and video-tape the proceedings. He needs to fulfill his special role at the birth. He is an important member of the team. But the father should not always be expected to be the sole birth coach. First-time fathers are inexperienced and may not be as reliable as we would like. A third party, such as a birth assistant or *doulah,* may be a great help. She also provides continuous, familiar care, espe-cially in a hospital setting where nurses leave after the end of their shift.[63]

If the father talked to his child (via the mother's abdomen, of course) for some months before the delivery, the baby will bond to the father more quickly postpartum. After birth when the baby hears this familiar voice, he/she is alert and aware as if to say, "Well, here's an old friend."

Most women who favor the home delivery appreciate the freedom and control over their environment, and the comfort and familiarity of their own home. Women remember the births of their children even twenty years later. The more in control they felt during delivery, the more positive was the experience. Also, evidence shows that less pain and fear during childbirth means a shorter labor. From time immemorial women delivered in the vertical, squatting position, but in the last century science has con-verted this to the supine, so the obstetrician could see the process more clearly. The water birth is a gentle form of delivery; the baby makes its tran-sition into the world a gradual one. Because the baby is still attached to the mother via the umbilical cord, breathing is not necessary until the baby is lifted out of the water and the placenta is delivered.

A concern of many women is whether they will need a cesarean section. In the past twenty years, the incidence of C-sections has steadily risen from less than 6 percent in 1970 to almost 25 percent in 1990. The Centers for Disease Control says this is way too many. They estimate that in 1991, 349,000 unnecessary sections were performed at a cost of $1 billion.[64] The World Health Organization states that no region in the world is justified in having a C-section rate greater than 10 to 15 percent. The operation carries documented risks to the mother: infections, bleeding, anesthesia compli-cations, and a maternal mortality four times greater than that of a vaginal birth. The infant might be delivered prematurely and is often at risk for res-piratory complications, as his lungs were not compressed during the pas-sage. Mother-newborn bonding is impeded. Forty percent of the sections are repeats, which are two to four times riskier for the mother compared to the vaginal birth.[65] Now mothers are opting for a trial of labor even after a previous section. The reasons for C-section are past section (35 percent), abnormal progress of labor (30 percent), breech presentation (12 percent), and fetal distress (9 percent).[66, 67]

Money is a big incentive to perform C-sections for both the hospital and the doctor. The hospital makes more money because this operation requires longer patient stays, and the doctor can charge more because surgery is involved. The fear of malpractice, another motivator, also spurs obstetricians to choose surgery over a vaginal birth if there is any risk at all to mother or baby. Parents should know that a C-section is major abdominal surgery. But when necessary, it can be lifesaving for the mother and the baby.

Babies delivered via cesarean with no labor may develop breathing problems because the normal mechanical and biochemical forces have been circumvented. Also normal labor releases hormones and increases circulation to vital organs.[68] A trial of labor seems prudent.

The point here is that prospective parents should be free to make well-informed choices about where they want to deliver their children. Childbirth at home is more than gathering newspapers and boiling some water. Your caretaker will give you a list of supplies.

It also seems appropriate to visit a hospital or birthing center well in advance of making any choice. You must be comfortable with the birthing place: home, center, or hospital. If you elect the hospital, be sure to find out about the consent form you sign. It is not necessary to shave your pubic hair, and not everyone needs an enema. You might want to question whether you have to have an episiotomy and if your son should or should not be circumcised.

Hospitals have their place in the childbirth process. If there are complications, modern medical facilities can be a blessing. But when medical interventions become routine, it is time to call a halt to some questionable procedures.

You do have some choices when it comes to selecting your birth attendant. The M.D. obstetrician is one choice, but you may only need him/her if you have complications. A naturopathic physician who has had additional obstetrical training may be just right for you. In addition they can utilize many natural therapeutics to deal with complications of pregnancy and labor. These include herbs, homeopathy, manipulation, and nutritional counseling. A naturopath or a midwife is more likely to give you more options in your care and delivery method. Labor companions have been shown to diminish the rate of intervention substantially—as an example, by almost halving section rates.[69] Richard Horton in the *Lancet* in 1994 suggested that physicians should be paid the same amount for vaginal and cesarean deliveries, so as to remove the financial incentive to operate.

It takes a few months for most mothers to recover from the pregnancy and the birthing stress. "One month after delivery, women still complained of breast problems, fatigue, hemorrhoids, poor appetite, constipation, increased sweating, acne, hand numbness or tingling, dizziness, and hot flashes. Three months after delivery, many of these symptoms continue… while forty percent of mothers also reported pain during sexual intercourse, as well as respiratory infections and hair loss at three to six months."[70] New mothers need a support system. It also sounds as if they need some nutritional counseling, as most of those symptoms sound like deficiencies.

The homeopathic remedy arnica should be taken within minutes of giving birth. It minimizes bruising and promotes healing. It reduces and may stop pain.

Checklist of issues to address before a home birth (courtesy Lauri Aesoph, N.D.):

1. The decision. Make sure this is a decision both parents-to-be agree upon.
2. Education. Learn as much as you can about birthing or delivery options in your city.
3. Classes. Take prenatal classes.
4. Backup. Friends, family, transportation, and emergency care if needed.
5. Prepare your home. Get a list of essentials from your midwife or obstetrician.

CHAPTER 2

The Newborn

Birth to One Month

"A baby is God's opinion that the world should go on."
—Carl Sandburg

There are a number of decisions the parents should make *before* this natal day. Mother Nature has given you about nine months to think about the things that will impact on your child's health for the rest of his/her life. Your choice of a general practitioner, pediatrician, naturopathic doctor, or chiropractor as your main healthcare provider should have been made by this time.

Here are a few rights to which all babies are entitled: To be born to a loving family; to be delivered by a knowledgeable birth attendant; to have as few drugs as possible; to be held and stroked by parents as soon after birth as possible; to be spared unnecessary "routine" medical procedures; to be breastfed on demand; and to receive unconditional love.[71]

THE FIRST FEW DAYS

You have figured out that breast-feeding is the right way to feed your baby, and, with a little help from a lactation expert, you are on your way. The following two things need to be decided upon before this day: *circumcision* and the ***hepatitis vaccine*** shot. If you are to deliver in a hospital, the admitting attendant may have you sign a consent form that includes these two procedures as "routine care." Don't sign anything that gives away your right to decide what is best for your child!

Putting silver nitrate drops in the babies' eyes to prevent gonorrheal ophthalmia has become such a routine that no one seems to question the practice. The assumption is that every woman in the country has gonorrhea. If the child does develop GC ophthalmia, he will have to be treated with a systemic antibiotic. (In Canada a few years ago, a couple went all the way to the Supreme Court of Ottawa and proved to the presiding judge that the woman did not have any venereal disease, and the judge exempted her baby from having the drops put in the eyes at birth: "It means that Canada discovered the first woman in their country who was free of gonorrhea. In the U.S. we are still looking for that woman." Source of quote unknown.)

Mothers should be allowed to hold and bond with their newborn baby right after birth—whether at a home delivery or in the hospital. Mothers should insist vehemently on this right.[72] With all the lights and noises the baby is subject to at that moment of birth, it has to mean stress. Frederick Leboyer, the French obstetrician, suggests, "In order to calm this vast terror, this panic, what is essential is a coming together with the mother, a reuniting." Infants are programmed for the human face at birth.[73] The newborn should be put to the breast immediately after the delivery. No bottle, not even water, is allowed. Don't put the baby alone in a plastic box; babies need that early human contact. If the baby can suck and swallow, it means the nervous system and the intestinal tract are relatively normal.

The Newborn Exam

But before the baby is moved from the mother's pelvis to her chest for some colostrum, a brief search for any abnormal conditions of the head, neck, heart, lung, abdomen, genitalia, and the whole skeleton is next in order. The hips must be checked for any congenital dislocation. Every baby should be tested for this weakness at birth and again at the six-week checkup. Treatment is much easier if the diagnosis is made early; sometimes just bulky diapers are sufficient to force abduction (see Gait Disorders, Chapter 5). The brief inspection of the infant in the presence of the parents is useful to indicate that all is well. A more complete examination of the baby is to be done in the following twenty-four hours with these points in mind:

A chiropractor is most helpful for evaluating the newborn spine at delivery time or shortly thereafter, especially if the baby was born after a tumultuous delivery. A chiropractor who has had experience with newborns would be most appropriate. There are tremendous stresses placed on the neck and head of the baby during the birth process, and these frequently escape diagnosis. Subluxation of the atlas (partial dislocation of the first cervical vertebra) can be the cause of an infant who is irritable, who sleeps for only short periods, and feeds poorly because of irritability in a particular feeding position. **Colic!** The chiropractor's evaluation and treatment can allow the child to develop to his/her full physical and mental potential. Respiratory depression in the neonate is a cardinal sign of injury to the spinal cord or the lower brain stem. In infants who survive there may be lasting neurological defects reflecting the primary injury as cerebral palsy due to lack of oxygen.[74]

We know that many cases of hyperactivity or attention deficit syndrome can be causally related to birth injuries or lack of oxygen at birth. Chiropractors, midwives, and obstetricians frequently work together in the birthing centers in some countries to evaluate spinal problems that may have happened during the birthing process.

Dr. Towbin believes that if the baby does not succumb to the damage to its spinal cord at birth, it may become a later casualty (days or weeks) and the situation be written off as SIDS. He has found that a careful autopsy, including examination of the cervical spinal cord, may reveal an epidural hemorrhage: "A hemorrhagic gelatinous coating over the dural sheath of the cervical cord was evident."[75] (Is it possible that extra vitamin C and bioflavonoids during the pregnancy might prevent some of this hemorrhage?) In many cases the pathologist doing the autopsy might stop when lung congestion is found, and sign out the case on that basis; however, it is the respiratory depression that led to the congestion. The brain stem contains the centers for respiration; this is where the damage occurred: "One cannot find what one is not looking for," and "Manual treatment of birth trauma...could be beneficial to many patients, and it is well within the means of current practice in chiropractic medicine."[76]

When the baby is suspended by its feet, the head should not deviate to one side or the other. If a subluxation is suspected, the adjustment can be made right then. This will save many days of discomfort. This exam is especially important if the delivery has been long and arduous.

At birth the baby is covered with a vernix (a cheesy, off-white substance) that helps to prevent intrauterine maceration of the skin. Only the excess on the face, armpits, and groin needs to be removed; the remainder disappears spontaneously. (Dr. L. Howard Smith, my father, was mentioned in *Time* magazine in 1934 because he found that bathing babies right after birth often led to impetigo. "Leave them alone!" he said. The vernix disappears spontaneously in a few hours. He was labeled "the dirty doctor.") If this vernix and the nails are bile-stained, intrauterine oxygen lack is suggested, as a stressed baby passes stool into the amniotic fluid if anoxia (lack of oxygen) has occurred.

If the baby's heart and lungs are normal, vigorous crying will increase the oxygenation of the red cells, and the skin pinks up. If cyanosis (blue-tinged) is increased with crying and struggling, heart anomalies or lung pathology are surely present. The right side of the heart receives the blood returning from the body, and pumps it into the lungs, where carbon dioxide is removed from the blood and oxygen is picked up by the red blood cells. This blood then returns to the left side of the heart that pumps it out to the body. Defects of formation of the heart develop during the first five to eight weeks in utero. These are fortunately rare, occurring in about one baby in two hundred.

Skin: Blue skin discoloration is produced when five or more grams of hemoglobin per one hundred cubic centimeters of blood are not oxygenated. Frequently a newborn has eighteen to twenty grams of hemoglobin and appears blue-tinged, as it is difficult to oxygenate all that hemoglobin. When he is quiet, breathing shallowly, and with a stomach full of milk, he may appear dusky and/or cyanotic. A few lusty cries, and he pinks up immediately because he has oxygenated all his hemoglobin.

Mongolian spots are blue discolorations of the skin on the lower back and buttocks, characteristically seen on Asian, Indian, and Mediterranean types. This resembles a bruise and fades with age.

The skin of a normal, full-term baby has a soft, velvety texture. Dry, cracked skin suggests postmaturity, which can be associated with lowered oxygen to the brain.

Little white pustulelike spots on the baby's face that resemble acne are called milia, and are considered a reaction to something the mother ate the day before delivery. They disappear in a day or so. A "spider" angioma is a loop of dilated blood vessels found in the skin from which radiate capillaries (like the legs of a spider). They measure only a few millimeters in size. With pressure, the vessels blanch. They fade with time. Stork bites are areas of dilated capillaries (pink skin) on eyelids, center of forehead, and back of neck. They fade by age one or two, but will recur with excitement or crying. (If your five-year-old denies lifting the quarter from your purse, look at the back of his neck; if the red splotch has returned, chances are good he has the quarter.)

Eyes: The cornea is the transparent tissue in front of the pupil and iris through which light must pass. It should be clear. Increased tension of the eyeball, as in glaucoma, can be felt through the eyelids.

Reflexes: The baby should be alert and responsive when awake, suck well, blink her eyes when a bright light is flashed into them or a loud sound is made nearby. She cries and withdraws her foot when pinched. A baby should resist having her face covered with a cloth. Movements of right and left extremities should be equal. When the baby is held prone in the examiner's hand and the spine is massaged, the baby will arch her back and lift her head, arms, and legs in an arc. When she relaxes, her head, arms, and legs will droop with gravity. The normal newborn will make alternating stepping movements when held upright with her soles allowed to touch a smooth surface. When held upright with her trunk in the examiner's hands, if the top of her foot is placed against the edge of a table, she will bend her knee, lift up her foot, and step onto the tabletop. If all these tests are present, her nervous system is adequate.

Experts in neurodevelopment have found that these primitive, automatic reflexes should disappear after they have served their usefulness. If they are retained after certain specific times, it suggests developmental delays. The orderly development and myelination (insulation) of the central nervous system is genetically determined. Hurts to the nervous system due to birth injury, lack of oxygen, nutritional, vaccine damage, febrile, and toxic insults may truncate this orderly march to maturity. One can expect symptoms and signs of those hurts to appear later in childhood, depending upon what level of the brain was injured (see Cerebral Dysfunction, Chapter 9). The following reflexes should appear and then be replaced or stored away:

Example: **the Moro reflex.** When the new baby is moved suddenly, subjected to bright light or loud noise, or is roughly handled, she will show the startle response with arms extended and hands opened, then gradually bring her arms across the body into a clasping posture—instinctively trying to hug her mother. This reflex is an immature "flight-or-fight" type of response to a threat, and is accompanied by an adrenaline release, a deep breath, an increase in heart rate, and a rise in blood pressure. It is a primitive survival mechanism directed from the brain stem that alerts the baby— and the mother—that something dangerous is happening: "Help me! I don't understand! I'm scared!" The swat on the bottom when the lethargic baby is born is intended to initiate this first "breath of life"—the Moro reflex has saved the baby's life.[77] When the baby boy is circumcised, he is strapped down and cannot perform this protective reflex; he is obviously panicked. Suggestion: Don't let him be circumcised. He has had enough trauma from the delivery; he may get suspicious about his parents' love if they let some stranger do *this* to him. (See Circumcision, this chapter.)

If this crude response does not turn off, the emerging child will be hypersensitive and will overreact to stimuli and be emotionally immature.

The **palmar reflex** is present at birth and represents another primitive life-saving response. A light touch to the palm of the newborn's hand will make his fingers close on the stimulus. (One can imagine the baby clinging to the mother for dear life while they swing through the trees.) Sucking movements will often elicit this palmar reflex and kneading movements in the hands, a sign that hands and mouth are already connected at that stage. If a child is having a hard time learning to write, he will make constant movements with his lips while writing. This connection is called the Babkin response.

Asymmetrical tonic neck reflex (ATNR), also called the fencing reflex: When the head is turned to one side, the arm and leg on that side will extend, while the arm and leg on the opposite side will flex. This reflex should disappear by six months of age. This ATNR reflex is important for muscular and vestibular (inner ear) stimulation as well as helping the baby in her passage through the birth canal. It is the first eye-hand coordination to take place, as if the brain knows that the head and eyes are turned to the hand that might be holding an object.

The rooting reflex is a lifesaver for the newborn. Just a light touch to the lips or the cheeks will cause the baby to turn her head toward that stimulus, open her mouth, and extend her tongue to initiate the sucking that begins breast-feeding. It is obviously present at birth, is strongest in the first few hours after birth, and then weakens somewhat if not used. (Put the baby to breast as soon as possible after the delivery.) A premature baby stuck in the incubator can be seen rooting, and if this reflex has not been fully utilized at the appropriate time, it may still show up in a weakened form after it should have disappeared normally.

Spinal Galant (lateral hip flexion) and **tonic labyrinthine reflex** (forward and backward) provide the newborn a method of response to the problem of gravity. **Symmetrical tonic neck reflex,** flexion and extension, appear for just a few months in the second half of the first year of life and allow the baby to rise up onto hands and knees. These reflexes facilitate the development of locomotion and eye-hand coordination. "It is through creeping that the vestibular, proprioceptive (internal stimuli), and visual systems combine to operate together for the first time, to provide a sense of balance, space, and depth."[78] (See Reflexes, Chapter 4.)

The genitals are the external sex organs. Parents are well advised to call these organs by their proper names and not "privates," "bottom," "down there," or "peepee place." (Find out what term is used in your neighbor-hood so you won't be surprised someday when your child comes home with a new anatomical name.) The male has a penis and a scrotum (or bag, often temporarily enlarged, especially if he was a breech delivery) contain-ing two testicles. The head of the penis (or glans) has an opening for urine and sperm (urethral orifice) that should be a one-sixteenth-inch slot—not a pinpoint hole.

Circumcision is the surgical amputation of some or all of the foreskin that covers the glans or head of the penis. (If you have your baby in the hospital, you will be asked to sign a consent form that usually includes the "routine" circumcision.) The foreskin is a mobile sheath of skin con-taining sensitive nerve endings and a mucous membrane that covers and protects the glans, keeping it soft, moist, and sensitive. During the oper-ation the foreskin must be torn away from the glans with a blunt probe as these two tissues have not yet separated naturally. This very painful tear-ing creates scarring and thickening over the normal mucosal surface of the glans, which results in progressive sensitivity loss that will affect your son as an adult.

During sexual activity, the *intact* foreskin slides back off of the glans and covers the tumescent shaft. The skin is loosely attached so there is freedom of motion back and forth over the body of the erect shaft. The erect and turgid penis of the *circumcised* male has none of this mobile skin, since what is commonly termed a "small snip" (when the doctor is minimizing the surgery) actually removes what would become one third to one half of the penile skin necessary to accommodate a full and comfortable erection. Those erections in the circumcised male are often painful, and the sex act must be well lubricated or the friction is disturbing to both participants. Since many of the sensitive nerves have been removed when the foreskin is cut off, the sex act may be less than satisfactory. Women who have had sex with both circumcised and intact males often comment that the intact penis offers a level of lubrication and comfort not found with the abnormally taut and dry circumcised penis. (Maybe the prudish authorities who thought the male should be circumcised felt that sex would not be so important if the fun part was removed.)

The practice of medical circumcision in the United States became prac-tically universal in English-speaking countries prior to its present-day decline.[79] It began in the nineteenth century when it was believed that it would stop masturbation, which "everyone knew" caused all sorts of diseases, from psychosis to epilepsy and bed-wetting, in addition to hair growing from the palm of the hand of the miscreant.[80]

Reasons for NOT circumcising:

• Circumcision does not prevent cancer in later life; cancer of the penis is found in the circumcised as well as in the intact.

• Circumcision does not have a significant impact on the incidence of urinary tract infections.

• The American Academy of Pediatrics, the American College of Obstetrics and Gynecology, and the American Pediatric Urological Society have stated there are no valid medical indications for the routine newborn circumcision.

• It is surgery. There are risks. The penis can be damaged. Newborn circumcision accidents are usually settled out of court and require parents to remain silent about the mishap. Bleeding has caused rare deaths. Infections in the wound are not uncommon. There are psychological scars as well.[81, 82] If your doctor is a circumcision advocate, ask him why he wants or needs to perform this procedure on your son: There are no valid reasons for this operation.

• Circumcision is a needless, destructive, and harmful surgical routine. The foreskin protects the head of the penis (glans) from diaper rash, urine, and feces. A diaper irritation can produce ulcers just inside the meatal opening of circumcised boys. When they heal the opening is but a small pinpoint, instead of the normal one-sixteenth inch slit. This may cause back pressure and hurt the bladder and the kidneys. (See Urinary Difficulties, Chapter 11.)

• The newborn foreskin is almost always adherent to the underlying glans. Some doctors feel this is congenital phimosis, and a vigorous effort must be made to break up those adhesions by a forced retraction of the foreskin. This is a dangerous practice as it usually leads to scar tissue, which may require a circumcision later on. Studies have shown that only four out of one hundred babies have a foreskin retractable at birth. Even 50 percent of ten-year-olds had some adhesions. Close to 100 percent of boys have a fully retractable foreskin at age seventeen. If adhesions were present in adolescence, it was usually due to forcible retraction in infancy and subsequent scarring.

• This "rape of the penis" is becoming less of a routine in the United States, especially since some insurance companies will not pay for the operation unless truly medically indicated. Foreskinectomy still generates a quarter billion dollars per year in revenue for physicians and hospitals.[83] Now, with less chance of payment, some doctors are losing interest, but they still acquiesce to the wishes of the parents. Furthermore, some insurance companies feel that if they do not pay for this surgery, parents will look elsewhere and premiums will be lost. The incidence in Britain is down to less than one half of one percent as the National Health Service has not paid for it since 1949, because, as they report, "It serves no useful purpose." (Gairdner's "The Fate of the Foreskin," published in the *British Medical Journal,* caused the NHS to stop payments.) In Sweden, Germany, and France, less than 5 percent of male infants are now circumcised. In the United States it is running about 60 percent, but less (perhaps about 30 percent) on the West Coast.[84]

In Europe circumcision has never been routinely performed except for members of the Jewish faith. The *bris* is performed when the boy is eight days old and this ritual is integral to Judaism, as is the circumcision ceremony performed on Muslim boys. The original Jewish *bris* was begun as a blood ritual, not because of hygiene. It removed only the distal tip of the foreskin, leaving most of it for protection, comfort, and pleasure. Modern Jewish and non-Jewish circumcisions are much more radical, removing the entire foreskin. Many Jews are now by-passing this ritual, as they have come to better understand that maternal heritage is the most important factor in determining one's Jewishness. Now they have a naming ceremony without the blood ritual.

In August 1993 Louanne Cole, Ph.D., columnist for the *San Francisco Examiner,* wrote: "Isn't it insulting to the average male's intelligence to think that surgery is preferable because he can't be entrusted with washing his genitals when somehow he manages to brush his teeth, clean his ears, and blow his nose?"

• Some authorities feel that the only reason to continue circumcision is so boys won't feel "different" in the locker room. "Circumcision has moved from being a medical issue to one of social custom."[85] However, with circumcision rates declining, plus the growing foreskin restoration movement, it may well evolve that the circumcised boy is the one who is "different." Regardless, many circumcised men believe conformity is not the issue. They feel respecting the child's rights to body ownership and self-determination is a more important consideration than "matching" Dad or the guys.

• The most obvious reason for stopping this assault on the penis is that it is so very painful to the helpless little boy. If mothers and fathers were forced to watch this mutilation, they would never consent to have it done to their sons. Even with anesthesia, there is nothing that can eliminate the overwhelming pain of this surgery or its postoperative agony. The best way to avoid the pain is to avoid the circumcision. These issues aside, circumcision forever deprives your son of making his own choice and of knowing his full sexual functioning as nature intended.

A San Francisco Bay Area nurse, Marilyn Fayre Milos, tried to educate parents, nurses, and doctors at the hospital where she worked. She gave parents the information she wished someone had given her before her own sons were circumcised. She helped the new mothers say "No" to the surgeons. "I believe every parent has the right and an obligation to know the consequences of a surgery most of the world scorns," she declared. Hospital officials told her not to talk to patients about circumcision because some of them became upset when she told them what circumcision is, what would actually be done to their baby, how the baby reacts, and the consequences. "The baby is a patient, too," she said, "and no one is more upset by circumcision than he is." In 1985 the hospital fired her.[86]

She believes it is a human rights issue. Milos reports on the convention in 1989 of the First International Symposium on Circumcision. The group adopted tenets including:

"The inherent right of all human beings to an intact body... a basic right."

"Parents or guardians do not have the right to consent to the surgical removal of their children's normal genitalia."

"The only persons who may consent... are the individuals who have reached the age of consent"

"Physicians who practice routine circumcision are violating Article V of the United Nations Declaration of Human Rights: 'NO ONE SHALL BE SUBJECTED TO TORTURE OR TO CRUEL, INHUMAN, OR DEGRADING TREATMENT...'"

Here is the complete article by Paul Fleiss, M.D., a pediatrician in Los Angeles, entitled "Care of the Intact Penis: Leave it alone!"

If it ain't broke, don't fix it. Summary: Leave it alone.

The female genitalia consist of two labia (or lips) that converge at the pubic bone over the clitoris. The latter may be slightly enlarged at birth but is usually completely covered by the labia by childhood. Upon separation of the labia, the vaginal opening is about one-fourth inch in diameter, the bottom margin formed by the hymen, a crescent of tough but tender tissue.

The urethral opening, about halfway between the clitoris and the vaginal opening, is a barely detectable pinhole. The most common adhesion seen is in infant females; the labia may be joined together, producing an abnormal appearance to the vaginal opening. If the opening of the urethra is occluded, the adhesion may be separated by the application of an estrogen cream. Forceful tearing apart of the labia is painful, and the raw edges are more likely to readhere. Because this problem is almost never seen in the older girl, we assume it relieves itself.

Breasts of the newborn baby are usually enlarged as a result of the mother's hormones that passed through the placenta. Even some milk (witch's milk) may be expressed from them. (Don't do it, though; infection may follow.)

The anal ring is a membranous tissue, like the iris of a camera, found in one quarter of all babies at birth. Its location, about half an inch inside the anal opening, serves as a partial obstruction to the easy passage of the stool and is a cause of colic. It is not serious but can cause grunting and straining at bowel movement time. A lubricated little finger inserted gently into the rectum for about an inch at that first exam will diagnose it. A drop of blood followed by the passage of a stool will be the reward when the finger is removed. The baby hates this invasion but will sigh with relief afterward. ("Thanks, Doc, I needed that.") Most mothers will then comment on how relaxed and easy the baby became after this manipulation. This finger test is also the treatment and saves the baby much colic.

Immunizations: The first big medical/political/philosophical question facing the parents of any newborn is whether to have their child immunized. Parents must be alert, as hospital babies will get the hepatitis B injection on the first day or so of life if the parents assume the hospital knows best, and have signed the consent form unknowingly.

The hepatitis B virus is transmitted through blood or body fluids. If the mother is chronically infected with that virus as determined by a blood test (carrier rate is 0.1 percent of the population), it makes sense to immunize the baby, as the vaccine is 90 percent effective. The American Academy of Pediatrics states: "To reduce transmission of HBV [hepatitis B virus] as soon as possible and, eventually, to eliminate it, universal immunization is necessary."[87] (And the babies are accessible.)

This seems laudable if the vaccine (HBV) could give permanent immunity (immunity to HB lasts just a few years), if you are a carrier, or your child might grow up to be a prostitute, a drug addict, an active homosexual, or a needle user. The American Academy of Pediatrics (AAP) again: "The need for booster doses will be assessed as additional information becomes available." "Allergic reactions after the HBV have been reported but appear to occur infrequently." However, the newborn liver may become dysfunctional as a result of this shot.

Who gets this HBV? According to the AAP, the newborn is to get one on that first day or two; it is repeated in the one- to two-month-old, and again in the eighteen-month-old toddler. Are you a bad parent if you refuse to have your child get this shot? Answer: No. It does not make sense to load a vulnerable newborn's immune system with an antigen that he/she does not need. The parents should take the responsibility of what goes into their baby. (See Chapter 7 for information about the other vaccines.)

Down syndrome is a genetic condition manifested by mental retardation, short stature, hypotonic musculature, umbilical hernia, epicanthic eyelid folds, protruding furrowed tongue, small teeth, and a simian crease in the palms. Most cases are felt to be due to a chromosomal breakage and fertilization of an egg with twenty-four chromosomes instead of twenty-three. Each body cell thus contains forty-seven chromosomes, which apparently distorts maturation enough to produce the above anomalies. Chromosome analysis of the child and parents may be helpful in evaluating the risk of recurrence. About one child in seven hundred has Down syndrome, and the incidence increases along with the mother's age. An Israeli study reported in 1994 showed a higher risk of the Down syndrome in women who have borne more than six children.[88]

Some parents, when told by their doctor that they have a Down syndrome child, elect to have the child placed in an institution. However, more and more parents now rise to the challenge of rearing a different child. The parents are the decision makers and must be comfortable with their choice. Friends, relatives, and family doctors must support their decision, whatever it is. They should be aware of the high incidence of the following:

- Fatal heart anomalies can occur.
- Leukemia incidence is twenty times higher in Down children than in others.
- Down children have a poor immune system and have about one hundred times the rate of respiratory infections.
- Most are sensitive to dairy products.
- Many have a subluxation at the atlantoaxial junction (partial dislo-

cation at the first and second cervical vertebrae; chiropractic care can be very helpful).[89]

- Many are deficient in thyroid hormone.
- They frequently have hearing, speech, and visual difficulties.

To some parents the situation is a devastation, but many parents have felt rewarded from the experience of rearing their child with these problems. According to Dr. John Unruh, "They can give the child an efficient nervous system capable of processing information in an organized manner."[90] Within the genetically determined guidelines, "there is plenty of room for environment to play a significant role." The behavior of these children can vary from socially acceptable (high-functioning) to obstinate and overreactive. (The ones who need to be institutionalized have uncontrollable behavior that the families cannot tolerate or change.) Unruh believes that these children need an "individual success-oriented program that will be motivating and productive, even if it takes longer."

As we now know, brain function can be improved by imprinting appropriate pathways into the nervous system. As infants, Down children need floor time with crawling and creeping. Appropriate doses of vitamins and minerals and even the use of thyroxin hormone have improved mental and physical functioning in many children with this condition.

Breast-feeding: Your baby has been born with all parts intact and your life will never be the same! No matter where or how the delivery took place, the baby and your breast need each other. They were made for each other. "No matter what the cicumstances of your babies' birth, it is possible to breast-feed. Mothers have breast-fed multiples when they have had a cesarean birth, 'surprise twins,' premature babies, complications related to the delivery, small children at home, little or no household help, work outside the home, or a combination of several of the above difficulties. You can feel confident in your body's ability to adapt to your particular situation."[91] We hope you have had the opportunity to learn about breast-feeding by attending a breast-feeding mothers' support group meeting, such as a La Leche League gathering, during your pregnancy. Prenatal breast-feeding classes are available in many areas, too. A certified lactation consultant (LC) also may be consulted a few months before delivery to dispel worries and to offer instruction, encouragement, and support.

Early problems that sometimes discourage mothers from continuing breast-feeding are: (1) baby's response to an inexperienced parent's "rough" handling during latch-on, (2) improper positioning of baby at the breast, resulting in sore nipples; (3) infrequent or ineffective breast-feedings due to a sleepy baby, or a hospital or self-imposed schedule, giving bottles or pacifiers with subsequent poor breast-milk production; and (4) mishandling of severe engorgement.

A full-term, healthy newborn usually is alert and actively searching for the first meal at the mother's breast within thirty to ninety minutes of birth. You should not miss this golden opportunity, because after this period the baby's interest may diminish a bit for hours or days. If you are feeling tired after the delivery, ask a nurse, midwife, or lactation consultant to help you bring your baby and your breast together for the first time or two.

Nothing should get in the way of this mutual supportive and health-giving union. Keep baby with you and cuddle chest to chest after birth. This helps your baby regulate body temperture; it also allows you to take advantage of your baby's early feeding cues, such as sticking the tongue out, rooting, and bringing those little hands close to the mouth. Early feeding cues tell you that your baby would like another lesson in latching on to the breast. Your baby may have more difficulty and you may find it more frustrating if you wait for the last feeding cue, which is crying, before beginning a breastfeeding. If you are not yet certain that what you are seeing are feeding cues, attempt to breast-feed every half hour or so until you catch your baby at the best time. No bottles allowed for your alert and latching baby. The confusion this produces often leads to poor breast-feeding patterns for your baby and to sore nipples and decreased milk production for you.

Get comfortable before putting your baby to breast. Prop up your feet and put a pillow under the arm supporting the baby's body. Your baby's head and body should be in a straight line, as it is difficult to swallow when one's head is turned. (Try it.) When using either a cradle or cross-cradle hold, "roll" your baby's body toward your body so that you are belly to belly. Many women, out of sheer exhaustion, learn how to nurse their babies while lying down, both in bed and on the couch. One can be quite creative with the use of pillows to facilitate this. If you hold him so his head is slightly tipped back, he will be able to breathe more easily. When baby's head rests snugly in the crook of your arm or you use one hand to cup the back of baby's head and neck, your baby will still be able to adjust the position of the head without feeling "smooshed" into the breast.

Once your baby is in position, support your breast by placing your finger underneath and your thumb on top, so that your hand forms a large *C* around the breast and looks as if you are holding a large sandwich. Be sure your hand is well behind the areola, especially those fingers underneath, as you don't want to cover any of the area where baby's mouth needs to be. You may express a few drops of colostrum (with its valuable antibodies) to get the action started. Then touch your nipple to your baby's lower lip and watch the demonstration of the open-mouth reflex. Make sure that the baby's mouth is wide open—like a yawn—with the tongue down and protruding over the lower gum. Only then is the baby's head drawn against the breast so that the gums latch on over the milk-storing reservoirs (lactiferous sinuses) located just beneath the areola, and the baby's lips flare out to cover most or all of the areola. Don't let your baby just suck or hang on your nipple itself; he must take a large portion of the stretchy areola into his mouth. It is called breast-feeding—not nipple-feeding—for a reason! Nipple-feeding is responsible for many cases of sore and cracked nipples. If it is not comfortable, something is wrong. So break the suction by putting a (clean) finger between your baby's upper and lower gums, and start over. Breast-feeding should feel so comfortable—after a few tries—that you might even drop off to sleep.

In a seven-year study of one thousand newborns observed and treated for breast-feeding difficulties, a chiropractor found 80 percent had a birth-induced temporomandibular joint (TMJ) dysfunction. In all cases the babies were treated with cranial and spinal adjustments, with excellent results in 99 percent of the cases. Birth trauma caused a cranial distortion leading to TMJ dysfunction, which interrupted proper sucking mechanisms. Headaches and gastrointestinal disturbances were the result.

When the baby has completely latched on to the areola, his tongue rolls from front to back against his hard palate. This drains the milk from the lacteals; a back-and-forth movement of the mandible is essential for this manipulation. With a TMJ malfunction, the baby cannot open his mouth wide enough and thus is unable to latch on completely—sore, bleeding nipples are the result. Breast engorgement follows. Baby wants to suck all the time because of hunger, but can never get satisfied. The mother has a frowning, nervous, frustrated, colicky baby; she feels the same and tends to give up nursing.

Only 1 to 5 percent of women have some physical problem that interferes with their ability to breast-feed. Even twins, triplets, or more can be breast-fed successfully; the breast is a very efficient factory, and the quantity of milk produced is based on the demand placed upon it. Your baby's "emptying" of the breasts during feedings is the only way to stimulate milk production. (They are never really emptied. More milk is always being made.) The key to establishing and maintaining sufficient milk production is to breast-feed often—about eight to twelve times every twenty-four hours.

"The baby needs to get the milk as much as the breasts need to be stimulated. It is better to awaken a sleeping baby."[93]

A normal, alert baby knows how long to feed. Unrestricted, or demand, breast-feeding—not just occasional nibbling—is best for both participants; rooming-in is the best way to achieve this in the hospital. Babies have different personalities and different feeding styles. One baby may look at the breast and seem to know precisely what to do from the get-go. Another takes it slow and easy. "Drive-through" babies are fast and efficient feeders—quick in and out. Other babies want to linger and enjoy this special time, relishing the ambiance of "Mom's Diner." You learn to trust your baby to know how much and how often breast-feeding is needed. The signs that breast-feeding is off to a good start during the first week: (1) Your baby "asks" for at least eight and up to about twelve feedings every twenty-four hours, and (2) you are changing more wet and dirty diapers with every passing day.

Engorgement is a normal phenomenon during the first week after delivery as milk production steps up and mature milk gradually replaces colostrum. You may notice that your breasts become tighter and fuller when your milk "comes in" at about two to four days after delivery; this "normal" engorgement diminishes within a day or two—although you may feel a bit engorged whenever baby goes several hours without a feeding. Part of the fullness is not the milk itself; it is swelling of the breast tissues due to the arrival of the extra blood and lymph fluid your body sent to the breasts to help them make the components of milk. Frequent breast-feeding is the best response to this temporary fullness. Relief from this discomfort can be obtained by soaking towels in hot water, wringing them out, and applying them to the breasts (Ah!). Massaging the breasts ever so gently through the towel helps. You can apply packs of frozen peas or corn in sealed plastic bags between feedings to help reduce the swelling. Fresh green cabbage leaves used occasionally as a compress on each breast will help.

If the breasts are so full and tight that they feel like they are stuffed with a million small, hard, painful pebbles, your baby will have trouble latching on and obtaining a sufficient hold just beyond the areolar border. You can soften this area by manually expressing some milk and then flattening it by manually squeezing it to a size that can be accommodated by the baby. The baby does the rest, but after a few minutes of sucking, he may tire and drop off to sleep without emptying the canals holding the milk. The baby may need to be awakened and encouraged to nurse longer. If that doesn't work, you can do the job by manually expressing the milk or by using a good breast pump. You can empty both breasts at once if you use a hospital-grade electric pump with a double collection kit (see Appendix B for names of companies).

One possible explanation for full, painful breasts is that the milk is too alkaline and the calcium becomes somewhat insoluble and cannot move through the ducts; it needs to be acidified. One teaspoonful of apple cider vinegar in a glass of water two or three times a day should allow the milk to flow more freely. If it tastes good, it is the right antidote.

Within ten to fourteen days the baby and the mother work out a rhythm and a flow to achieve an adequate supply that permits satisfaction of hunger and growth needs.

Many herbs have the power to act as a stimulant for milk production: Fenugreek (a component of Lydia Pinkham's Vegetable Compound, and now found in artificial maple syrup), alfalfa, basil, borage, caraway, cumin, dandelion, dill, fennel, ginseng, hops, lavender, red raspberry, and parsley are a few of them. Chamomile, skullcap, passiflora tea, and catnip, may help to relax the distraught mother with a demanding newborn. Removing stress will increase milk production. When women listened to a progressive relaxation exercise tape, followed by guided images of pleasant surroundings, milk increased 60 to 100 percent.

The baby knows how often he needs to nurse. Demand feeding—not nibbling—is best for both participants; this is ideal if rooming-in arrangements are made in the hospital. Doctors and nurses are finally becoming more supportive of breast-feeding and do not automatically provide a bottle of formula in the nursery because the "baby was so hungry." Rooming-in and home births provide the opportunity to feed on demand, and will allow for more effective bonding. "True" milk usually does not appear until the second to fourth day. Having your baby "remove" the colostrum is an important prelude to the later flow and production of milk, and provides important immunity. It also has a laxative effect, which helps the baby eliminate the sticky, tarry meconium. (If your baby is unable to breast-feed well immediately, any colostrum you express or pump should be given to your baby some other way. It is important.)

Frequent feedings are to be expected. Because human milk is so digestible and your baby grows rapidly, your milk does not provide much staying power in such a small stomach. This is because human milk is low in fat and protein, especially the casein, or curd-forming, portion. Artificial cow milk formulas are higher in casein, and the curds that form in the stomach take time to break down, which is why bottle-fed babies usually go longer between feedings. The digestibility of breast milk puts less stress on every system in baby's body, but it is low in sustainability. Apparently Mother Nature intended that human mothers should carry their babies with or on them for the first few months.

Mothers usually find that they do better at home where they may cooperate with the baby's erratic schedule; the trick is to nurse him when he is vigorously hungry. Some babies cluster-feed: They will eat frequently for a few hours and then sleep several hours before feeding again. Others seem to be built with a stopwatch that "tells" them to eat every two or three hours on the dot. Both patterns are normal as long as your baby is feeding well at least eight to twelve times every twenty-four hours. Most mothers learn to nap between feedings. Encouraging feeding every two to three hours during the day may allow the baby to sleep longer at night—if he is cooperative.

Breast-fed babies swallow very little air, so burping may not be necessary. When the baby has finished nursing from one breast, it might be wise to burp him before you let him latch on to the other breast. Thumping on his abdomen as you would test a melon for ripeness should tell you if he has some air in his stomach. (A low-pitched hollow sound means burp him.) Gently rolling the baby from side to side, and then sitting him up again, might finally get the air to come out.

Watch your baby, not the clock. Breast-feed whenever your baby seems interested or is vigorously hungry. The baby's frequent feedings may tempt you to offer a cow milk supplement in these early days, but this usually weans him off the breast, as the bottle is less work for him. When the baby breast-feeds, messages are sent to your breasts and brain to make a certain amount of milk. Frequent feedings send more messages, which tells your breasts to step up milk production. If you supplement, your breasts and brain receive fewer messages, so production slows down and less milk is made. This vicious circle leads to less milk production, and you will have to supplement more and more. Also, babies use different mouth and tongue movements when bottle-feeding, which confuses most babies.

A few babies are too sleepy to feed well—either they don't wake up alert and eager to eat at least eight to twelve times every twenty-four hours, or no sooner do they latch on than they fall back to sleep again without "emptying" the breasts. The baby may develop a dehydration fever on the third day if fluids are insufficient and the ambient temperature is high. If urine is scanty—less than three or four times a day—breast-feeding management needs to be evaluated. Water is not recommended; the baby is to suck at the breast for his fluid. In this instance a mother should express or pump her milk and feed it to her baby in a different way until he becomes more alert and ready to learn to breast-feed. This way the baby gets fluid and the calories, and you will be able to maintain your supply. Your lactation consultant should help monitor your situation. If God wanted babies to have water, He would have provided a breast with water.

Unfortunately, breast-feeding has largely declined in our country because of the availability of easy-to-prepare milk substitutes, the pressure on working mothers to return to work in a month or so, the lack of encouragement for rooming-in on maternity units, early hospital discharge without good follow-up by someone knowledgeable about breast-feeding, and, I might add, the negative attitude of some obstetricians, pediatricians, and other health-care providers. Did you know that:

- In 1900, 90 percent of babies were breast-fed; at age five months, 80 percent were still at it.
- In 1958, only 20 percent were breast-fed. Most were on evaporated milk formulas.
- In 1980, it had risen to sixty percent, but with only 30 percent still breast-feeding at six months.
- In 1989 breast-feeding rates had dipped again to about 50 percent initiating breast-feeding with less than 20 percent still breast-feeding at six months.

One of the "Healthy People 2000" goals for our country is to have at least 75 percent of babies breast-feeding soon after birth, with at least 50 percent still breast-feeding at six months.

Obstacles to Successful Breast-feeding: Most new mothers haven't grown up seeing babies breast-feed, so they often don't understand how breast-feeding works. Because of this a mother may believe that her baby wants more than she can supply in the first ten days, and thus discouraged, she quits.

• The new or naive mother needs to know that breast-fed babies eat frequently and that just about the time her breasts are not feeling as full from engorgement, her baby has a growth spurt and wants to eat more often for a few days.

• A baby may have trouble latching on to a flat or inverted nipple. There are ways to help both the nipples and the baby.

• Painful cracks or fissures may develop on the nipple or occasionally on the areola if the baby is not latching on correctly. (Try purified lanolin.) Your areolae produce their own cleansing agent, so there is no need to wash with anything other than ordinary water. Avoid soap as it is drying to the skin. Pat nipples and areolae dry after washing and after feeding. Vitamin E oil may be rubbed on the tender, cracked areola and will not harm the baby, but these will not heal the sores that result from poor latch-on technique. Talk to a certified lactation consultant if the sore nipples do not improve by the time the baby is one to two weeks old. Calendula ointment is safe and promotes healing. Breast shells allow air to circulate and prevent friction from the bra. Sunshine exposure is not recommended anymore.

• The boss at work may discourage demand feeding of baby or expressing/ pumping milk and insist that the baby can be fed a bottle of artificial formula at home by a sitter. The boss should be told that the mother who is allowed to feed or pump often enough is less likely to miss work for infant illness or because she's developed a breast infection.

• Some women are embarrassed to feed their babies in public, often because the only pictures they've seen of breast-feeding show a woman with her breast exposed. Most mothers can learn to breast-feed very discreetly without any breast exposure.

A couple of years ago the states of Florida and Virginia passed legislation protecting the rights of nursing mothers to breast-feed their babies in public. Mothers have been harassed by security guards and store proprietors for baring chest skin to nurse their babies. It had been called "indecent exposure" before. The Florida law states that breast-feeding should be encouraged in the interest of maternal and child health.[94]

• A mother must be prepared to eat an adequate diet; she may need to refrain from certain foods that might get in her milk and upset the baby. (Cow milk is the most common offender, but cabbage, garlic [a study several years ago found babies "liked" garlic in milk], onions, theobromine in chocolate, and beans may produce gas and cramps.) A sleepless baby may be due to the mother's ingestion of caffeinated tea or coffee. Her lack of sleep may encourage her to drink more to stay awake—a vicious circle. The caffeine may rock around in the blood of the baby for as long as one hundred hours. Abstinence from caffeine for a week should solve the problem.[95]

• A mother may feel guilty and inferior if her baby does not thrive or cries unduly. Her doctor might like to encourage nursing but cannot insist that she does so. Often when faced with a baby not gaining in the first two weeks, he might discourage breast-feeding too quickly at times when what a mother really wants is encouragement and the number of someone experienced in helping with breast-feeding problems. A mother must let her doctor know what she really wants. Whatever decision she makes, her doctor—and her family—must encourage her and provide comfort, quiet, and freedom from anxiety.

Preparatory information and exercises permit the easiest introduction to breast-feeding on the natal day. A breast-feeding mothers' support group or a certified lactation consultant will have practical suggestions to work through almost any obstacle.

Advantages. Sir William Osler, the father of American medicine, said, "A pair of substantial mammary glands has the advantage over two hemispheres of the most learned professor's brain in the art of compounding a nutritious fluid for infants." Human milk is ideally suited to human babies because humans' main characteristic is the development of a relatively large brain with special growth of the frontal lobes. The protein content of human milk is much lower than cow milk. The nutrients that help form the brain are all present in appropriate quantities.[96] It is not for oxen, elephants, or rabbits. Human milk changes from morning to evening, from day to day, and changes over the months of nursing. The first milk, colostrum, is rich in both protein and antibodies against a number of bacteria and viruses. Transition milk comes in for a few days and also helps with immunity. Mature milk arrives at about two weeks, and may look weak as it has a bluish color. Birth weight is not regained until about two weeks of life. After five or six months the fat content drops to about two percent. Human milk contains about *eight* times the levels of linoleic acid as does cow milk. It also contains a higher amount of cholesterol than cow milk. These fats are necessary for the myelination of the nerves going on in those first few important months. Cow milk has much more protein, minerals, sodium, and phosphorus than human milk, but a calf needs all those items for its rapid growth. Does a calf need to think?

Human milk is cheap, safe, delivered at the proper temperature, free of bacteria, discourages many infections, and helps provide an important intimacy between mother and child. Babies are not allergic to it, *but may be sensitive to the foods the mother has eaten*. Breast-fed babies are almost never constipated. The huge milk curd that forms in the stomach from cow milk often turns to a hard ball of dust by the time it gets to the rectum, defying expulsion. It is like a golf ball plugging the anal opening. Some have been as large as a croquet ball. Breast-fed babies usually have a soft, unformed, yellowish bowel movement with a mild yeast smell—like bread baking in the oven. That pleasant smell is from the *Lactobacillus bifidus* which comes from maternal skin. The baby acquires this microorganism from the mother during nursing and then continues to be supplied with it throughout breast-feeding. It is important to help the infant ward off pathogenic bacteria and viruses. These soft stools may come a few times a day or may only come once every few days; the soft consistency is important. The frequency is not important. When the baby is nursing, the mother's uterus contracts—sometimes painfully—and returns to normal size more quickly. Women who breast-feed for a minimum of six months have less risk of premenopausal breast and ovarian cancer.

One study of eighteen-month-old children who had been nursed totally without any solid foods all that time revealed that they were healthy, of normal weight and height, and were not anemic. They seemed secure and free from infections and allergies. Of one hundred babies in the hospital with intestinal flu, only one of them was breast-fed. No other foods need be given until the baby begins to grab food off the table, out of the dog dish, or off the floor. Nutrition research by allergists and the American Academy of Pediatrics indicates that early feeding of solids benefits only the baby food companies, and tends to set up allergies to those early-introduced foods that may never be outgrown. Early feeding of solids also tends to encourage obesity in adulthood. Breast milk has iron, zinc, calcium, protein, sugar, essential fatty acids, and everything else the baby needs. There is a little iron in all mammalian milk, but it is species-specific and, consequently, well absorbed by the baby of the same species. If a mother's diet is adequate, her human baby will get the iron it needs from her breast milk, but not from cow milk. (Breast milk has 0.8 milligrams of iron in a liter of milk, but it is 50 percent absorbed. Cow milk has 6 to 12 milligrams of iron per liter, but the amount of iron absorbed by human babies is but 0.4 milligrams.) Cow milk has iron for the calf; human milk has iron for the human baby. But the iron in cow milk is not available to the human baby.[97]

Early feeding of solids was intended to prevent milk anemia, which is common if a baby is only getting cow milk. Even if the nursing mother is slightly anemic, the baby will get some iron from her, like the parasite he is. A well-balanced diet is obviously important for mother and baby.

Nursed babies grow up to have a better jawline and require less orthodontia. Human milk is more acidic, and the minerals are more available to supply the growing jaws. Breast-fed babies have to work harder, coordinating tongue and jaw movements differently to get the milk from the breast, so facial bones and muscles are more developed. Francis Pottenger notes that if a baby is nursed for more than three months, the bimalar (cheekbone to cheekbone) distance is greater than the biorbital (temple to temple) distance. Bottle-fed babies often develop tongue-thrusting habits because the milk is coming out too fast. The tongue pushes the frontal teeth forward: beaver-mouth. If orthodontia is needed, it means that the diet has been defective. Females with a good dental arch usually have an adequate pelvis for childbirth.

Dr. Steven Bell, associate professor of psychology at the University of Georgia, studied breast-fed babies. The key indicator of competence and responsive behavior in children (i.e., trust, autonomy, obedience, attachment, persistence, and tolerance) was highly correlated with breast-feeding.

Mothers have breast-fed adopted babies in order that they and their babies have the opportunity to experience the closeness breast-feeding offers. Although many adoptive mothers can get some milk to flow, it usually is necessary to provide their babies with a supplement as well. It takes a little doing, persistence, and motivation, but it works. The feeding systems consists of a bag of artificial milk attached to the mother's chest. Although the baby is sucking on a dry breast, the baby is rewarded with some milk from a small tube connected to the bag of milk and ending at the mother's nipple. He is rewarded for sucking. Sucking stimulation to the breasts sends a message to the thalamus in the mother's brain: "Hey, there's a baby out there. Send down some milk." The thalamus, in turn, signals the pituitary to send hormones to the breasts. (The brain thinks, "Why didn't the uterus say something?" But without a normal pregnancy and delivery, there was no message to tell the brain to send out the lactogenic hormone. The uterus is basically just a muscle.) It takes one to two weeks, so one must believe and be determined. (A patient of mine adopted a three-month-old baby with severe eczema. Within two weeks, using donated breast milk and her own when it was finally produced, the rash healed, probably from the intake of essential fatty acids. The mother continued to nurse him for a year. In some third-world countries when the nursing mother goes off to work, Grandmother [the babysitter] will often put the hungry baby on her breasts, which have not been used for years, and some milk will come. It is called relactation.)

A kangaroo-style method of nursing small babies has been successful in some countries. If the baby is alert, he can be put to the breast and allowed to nurse as long and as often as needed. The mothers keep their babies warm by carrying them skin to skin beneath their blouse in an upright position between their breasts.

Your milk is a living food. It changes throughout the months or years your baby nurses to meet baby's special needs. It also provides your baby with antibodies to any disease that you've ever had during the entire time that baby breast-feeds. No other milk can come close to providing such a benefit. In a British study, all but one of 339 infants hospitalized with gastroenteritis were bottle-fed. One third of the children in this group were dehydrated, and five died. The one breast-fed infant was not even dehydrated.[98] Overall, breast-fed infants in modern societies suffer only one third to one half the incidence of significant illness of bottle-fed infants.[99]

Mothers who have nursed their babies successfully may seem evangelical in their efforts to encourage others to do likewise, but who else will do Mother Nature's marketing if not her satisfied customers? La Leche League International (LLL), an organization offering mother-to-mother support for breast-feeding, finds that most women, given enough encouragement and the facts, are able to breast-feed their babies.[100] Lactation professionals, such as certified lactation consultants, are growing in number and acceptance, and they are able to help most new mothers to breast-feed successfully. "Training" begins during the pregnancy.

We wimpy pediatricians allowed the cow milk formula companies to move into the newborn nursery and sabotage breast-feeding efforts. "Here's a little formula so the baby won't be so hungry, dearie," they said to the exhausted, vulnerable new mother who welcomed the rest. Well, that pretty much stopped her milk flow. Some smart aleck said that if women's breasts had been provided with flow meters, there would be no problem about encouraging nursing; we could then be sure the little suckers were getting enough. (If you can't check the flow as it goes in, check it as it exits at the baby's other end.)

All babies are born somewhat waterlogged, and they lose that water before they begin to gain some real weight. Doctors tend to compare bottles and breast-fed babies; they might suggest to mothers that they abandon breast-feeding because the baby is not up to the weight gain shown by the bottle-fed ones. The bottle-fed ones usually get to birth weight by one week; breast-fed babies take longer, maybe up to two weeks. We know that to gain weight, a baby needs about two ounces per pound of weight per twenty-four hours. Weighing the baby before and after each feeding usually creates stress and discouragement. Why not just ask the mother, "How are you doing?" or "How are the feedings going?" and weigh the baby every few days. As long as the baby is breast-feeding well at least eight times every twenty-four hours and is having enough wet diapers, all is well. (Once a weight gain is established, it isn't necessary to check baby's weight this often.)

The new mother should aim for a year or two of nursing. We must get all mothers to nurse, nurse, nurse. Some authorities feel mothers should stop nursing when the child can unbutton the mother's blouse, or stands up to nurse. Why stop then? Stop when the *baby* is ready to give it up. Henny Youngman said, "The best years of my life were spent in the arms of another man's wife—my mother." It makes sense.

From a correspondent in Eugene, Oregon: "Our three-month-old son had a low-grade weeping, purulent infection in his eye from birth. The pediatrician prescribed erythromycin, which we diligently put in his eye a bit at a time—with no results. A friend suggested that we put breast milk in his eye. In two days the eye cleared, and has been clear ever since! The advantages of mother's milk!"

Maybe we should have a national breast-feeding day, at which time all mothers would come to a downtown park and nurse their babies in public. We must get the world to realize it is a normal, healthy physiological function.

Weaning from Nursing. Breast milk is a complete food for most of the first year, but teething can interfere with nursing comfort. The eruption of teeth is nature's way of telling the mother that solid foods could now be introduced.

Mothers around the world nurse their babies for two to three years. At about eight to ten months, after the baby sits well and sees others eat, he will want to imitate self-feeding. Breast milk supply will decrease because of the law of supply and demand. At nine months or so, one nursing at the breast may be replaced with a four- to six-ounce bottle of milk or cup of vegetable juice or water. (Commercial fruit juices have too much sugar in them. Squeeze your own.) After four weeks, another nursing is replaced by a bottle or cup. This gradual diminution of amount and frequency of milk intake is easier on both participants. Cow milk is less important after ten months, but adequate protein must be supplied by the solid foods. Babies from allergy-prone families are usually breast-fed for the whole first year without any solids being offered until after that time. Many infants and their breast-feeding mothers find it convenient and comfortable to continue nursing on a limited basis for years. This does not spoil the child, but serves to provide security and pleasant bonding. Many mothers have found that if the baby is breast-fed long enough, he/she never gets addicted to the bottle or pacifier.

Attachment to an accepting adult is the only opportunity a human has to learn mutual trust. If a child is shut off consistently from attachment within the first two years of life because of severe neglect, abuse, or shifting about from one family to another, he is going to be hard-pressed to fulfill his role as an adequate social human. The human organism appears to force itself onto its environment with age-related mechanisms calculated to satisfy its needs: The hungry baby cries and is fed.

"All babies are good, but can know it themselves only by reflection, by the way they are treated. There is no other viable way for a human to feel about himself, all other kinds of feeling are unusable as a foundation for well-being. Once a mother realizes that carrying her baby about, for the first six or eight months, will assure his self-reliance and lay the foundations for his becoming social, undemanding, and positively helpful for the next fifteen or twenty years he will be at home, even her self-interest will tell her not to spare herself the 'trouble' of carrying him while she is doing her housework or shopping. Without waiting to change society at all, we can behave correctly towards our infants, and give them a sound personal base from which to deal with whatever situations they meet. Once we fully recognize the consequence of our treatment of babies, we cannot fail to discover a great deal more of our potential for joy."[101]

The accepted belief is that psychologically deviant children were detoured into their unacceptable behavior because of some distorted parent-child relationship. The mother—and sometimes the father—did not cuddle, massage, hold, love, accept, reward, and encourage the growing infant. The child felt lost, left out, abandoned, unloved, and rejected, and ends up depressed, angry, paranoid, selfish, sickly, or withdrawn. The mother is usually blamed for any psychopathology in the child as she was more intimately involved in the day-to-day care. Genetic influences from either the mother's or father's side might determine the final type of psychopathology, whether it be a neurosis, a psychosis, antisocial behavior, or chronic anxiety. The growing child needs to hear good and encouraging words from both parents. The ratio should be about twice as many good vibes as negative ones—no matter which parent is offering the goodies.

Old wives' tale: "Don't pick him up so much. You will spoil him." Wrong! If babies are responded to in those first few weeks, they cry for shorter times later. "The relative lack of carrying in our society may predispose to crying and colic in normal infants."[102] If babies were left to fall asleep alone after feedings, they were more likely to be habitual finger and thumb suckers as children. Putting babies on a rigid schedule may produce just what you are trying to prevent—a nervous, anxious, and insecure child.

The attachment the newborn baby makes with the significant parent usually sets the tone of the whole next eighteen years. If the mother is not too exhausted after a drug-free delivery, she is happy to bond with her baby by placing the naked infant on her naked chest and encourage this "reflex bundle" to suck.

Ashley Montagu says it well. "Tactile experience plays a fundamentally important role in the growth and development of all mammals thus far studied."[103] If this need is denied, these infants may develop failure-to-thrive or behavioral problems.

As a baby's nerve fibers in the higher cerebral centers become capable of storing information, she incorporates the fact that a warm, loving, accepting adult is a dependable, necessary part of her existence. If she laughs, smiles, and eats, then this adult responds with love and satisfactory care. She is rewarded for being pleasant, and is loved for being loving. This early attachment is necessary to develop a conscience as well as a good self-image. Mutual trust results.

During the formative periods of brain growth, sensory deprivation—lack of touching and rocking by the parent—results in incomplete or damaged development of the neuronal connections that control affection. These same systems influence brain centers associated with violence; deprived infants may have difficulty controlling violent impulses as adults. James W. Prescott, Ph.D., believes that children in some societies may be unable to experience certain kinds of pleasure, and might be predisposed to anger.

"I found that when levels of infant affection are low—as among the Comanches and the Ashanti—levels of violence are high; where physical affection is high—as among the Maori of New Zealand and the Balinese— violence is low."[104]

Tactile and kinesthetic stimulation was given to twenty preterm neonates in a neonatal intensive care unit for fifteen-minute periods three times a day for ten days. These stimulated infants averaged a 47 percent greater weight gain per day, were more active and alert, and showed more mature behavior than the control infants. The hospital stay was also shorter.[105]

Bathing removes body odors for a time, and discourages a number of skin infections. Most odors people have are due to the growth of bacteria and fungi, but a persistent, offensive odor despite regular bathing may mean a magnesium deficiency.

Bathing a baby should be as simple, quick, and pleasant as possible for everyone. One must not make it a religious ceremony, but it is an opportunity to cuddle, massage, and talk to your infant. For a new baby, it is usually not necessary to do more than go over her dirty, sweaty areas with a wet washcloth. When she starts to sleep through the night, a full bath is usually necessary, or a somewhat disagreeable odor will develop in the diaper area and a rash is soon to follow due to germs or fungi. It is not necessary to postpone the full immersion bath until the navel is healed completely. It is worthwhile to bathe the area so bacteria will not have a chance to grow (see Navel, this chapter). Most soaps are alkaline and tend to dry and crack the skin. Bathing the baby in a plastic dishpan is probably preferable to the hard sink where she could bang her head. Use as little soap as possible; agitating the bar of soap in the water for a few seconds will lower the surface tension of the water just enough.

During bathing or drying is a good time to observe the infant or child for signs of dysuria (straining to urinate), frequency, and inadequate stream. The infant boy should be able to wet his feet easily while lying on his back; the girl should flood the diaper without straining.

Bottle-feeding, unfortunately, has become an easy (?) substitute for breast-feeding. However, if you have really tried breast-feeding, but it is not for you, the bottle is the next step.

Most authorities agree that a baby should be fed when she's hungry. Just a few decades ago, the popular pediatric belief was that if a baby was fed every four hours, hungry or not, she would develop the habit of those regular hours and not be a burden to the parents. It was a misguided idea. A baby can empty her stomach in just an hour and a half, and should be fed that often if she appears hungry. A normal seven-pound newborn baby who is reasonably awake and alert needs from fourteen to twenty ounces of milk every twenty-four hours. When mixed properly, there are about twenty calories per ounce in the milk she's consuming, so she should get at least two ounces for each pound she weighs in her first two or three months. If she wants to be fed every hour and a half or two hours, she will get her nutritional quota during her twelve waking hours and may possibly sleep all night long—the ideal schedule.

Here's an old wives' tale: "Gradually give the baby less and less milk at the 2:00 A.M. feeding and he will soon be sleeping through the night." (Told to mothers by a bachelor pediatrician.) If a baby needs eight ounces of milk in the middle of the night, the baby will not let you cheat him with six.

If he's growing at a terrific rate or he's very active, then he may have to be fed more because his hunger will undoubtedly be greater. A baby destined to be a small adult can get all his calories during his twelve waking hours and not have to wake up in the night; he is unlikely to eat as much as a baby who will eventually be six feet tall. But if he's active and going to be a good-sized adult—if both parents are five feet ten or six feet tall—he won't be able to sleep through the night until he's three or four months old, because he's growing too fast to get all his calories during his twelve waking hours. (I once figured out that if a baby continued to grow as fast as he does in those first ten days, by the time he is ten years old, he would be twenty-two feet tall.)

If the ambient temperature is high, an ounce or two of water should be added to each bottle as infant kidneys cannot conserve fluid. Most babies choke on plain water from the bottle as it squirts out so fast.

Just about any good type of milk (any of the standard prepared formulas to which water is added) will provide the necessary twenty calories per ounce. Incidentally, if it is safe for adults to drink the water without boiling it, it is not necessary to boil it for the baby. But if the caretaker has any disease or skin infection, or if one is not sure about the water, it is probably better to boil it for ten minutes before using it for the formula. The bottles need not be boiled. If a bottle brush gets the milk curds out, then washing them along with the dishes is good enough.

Ideally, bottle-feeding should attempt to simulate breast-feeding. The parent tries to hold and cuddle the baby when bottle-feeding, but a number of babies are upset if they are held. It suggests—but does not prove—

that he/she is low in magnesium if the baby prefers to have the bottle propped. But the feeder should be close and continue to sing and talk to the baby in a soothing fashion. These babies just do not want to be touched and handled when they are eating—it is too distracting. A nervous baby is more aware of his environment and is easily overstimulated. Many parents have found that if the bottle is propped, the baby is less likely to spit up the milk; he drinks the milk faster and seems to be more content. The stomach curves from left to right, so if he's fed while lying on his right side, the air bubbles will remain on the top and he's less likely to spit up his milk.

The feeder and the baby decide on the most comfortable way to accomplish the feeding. The warmth, the cradling, the loving, the cooing, and the satisfactory warm milk going down to fill his stomach tell the baby that these "feeding people" are to be trusted and that he belongs.

Try this: A quick way to prepare a feeding: At the first hunger cry, baby is picked up. Parent carries baby to kitchen. Parent talks reassuringly to baby, explaining that relief is on its way. Parent turns on hot water tap, puts previously washed baby bottle on counter. Parent opens refrigerator door, grabs can of concentrated formula, pours two ounces into bottle, puts can back, closes refrigerator door. By this time the water is running hot, and two ounces of hot tap water are run into the bottle. Parent shuts off water, screws on nipple, and puts nipple into baby's open mouth. Twenty-five seconds is the record. Sometimes the bottle can be held under the chin like a violin to free a hand to mop up the milk that has been spilled.

(Warning! Milk heated in the microwave oven may be too hot to drink, even though the bottle itself seems cool or only slightly warm. Test it, obviously, before feeding the baby.)

Sleep: The American Sleep Disorders Association, Rochester, Minnesota, reports that "newborn babies average sixteen to eighteen hours of sleep a day, spread out in about five sleep episodes." Within just a few days of birth, some babies sleep longer at night than during the day. Most babies have sleeping and waking periods for the first four weeks of life, with sleep periods of three to four hours day and night. The total amount of sleep is about the same for the first four months, but it gradually gets better organized, with longer sleep periods at night. You hope. The nervous system becomes capable of inhibiting arousal for extended periods. The amount of crying increases during the first three weeks and peaks at four weeks of three hours daily. It is appropriate for parents to respond with soothing, rocking, massage, and cuddling. This early response to crying may result in less crying in subsequent months. When the baby awakens at night at this young age, assume it is hunger. Keep lights low at night. Try to avoid stimulating activities. Pat the baby, or change a diaper without taking the baby out of the bed except to feed.

Temperature of a newborn is obviously the same as the mother's at birth, but may drop rapidly in the first few minutes if the infant is not covered. The premature baby, with little fat to insulate him, is especially susceptible to chilling, and increased oxygen is necessary if environmental temperature is low, relative to his body temperature. Overheating also requires extra oxygen, so the trick is to produce a crib temperature that neither overheats nor chills the newborn. Fever in a healthy baby on the third day is usually due to dehydration (see The Purpose of Fevers and Infections, Chapter 6). A quick method of assaying the body temperature is to feel down the middle of the back between the baby's shoulder blades. If the area is hot and sweaty, the baby is too hot and needs fewer clothes. The hands and feet are frequently cool when the baby is digesting, because the circulation is busy in the abdomen.

Tongue-tie in the old days (before 1965) was thought to be responsible for lisping or stuttering—or not talking at all. No one in the medical profession believes this now, but just in case there might be some truth to this old wives' tale, doctors still clip the frenulum if it is short. The frenulum is the web of tough tissue that is attached to the underside of the tip of the tongue and to the floor of the mouth just behind the lower gum. If it is short, the tongue will form a **V**, with the apex of the angle of the tongue held down to the gum level. It seems sensible to nip the membrane to allow the tongue greater mobility, but there are just enough horror stories about babies developing uncontrollable hemorrhages into the tongue muscle to warrant caution. The frenulum is stretchable; time and use permit more freedom of motion. After all, none of the sounds used in speech require the tongue to reach farther forward than the teeth. I knew an attractive, speech-perfect nurse with a tongue-tie; her only complaint was that licking stamps caused a small ulcer on her frenulum.

Torticollis is a spastic condition of the sternocleidomastoid muscle that runs from the front of the upper chest and attaches to the mastoid bone. The assumption is made that it was torn or injured during delivery, and as a compensation, the muscle goes into spasm. If untreated, it will become scarred and may require surgery to release the tension. Manipulation of the upper spine by a chiropractor was effective in almost all cases.[106] Parents can be taught how to gently stretch the muscle over a period of months. The infant should be placed in the crib so that he is forced to stretch the muscle when he looks out toward any activity.

AFTER A FEW DAYS OR A WEEK

Anal fissure is a crack or tear at the anal opening, usually due to a hard, dry stool or irritation from a food sensitivity. It is rare in the breast-fed baby, but cow milk is often constipating (see Constipation, Chapter 3). Softening the stool with dark Karo syrup might be enough. Lubricating the fissure with an ointment to "grease the skids" usually heals it within one week.

Many cracks or tears are due to vigorous rubbing with dry toilet paper in an attempt to clean the anal opening and the adjacent skin. The skin is abraded, bacteria are introduced, and inflammation follows. Use moist toilet paper or a wet cotton ball to cleanse the anal area. Blot, don't rub. Tucks pads (cotton pads saturated with glycerin and witch hazel) are ideal for cleaning up after a bowel movement.

Chapped lips, or cheilitis, is the cracking and scaling of the lips, usually due to a food sensitivity—milk in this case. An occasional baby becomes sensitive to the rubber nipple or pacifier. Yeast infections may be associated with this condition.

Colic is any crying that cannot be related to hunger. The usual explanation by pediatric authorities is that it is an overreactive intestinal tract in a baby who is being overstimulated by the environment.

The following possibilities should be considered when dealing with a fussy, crying, unhappy baby:

1. Hunger. If giving her an adequate supply of nourishing milk does not stop her screams, the condition is called colic. But if she is quiet for an hour and a half and then cries, her unhappiness is most likely caused by hunger, as a baby can empty the stomach in an hour and a half. If you feed her every hour and a half during the day, she might just be able to sleep for six to eight hours at night (that's ideal). However, if she gets an adequate supply of milk and bellows within twenty minutes, it is probably colic.

2. Allergy. If a baby is not suffering from hunger, but is bloated with gas, is vomiting, or has diarrhea or bloody stools, a change of milk is mandatory. If she is better within twenty-four to forty-eight hours after the change and remains so, it implies that she has a milk allergy or at least a sensitivity. If the original milk is again tried and screaming returns, she should remain on the substitute milk. A number of babies will get better after a change to soybean milk, but after a week or two, 20 percent will start to scream and cry with cramps as they have become allergic to the soy. Another substitute will have to be tried. Most outgrow the problem between ages one and two years.

If the breast-fed baby develops colic and passes green stools (bile), and shows other signs of sensitivities (circles under the eyes, a red ring around the anal opening), it suggests that the baby is reacting to something the mother is eating. The most common offenders are milk, soy, corn, wheat, peanuts, tomatoes, and eggs. Garlic, onions, cabbage, and beans are common gasmakers. These foods can go through her system and hit the baby's intestines like a hockey puck. Try this remedy: Add one teaspoon of apple cider vinegar to an eight-ounce glass of water. Offer the baby a tablespoon to an ounce of this acidic water every thirty to sixty minutes. It is safe and effective, as some colic is due to an alkaline, high-sodium condition. If the baby likes it, he needs it.

3. Position. Some babies do not like to be held when they are fed and seem to be irritated by any effort to soothe them. It is perfectly acceptable and *not* psychologically damaging to let him lie flat on his back or tipped slightly to the right (stomach curves from left to right) with the bottle propped. (I knew a mother who had to breast-feed her touchy baby by coming in on top of him—like a plane landing—while he lay supine on the floor.) Some parents get quite skillful at thumping the baby's abdomen in the upper left portion—as if testing a melon. When the *thoonk* is just right, she should be picked up and burped. Some feel that ear infections are more common in those babies who are fed in the supine position.

4. Nipple holes. Obviously nothing can be done about the nipple holes used by breast-fed babies, but many people assume that the manufacturers of bottle nipples calibrate them so they are exactly the right size. This is not so. In general, they're too small. To test rubber nipples: Put cold formula in the bottle and turn the bottle upside down. Without shaking, the milk should drip out at the rate of about one drop a second. If it doesn't, the holes are too small and need enlarging. The milk should flow into the baby's mouth at a rate that *almost* chokes him. A baby swallows *more* air if the nipple holes are too small, because he sucks air *around* the nipple. If the holes are large, he'll get less air and less bloat. Breast-fed babies get their milk at a rather rapid rate, so bottle milk should also come at a rapid rate. The baby should be able to take almost all his quota in five to ten minutes.

5. Inadequate feeding. A few parents report their babies are colicky after they gave them what they thought was an adequate amount of milk—eight ounces. Because the bottles held only eight ounces, they assumed it was enough. But when offered ten ounces, the babies were completely satisfied. This seems like an outrageous amount for a small baby, but it is clearly what some babies prefer. Before the parents stumbled on this concept, they were offering six ounces five times a day, but the babies wanted ten ounces three times a day. They were perfectly happy when they finally received this amount.

6. Obstructions. About one out of four babies is born with a slight narrowing at the anal-rectal junction, just one half or one fourth of an inch inside the anal opening. It acts as a partial obstruction. (See Anal Ring, this chapter.) Some babies have pockets of gas inside the anal opening; a glycerin suppository inserted into the rectum can help the baby express the stool and gas. This only relieves some of the gas in the last six inches or foot of the colon, not in the twenty feet of intestine between the stomach and anus.

The colic due to an incarcerated (stuck) inguinal hernia should be easily diagnosed by noticing a tender mass to one side of the base of the penis in the pubic area. This is an emergency.

7. Nonintestinal causes. Because the urinary department is located in the abdomen, a congenital urinary obstruction can sometimes cause colic. The doctor must be notified of any symptoms a child may have in this area—such as not being able to urinate for some hours at a time, or seeming to be in distress when he does urinate, or his urinary stream is thin and feeble. Any of these indicate some obstructive problem. Is the urethral opening at the end of his penis a slot or a pinhole? (See Genitals, this chapter.)

8. Cold feet. An old wives' tale says the baby has colic because his feet are cold. I had always thought his feet were cold *because* he had colic. Keep his feet warm anyway; if it soothes him, then *that* is the answer.

9. Pacifier. Most babies need to suck on something for digestion, relaxation, and security. If sucking pleasure (oral drive) is not satisfied during the feedings, the infant should be urged to suck a pacifier (Nuk is best) before thumb or finger sucking becomes a fixed habit. The pacifier can be "lost" someday when the child is older (about age six). Usually less orthodontia work is necessary if the pacifier is used rather than the bony thumb. Most breast-fed babies do not need to suck their thumbs or pacifiers.

10. Anxiety. A parent's anxiety may not cause the colic, but may perpetuate it after the baby starts to cry. In her effort to soothe the baby, Mom may be overstimulating him. Some hyperresponsive babies have to cry themselves to sleep. If the baby has been eating well all day and begins to cry after his 6:00 to 10:00 P.M. feeding, it may be assumed he has an over-loaded gut and needs to cry a little. Twenty minutes is about the standard time for allowing him to work it out for himself. If he is still at it after this interval, a little rocking, a homeopathic sedative, or some herbal tea might be a sanity saver.

11. Cervical and thoracic spine subluxations. "Temporomandibular joint dysfunction early on can lead to breast-feeding difficulties, headache, and improper feeding, which in turn can lead to colic."[107]

12. Nutritional causes. This infant cries after every feeding. His formula has been changed every four days (soy, goat milk, rice milk, amino acid milk, etc.). Multiple changes with no relief tend to rule out a milk sensitivity, yet nothing works.

• A key question for the mother: "Did you have backaches, muscle cramps, or charley horses during your pregnancy?" If she responds, "Yes, all the time. I couldn't get comfortable," the most likely reason for her discomfiture, and the baby's misery now, is a deficiency in calcium and probably magnesium. "But I drank a quart of milk a day," she may say defensively. "The doctor said I had to." Swallowing is not the same as absorbing. In my experience, when mother and baby receive calcium and magnesium supplements, both calm down in a week.

• Another fussy, unhappy, colicky baby has cradle cap (crib crust), yellow scales on his eyelashes, and a groin rash usually referred to as seborrhea. My question to the mother: "Did you have nausea and vomiting in the first three months of your pregnancy?" Often the reply is, "No, it was for the whole nine months." Aha! Mother and baby may need vitamin B_6 (pyridoxine). It works as a coenzyme in many metabolic processes.

• Here is another scenario. "I cannot run the vacuum or the dishwasher unless the baby is out of the house. He even stiff-arms me if I try to cuddle him. If I stimulate him, he will throw up. He is touchy." Some mothers have told me they were kicked out of bed by these restless, *unborn* babies. Some genetics play a role. The parents and the children often have the following symptoms in common: ticklishness, sensitivity, and often talkativeness. They experience little muscle cramps and are unable to relax and go to sleep. The giveaway: They love chocolate. Chocolate cravers are often low in magnesium; they are looking for the magnesium in the chocolate. Fifty milligrams of magnesium a day for a few days should calm such a baby. There is a pleasant-tasting liquid magnesium that should go down the baby's gullet if an eyedropper is used. The mother should take five hundred milligrams a day. These babies may turn into hyperactive children.

When all efforts have failed to reduce the baby's screaming attacks, parents should seek some professional help. Most medical doctors will prescribe a drug that has an effect on gastrointestinal spasms. These hyper-reactive babies simply notice their intestines more than others—they are unable to disregard the gas going sideways. I see babies who are burping, passing gas, and bloated, and it does not bother them at all. Others can get one little bubble in their intestinal tract and go wild. Their nervous systems are more easily stimulated.

Before parents "stone" their fussy baby with some tranquilizer, a visit to the chiropractor is in order; they can control colic with a simple neck adjustment. Naturopathic doctors use herbs and homeopathic remedies that are safe for babies.

These teas should be safe to try: Catnip, peppermint, fennel, anise, chamomile.

Cradle cap (one mother called it "crib crust"; another used "creeping crud") can be controlled if a few drops of mineral oil or flaxseed oil are rubbed into the yellow, greasy scales, which might then come off during the bath. Soap and a soft brush might help to remove the extra scales. Many are afraid to touch the soft spot at the top of the head, but the tissues there are tough, and one need not worry about poking a finger into the brain. These yellow scales may be a clue that there is a pyridoxine (B_6) deficiency. (If the mother had nausea and vomiting in the pregnancy and she has trouble with dream recall, a B_6 deficiency is a likely cause for the greasy scales, which are a manifestation of seborrhea.)

Cradle cap offers a fertile ground for the growth of bacteria and fungi. "A relatively old solution called 'colloidal silver' has regained popularity in the nineties. Colloidal silver has the effect of a germicidal. I have had success with colloidal silver on a cotton swab and painting the affected area. Within two to three days the cradle cap resolves."[108]

Candida, a yeast, loves to grow in the seborrheic skin. Frequently a secondary bacterial infection contaminates the weepy rawness behind the ears. This weepy ooze should first be treated with a bland cream like calendula, and if redness remains, a cortisone ointment might have to be used sparingly. For the groin and diaper area, a cortisone and anticandida cream works. A homeopathic tincture of candida may also work here.

Some oily material naturally found in the genitalia is protective, and vigorous effort to remove it is unwise. Dry the armpits and between the fingers and toes thoroughly. Try cornstarch for those areas. Perfumed oils are sensitizing and not necessary. Nonallergenic creams would be the best to use on scaly skin.

Drooling usually increases at about three months of age. The baby really does not care, so he lets his saliva run down his chin. Eventually, after a few months, he learns to swallow it, and no effort on the parents' part will speed up his social control. Most parents feel that a tooth is on its way, but they usually have to wait four months for that exciting day.

Moniliasis or candidiasis is a yeast infection, commonly found in the mouth ("**thrush**") and diaper area of babies less than a month old. It is rare after that unless the child has had heavy doses of antibiotics. It may regrow because of the temporary lack of competition from friendly bacteria.

Pregnant women frequently have a mild, unrecognized case of vaginal candidiasis, as her hormones make her more susceptible to this ubiquitous pest. The baby will acquire it during the birth passage. He may also get it in the nursery, as the yeast is almost impossible to eradicate, and he may then give it to his mother. They can pass it back and forth. In the mouth the colonies appear as white milk curds (that won't rub off) on gums, tongue, and inside the cheeks. The baby may be fussy, but he's not really bothered much. Mother and child are treated with acidophilus cultures and possibly Nystatin.

Nasolacrimal duct (tear duct) obstruction is a failure of complete formation of the passageway from the inner corner of the lids into the nasal cavity. This common condition prevents the tears from flowing into the nose; stagnant water allows germs to grow. The baby has a purulent discharge at the lid edge, and tears often run down the cheek. An antibiotic ointment or drop is used to control the infection; massaging the inner aspect of the lower lid against the nose may relieve the obstruction if it is but a mucus plug. If the obstruction continues after the first six or seven months, the ophthalmologist or optometrist can usually open up the duct by passing a probe down the passageway into the nose.

Navel, or umbilicus, is the small pit in the center of the abdomen through which the baby received nourishment and oxygen during uterine life. The umbilical cord contains a vein that transports blood and oxygen to the baby, and two arteries through which waste products and carbon dioxide are returned to the placenta and hence to the mother's circulation for removal. Directly after birth, the arteries in the umbilical cord constrict, and blood rarely leaks from them, although a clamp or umbilical tie is usually applied as a precaution. The cord dries up and sloughs off in seven to ten days, leaving a bit of raw stump, like a third-degree burn. Alcohol for cleansing is too drying to be used on this area as it may crack and bleed. Hydrogen peroxide is safe and effective. Calendula ointment keeps the area soft and pliable. Some babies have extra skin extending up the cord for one half to one inch. It takes several months or a year for this fingerlike protrusion to shrink and flatten down evenly with the surrounding skin. It has nothing to do with the way the obstetrician clamped the cord.

Sleeping position: Research has indicated that there is a risk for sudden infant death syndrome (SIDS) if babies are allowed to sleep on their stomachs in the prone position. It may not be a suffocation problem, but rather the result of inhaling toxic gases released from the chemicals in the mattress cover when the moist, warm air from the baby's lungs strikes the plastic. One hundred percent cotton bedding is available.

Dr. Hal Huggins, a dentist and researcher from Colorado, has found that back sleeping is the best way to promote good facial features and a well-developed dental arch. He notes that 80 percent of U.S. citizens need orthodontia, and part of that reason is because of nonbreast-feeding, but a significant blame can be placed on prone sleeping. Frequently the baby will rest his face against his fist, which acts like an orthodontia appliance. He says that American Indians have the best posture and body structure because of back or papoose sleeping. They also develop better balance and have no fear of falling (see Sleep Problems, Chapter 5).

Smoking: Researchers report that passive exposure to tobacco smoke from anyone smoking in the house will raise the risk of SIDS three and a half times. Recurrent respiratory illnesses, stunted intelligence, and shortened attention span are related to exposure to secondhand smoke. Smoking in the house lowered children's levels of the good HDL cholesterol.[109] (Are you motivated to quit?)

Tongue thrust is the forward pressure of the tongue against the teeth during swallowing or speech, sufficient to push the teeth forward or to interfere with articulation of *s* sounds (lisping). This habit may have originated from the rapid flow of milk from the bottle; the baby thrusts his tongue forward to slow the flow. Breast-fed babies are less likely to develop this habit. Speech pathologists claim that they can correct this impediment if the child is referred to them by age six or seven years. The dentist may place a "reminder" wire gadget just inside the incisors to break the habit of thrusting.

Vomiting is the rejection of stomach and/or intestinal contents. (Rule: If your baby throws up, he is telling you that something is wrong.) "Spitting up" to one observer may be "violent heaving" to another. It is difficult for a doctor to estimate the severity of a telephone report of "vomiting" without additional clues as to amount, frequency, duration, force, and content. The following may be helpful in evaluating relative severity.

The general condition of the vomiter is perhaps more important than what is coming up; if there is fever and lethargy in addition to the vomiting, the condition is more serious than it is in the child who vomits and then resumes normal play.

Spit-up or wet burp is common in babies who overload their stomachs with milk, or who may have swallowed air and bring up an ounce or two of milk when they burp. The milk may be slightly soured (a good sign that stomach acid is present). The stomach curves like a fish hook, so feeding a baby while he is lying on his right side may prevent this. (The bubble stays on top of the milk.)

Emesis is a nice way to say a small amount (two to six ounces) of vomitus is returned. If consistent with each feeding, a milk allergy should be considered. Most babies do well and gain normally. Smaller, more frequent feedings may be the answer. Thickening the milk with a tablespoon of baby food may make it more difficult to throw up. Propping the baby up after a feeding may allow gravity to aid retention. Acidified milk or buttermilk may be tolerated better.

Vomitus suggests a larger amount (four to eight ounces) is returned, and usually with some force. It may occur with an illness such as intestinal flu, meningitis, pyelonephritis, intestinal obstruction, or concussion. If the underlying condition is serious, the patient is usually lethargic.

Heaves suggest larger amounts and more forceful ejection of stomach contents.

Projectile vomiting is more likely to be associated with intestinal obstruction. The emitted fluid is often shot out three feet away from the victim.

Pyloric stenosis is the obstruction of the pylorus (outlet of the stomach) due to the hypertrophy of the muscles in the wall of this portion of the intestinal tract. It has an affinity for the firstborn male child in the springtime. (Of course, I once had a second-born female patient develop this in the fall.) The symptoms develop in the first six weeks of life.

Initially there is only an occasional spit-up, but after a few days, projectile vomiting shoots the stomach's contents across the room. The initial symptoms suggest a milk allergy, but it is quite obviously a mechanical problem when even water is blasted back. Urine and stools become scanty, and malnutrition, lethargy, dehydration, and alkalosis become late findings in the undiagnosed, neglected case.

The swollen muscle feels like an olive deep in the abdomen—above and to the right of the navel. After a few ounces of milk are swallowed, gastric waves can be seen moving through the upper left abdominal area toward the navel; they appear like a golf ball rolling under the skin, and indicate stomach contractions trying to force the milk through the narrow pyloric tunnel. In a questionable case, some radiopaque dye can be added to the milk. The X ray would show no stomach emptying, or a thin ("string sign") column in the pyloric area. Emesis is milk and stomach juices; bile returned indicates that the obstruction is farther down the duodenum. Surgery is the treatment.

Call the doctor!

CHAPTER 3

Diet for the First Few Years of Life

If Breast Milk Is Unavailable, Is Cow Milk Safe for Babies?

When I started pediatric practice in 1951, the word was out that bottled cow milk was just as good as breast milk. We were introduced to the various formulae by the company representatives who told us to "just add water," and this new manufacturing method produced a milk like mother made, which formed a small curd when it hit the hydrochloric acid in the stomach. The baby could digest it just as well as the real stuff. **Wrong!**

Dr. Frank Oski, head of the Pediatrics Department of the Johns Hopkins Medical School, has been able to list the problems if alternative milks are used for human babies:

• **Anemia.** Babies fed only cow milk will eventually develop iron-deficiency anemia.

• **Folic Acid Deficiency.** Preparing cow milk for human consumption may destroy folate as well. Megaloblastic anemia may develop.

• **Eczema.** Many babies had eczema and dry skin due to a fatty acid deficiency. Linoleic acid must be added.

• **Ear Infections.** Ear infections are uncommon in breast-fed babies. Otitis media occurs in only 1 percent of totally breast-fed babies but in more than 50 percent of totally bottle-fed babies.

• **Hemolytic Anemia.** When iron was added to cow milk formula, it tended to destroy the baby's red blood cells; iron plus oxygen caused this hemolysis. Excessive fatty acids—not the human gamma-linolenic acid—also contributed to the phenomenon.

• **Beriberi.** In 1965 some babies on soybean milk developed beriberi, as someone forgot to put thiamine into the formula.

• **Low Intelligence.** Between 1950 and 1970, preemies got a high-protein, low-fat milk. Since then, tests have shown the IQ of these high-protein-fed babies is but 89. The IQs of the control group of breast-fed babies is 112. Full-term breast-fed babies grow up to have a slightly higher intelligence than their bottle-fed peers. These good results are probably due to the essential omega-3 fatty acids that breast milk supplies. ("Observations of exceptionally bright children: none was artificially fed during infancy." [110])

• **Dental Arch.** Breast-fed babies grow up to have better dental arches and less crowding of the teeth. Bottle-fed babies may develop tongue-thrusting habits because the milk is coming out too fast. The now common temporomandibular joint syndrome (TMJ) is more likely seen in those who were bottle-fed as infants.

• **Diabetes.** Genetic susceptibility is important as a causative factor, but early cow milk exposure (in that first year) may be an important determinant of subsequent type I diabetes and may increase the risk of developing this problem by 1.5 times. A *New England Journal of Medicine* report found that of 142 children with diabetes studied, 100 percent had abnormally high levels of antibodies to bovine serum albumin, a milk protein. These antibodies destroy the ability of the pancreas to produce insulin.

• **Cardiovascular and Cancer Tendencies.** If adolescents were breast-fed as babies, eight out of thirty have evidence of coronary arterial narrowing. If bottle-fed, they will have two to three times as much narrowing. The incidence of lymphoma in adults is five times higher in bottle-fed than in breast-fed babies. A Swedish study indicates that the alpha-lactalbumin in human milk can interfere with cancer cell growth. Cow milk is low in zinc, taurine, carnitine, cysteine, nucleotidin, prostaglandin, and epidermal growth factor. These nutrients tend to suppress the occurrence of degenerative dieases. An XO factor in homogenized milk passes through the intestinal mucosa into the circulation and damages arteries. Finland, the United States, and Australia are the countries in which the people are ingesting the largest amounts of homogenized milk; they also have the highest rate of cardiovascular disease.

Toxic metals such as aluminum, lead, and fluoride may be found in canned milks.[111]

Using cow milk for humans may be dangerous to their health.

Cow milk is meant for calves, but many human babies can thrive on it. The calcium and phosphorus content are adequate. (My wife and I had a milk-sensitive baby who could not tolerate any of the formula samples we were given. We discovered that if we simmered two quarts of skim milk for five hours [then added the water back] and fed him that, he would sleep for a few hours and not scream, throw up, or have green stools. He continued to have trouble with cow milk all his life: ear infections, asthma, nosebleeds, headaches, and bedwetting.)

Many people can tolerate raw, fresh cow milk because of the enzymes therein. But it does contain some bacteria. As the milk stands in the refrigerator, these bacteria multiply slowly. They attack the histidine in the milk and easily change it to histamine, which may be the cause of the allergic symptoms. Vitamin C and digestive enzymes may take care of the histamine load.

If the infant cannot tolerate cow milk, the following milks are usually tried:

Goat milk is a satisfactory breast milk substitute and is occasionally used if a cow milk allergy is suspected. The kid goat grows at a rate similar to a human baby, so goat milk contents seem more appropriate as a substitute for breast-feeding. It is less allergenic than cow milk, so it is usually the first choice if the mother is unable to nurse. It has no iron, and the folic acid may be deficient, so these must be added. The fat in goat milk is more easily digested than the fat in cow milk.

We were told never to recommend goat milk for infants under a year of age, as there was not enough folic acid in the milk of those hoofed ones to prevent the infant from getting pernicious anemia. That seemed odd to me, as kid goats did not seem to get anemic, and unless the mother goat was subsisting on a diet of tin cans and newspapers, these herbivores must be getting folate from the fodder. (A mother reported to me that her one-year-old child was full of phlegm in his throat, and seemed to have a mixture of asthma and laryngitis: gurgling, "zonking" [making that terrible throat-clearing noise as if he had a bunch of rubber bands hanging from the back of his palate], choking, wheezing, coughing, sputtering, spitting up, and gasping. He thrived on breast milk for the first six months of life, except when the mother ate some cow products. When she weaned him to the cow, he developed all the preceding symptoms. Soy milk was not much better. But raw goat milk from a neighbor was perfect; he had no phlegm. But the baby's pediatrician said he was probably on the verge of a terrible anemia. So it was back through the mess of the various cow milks. Nothing worked until she went back to the goat. And it had to be raw.)

Albert Camp, president of the Brentland Corporation, purveyors of goat products, has told me of the hundreds of patrons who have had symptoms disappear when they changed from the cow to the goat. Much of his support comes from doctors trained outside the United States. Could he be biased? (Remember, most of the women of the world have raised their children on goat milk if unable to nurse.) Some decades ago goat milk was tested for folate and found lacking. But the goats who were tested were eating winter fodder—no folate in that. Of course.

Only here in the United States has the cow become the norm. If raw goat milk is used, one must be sure the nanny goat is living in clean surroundings. Because it is fairly concentrated, raw goat milk should be diluted about one to one with sterile water. Get a goat. They are clean and wholesome. You can add some folate if you are nervous about that. (You can bring the goat inside occasionally; they have cute, neat, little bowel movements that you can flick off the carpet. Can you say that for the cow?)

Soy bean milk is a reasonable substitute for breast or cow milk. It provides all the protein, calcium, and minerals necessary for growth and nutrition. If a baby vomits, has diarrhea, or is screaming with gas on a cow milk formula, two or more days of soy milk will usually quiet these symptoms if they are due to a sensitivity.

Meat and nut-based milks are the next step if the baby has trouble with goat, soy, and cow milks. When all else fails, some mothers will rotate the milks: boiled cow milk in the morning, soy milk at noon, meat milk at supper, and whatever is handy at night, like rice or almond milk. Apparently the baby is sensitive to *all* these milks but does not get too much of any one by using this rotation method.

Skim or 2 percent milk may be used if spitting up is a problem. Some babies cannot tolerate much fat in the milk. Boiling or simmering for a few minutes to an hour may further improve the digestibility of the milk if spitting, gas, and/or sloppy stools occur. Water lost during the boiling process must be replaced. Because of the low number of calories in skim milk, the baby may drink almost twice as much. It usually does not contain vitamin D, so this should be given as a supplement. Essential fatty acids must also be added, especially in infancy, when the brain needs fats.

Diet for the First Six Months of Life

If the baby is on breast milk or formula, nothing more needs to be added to the diet for the first six months of life. Milk is important for the rapid growth during those months. Water is obviously essential. Daily intake for a baby must amount to more than 10 percent of his body weight, depending on environmental heat and loss in the stools. A seven-pound baby needs about a pint of fluid daily. (An average adult could get by on four or five pints a day.) Almost half the water loss occurs through evaporation from skin and lungs; the remainder is excreted in the urine. A baby urinating but twice on a hot day needs extra fluid to prevent dehydration and/or fever. The kidneys of infants up to six months of age are unable to concentrate urine as well as adults. This is one reason for using milk as the main ingredient of the diet during this period: The infant's poor ability to process sodium via the kidneys in the first few months of life argues against the early introduction of solid foods with high sodium content. Because of this poor concentration ability, diarrhea during warm weather is especially dangerous. Extra fluid (watered milk) is important. Boiled skimmed milk is dangerous because of its high sodium content. It must be diluted.

Solid Food. Pediatricians used to advise parents to start rice cereal after milk intake had been established at about one month of age. We thought it would help the baby sleep through the night. **Wrong!** Most parents start rice cereal when pressure from friends and relatives is overwhelming. Intestinal amylase (the enzyme needed to digest starches) production is insignificant, and hence starch digestion is poor under four months of age. Boredom may also push a parent to start solids early. A doctor usually suggests using some cereal as soon as parents indicate they *want* him to suggest it. It takes about twenty minutes to prepare the cereal, and the baby may last twenty minutes longer before the next feeding. It does have some iron, but the baby's intestines usually cannot absorb it well in those first few months.

A milk anemia can appear in bottle-fed babies by six to eight months of age. Caucasian babies will look as pale as the milk they drink. African-American babies reveal their anemia by their pale mucous membranes. This anemia stimulated the baby food companies to put out baby food with iron, to feed these iron-deficient babies some "good food" and preclude the development of this anemia. Then the race was on. As time went by, it seemed that the only contraindication to the early feeding of solids was that the cord was not yet cut. It was ridiculous how early we had mothers shovel food down those reluctant throats.

Research has now proven that all we have done to those babies is make them allergic or sensitive to those foods we fed to them so early. We had no idea that their intestines were so immature that the foods would not be broken down or absorbed. In infancy the only safe food is mother's milk. The infants' intestines have not produced the enzymes necessary to break down foods into nonallergenic amino acids, simple carbohydrates, and fatty acids. (Sorry.)

Diet from Six Months to a Year of Age

The diet must provide adequate calories, protein, fats, minerals, and vitamins. A rigid adherence to a prescribed, balanced diet usually leads to frustration, as most infants consume either more or less than what is thought to be optimum. If offered eight ounces, he only takes seven; if one jar is opened, he wants a jar and a half. The science of dietetics must be permissive, as growth, intestinal absorption, and activity levels are quite variable.

The American Academy of Pediatrics recommends that solids be started at about six months of age. It is a ritual, and not based on any science. Rules: Wait until the extrusion reflex (the baby's tongue pushes out anything that is not milk) is gone; wait for normal esophageal motility (the gullet in infancy can move liquids on down to the stomach, but does poorly with solids); wait until the baby sits well; and wait until the intestines are less permeable to avoid allergies. This means to begin solids *after* six to eight months of age.

Whenever solid foods are started, the least allergenic foods are the best and safest: steamed zucchini, carrots, squash, yam, cauliflower, and asparagus. Commercial baby foods may be high in salt content; it is wiser to use home-cooked foods, either strained or pureed in a blender. The salt content can be more easily restricted this way; in addition, it is cheaper. Additional seasoning should not be added to the commercial baby food in the jar. Cooked, mashed zucchini is probably the safest food to introduce to the baby first, as it is a rare sensitizer; no one seems to eat enough of it to become allergic to it. In the beginning, the baby's food is made soupy enough to be easily sucked off the spoon. Some find it convenient to use a dull knife and wipe the food off the baby's upper gum, allowing the blob to fall on the tongue. Introduce one food every week or so in small amounts— given in the amount of two to ten tablespoons once or twice a day. If there is a reaction, the parent will know which food caused it. At nine months you might want to add these: papaya, nectarines, banana, pears, berries, cherries (pureed), beets, rice, and oatmeal. Breast-fed babies need no supplemental solids if they are gaining and the mother is on a good diet.

Veal, lamb, and beef may be added at eight or nine months of age, and are best used singly, not in mixtures, so if there is a reaction, one will know which is the villain. Two to four teaspoonfuls can be given per day, and may be combined with fruit or a vegetable.

If the baby is bottle-fed, the solid foods are to be offered first—before the milk—after seven months of age in an effort to cut down on milk consumption. Iron-bearing foods become more important after six months, because of the anemia. (This is not a concern for the breast-fed infant.)

At eight or nine months, four-ounce meals of cereal, fruit, and vegetable, along with some vegetable or animal protein, are offered three times a day. Teething biscuits might be tried at this time; use any but those containing wheat. At about ten months, six to eight ounces of solids are offered three times a day followed by goat, soy, or cow milk, determined by the baby—depending on *his* requirements. Some big, active babies still consume eight ounces of milk three or four times a day; small, quiet ones may only need two to four ounces after their meal of solids.

It would be best to avoid the common allergens—wheat, corn, eggs, citrus, peanut butter, chocolate—until the baby is one year old, as they are more likely to cause reactions in the younger infant. It is possible to keep people from becoming allergic to foods if we wait to introduce the more likely sensitizing ones until the baby is a year old.

Although starches are hard for infants to digest, rice is the safest of the cereals, but it is somewhat constipating. Barley and oats have some laxative action, but cereal with wheat is the most likely to cause reactions: gas, cramps, and diarrhea. Try these at one year: applesauce, tofu, parsnips, avocado, peaches, egg yolk, and split pea soup. Squash is safe, but because it is a starch, it may be hard for the baby to digest. Avoid oils and sweets. (Primitive mothers will chew up the food and introduce that bolus to their baby.)

Animal protein is an efficient provider of all essential amino acids and B vitamins, but all the essentials can be obtained from vegetables and grains, properly combined.

Self-feeding after twelve months of age allows the child to take some responsibility in balancing his own caloric requirements. If appetite falls off, the starches, fats, white foods, and milk should be the first foods subtracted from the diet so that the child will get the basic protein and fruit. Egg, peaches, and green vegetables may be added at one year, cautiously, and one new food every few days. Finger foods are fun; but no raw carrots or nuts because of the potential for choking. Rotating the foods will help prevent some of the sensitivities. Cooked carrots are fun as the infant can squeeze them and eat the parts that come through between the fingers.

Protein and fruit or vegetables provide the essential ingredients. (Milk and starches are used as "fillers.") Protein requirements are greater for infants than for children and adults. Amino acids are the basic chemicals (containing nitrogen) that constitute protein. Milk will supply the protein needs until vegetable or animal protein (legumes, grains, veal, beef, lamb) is added to the diet after seven or eight months of life. It is easier to supply a child's amino acid requirements with animal protein than it is with the protein found in grain, beans, peas, and nut butters. About one teaspoonful of protein for every four or five pounds of body weight per day should keep the infant and child in positive nitrogen balance. One serving of rice and beans, or a small low-fat hamburger patty, should be enough each day for the growing child.

Supplementary vitamins should begin early and continue throughout life. I suggest these doses of vitamin C: one hundred milligrams per day per month of age. A six-month-old would get six hundred milligrams per day. The one-year-old would get one thousand milligrams a day. The two-year-old would get two thousand milligrams daily. This is increased one thousand milligrams for each year. After age five years, the five thousand-milligrams dose is continued daily.

The B-complex vitamins are usually included in the milk formulae (at least 10 milligrams of each of the Bs), but extra B_6 (pyridoxine) at twenty five milligrams a day might be helpful to suppress the possibility of SIDS. (See SIDS, Chapter 15.) (The twenty-four chemical blood tests will reveal protein deficiencies.) If vitamin D is not in the formula, four hundred units should be given daily, in the winter, at least. Vitamin A is usually incorporated in the formula; if not, 5,000 units daily is the dose. Beta carotene, ten thousand units daily, is a health promoter. Fluoride has been found to be a toxin and not to be used for babies (see Fluoride, Chapter 7).

Clara M. Davis, M.D., ran a famous diet experiment in 1927. She offered infants of seven to nine months natural foods, unmixed, unseasoned, and some cooked. No soups, bread, or custards. They were all breast-fed. She noted that with this self-selection they became omnivorous. They liked most of the foods, but rarely ate more than three solid foods in any considerable quantity at one meal. They had their favorites and continued to take eleven to forty-eight ounces of milk a day. They might eat one to seven eggs or none; and one to four bananas. They had waves of preference that lasted several days. There was no particular preference between raw or cooked foods.

Their favorites: (1) Fruit—banana, apple, orange, tomato, peach; (2) bone marrow; (3) raw milk; (4) cereal, whole wheat, oats, Ry Krisp, corn, barley; (5) chicken, beef, lamb; (6) egg; (7) thymus, brain, liver, kidney; (8) vegetables—potato, beets, carrots, peas, cabbage, turnips, cauliflower, spinach, lettuce. They were healthy by examination and blood tests. Can you do this for your children? Maybe they know more than we do.[112]

Weaning a baby away from the bottle may take months, but most parents find it not worth the fight to stop it suddenly. Most continue with a pacifier, or a bottle with only water. *No juice or sugary fluid is allowed as the teeth will be destroyed.* The sugar just sits on the enamel and allows the germs to make the cavities.

Cow milk after infancy has been highly overrated, chiefly by the American Dairy Council, which exists solely to promote the ingestion of dairy products. Dietitians teach medical students that milk is the perfect food; doctors thus carry this message to their patients, so the myth is perpetuated. Most doctors have discovered, to their surprise, that a number of their patients are in excellent health despite a low milk intake, or even *because* of an absence of dairy products in their diets. We all have found from experience that growing children who consume excess milk are more likely to become anemic. Anemic children may have double the respiratory infections than the nonanemic. When a child becomes anemic, for some reason, he dislikes the very foods that would correct his anemia and prefers to drink milk and eat white foods (white breads, starches, potatoes, macaroni, rice). Because these foods are lacking in iron, he becomes more anemic and aggravates his original problem.

• Cow milk is a common allergen. About 50 percent of babies are sensitive enough to milk to require a substitute. If a baby or child has any chronic respiratory, ear, intestinal, skin (a red ring around the anal opening), or urinary problem, milk and dairy products must be withheld from the diet, as they may be the cause of the problem. Some wet the bed because of it. Milk ingestion in some people makes the intestinal lining leak blood from damaged capillaries. Headaches, pallor, and irritability can frequently be traced to milk in the diet (see Tension Fatigue, Chapter 12). Homogenized milk contains a substance called xanthine oxidase that is believed to damage the lining of the blood vessels. Calcium can be found in other foods, and animal protein provides a greater variety of amino acids than does milk. Many babies have minor gas, snorting, and rash problems from milk; if these symptoms are not serious, a substititute may not be necessary.

• Cow milk is constipating to most people. Bovine milk has been found to stimulate exorphin production in the small intestine. Exorphins are opiate receptor-active peptide fragments that decrease intestinal motility. The frequent use of laxatives in our country is probably directly related to the high milk ingestion.

• Cow-milk-fed babies are more likely to grow to have multiple sclerosis, probably because it has only one fifth the amount of linoleic acid as human milk. Linoleic acid is needed for the myelin sheath surrounding the nerves.

The human is the only animal that drinks milk after infancy; the other mammals stop nursing when their teeth begin to bite the nipples. Children are normally poor eaters from two to four years of age; cow milk should be restricted at that age. Many people have beautiful teeth and bones and are infrequently sick, yet had no milk from infancy because of their allergy.

Parents say: "I don't care if he doesn't eat as long as he drinks his milk." This should be changed to "Stop the milk and maybe he will eat better."

However, having said all that, milk can be a good source of calcium and protein if it is suitably modified with the addition of an electrolytic solution containing water, sodium, potassium, chloride, carbonate, sulfur, and magnesium.[113] This changes it so the allergenicity is less, and the absorption of the calcium and protein is enhanced. A blood test for calcium, nitrogen elements, and protein would be the best way to monitor the level and the need for calcium. Despite health science researchers' efforts to make cow milk safe for humans, Dr. Thom still finds cow milk is a problem with many people.

Intestinal Problems of the Infant

Constipation is the passage of hard, usually dry, usually large stools, and is a common complication of a low-roughage diet. Constipation is determined by the *consistency,* not the frequency of the bowel movements. The chief cause of constipation is the consumption of dairy products (milk, ice cream, and cheese) and foods low in roughage (meat, gelatin, and most white foods—white breads, starches, potatoes, macaroni, rice). These foods hold little moisture, so they become dry and packed by the time they get to the rectum. Just some "dust" is passed. Inattention to the call of nature can lead to constipation also. Ritalin (commonly given to calm the attention-deficit-disability child) may cause constipation. Some just need more water, although that usually just makes more urine. Congential defects and hypothyroidism are possibilities.

A child may withhold his movement because his last one was painful, thus setting up a cycle: The longer he holds it, the harder it gets, and the more it hurts when he *does* go. He may refuse to defecate on command when he is being toilet-trained because of a stubborn, passive-aggressive attitude, and thus become constipated. His psychological refusal may allow a large fecal impaction to build up inside his rectum, causing cramps and irritability and occasionally a paradoxical leakage of soft stool around the mass, staining his underwear. This soiling usually does not occur until he has retained his stool for some weeks (see Encopresis, Chapter 5). Some children cannot use the toilets at school because there are no doors on the stalls.

It is also possible that he does not know exactly where his body is; he is unaware of the rectal message, as he may think it is coming from his knee or his toe. It may be that he has a retained infantile Galant reflex (see Chapter 4).

Treatment for constipation: Addition of high-roughage foods is critical. Prune juice or grape juice may help. (Dr. Thom: "I use external castor oil packs routinely with great results without producing any dependency.")

Along with roughage, the following might give a person normal bowel movements: aloe vera juice, flaxseed oil, apple pectin, psyllium, acidophilus. "Chiropractors have found that doing abdominal massage along the iliocecal sphincter [lower right area of abdomen] has produced remarkable results in relieving constipation."[114]

Laxatives are agents that soften the stool by holding moisture and increasing intestinal activity. Bulk laxatives take about three days to get down to where they will benefit. If the stools of the bottle-fed infant are hard, one or two teaspoons of dark Karo syrup in each bottle may help hold moisture in the stool. One half to one teaspoon of milk of magnesia in one bottle a day may keep the stool soft.

Some people feel that a daily bowel movement will prevent sickness or insanity. We all have different rhythms for elimination, varying from three bowel movements a day to one a week, but they should be soft and easily passed. If the stool is hard and big enough to cause pain and fissuring, changes in the diet must be tried first. The constipatee might become dependent on cascara or castor oil; a purge on Monday might produce the previous four days' movements on Tuesday. He might be so cleaned out that when Friday rolls around and nothing happens, the purge would be repeated. With this method he will never be able to rely on nature.

Mineral oil will lubricate the passageways, but may be overdone. (One of our professors in medical school told us, "In America, the only contraindication to mineral oil seems to be a slippery pavement.") It may inhibit the absorption of vitamins A and D (which are oil soluble) and will sometimes produce an opacity in the lungs if an occasional drop has been inadvertently aspirated. If used, a thirty-pound child needs about two or three teaspoonfuls a day to do the job. Try to avoid it.

Occasionally the physician may have to insert his lubricated finger into the rectum to break up and remove the big, dry chunks. These manipulations are painful and, if repeatedly necessary, can cause some psychological problems; it is better to soften the stools via the oral route. On a high-roughage diet, defecation usually becomes a once-a-day ritual.

Enema is the removal of stool from the rectum by hydraulic pressure. Enemas may be required to dislodge the first impacted portion. Fluid (water, salt solution like Fleet's, or oil) is forced into the rectum, hopefully above the stool. This stretches the wall of the intestine, which responds by contracting, and thus the stool is pushed out. Large amounts of plain water may lead to water intoxication (cerebral edema), as the large bowel absorbs water very efficiently. High, hot, and heavy enemas given to a victim of appendicitis have been known to burst the appendix even though it is five bowel feet away. However, a rectal insertion of six ounces of water plus two pinches of salt might rehydrate a vomiting infant.

A struggling child might be given an enema more easily by placing him facedown (prone) on a chair by the bathtub so his legs are hanging down into the tub. The operator can see what is being done and is able to place his knee on the child's back to stabilize the moving target. Some type of lubricant facilitates the passage of the enema tip.

Stool is perhaps a better term for a fecal evacuation than "go-go," "number two," "big job," or "big potty." Doctors use "bowel movement" (BM) or "defecation." Families would be well advised to use a specific medical term that will never be confused with some other activity. (If you say, "Let's go-go for a ride," and the child runs to the bathroom instead of the car, it would be wise to revise some terms.)

Diarrhea is the passage of frequent, loose, or watery—usually bile-colored—stools. Any diarrheal disease is dangerous in infants, because of their susceptibility to dehydration and salt imbalance. Diarrhea in the first few weeks of life is most likely due to a **milk allergy** (a breast-fed baby may be allergic to the cow milk in the mother's diet), a fat intolerance, or a congenital absence of one of the sugar enzymes. Antibiotics are notorious for causing diarrhea, and valuable magnesium, zinc, and other nutrients are lost as a result. When these nutrients are lost, immune function is compromised and more infection will follow. Healthy colonies of beneficial bacteria—*L. acidophilus, L. bulgaricus*—can discourage the growth of harmful bacteria by acidifying the colon contents. Homeopathic remedies (such as arsenicum album, chamomilla, mercurius vivus, podophyllum, sulfur) allowed children to recover from diarrhea much more quickly than those taking a placebo.[115]

Viral gastroenteritis. This starts with a day of vomiting, and then moves to diarrhea for seven days. (see Gastroenteritis, Chapter 6).

Mild diarrhea: home treatment. Give nothing by mouth until vomiting has stopped, then give a water-sugar-electrolyte solution (six ounces of water, one half teaspoon of sugar, and a pinch of salt). (This is a better one: sodium chloride, 3.5 grams; sodium bicarbonate, 2.5 grams; potassium chloride, 1.5 grams; glucose, 20 grams, in one liter of water.) One ounce of this should be given every one half to one hour for six to twelve hours as the only nutrient. Try to get a quart of this down in a twenty-four-hour period. On the second day give four to eight ounces of this solution three times a day; then four to eight ounces of a solution containing half skim milk (unboiled) and half water, three times a day. The third day change to skim milk (do not boil); on the fourth day give whole milk or formula. If symptoms are immediately exacerbated, a nonmilk (soy or meat) formula might be tried while waiting for the seven-day period to pass. Resting the gut is the idea.

Miso soup, rice water, and rice are helpful. Charcoal will absorb toxins. Zinc and vitamins A and C will promote healing. The Life Balances electrolyte solution is ideal here.

Anything can do anything. This means that food sensitivities may be responsible for diarrhea (see Gastrointestinal allergy, Chapter 12).

These might help: slippery elm, red raspberry tea, goldenseal, marshmallow root, dill, ginger, agrimony, echinacea, comfrey, catnip tea. Lactobacilli may help to control the diarrhea.[116]

Celiac disease is now called gluten-induced enteropathy (disease of the intestinal tract). It was formerly thought that the gliadin fraction of the gluten found in wheat, rye, and other grains was the problem, but now

Corey Resnick, N.D., of Gresham, Oregon, tells us that the carbohydrate part of these grains (glucose, galactose, xylose, and arabinose) is the source of the toxicity. It is probably genetic and thus a lifelong problem, but its manifestations may vary depending on age, being more severe in infancy. Despite the wasting of the buttocks and general malnutrition from the diarrhea, these children have a normal facial appearance. The stools are large, foamy, foul-smelling, and greasy, as fat absorption is also affected. Resnick suggests that fungal enzyme therapy (Aspergillus-derived) will help to solve the problem.[117]

Chronic nonspecific diarrhea is the name given to the passage of three to ten big, sloppy stools a day running clear down to the child's shoes. There is no fever or other sign of illness. The child is happy, plays well, and even gains weight. No cause can be found. It usually begins as an ordinary attack of gastroenteritis with vomiting and diarrhea, but after the usual seven days it doesn't stop. Diet changes are of no value. A temporary enzyme deficiency is blamed but is unproven. No pathological bacteria can be demonstrated in stool culture. Intramuscular B complex and C vitamin injections are often curative.

Sometimes giardia (an intestinal parasite) is overlooked in children. There is a specific antigen test for it. (See Great Smokies Diagnostic Laboratory, in Appendix B. Diagnostics in Seattle does this testing also.)

If the usual pathogens are not found in the stool culture, a diet of fruits and vegetables, but no milk and no grains, seems to work for some. Sometimes certain carbohydrates remain in the digestive tract, allowing the growth of bacteria and yeasts that give off toxins that can affect the nervous system (mental confusion, epilepsy, poor memory).[118]

Malabsorption is the general wasting of body tissues that occurs when food passes through the intestines without being digested and/or absorbed. Stools are usually bulky, greasy, foamy, loose, and malodorous. This is called steatorrhea (fat diarrhea), but impaired fat digestion is not the primary cause; the greasy stools just contain a great deal of unabsorbed fat. The stomach acids, as well as pepsin, bile, and pancreatic digestive enzymes (lipase, protease, and amylase), may all be working efficiently to digest and emulsify the fat, protein, and carbohydrate in the meal. The pathology lies in the lining of the small bowel. It has lost its ability to move these products of digestion from the lumen of the intestine into the capillaries and lymph channels on the other side of these lining cells. Bacteria digest the unabsorbed protein and sugar, causing gas and cramps. Fat-soluble vitamins A, D, and K are poorly absorbed, and skin changes, low calcium tetany, and bleeding problems occur. General body wasting is the rule. Vitamins by injection may help.

Lactase deficiency is due to the inadequate production of lactase, an enzyme that converts milk sugar (lactose) into glucose and galactose, the simple sugars. The lactose molecule has a diarrhea effect, and like a dose of salts, produces watery, gas-filled stools that burn the anal opening. (A common, temporary lactase deficiency may follow a bout of dysentery or gastroenteritis, which can erode the intestinal cellular lining wherein the enzyme is produced.)

Some people are born with the condition and can tolerate only a small amount of lactose. Seventy to ninety percent of Africans, South Americans, some American Indians, and Asians are more likely to be deficient in lactase, and can tolerate no more than a few ounces of milk with its lactose. (As part of foreign aid, our country has sent much skim milk powder to the very people who cannot tolerate it. They may become severely ill and assume their "friends" in the United States have sent them "bad" skim milk powder. Many of them use the milk to whitewash their homes and fences.) "A sharp deterioration in lactose tolerance was observed after the age of three, and all the subjects above the age of twelve had flat tolerance curves [sugar not absorbed]. Age is the only consistent factor determining a subject's ability to hydrolyze and absorb lactose."[119] Adding the missing enzyme, lactase, to the diet is the method of control.

The Diet from Two to Four Years

Age two to four years is traditionally a poor eating age, mainly because of the slow growth during this period. An average two- to four-year-old child gains but two to three pounds each year. Thus this nursery school child will need about the same number of calories in a year that he needed for *one month* when an infant! If the parents are not aware of this normal appetite loss, mealtime could become a battle, and the child learns to manipulate his parents' frustration and tyrannize the family. The child wins.

A tablespoon of some protein food, a quarter piece of bread, and six peas, plus about two ounces of soy, goat, or rice milk, is a big dinner to the toddler, and would provide most of his protein, minerals, iron, and vitamins for the day. He may want to eat all yellow foods for a month, then all ground meat, then nothing but white foods, but almost never any green foods. She may not eat anything on her plate at all, simply because the mashed potatoes happened to touch the peas. Some toddlers find one poor meal a day quite satisfactory. Small amounts are more readily consumed. A child may be completely discouraged when she sees a big helping in front of her. Let her ask for more; it's a better ploy.

If the child can get up, walk, run, urinate, have a soft bowel movement occasionally, somewhere, and smiles and laughs more than she cries and frowns, she is okay. So many children "forget" or "refuse" to eat at about that two- to three-year-old age range, we feel there must be something wrong if they don't eat three "good" meals a day. Many parents will cuddle, cajole, bribe, distract, fight, push, and try almost anything (juggle) to get the uncooperative passive-aggressive beast to eat *something*. (Don't say anything about the starving Armenians.) She may realize that not eating drives you nuts. She may even be hungry, but the joy of seeing you get red-faced and blow your top is a great power trip. She may eat better if she attends a nursery school. Many children eat better if their peers are eating. (It is the same with toilet training; if something looks like fun, most children will try it.) She may be following in the genetic growth pattern predetermined by the genes from some slight grandparent. Does she look like Grandmother Bitsy, who is but four feet tall? This child may just have a very efficient digestive tract, and get more out of her food than others.

Loss of appetite occurs as the first symptom of almost all diseases, but if the child's general attitude and physical behavior do not change, it suggests that the anorexia is physiological and not due to disease or emotional factors. Many children—and adults—have major food likes and dislikes, sometimes based on allergies, and sometimes on a mysterious built-in mechanism the body uses to provide internal balance (fluid needs, acid-base balance, various mineral requirements, etc.). These should be respected. If a child loves vinegar, it means that he is somewhat alkaline due to a greater than average sodium level in the system. It is perfectly fine to allow the child to consume what he wants of that food. (Vinegar, pickles, and salsa are acidic foods as they contain acetic acid, which removes sodium from the body. Some alkaline people will drink the vinegar right out of the pickle jar.)

A good rule for the anorexic child: If he eats some protein and fruit almost every day, his bodily needs are almost satisfied. Ingesting a multi-mineral and vitamin supplement would assure one that the child is getting the known essentials.

ANOREXIA—"WON'T EAT"—APPETITE LOSS

Sick		Not sick, activity same	
Nausea, vomiting or	Pain on swallowing	Normal two-year-old or	Psychological
		wants to feed self	neurological
Intestinal flu	Tonsillitis	Too much milk	
Mesenteric adenitis	Ear infection	Anemia	
Head injury	Aphthous stomatitis	Constipation	
Bladder infection	Canker sores	Stubborn 2- to 4-year old	
Brain tumor	Foreign body	Emotional upset	
Intracranial bleeding	Herpangina	Tension at table	
Lead poisoning		Hyperactive (ADD)	
Mercury poisoning		Allergy	
Use of aspartame			

A checkup for anemia is worthwhile. Some need zinc, as that mineral is responsible for our sense of taste and smell. Check the nails for white spots.

Insisting that your two-year-old use proper table manners *all* the time can create some pretty nasty mealtime fights. ("Don't spill. Don't play with your food. Eat your broccoli!" is enough to wreck the appetite of the already poor eater. Child's response: "I say it's spinach, and I say to hell with it" [from a drawing by Carl Rose, *New Yorker,* 1928].) If you find your child regressing to the point where he refuses to use his silverware or won't eat at all, you might be asking him to be more grown-up than is possible for his age. If you use knife, fork, and spoon, your child will eventually do likewise. Back off. You might avoid a fight by feeding a child earlier in the evening to improve her blood sugar and then having her sit when the grown-ups are eating and chew on a salad or a piece of melon, and then be excused.

Pica is the persistent ingestion of nonfoods. (Consumption of dirt, sand, plaster, animal excreta, paint, glass, and grass—even five-dollar bills—have all been reported.) This perverted craving is most often due to an iron-deficiency anemia, but vitamin and other mineral (zinc) lack may also account for it. The toddler is looking for the missing elements his body needs. He also needs to orally investigate most things. He might also be getting some attention from this behavior, albeit negative. Somehow the parents have to pretend they don't care, and at the same time the child must have a balanced diet, extra iron and zinc, and plenty of opportunity to satisfy oral drives: Permit and encourage pacifier and thumb-sucking, let him mess in his food, let him place harmless toys in his mouth. Sometimes the pica produces other diseases (lead poisoning, worm infestation, mercury poisoning) that, by their nature, heighten irritability and might foster more pica. The hair test, a twenty-four-chemical-screen blood test, plus a complete blood count would reveal some obvious deficiencies.

Diet for the Four- to Six-Year-Old:

Children this age show great variations in appetite. Definite food likes, cravings, and dislikes are the hallmark. Parents know that if their child would eat better, he would feel better. The more the parents cajole, force, and bribe, the more the child seems to insist on his/her favorite: peanut butter and jelly or macaroni and cheese. White bread and hot dogs are goodies. Ice cream and other sweets seem to slide down easily, but vegetables are yucky to them. Most of these preferred foods are low in roughage, so constipation could be a problem with this age group. It is too bad that junk foods are promoted on television and are so readily available everywhere. Parents must be tough and restrict the intake of nutritionally impoverished foods. It is a far cry from running naked through the woods eating bark, leaves, and berries as the human body was meant to do.

Malnutrition may be caused by insufficient food or dietary imbalance due to poverty, ignorance, or emotional factors. Iron, magnesium, and vitamin C deficiencies are the chief deficiencies in the American diet, but inadequate protein intake is a close fourth. Many children, and adults, are suffering from subclinical deficiencies of various vitamins and minerals. An all-purpose, high-quality vitamin and mineral preparation should be given to everyone, because even with the best diet, *modern foods are deficient.*

The trouble is that junk foods, laced with sugar, taste good. Two thirds of the staple American diet is sugar, bleached flour, and processed hydrogenated fat. But the only foods that the human body can use have to be fresh, wholesome, and of good, natural flavor. A century ago, America's food was good because it was fresh. When picked, fruits and vegetables die and start to decompose; they spoil. Stale foods contain oxidized lipids and free radicals, which make us sick. To prevent spoilage, processed food is fractionated for shelf life. Natural flavor leads us by our senses of smell and taste to the foods we need. This is not as possible anymore because of what has happened to the foods we eat. Negative modern foods such as potato chips, ice cream, candy, pastries, french fries, deep-fried foods, pasta, margarine, commercial peanut butter, nondairy creamer, doughnuts, imitation cheese, pancakes and waffles, and most breakfast foods have had the B vitamins and most of the minerals removed to prolong shelflife. Therefore, the body must steal B vitamins and minerals from its stores to digest and metabolize them.

In 1933 the U.S. Department of Agriculture announced that American topsoil was deficient. It was being blown and washed away because farmers did not have the know-how to preserve it. Much of the commercially farmed land is now fed with artificial fertilizers that are high in nitrogen yield a larger crop. Apparently this suppresses the take-up of trace minerals from the soil. We are all getting cheated, even when we eat fresh food, because the topsoil does not, cannot, put the nutrients into the plants if the goodies are not there in the first place.

"Artificial fertilizers are the junk foods of plants. The vegetables produced on this soil are unhealthy, lacking in flavor, and have poor storage-keeping qualities. The food system of the United States has to be overhauled from beginning to end. A start must be made to rebuild the soil to the quality it had a century ago. This could be done in a few years. We have the know-how." Meat should be slaughtered locally for daily delivery. "Wheat flour should be ground locally so fresh flour, with the wheat germ in it, can be supplied daily. The fragile oils need to be pressed locally so fresh cooking oil is available daily." Again: "There should be no taxes on healthy foods, so that the high-quality food is made as inexpensive as possible." Our ministers should tell their congregations what foods to eat. "It was the ancient duty of the religious teachers to tell people what was fit to eat and what was not fit to eat."[120]

Until this happens, we should shop only where the fresh fruits and vegetables are on display, and try to avoid all the packaged, processed foods. It is not perfect for optimal nutrition, but it is a start. Until the Department of Agriculture gets the food to us the way it was a century ago, we will have to eat fruits and vegetables as raw as possible and take supplements. We can ask our grocery store managers to provide organic foods. This might just turn the entire food industry around!

If parents have not begun a regimen of extra nutrients, these are the essentials needed in any diet:

Essentials for Any Diet. (Universal truism: Food is an important part of any diet.) The ideal diet provides:

- Sufficient calories for growth and exercise;
- Adequate protein for muscle and brain;
- Enough minerals for blood and bone;
- Vitamins to prevent deficiencies;
- Fat for energy and palatability: essential fatty acids omega-3 and -6. If normal, the human being has a fantastically accurate set of regulators that signal the brain to eat more or less, and to consume more grains, fruits, or meat in order to meet the individual's needs.

Cultural, family, and hereditary differences, plus individual response to food intake, will determine overall body size. Most fat children eat a great deal, but so do some thin children. All the beautiful charts prepared by doctors and dietitians, indicating what and how much food is to be consumed, are usually disregarded by the harassed parent trying to cater to a variety of caloric needs and food prejudices within the family. Sugary foods (sweet drinks, ice cream, cookies, jams, jelly) should be considered bonus foods, and offered rarely, like at a couple of birthday parties a year. One trick is to fill a child up with good, nourishing foods before Halloween, Christmas, and parties; he may not eat as much at party time. My wife and I inspected our children's trick-or-treat bags when they came home and threw out the hard candy. We were mean. Now, forty years later, they thank us.

Urging a small child to eat large amounts of food may create a lifelong pattern of overeating and the related problems of obesity, including diabetes and hypertension. Some families are mistakenly convinced that a big appetite is equated with health, or that extra fat will protect the body from disease. The new nutrition labeling is a step in the right direction, but whole foods with no labels might be the better choice. (See Obesity, Chapter XIV.)

Fat in the diet is a source of energy essential to metabolism, and makes food taste better. A palatable diet usually derives about 20 percent of its calories from fat; present-day studies suggest that we should derive less than 20 percent of our calories from fat. Fat provides more than twice as many calories per ounce as carbohydrate or protein. Small amounts of butter appear to be safer than the solid margarines. Trans fatty acids in hydrogenated fats like margarine hurt the cell walls, are more sticky, and encourage fatty deposits in the arteries. Margarine eaters are more likely to need orthodontic care later in life as the essential fatty acids (EFAs) are needed to absorb nutrients for skeletal formation. Use "better butter": half olive oil and half butter. Research indicates reducing fat intake and substituting unsaturated fatty acid preparations will cut down the incidence of vascular accidents.

Healthy fats must be cold-pressed and protected from light, heat, and oxidation; they must be fresh; they must be packaged in amber glass (not plastic) bottles; they must not be used for frying. EFAs, omega-3 (cold-water fish like cod), and omega-6 (primrose and borage) can be obtained in the health food stores. Hemp, flax, soybeans, fish, and walnuts are high on the list of the fats that heal.[121]

EFAs form part of all cell membranes, constitute 20 percent of the brain by weight (important for the growing brain), and are the precursors of prostaglandins, hormonelike substances that help regulate functions of all tissues. Linoleic acid is an unsaturated acid (some double bonds between carbon atoms) that cannot be synthesized by the body, so it must be supplied in the diet. EFAs are needed to keep the skin waterproof and supple. ("Alligator skin" means a deficiency.) These unsaturated fatty acids are more prevalent in vegetable oils, and are safer for continued use than dairy and animal fats.

Carbohydrates are the chief sources of energy for the body. Enzymes to digest and metabolize foods for energy need B vitamins and magnesium for their digestion, yet these are the very nutrients that are processed out of food so that they will not rot on the shelf. Saliva and pancreatic digestants reduce starches to sugars that can then be split by enzymes in the cells that line the intestinal tract. Raw foods provide their own enzymes for digestion and should compose more than half of the diet. Chewing grains and vegetables until they are soupy (chewed thirty times, à la Fletcher) will make them more digestible and absorbable due to their contact with salivary enzymes.

Proteins are the building blocks of the body. Medical teaching indicates that animal proteins best provide the protein needs of the human. People with the fewest somatic complaints were eating the highest amount of animal protein.[122] Among chronically protein-malnourished adults, the incidence of postoperative wound infections, bacteremia, and pneumonia was 23 percent compared with 5 percent among those considered well nourished. Hypo-gammaglobulinemia is noted in children on a low-protein diet; the risk of infections is double in those on this low diet.

With a little study and care, however, a vegetarian diet has all the amino acids the child needs. Grains and legumes do not have to be eaten at the same meal to provide complete protein, just so the full complement is incorporated within a few hours or a day. Dairy, eggs, fish, and fowl in the diet make it easier to supply all the amino acids. Strict vegan vegetarians (no meat, no dairy, no eggs) must be careful, as they may suffer from hypoproteinemia, because it is difficult to ingest a diet complete in all essential amino acids without consuming an uncomfortable amount of nuts and beans. A few bits of fish or fowl every day are often sufficient to supply the amino acids the body is unable to manufacture. Red meat is hard to digest, and its ingestion is associated with the high incidence of hypertension, obesity, osteoporosis, and cardiovascular disease. "Meat may contain pathogens responsible for brucellosis, hepatitis, leukemia, toxoplasmosis, trichinosis, tuberculosis."[123]

Flesh eaters, moreover, may show less endurance than the vegetarians, perhaps due to the low intake of potassium. One physical observation suggests that we are at least omnivores: the length of the intestinal tract. "An herbivore has a ratio of ten to thirteen times the length of the body." The human has a ratio of only five to six times the length of the body.[124]

For their balanced diets: in the Mideast, bulgur wheat and chickpeas; in India, rice and lentils; in the Orient, soy and rice; in Korea, soy and barley. Remember, the more protein we take in, the more calcium we lose, regardless of how much calcium we take in. Meat, eggs, and fish are acid-forming and cause calcium to be drawn from the bone to restore the acid/base balance.

Perhaps what both groups (vegetarians and meat eaters) are saying is that we need to eat some vegetables and some meat. The ectomorph, more susceptible to hypoglycemia, might do better with small amounts of meat protein eaten throughout the day. (Their intestinal tract is a short twenty feet.) The endomorph types with their susceptibility to obesity might control their weight better with a predominately vegetarian diet. (Their intestinal tract may amount to an efficient forty feet.)

For adequate growth and nutrition, a child requires about three times as much protein in proportion to weight as does the adult. The average adult needs about two or so ounces of protein per day. A fifty-pound six-year-old should get almost as much to insure optimum nutrition, about two ounces of hamburger, for example, or a dish of rice and beans, or some almonds and whole-grain bread.

Amino acids are the nitrogen-bearing chemical compounds that form protein. Two dozen different amino acids have been identified; their number and arrangement in different combinations give protein its various characteristics. When ingested, meat, milk, fish, eggs, nuts, and beans are broken down into amino acids by the intestines. These acids are then absorbed and circulated to all cells of the body, where they are synthesized (especially in the liver) into human protein. If a particular amino acid is not present in the cell when needed, the corresponding protein cannot be manufactured—hence, a deficiency. It is important that all the essential amino acids be supplied daily.

Essential amino acids are those the body is unable to synthesize. They are histidine, isoleucine, leucine, lysine, methionine, phenylalanine, threonine, tryptophan, and valine. They must be included in the diet almost daily or the body is unable to manufacture the more complicated proteins necessary for structure and function. A carefully planned vegetarian diet can provide all the amino acids needed for health. Some find that powdered amino acid mixes are palatable enough to supply all the essential ones. The standard chemical screening test will help indicate if the diet is adequate in protein.[125] A special twenty-four hour urine test can tell if one has specific deficiencies of one or more amino acids.

Some genetic diseases arise from a lack of an enzyme responsible for changing one amino acid into another (phenylketonuria) or for manufacturing protein molecules from amino acids (agammaglobulinemia).

Calories are a measure of the energy stored in food. Water has none; fat has the most. If a person consumes and absorbs into his system more calories than he uses, he gains weight.

Glucose is the simple sugar used for energy in the metabolism of the body. It is the only compound the brain is able to use, hence a constant level of blood glucose is essential. Glucose is the end product of the breakdown of starches, milk sugar, table sugar, glycogen, and amino acids. Using various enzymes and hormones, the glucose is metabolized in the cells for energy, or into the formation of amino acids, fatty acids, acetone, or pyruvic and lactic acids, thence into carbon dioxide and water. The hormones insulin, adrenaline, and the glucocorticoids are the agents responsible for maintaining a reasonably constant level of glucose in the blood and tissues. Glucose and sucrose (table sugar) are more likely to be transformed into fat, and are more likely to cause a rapid rise and fall in blood sugar (see Hypoglycemia, Chapter 9). People who later develop diabetes may have had hypoglycemia earlier in life.[126] If glucose in the diet is accompanied by some protein, the rapid rise and fall of the blood sugar can be avoided.

Salt, or sodium chloride, makes food more palatable, but an excess is known to be related to the development of hypertension in susceptible people. Some salt is necesssary for the body. As one ages, the level of sodium should be monitored. There is a strong correlation between high serum cholesterol and low blood pressure. Low blood pressure prevents the fats and cholesterol from being pushed through and cleared from the arteries as they should be. Sodium is one way to get the blood pressure up to a more normal value. Salt should not be restricted from the diet unless the blood chemistry shows the sodium level is high. People with high sodium levels usually love vinegar. French Celtic salt or at least sea salt are more appropriate for everyday use than ordinary table salt (sodium chloride).

Boiled skim milk is a concentrated salt solution; salt poisoning may occur if boiled skim milk is given to a baby already experiencing dehydration from diarrhea.

Supplements

It is well documented that (1) our children cannot get all the vitamins and minerals they need for metabolic competence from the standard American three meals a day; (2) when their bodies are stressed by drugs, pollutants, injury, tough teachers, sickness, and the "slings and arrows" of everyday life, nutrients are lost, and if these specific nutrients are not replaced, the child's ability to withstand stress or fight off disease is reduced; and (3) our ancestors, two to twenty million years ago, existed on raw foods, fruit, vegetables, and lean meat. We have a similar intestinal tract to theirs, and it has not evolved to handle Twinkies, white sugar, or potato chips. We need fewer calories because of our sedentary lifestyle, but with fewer calories we tend to get less iron, zinc, calcium, magnesium, and the B vitamins; we are all getting short-changed. There are too many tasty, but devitalized, foods that simply leap into our children's mouths; children need extra vitamins and minerals in order to digest and metabolize them.

Minerals

Boron has been found to be important for the integrity of the bones and is especially helpful for the control of osteoporosis.

Calcium is a mineral found chiefly in bones and teeth, and is a necessary blood element to aid clotting and neuromuscular function. If the level of calcium in the blood is decreased, tetany may occur. Calcium acts as a protector of each cell wall. A deficiency may show as muscle cramps, arm and leg numbness, tingling of lips, tongue, fingers, feet, carpopedal spasm, sensitivity to noise, and increased susceptibility to tooth decay. People who need calcium are those who get little sunshine, are on a poor diet (no dairy and no vegetables), a low-fat diet, or have malabsorption. Calcium has a calming effect on hyperactive children. Some people are relaxed and sleep better after taking calcium and magnesium supplements. Some just need the calcium. (Some just need the magnesium.) Surveys show most people in the United States are taking in an amount below the RDA. Calcium is absorbed from foods more efficiently than from inorganic pills. Optimal daily calcium intake for infants from birth to six months of age is four hundred milligrams six months to one year, six hundred milligrams. For children age one to five years, eight hundred milligrams; for children six years to ten years, eight hundred to twelve hundred milligrams daily. These foods are high in calcium: amaranth flour, garbanzo flour, soy meal, parsley, tofu, almonds, filberts, sesame seeds, sea vegetables.[127] People who crave dairy products usually have a low calcium level in the blood. Their sensitivity to cow milk prevents the absorption of the calcium from this often-recommended fluid.

Chromium is essential for the utilization of insulin. A deficiency might show as insulin resistance, poor glucose tolerance, and elevated serum fat levels. Diabetics may be able to lower their insulin requirements if they take chromium.

Copper is needed for oxidative enzymes, in the development and function of the nervous system, and is necessary along with iron to make hemoglobin. Too much from copper pipes can adversely affect the brain; zinc and vitamin C would help lower a toxic level.

Iodide is a salt essential to the function of the body, especially the thyroid gland. A deficient intake will lead to simple goiter or endemic cretinism. People who live in areas where there is a natural deficiency can be maintained easily with the use of sea salt or kelp in the diet. It is especially important for the pregnant woman, as the developing fetal brain needs thyroid for cell division.

Iron, a metal, is an essential part of the hemoglobin molecule and muscle protein. Inadequate amounts in the diet are usually due to excessive milk intake and inadequate ingestion of meat, fruit, and vegetables. Most of the dietary iron is passed out in the stool; however, if the body is low in iron, the intestinal tract adapts by becoming more efficient in absorbing the iron that is ingested. Iron must be in the ferrous state to be absorbed; absorption is enhanced if it is accompanied by vitamin C. Some foods, such as phytic acid in unleavened breads, bond with iron and prevent its absorption. An iron tonic can safely be given to growing children who "eat poorly." It is best to monitor the hemoglobin and serum iron levels in the blood with a blood count every six to twelve months. Iron is the most common deficiency worldwide. Too much, however, can lead to a buildup of iron storage in the liver and impair its function. A disease named genetic hemochromatosis is the result of too much iron in the blood and can cause arthritis and a host of debilitating diseases. It is even possible that iron supplementation for babies in the first few months of life might contribute to SIDS if the baby is genetically susceptible to hemochromatosis.[128] A blood test for serum iron, total iron binding capacity, and ferritin is prudent. No one should take an iron supplement unless the tests show that it is really needed. Read the label.

Magnesium is needed as a coenzyme in at least five hundred functions of the body. Seventy-five percent of us are low in this mineral. Its excess or deficiency depends on vitamin D, parathyroid function, calcium ingestion, diarrhea, malabsorption, or severe malnutrition. A deficiency might produce these symptoms: apathy, irritable nerves and muscles, twitches in feet and legs, apprehension, weakness, confusion, depression, hyperactivity, paranoia, anorexia, nausea, vomiting, sensitivity to noise, irregular heart beat, ticklishness, chocolate craving, insomnia, hypothermia, hand tremors, body odor, asthma. Children who need magnesium are usually those who have been on a poor diet with no green vegetables, nuts, or seeds, or have had stress, diarrhea, diabetes, or kidney disease. The usual American diet supplies but half of the recommended four hundred milligrams daily. If calcium is taken for muscle cramps, magnesium tends to leave the cells. Our ancestors had a low-calcium but high-magnesium diet. Calcium and magnesium seem to work best if taken together.

Manganese is found in grains and vegetables. It is a part of superoxide dismutase, which is needed to combat free radicals. It is important for enzyme activity relative to the digestion and utilization of food; it supports insulin in the control of blood sugar. Low manganese will show as slow growth and bone deformities. It is essential for the formation of joint fluid. It can calm "growing pains" and speed tissue repair, especially after tendon injuries. It can aid memory and may help those who suffer from recurrent dizziness.[129]

Molybdenum may be more important for the teeth than fluoride. It helps regulate iron stores, helps metabolize carbohydrates, helps detoxify sulfites, and some other functions. It is in most foods, but fifty to one hundred and fifty micrograms daily for children would be a safe dose.

Phosphorus is a mineral important to bones and teeth, and is present in the nuclei of cells. It is important for the metabolism of chemicals and foods, and for nerve cell function. It is found in most foods, especially grains and dairy products. A high intake, as from excessive consumption of meats and soft drinks, will remove calcium from bones.

Potassium is a mineral found in every cell. It is essential for nerve conduction, muscle contraction, and sugar metabolism. It acts in a reciprocal manner with sodium. If much sodium is ingested, potassium is excreted as a compensation, but if potassium falls to low levels, aldosterone secretion is reduced, and the potassium level will rise. The diet should provide more potassium than sodium. Diets high in sodium and low in potassium may lead to hypertension. Potassium deficiency is common in the United States. Fruits and vegetables provide potassium. As the potassium intake decreases, muscular strength decreases also.

Selenium is an important part of the antioxidant enzymes and works in glutathione along with vitamins A and E. It prevents and retards tumor development; early supplementation is important for future health.

Silicon is necessary for bone and tooth calcification. It is important for collagen, the major protein in connective tissue, or cartilage. Joint problems may be a clue of a deficiency.

Silver as a colloidal solution has proved effective against a variety of germs and viruses.

Sulfur, an essential nutrient of body protein, is found in almost all tissues, incorporated as part of certain amino acids. The body can only use the sulfur that is consumed as organic or amino-acid-bound sulfur. It helps to remove lead, cadmium, and mercury from the body.

Zinc is needed by the body as it is essential for the function of more than one hundred enzymes; it works with vitamin A for the integrity of the eyes and skin. Its absence from the diet can result in anemia, depressed immunity, iron deficiency, poor growth, hypogonadism, infertility, impotence, prostate swelling, anorexia, acne, diarrhea, apathy, birth defects, slow growing and brittle nails and hair, hair loss, depression, eczema, fatigue, stretch marks, hypercholesterolemia (high level of cholesterol in the blood), poor wound healing, malabsorption, and memory loss. A common sign of a deficiency is white spots on the fingernails, and distorted taste (dysgeusia; see Anorexia Nervosa, Chapter 10). If a mother has been deficient in zinc during the pregnancy, the baby will be born with little hair and be susceptible to diaper rash. Low zinc in the pregnant woman's diet may prolong labor. Zinc is especially important for the integrity of male sperm, and for sexual function and maturity. People who need zinc have either been on a low-zinc diet, a starvation diet (as in anorexia), or have regularly eaten unleavened bread or a diet high in beans and legumes. (The zinc becomes attached to phytic acid in these foods and is taken out of the body.) Fifteen milligrams a day is the maintenance dose and is usually not consumed by the typical American. It is abundant in most meats, wheat germ, and oysters.

Vitamins

Vitamins are compounds that the body is unable to synthesize. They are necessary, along with minerals, in the various enzyme systems of the body. They must be provided in the diet or, as in the case of vitamin D, by sunshine.

Deficiency Symptoms and Signs. "Your body might need doctors and drugs during a crisis, but will cure itself if given the proper tools."[130] Here are some of those tools:

Vitamin A is a fat-soluble vitamin found abundantly in egg yolk, liver, fish oils, milk fat, green and yellow vegetables, and yellow fruits. It is needed for retinal pigments (allowing vision in dim light), bone and tooth development, and integrity of skin and mucous membranes. Its absence causes night blindness, thickening of skin and membranes, "chicken skin" on upper arms and thighs, warts, susceptibility to bronchitis, asthma, colds, inner ear disease, acne, dandruff, dull hair, brittle nails, loss of appetite, diarrhea, dry eylids, and sensitivity to glare. Exposure to stress, pollutants, and cortisone therapy increases the need for vitamin A. Zinc is necessary to make vitamin A work. The leading cause of blindness in developing countries is due to lack of vitamin A. Improved vitamin A nutrition could prevent one million deaths per year in children, mainly due to the serious complications of measles. Mothers positive for HIV but with a high vitamin A level were less likely to transmit HIV to their infants as opposed to mothers who had a low vitamin A level.

Vitamin A deficiencies are becoming more frequent since many children are being served low-fat diets. Eggs, liver, and butter—the normal fats that the body has utilized well for thousands of years—are replaced with man-made substitutes that are slowly destroying them. Since vitamin A depends on the natural fats for absorption, vitamin A deficiencies will more likely occur in the absence of adequate fat intake. The body knows the difference between the synthetic and the natural vitamin A in fish liver oils; "the body utilizes the fish liver oils without problems."[131]

Its excess will lead to enlargement of liver and spleen, bone pain, double vision, a constant headache, appetite loss, and yellow, cracked skin. These symptoms and signs are reversed when the intake is stopped. (Some evidence indicates that exceeding ten thousand units daily during pregnancy might allow a congenital orofacial defect to appear.)

Vitamin B is a mixture of about six distinct vitamins. All are contained in cereal, meat, fruit, vegetables, and milk, so a deficiency of one is usually associated with the deficiency of another. All the B vitamins are essential in the proper use of ingested carbohydrates. Some people simply do not ingest enough of them in their diets. The B vitamins are largely destroyed when food is processed to prolong shelflife. The deficiency signs that are common for all the Bs: fatigue, irritability, depression, reduced ambition, irritability, anxiety, insomnia, confusion, memory loss, numbness and tingling, clumsiness, increased sensitivity to noise and pain.

Vitamin B_1 is thiamine, the antiberiberi vitamin. It is water-soluble and is stored only briefly in the body, so it must be supplied almost daily in the diet. Thiamine is needed in the formation of certain enzymes that regulate carbohydrate and nerve metabolism. Beriberi is a composite of symptoms and signs resulting from the deficiency of thiamine. The symptoms are vague and generalized: weakness, appetite loss, paranoia, learning disability, heart irregularity, and abdominal pain, along with the other signs of B vitamin deficiency. Supplementation with B_1 relieved the behavioral problems of some junk-food-eating teenagers. Thiamine deficiency may reduce the availability of serotonin in some people. The mercury in amalgam fillings may bind with the sulfur in thiamine and further deprive the body of this essential nutrient. A baby with this deficiency becomes apathetic, pale, and flabby.

If the open bottle of thiamine smells good, the person needs it. If it smells putrid, that person's body has enough, and thiamine is not needed that day. Some people find that oral thiamine every four to six hours acts as a mosquito repellant.

Vitamin B_2 is riboflavin, one of the B-complex vitamins. Abundant amounts of B_2 are found in meat, milk, eggs, and cereals. A deficiency will cause burning, itching, and redness of the eyes and lids, photophobia, red, cracked lips, dermatitis, and a smooth, magenta-colored tongue along with the preceding symptoms and signs. People who need B_2 have usually had a poor diet with excess sugar, stress, trauma, pregnancy, lactation, high energy needs, fever, or antibiotic use.

Vitamin B$_3$ is niacin, necessary for a number of enzyme activities. Pellagra is the disease that occurs as a result of its absence from the diet. Only ten to twenty milligrams of this are necessary in the daily diet. It is found in meats, peanuts, whole-grain cereals, and green vegetables. It takes a really poor diet for pellagra to develop. If diarrhea, red, scaly dermatitis on exposed areas (hands and face) that looks like sunburn, paranoia, sore, red tongue, and sore lips are present, it is pellagra. (The mnemonic we learned: dermatitis, diarrhea, and dementia. Death follows.) "If all the niacin were removed from our food, everyone would be psychotic in one year."[132]

Niacin forms a part of certain enzyme systems; thus, its absence causes generalized body symptoms listed under vitamins B$_1$ and B$_2$. Other symptoms and signs: high cholesterol, headaches, ringing in the ears, unmanageable hair, canker sores, low stomach acid, halitosis, arthritis. Children who need extra B$_3$ have usually been eating too much sugar and starches, are engaged in strenuous exercise, or have had trauma, rapid growth, or prolonged antibiotic use.

Some forms of schizophrenia have been controlled with large doses of niacin (three thousand milligrams along with the same amount of C).

Vitamin B$_6$ is pyridoxine, normally found in milk, grain, meats, and vegetables. Some people only need a small amount daily. Despite that small requirement to prevent a deficiency, 80 percent of us are low in B$_6$. It is involved in the metabolism of almost all nutriments. Its absence from one brand of canned milk in 1950 was responsible for convulsions in infants receiving this milk as their sole food; when cereal was added or B$_6$ given, the seizures promptly stopped. Signs and symptoms are listed in the preceding sections. Also: low blood sugar, dandruff (seborrhea), eczema, premenstrual syndrome, asthma, allergies, anemia, stiff joints, cheilosis, conjunctivitis, geography tongue, stunted growth, poor wound healing, carpal tunnel syndrome, hyperactivity, cancer, and kidney stones. Many autistic children respond to B$_6$. Children who need B$_6$ have usually been on a poor diet or a fast, have had infections, were getting X radiation, or have had stress. If a person appears to be twitchy, jumpy, restless, a worrier, or have insomnia, extra B$_6$ might relieve these symptoms. Magnesium might be given with it, as high doses of B$_6$ (more than six hundred milligrams) might deplete this mineral. Children taking B$_6$ and magnesium become calmer and friendlier. B$_6$ in high doses can increase the brain serotonin levels. (Maybe hyperactivity is due to a relative insufficiency of norepinephrine in the limbic system plus decreased amounts of serotonin in the other areas of the brain served by that brain chemical.) An adequate amount may be able to prevent heart attacks or SIDS because it helps convert homocysteine (which causes vascular damage) to the nontoxic cystathionine.[133]

Vitamin B$_{12}$ and related compounds are essential to prevent the occurrence of pernicious anemia and some types of neuritis. Along with the preceding deficiency signs and symptoms: depression (especially postpartum), asthma, malabsorption, sore and beefy red tongue, anorexia, postural hypotension, body odor, palpitations, yellow pallor to skin, psychosis, paranoia. Children who need B$_{12}$ are strict vegan vegetarians, chronic laxative users, or those who have had heavy bleeding. (If the soil in which plants grow is fertilized with organic materials like manure, the B$_{12}$ content increases in the plants. The use of chemical fertilizers and the effects of acid rain has resulted in the die-off of bacteria necessary for the formation of B$_{12}$.)

Folacin or folic acid is another one of the related B vitamin nutrients, the absence of which causes megaloblastic anemia. Folic acid is found in a wide variety of foods; it is present in both cow milk and human milk. Some goat milk may be deficient in this. If the label does not say it is fortified with folic acid, it must be added. Lack of folic acid can cause the preceding symptoms and signs plus numb, weak, unstable, restless legs; a smooth, sore, red tongue; mouth ulcers; growth retardation. Children who need folic acid include those not eating leafy vegetables, those with parasites, bleeding, stress, malabsorption, and diarrhea. Most Americans get but half of the recommended four hundred micrograms daily. All authorities agree that everyone should be on a folic acid supplement because the deficiency is so common.

Pantothenic acid is considered one of the B vitamins as it is usually found in the same foods. It is a precursor to cortisone, and therefore a help with allergies. If a child is deficient in pantothenic acid, the following symptoms might be observed along with the preceding symptoms and signs: poor coordination, faintness on arising, joint and muscle pain, allergies. People who need pantothenic acid have usually been on a poor diet, have had stress, used cortisonelike drugs, or have malabsorption. "As much as ten years can be added to the human life span through supplementation with pantothenate."[134]

Vitamin C is ascorbic acid. The absence of it will lead to scurvy, the chief manifestation of which is internal bleeding or seepage of blood and easy bruisability. Vitamin C is not stored well in the body, so daily ingestion is prudent. Fresh fruits are good sources, as are lightly cooked—preferably steamed—vegetables.

Vitamin C facilitates many enzyme systems in the body and enhances the absorption of iron. Its ability to control viral and bacterial infections has been proven since the 1930s. The usual reason it "does not work" is that people are reluctant to give a dose adequate to control the problem. The severity of the condition dictates the dose. Most of us who use alternative medical methods recommend the daily maintenance dose of one hundred milligrams per day per month of age for infants and children. But infants with colds, bronchitis, ear infections, or whatever should get about one thousand milligrams each waking hour. The dose is titrated to the state of the bowel movements: It is increased until the stools get sloppy, and then reduced to a subdiarrhea dose.

Most animals can synthesize their own ascorbic acid. Primates and guinea pigs need vitamin C supplied in the diet, or they will get scurvy. Some dogs with the Old Stiff Dog syndrome have been helped with large doses of vitamin C, even though they can make their own. Apparently with stress and ingestion of modern dog food, they cannot make enough for their needs.

Ascorbic acid is responsible for the integrity of collagen and connective tissue, which holds the body together. A deficiency, therefore, will lead to hemorrhages (because the capillaries are fragile), loose teeth, and disorganized bone growth. (Calcium is deposited, but the bone's connective tissue is not adequate, and hemorrhages form between the bone and the periosteum.) Other signs of a deficiency: alkalinity, irritability, fatigue, anxiety, anorexia, indigestion, easy bruisability, bleeding, receding gums, slow wound healing, hair loss, labored breathing, gallstones, allergies, anemia, and frequent infections. We cannot forget that vitamin C is found in nature with bioflavonoids. This part of the complete vitamin C is probably responsible for capillary fragility. Habitual aborters can carry a pregnancy with citrus bioflavonoids (two hundred milligrams three times a day) along with vitamin C. This therapy toughens the fragile capillaries responsible for intrauterine bleeding and spontaneous abortions.[135]

Children who need C are those who are exposed to secondhand smoke or other pollutants, have had stress, injuries, fevers, infections, excessive physical activity, burns, antibiotic use, drugs, addictions, cortisone, or have cancer, arthritis, or anemia. A fit of rage can use up to three grams of C.

Five hundred milligrams of vitamin C daily will add seven years to your life (UCLA study in 1992). In other words, everyone needs it.

A baby rarely has scurvy at birth unless the mother's diet has been wholly inadequate. If an infant's diet during the first year is limited to formula milk (breast milk has sufficient vitamin C in it), without fruit, juice, or vitamin supplements, he begins to show irritability, lethargy, and bone tenderness at about age six to ten months. His gums, especially surrounding erupting teeth, will be swollen and hemorrhagic. Leg pains will progress to the point of his refusal to move, and he will assume the frog position because of the pain. Knobs of bloody, swollen bone tissue appear on the ribs. Blood in the stools or urine and skin hemorrhages are common. X rays of the bones of a child suffering from scurvy will reveal the characteristic changes. The low vitamin C blood level helps to confirm the history of poor intake.

A parent who boils fruit juice to kill the bacteria will also destroy this heat-susceptible vitamin. One obvious scurvy case was confusing because the mother insisted that she gave the baby orange juice. After the third interrogation session, she mentioned the name of a popular brand of orange pop.

If the body needs vitamin C, it will soak it up from the intestinal tract like a sponge. In the well-vitaminized body, a dose of vitamin C will be excreted in the urine in the subsequent few hours. In a case of scurvy, almost none will be found in the urine, as the tissues will have absorbed it. People on a reasonably balanced diet with fruits and/or vegetables will get the recommended daily allowance of C (sixty milligrams), but if they want optimum health, they will take about five hundred to seven hundred milligrams per day. Research shows that people on that higher dose daily are in optimum health.[136] I read about an eccentric who existed on eggs and wine for six months; he finally got scurvy. It does take some doing to develop the disease, but subclinical scurvy is a common problem in the world. The bioflavonoids must accompany the C for optimal effects.

Many of the studies that prove vitamin C is beneficial cannot get published in standard, peer-review journals, as the editors of those journals are beholden to the pharmaceutical industry.

Vitamin D is transformed in the liver to calciferol. This metabolite moves to the intestines and bones, where its chief effect is to move calcium into the circulation. Calcitonin, an enzyme secreted by cells in the thyroid, has the job of depositing calcium in the bone. Vitamin D is the "sunshine" vitamin; sunshine converts a vitamin precursor contained in the skin to vitamin D. Years ago Scottish fishermen prevented rickets with sunshine and cod liver oil. Sunshine through window glass is of the wrong wave length to effect this change, hence rickets is more common in the northern climes. Vitamin D must be provided artificially in milk or vitamins, or by a sunlamp. Breast milk contains enough if the mother is getting it. Dr. Garland of Johns Hopkins University feels that cod liver oil along with sunshine may prevent colon cancer.

Rickets, or vitamin D deficiency resulting in soft bones, has largely disappeared because of the universal knowledge of its cause and the addition of vitamin D to most milks. The disease is due to the deficient mineralization of bone; the connective tissue and cartilage are normal, but the calcium and phosphorus are not deposited therein.

Usually a baby must be deprived of vitamin D for the whole of his first year before developing rickets. Then the skull bones are soft, plunking in and out like a Ping-Pong ball when squeezed. Knobs appear on the ribs. Wrists and ankles become thickened. The leg bones curve, and the toddler displays an exaggerated bowing to his legs. Treatment is the giving of five to ten times the usual daily dose of vitamin D (usual dose—four hundred to eight hundred units) for several weeks. Vitamin D is a storable, fat-soluble vitamin, so a three-month supply may be given once every three months with the same beneficial effects.

Grandmothers often discouraged early walking because they feared the development of bowed legs. If an infant wants to walk early and is receiving prophylactic vitamin D, he will show no more than the usual physiological bowing of the normal ten- to twenty-month-old.

Vitamin E is a group of related compounds called tocopherols. They are oil-soluble. Their action is necessary for the integrity of the vascular system. A deficiency is rare and is usually associated with chronic diarrhea. Anemia, muscle weakness, and wasting are present in vitamin-E-deficient people. Along with C, beta-carotene, and selenium, vitamin E helps the body counteract the damaging effects of the antioxidants in our food, our air, and our water. "A slight stress, such as a marginal deficiency in vitamin E, could impair the immune response."[137] It has an effect on many enzyme systems; it aids the liver enzyme systems involved with the metabolism of drugs and poisons. The Russians have found that exercise reduces the body stores of vitamin E. This must explain why it has proved effective in reducing muscle cramps. (Calcium, potassium, and vitamin D also help.) E is an antioxidant and free-radical scavenger; its recent reputation for reducing the risk of heart attacks, strokes, and tiredness has been proven by research. It has antihistaminic effects. About four hundred units of E for anyone who is breathing, drinking, or eating makes sense, but most Americans are not getting even the paltry RDA of thirty units daily.

Vitamin K is a chemical necessary for the production of some blood coagulation factors.

The Diet After Age Six Years

There is little control over what goes into the mouths of children from here on. They are subject to peer pressure, TV ads, their hunger pains, and the convenience stores between home and school. Leaving fruits and raw vegetables around as snacks seems to be the most acceptable way of getting good food into children (and adults). It is tough to change, but everyone will be rewarded if we all eat more raw foods. Arthritis is a cooked-food disease. Cooking destroys the enzymes that are naturally found in plants and animals that serve to digest themselves, if given a chance. Eating a salad once a week and munching on an apple a day is not enough.

We can learn from other humans and some animals about eating. If a python, for example, chokes down a pig, that animal may not have been dead when he swallowed it, but it soon suffocates inside the snake's stomach. But no snake has enough digestive enzymes to break down that pig into the four food groups; it relies on the autolysis of the cells of the ingested porker. The enzyme in all cells just waiting for us to shut down is called *cathepsin*. The intestines of the python have some proteases, lipases, and amylases along with some acid to dissolve the bones. But the snake cannot get much benefit from the ingestus if the ingestus does not help out a little bit. Apparently Mother Nature wants all of us to dissolve when we are no longer useful as living entities. Our decomposed residua become the minerals and organic material for the following generation.

Eskimos (which means "he eats it raw") do not have firewood or charcoal for a barbecue. They eat raw or fermented and autolyzed meat. They arrange for outside enzymes to help digest their food. They store the meat until it undergoes some autolysis and produces new flavors. "Walrus meat tastes like old, sharp, rich cheese." After a walrus hunt, they would have a dinner of almost raw clams eaten right out of the stomach of the walrus. The raw whale blubber has its own lipase that breaks down the fat into fatty acids, usable by these hardy people. They had clean blood vessels until our civilized methods of food preparation caught up with them.[138] The Masai do well on raw blood and milk from their cattle. Weston Price found that none of the groups he studied were able to maintain good bodies if they ate plant foods exclusively.

We have the same intestinal tract our ancestors had two million years ago. They did well as hunter-gatherers. We must try to imitate that diet: One third of their diet was wild game, frogs, snakes (cholesterol at about six hundred milligrams a day), and two thirds of the diet was fruits, vegetables, and tubers, which included about fifty grams of fiber a day. All this gave them four hundred milligrams of C a day, sixteen hundred milligrams of calcium a day, and a potassium-to-sodium ratio of about sixteen to one. (Present diets are 1:1.) It was a two-food-group diet, as they had no dairy nor grains.[139] Most of the food was raw.

"The cooking, canning, freezing, and preserving of foods virtually eliminates their active enzymes, as well as removing many of their nutrients."[140] People and animals who eat cooked foods have larger digestive glands than those who eat foods raw. The body has to compensate for this lack of food enzymes. Eat more raw foods. Taking the proper vitamins and minerals is not enough if you do not have the appropriate enzymes to help you digest the foods down to their basic, nonallergic simple carbohydrates, fatty acids, and amino acids. Let your kids eat frozen mixed vegetables right out of the bag—sometimes while they are still in the grocery cart. Healthy recipes for zucchini bread, carrot cake, and squash muffins are good ways to sneak veggies into a reluctant eater's mouth. A tasty dip like peanut butter would help.

Raw meat for us civilized folk would probably give us *E. coli* and parasites. Give your children some digestive enzymes with their meals. We know that the diet can affect performance academically and have an impact on the emotions.

Consider the following: (1) The rate of obesity in children has roughly doubled since 1980; (2) children age one to five are as likely to drink soft drinks as they are orange juice; (3) A child's diet contains five to ten times more sodium than he or she needs; (4) experts have found that kids who watch the most TV have the worst diets and the lowest level of nutritional knowledge; and finally, (5) at least one in four children in grades one to twelve does not eat even one serving of vegetables a day. French fries do not count.[141] Catsup is not a vegetable.

The National Institute of Health recently reported that residues of DDT, chlordane, dieldrin, and heptachlor are found in the blood of children and adults, although they were banned from use in our country two decades ago. Most of these residues are in the fat and skin of the animals who have eaten those products. Remove the fat and skin of animal carcasses you cook and eat. Maybe there is a connection: In a study by researchers at the University of Southern California School of Medicine, the incidence of leukemia in children under ten years was higher in those children who regularly ate more than twelve hot dogs a month. It might be the nitrosamines that come from the nitrates used to preserve processed meats.[142]

When cow milk is completely eliminated from the diet, the result is an abnormal chemical imbalance of calcium, phosphorus, and magnesium that affects the circulation. If cow milk is modified with an electrolyte solution, it becomes less allergenic to humans, and the calcium and protein in it are bioavailable.[143] Normal use of salt and milk with adequate C and vinegar results in general good health and circulation.

Eating should be associated with pleasant, warm, secure feelings. Parents may force-feed a reluctant child, only to find the child goes hungry for attention or complies by becoming fat. So many factors are involved with the eating process that a simple overall statement about "normality" is impossible. Some children eat huge amounts and stay thin; others eat "nothing" and get fat. If there is a rule to follow, it would be that if a child seems happy—laughs more than he cries, plays normally, and grows two to three inches a year after age three—he is probably taking in at least enough calories to maintain his energy requirements. The usual error is allowing him to fill up on impoverished foods. Many mothers will add chocolate syrup to the milk in an effort to get it down! Six ounces of chocolate milk might have enough calories to destroy the six-year-old's appetite for the next twenty-four hours.

Eating habits are big concerns for parents, especially those who feel that a child who eats well *is* well. The following idiosyncrasies should be respected within the context of good nutrition: An aversion (but also a craving) may represent an allergy; a craving for sweets may suggest hyperactivity or hypoglycemia; liking sour food may suggest the body's desire to stabilize a faulty acid-base balance. Most hyperactive children eat little because of distractions at the table. Some eat huge amounts but gain little (malabsorption?) because of their perpetual motion, which burns up calories as fast as they are consumed.

when various eating styles are scattered through the family. Some children are nauseated by breakfast and can barely choke down some juice; some need a hearty breakfast with protein, or they faint at 11:00 A.M. Compromise, compromise. Some cannot chew grown-up foods until all the molars are in at age twelve years. Some nervous children have such an active gag reflex that pushing a pea down that reluctant child's throat is just asking for a return of the same.

If a child is difficult to awaken in the morning and refuses to eat breakfast, a prudent parent might set the alarm for about thirty minutes before the hoped-for arousal time, get the child to swallow a glass of orange juice, and then note the child is at least a little more eager and awake at the get-up gong. Low blood sugar bothers a lot of people. Massage can have the same beneficial effect as food.

Appetite is related to parental attitudes, congenital factors, ability to absorb and digest food, state of the bowels, state of mind, age, and rate of growth. Walter L. Voegtlin, M.D., says, "Because of hunger we have restaurants, but because of appetite the restaurant has a menu. Appetite is acquired, a conditioned reflex. Hunger is innate, an inborn, unconditioned reflex."[144] The wise parent can whet the child's appetite by offering nourishing meals pleasantly served in congenial, unhurried surroundings. Although a bad appetite does not imply ill health, a good appetite is generally a good sign that all is well. A *change* in appetite suggests a possible problem.

When your child is twenty-two years old and comes home to tell you that you should have made him eat more vegetables, you will say, "I tried." He will counter with, "You should have tried harder." Your stock answer: "Wait till you have your own kids."

CHAPTER 4

Development From One Month to One Year of Age

The following is a very sketchy developmental outline of what is near normal. There is a relentless progress toward maturity that is unique to every child. If, however, the infant does not progress within these parameters, neurological therapy can help. Some of the following comes from Florence Scott of the Northwest Neurodevelopmental Training Center.

DEVELOPMENTAL SCHEDULE

Newborn: Eyes react to light. Auditory function is the startle reflex; a sudden noise will make him jump and his arms and legs move out. Touching his cheek will make him turn his head to suck an object—we hope it is the mother's nipple (see Reflexes, Chapter 2). He has a pain cry, also. All these functions mean that the myelin sheath has grown over the spinal cord nerves and to the base of the brain stem, the medulla.

One Month: By six weeks the prone infant can raise his head and hold it there for several seconds. All the lower, brain-stem levels of response are needed for newborn survival. They remain within us throughout life, but must not predominate, or we cannot mature to higher levels of functioning. The infant is able to progress through these levels to maturity only by storing or putting aside those initial, primitive reflexes. "Specific movement patterns made in the first months of life contain within them a natural inhibitor to the primitive reflexes: It is the absence or inadequacy of these movements in early life that have permitted the primitive reflexes to remain active."[145] Central nervous system development progresses by repetition of movement responses. Neural pathways are being laid down simultaneously with the myelin around their sheaths. The infant must be allowed to practice these movements and become skilled. Like a well-practiced performer, continued use of the neurons promotes facilitation; neuronal pathways are laid down in this critical first year.

Two to Three Months: He can lift his head well above the horizontal and hold it there for several minutes. He has the "social smile"; he smiles and laughs at people; all human faces look alike to him. This indicates the development of the areas of the nervous system that allows for arousal without crying and sustained sleep periods. The nerves have matured to the pons area of the brain. The functions that are dependent upon the pons are for life preservation. Heart rate and respiration originate in this area. The pons is responsible for horizontal eye movement; he can watch his parent coming and going. (This function is critical for later reading skills, to track words across a page.) Loud noises produce less of the startle response. If the infant perceives heat, cold, pain, or hunger, he will cry for help. He may crawl away from the perceived danger. When the infant cries for any of the above reasons, an adult, usually a parent, must come to comfort him. The adult response establishes an engram in the baby that becomes a foundation for future relationships with other humans. That vital cry has immediate and long-term implications. The palmar reflex is usually gone by this stage.

Three to Six Months: As the baby should be able to reach and grab by six months, toys worth using are crib mobile, crib gym, bright balls, rattles, squeeze toys, and washable dolls. Let him spend a good deal of time on a blanket on the floor with a variety of small objects and a few containers to put them into.[146] He should be crawling on the floor on his stomach like a lizard. ***Never use a walker;*** this bypasses the crawling and creeping so important for later brain function. Florence Scott of the Northwest Neurological Developmental Training Center wrote in 1987: "For the past thirty years, I have done functional neurological examinations on both children and adults. I've seen an increasing number of children and young adults that present a particular syndrome—one that I have come to recognize and call 'the walker syndrome.' The one common factor in their histories is that between two to three months of age and the time they began to walk they have spent a period of time in walkers. I am alarmed at the damage that is being done and want to warn parents of the danger that may not become apparent until children enter school." The state of Washington has outlawed the use of walkers in government-funded day-care centers.

He can now press down with his forearms to lift his head and upper torso, stretching his limbs and "swimming" in this position (**Landau reflex**). With support under the stomach, the arms, legs, and back are extended. It supercedes the tonic labyrinthine reflex. It is important for future movements. But if a child maintains the Landau after age three years, he will run in an awkward fashion, and hopping, skipping, and jumping will be difficult.

An **amphibian reflex** occurs at about four to six months of life. When the pelvis is elevated, the arm and the leg are flexed on that same side. This facilitates crawling and the future ability to creep. If an infant does not develop this amphibian reflex, it might interfere with her sports ability when she is older.

Six to Seven Months: Provide balls of various sizes. Locomotion starts. Burton White warns us, "Make it a safe place for the baby to be, and to explore; make it safe *from* the baby."[147] Two lower central incisors erupt; the upper central incisors follow soon. The myelination of the nervous system has now reached to the midbrain. The next level of reflexes, called postural, are mediated though the midbrain, a higher level of involvement. They are concerned with posture, movement, and stability. The **righting reflexes** show up at about three months and allow the infant to maintain the head when the body position is changed. Rolling, crawling, and creeping are the noticeable manifestations of these reflexes. The eyes and the labyrinthine (vestibular or inner ear/balance) apparatus are involved along with the cerebellum, whose nerves are being myelinated at this time. The eyes and the vestibular system must operate in concert; they supply the data upon which the head position is adjusted. (Like a cat chasing a mouse: The head and eyes remain fixed on the prey; only the body moves.) If there is some interference in these connections, the child's balance, eye movements, and visual perception may be impaired. This bodes trouble for future ability to read smoothly.

The baby must use the midbrain areas to help him figure out the world and his place in it. He is gathering data about balance, three-dimensional aspects of his environment, details— especially of faces—and he begins to discern emotional tones. The tone of voice has meaning for him; if parents are cheerful, he will usually imitate that cheerfulness.

The **segmental rolling reflex** appears: He can roll from prone to supine. When developed well and used consistently, it will set up the nervous system for future proficiency in running, jumping, skiing, and other sports. He develops vertical eye movement. He can perceive soft, fuzzy, rough, etc. He can play with his toes. He can creep on hands and knees, and moves toward objects of interest. He can create meaningful sounds: cooing, babbling, shrieking, and giggling. He can grab things with his whole hand. The midbrain also acts as a filter to help him disregard unimportant stimuli (see The Nervous System, Chapter 8). If this area does not function properly, learning difficulties may show up at schooltime. The midbrain helps us make adjustments when stressors are impinging on us. The midbrain contains the hypothalamus, which moderates sleep, blood pressure, temperature, hormone output, digestion, and neurotransmitter output. In short, it controls the autonomic nervous system.

Eight to Nine Months: Toys worth using are an unbreakable mirror, a roly-poly doll that bounces back, cloth books. The child becomes shy, nervous, even paranoid, and experiences stranger anxiety—he can distinguish between familiar and unfamiliar faces. "During its waking hours for the next few months, this infant should be provided with ample opportunity to remain on its stomach, to assist the development of the cervical and thoracolumbar muscles as they are lifted against the force of gravity. This begins development of the lordotic cervical and lumbar curves, that will be enhanced during the next stage of development, at approximately six months of age or so, of cross-crawling. It is unfortunate that these patterns are often interfered with by the extensive to excessive use of infant seats, baby swings, play chairs, and walkers...instead of encouraging them to develop and perfect their cross-crawl patterns that enhance neurological organization from pons to midbrain to cortex."[148]

He should be allowed to creep on hands and knees all over the house. His ability to converge his eyes on objects is accomplished only if he has done the crawling and creeping. Do not let him spend time in a walker, as he will not get the nervous stimulation he needs for future reading, and he may roll himself off the porch or down the stairs. Each year, according to the Consumer Product Safety Commision, twenty-three thousand emergency-room-treated injuries to infants and children were related to children going down the stairs in their walkers.

Ten Months: He sits well alone. The lateral incisors will appear, but some are delayed to fourteen months. He grabs objects and plays peekaboo. Some can stand, hanging on to a chair. He has thumb-finger grasp. He imitates speech. He resists toy removal. He cries upon separation. Chiropractors suggest a spinal evaluation at about this time because the secondary spinal curves are forming in the neck and lower back. It can be seen that the period of fastest growth, the first year of life, is also a period of considerable trauma when the child is learning to walk. Spinal adjustments for infants and young children involve very light fingertip adjustments to correct malfunctioning spinal structures.

One Year: He feeds himself using finger food because he can use his thumb and forefinger in a pincer movement. He shows temper, waves "bye-bye," imitates gestures. The myelination of the nervous system has progressed up to the cortex, the part of the nervous system that differentiates us from the lower animals. This is where the conscience is located. She uses both eyes to look at an object (called convergence). Somewhere after this age she develops symbol recognition, the highest function of the human nervous system and necessary for reading. A female will be twenty-eight to thirty inches tall, and a male, twenty-nine to thirty-one inches.

Summary of the First Year

In this first year of life the newborn has risen from a "reptile" (head lift, squirming, rolling) operating on his lower reflex brain, through the midbrain level (the "animal" in all of us: pons, thalamus, hypothalamus, cerebellum, which allows for crawling, sitting, creeping, and standing), to the highest cerebral cortical level, which makes him a human being. If all is well, normal development leads the infant to cortical or voluntary control. **Learning waits on maturation of the nervous system,** which waits on the myelinization of the nerves. The highest level of human function is the cortex: purposeful behavior. The nerves are there, but must be stimulated, like Sleeping Beauty being awakened by the kiss from the prince. If there has been a hurt during pregnancy or the delivery, it might show itself in this first year or two.

The primitive reflexes, superseded by the postural reflexes, indicate normal functioning of the brain stem and then the midbrain. If the subcortical systems (primitive and postural reflexes) remain dominant after they are supposed to have been stored away in this normal progression, it suggests there was a lack of use at an early stage in development (child not allowed to crawl and creep because he was put in a walker); lack of inhibition; metabolic or pathological conditions (immunization shots, heavy-metal poisoning, high fever); or some direct injury. Neurological therapists can detect if these primitive and postural reflexes are still functioning, and can then determine what level of remediation is required. They can find where the system is "broken."

The following reactions might indicate that the infant is at risk for social or academic problems later on in life. In the first year of life the following clues suggest that the baby has suffered from some hurt that can be corrected.

1. Severe and prolonged colic suggests an inadequate screening mechanism in his brain (limbic system). If the **Moro reflex** is not replaced, the child may become sensitive and overreact to stimuli. He might perceive the sound of the vacuum cleaner as painful and the doorbell as a stab in the back. He would also tend to stiff-arm the parent when an attempt was made to cuddle him; he does not like to be held. He overreacts to touch. He is immature. He may resort to self-stimulation, like rocking or sucking his thumb, which would help to calm him and help him disregard the environment. Neurological therapy can transform the Moro reflex into an adult startle reflex—a normal mature response.

2. The palmar reflex (see Newborn Reflexes, Chapter 2) should start to disappear at about three months of life and be replaced with the voluntary grasp, and subsequent refined finger control with the pincer grip at about nine months. If this reflex does not disappear at about five months of age, it could interfere with manual dexterity, and, of course, handwriting (lack of a mature pencil grip), speech, and articulation will be affected.

3. The ATNR (fencing) reflex should be inhibited or stored away by six months of age so that more complex skills can be acquired. Crawling and creeping cannot function if the ATNR is still present. These crawling/creeping activities must be encouraged as they are important for hand-eye coordination and the integration of balancing connections with other senses. These movements help myelinate the entire nervous system. This child cannot establish handedness, and the ease of bilateral movement is impaired. Eye movements are interfered with. His balance will be affected.

4. The rooting reflex, which allows the baby to find the nipple and be nourished, should have disappeared by the fourth month. If the rooting reflex is not stored away at the right time, the oral muscles used for feeding may not be ready for babbling and later speech. Manual dexterity may be affected also.

5. The spinal Galant reflex, which permits hip flexion, should disappear by six to nine months of age. If it does not disappear, the child will be restless—an "ants in the pants" child, who hates belts. Every time something touches her lower back, her hips will want to kick sideways. She may have gait disorders. If she develops scoliosis, this reflex will have been retained.

6. The tonic labyrinthine reflexes (forward and backward movements), if retained, will lead to poor posture like a stoop, or walking on toes with stiff, jerky movements, and balance will be off.

7. The symmetrical tonic neck reflex allows the baby to rise up to the hands-and-knees position for the transition to creeping: When the head is extended up, the arms straighten and the knees flex. This sets up eye training for later reading: Focusing is now adjusted to arm's length, just the distance needed for reading. It is through creeping that the vestibular, proprioceptive (tells where one is in space), and visual systems combine to operate together for the first time, to provide a sense of balance, space, and depth. A high percentage of children with reading difficulties omitted the critical developmental stages of crawling and creeping in infancy.

If the normal process of achieving these developmental milestones does not meet these criteria, neurodevelopmental training can help get the child back on track. "If he does not have the opportunity to do the activities that correspond with each stage, then he cannot reach his neurological potential. Each of the developmental activities has a very specific role in triggering the advent of new functions."[149] We must remember that 70 percent of us are "brain-damaged" to some extent, and the earlier we take remedial steps to help the brain reconnect, the easier it is for the child to make normal adjustments later in life. "An interruption of normal neurological development, even of just a few months, has serious consequences."[150] The brain has all the nerve cells it will ever have by the end of the child's second year. But the dendrites and axons of those cells can be stimulated to grow and form new connections all through life.

GROWTH

Growth is the increase in weight and length from conception to the end of adolescence. It will vary depending on heredity, intrauterine conditions, environment, disease, hormones, emotional factors, and diet. Under optimum conditions it is predictable—once a pattern has been established in the first year. Adult weight is too variable to be estimated, although a grossly fat baby at one year of age is destined to be an obese adult.

Growth is most rapid in utero, but is still accelerated in the first few months of life. Growth is predetermined by genetic factors, but intrauterine nutrition, postnatal diet, and environmental influences may alter the rate significantly. Protein, iron, calcium, zinc, vitamin C, and phosphorus seem to be the key nutrients for optimum growth.

Average weight at birth is seven pounds. Water loss accounts for the weight loss in the first few days, but he should be back to birth weight within seven to ten days. Twenty inches is the standard length at birth, but it is difficult to measure a squirmy baby. Between three and five months the baby will double his birth weight, and his length at six months should be close to twenty-five or twenty-six inches. Over the remainder of the first year, he adds only three or four inches to his length, and perhaps another six or seven pounds.

Weight gain is much more variable than linear growth, and is frequently related to hereditary predisposition toward obesity. Efforts to alter the weight increase are usually fruitless; it seems axiomatic that the harder the mother tries to keep her fat child slim, the more obese he becomes. There was a time when doctors suggested an ideal weight to go with a certain height. The rule now is that if a person looks thin, he is thin; if he looks fat, he is fat.

Some prediction can be made. Doubling the length of a girl at eighteen months gives close to her ultimate height as an adult; for a boy the two-year-old height should be doubled. If he is thirty-six inches at two, he might just become six feet tall when mature.

Slow Growth

Dwarfism means less than optimum growth for any reason. Congenital anomalies, associated with metabolic defects or enzyme deficiencies, are rare and largely untreatable. One cause seen in practice is due to malabsorption or intestinal allergy; growth resumes its normal rates when diagnosis and appropriate diets are established. If calories and protein are not being supplied to the body cells in adequate amounts, growth will fail. A diabetic child with blood sugar out of control would not be nourished well enough to grow. A cretin child with inadequate thyroid hormone would not grow well because all cells require this hormone for optimal function. Chronic infection, diarrhea, kidney disease, parasite infestation, and anemia might slow growth somewhat. A congenital heart lesion with cyanosis would retard growth because of lack of oxygen to the tissues. Emotional deprivation might cause growth retardation, apparently not from just a low-calorie intake.

The pituitary dwarf is very rare; growth hormone from the pituitary gland is not formed, because a tumor or inflammation has destroyed the cells responsible for the production of the homone. Constitutional growth delay may be diagnosed by a family history of retarded growth and delayed onset of puberty in relatives. Bone age is usually delayed, but ultimate height is within normal limits. Familial short stature accounts for the vast majority of syndromes.

A standard workup for a short child should be conducted by an endocrinologist who specializes in children.

Failure to thrive is a multifaceted syndrome in which a baby appears underweight and apathetic. Sometimes a malfunction of the heart, lungs, kidneys, or intestines can be found. All too often, however, failure to thrive results from physical or emotional neglect. The parents are unwilling or unable to accept the responsibility for the care of their newborn baby.

Neglect can begin as early as the pregnancy. If the mother's diet is low in protein or lacking in nutrients such as iron and folic acid, development of the baby's brain cells may be impaired, causing irreversible brain damage.

This physically deprived baby may now be further insulted by an environment of hostility, low stimulation, brutal reprisals for disrupting the status quo, or constant shifting from one home to another. If he is not battered, he will at least be unloved. This neglect will soon make him suspect he is unwanted. He will avoid human contact, as he has learned love is dangerous: "If you show love, you may get hurt." He will not understand how to love. Self-stimulation, poor growth, and rumination (self-induced vomiting) are the results of this maternal deprivation.

The process is felt to be reversible if interrupted in time and if persistent love, warmth, and acceptance are offered. Early compensatory intervention is essential: A doctor, a visiting nurse, a dietician, and a social worker are the minimum needed to restore the child to health.

Hypothyroidism appears if the thyroid hormone is less than adequate to maintain metabolism. If congenital, it is called *cretinism*. If it develops after a few years of normal functioning, it is usually due to thyroiditis, most likely an autoimmune disease.

The child gradually grows sluggish, sleeps a lot without becoming refreshed, and becomes constipated, and the skin is cold, dry, and waxy-looking. Obesity is rarely a result of hypothyroidism. If the child has warm, moist palms and grows two inches a year, he is just fat, not low in thyroid. In the low thyroid condition, growth stops or decreases to an inch or so in a year; the yearly checkup provides a way to keep an accurate growth record.

A few reliable blood tests are available. Treatment is lifetime hormonal replacement with a daily dose of thyroid extract (animal source is best). Wrist X rays are taken in evaluating growth failure. The epiphyses have a characteristic appearance in rickets, scurvy, lead poisoning, and in epiphysitis.

Diabetes mellitus is an inherited disease in which glucose is poorly metabolized and/or stored. When the amount of glucose in the blood rises to a critical level, it appears in the urine. This produces excessive loss of water, leading to dehydration. Without sufficient glucose to convert to energy, the body burns fat and protein, which leads to acidosis and weight loss.

Diabetes research indicates a number of factors are involved: low insulin production, lack of tissue response to normal amounts of insulin, antibody production against insulin, and the formation of defective insulin. An increased incidence of diabetes is seen in children fed cow milk in the first year of life.

The overt disease may be precipitated by infection, stress, or rapid growth. Juvenile diabetes usually has a rapid, dramatic onset with thirst, weakness, and coma. Children's insulin requirements are remarkably changeable for the first year or two of their disease; the daily dose is usually given as a regular or short-acting insulin. Quick sources of sugar must be nearby for the occasional low-blood-sugar reactions. Small doses of regular insulin five times a day will keep the blood sugar more even.[151] Long-acting insulin may be substituted when the insulin requirements become more stable. Rapid growth at puberty, or a sudden crisis like an infection, require careful adjustment of insulin to avoid reactions.

Guidance and encouraging personal responsibility are essential. The family and the doctor must foster the notion that the child is normal but has a controllable defect.

Sir William Osler said, "Get a chronic disease and take care of yourself, and you'll live a long and healthy life." I agree with that 70 percent of the time.

Glycosuria is the presence of glucose, a simple sugar, in the urine. This usually means diabetes mellitus, and is one of the chief reasons for doing a routine urinalysis. The kidneys usually do not allow glucose to appear in the urine.

The Heart

Heart murmurs are the hums, squeaks, whooshes, and growls heard between the normal heart sounds. (LUB-DUP are the sounds when the heart valves are closing.) Most commonly murmurs are functional or innocent; no defects are demonstrable in the heart. It is assumed that they are due to swirling of blood about the cords and muscles in the chambers. A third of all children have these at various times; most disappear by adolescence. Reassurance is the only treatment. (When we move the stethoscope around the chest to hear the various noises, some smart-alecky children will ask, "What's the matter, Doc? Can't you find my heart?")

Organic murmurs are produced by septal defects and valvular anomalies. Their intensity, duration, timing, and location will provide clues as to the underlying disease process, but X rays and cardiac catheterization may be necessary to find the true nature of the lesion. Is the defect surgically repairable?

Heartbeat or pulse is the pressure wave noted in the peripheral arteries (the wrist is the one traditionally used) synchronous with systole, or the emptying of blood from the ventricles. A rapid pulse persistently elevated over 150 to 120 beats per minute suggests hyperthyroidism (sleeping pulse stays elevated), Wolff-Parkinson-White syndrome, or an adrenaline-producing pheochromocytoma.

Any person may become alarmed by the occasional skipped beat that feels as if the heart flipped over inside. The heart fills with twice as much blood as usual during the pulseless interval. Then, when it beats, the force makes the heart bang against the ribs. This is common and innocuous. If these are frequent, it suggests that the person is consuming caffeine (soft drinks) or that the blood sugar is bouncing up and down and the adrenaline produced is making the heart beat thusly. Low magnesium in the body may allow this to happen also.

The pulse is rapid in the newborn (80 to 150 beats per minute, average 120) and gradually slows to 80 to 90 in childhood. An athletic adolescent in training may have such an efficient heart that its slow beat can alarm the observer. (It may be as low as 40 to 50 beats per minute.)

Rapid rates (over 180 in the newborn or persistently over 120 in a child) suggest heart disease or conduction anomalies. An electrocardiogram is called for.

Irregular

Sinus arrhythmia: Almost all normal children have this. The heart speeds up when the child inhales and slows when he exhales. This is caused by the vacuum in the chest increasing the return of blood to the heart (more rapid on inspiration, slower on expiration), requiring a faster beat to move this blood forward.

Rapid

Tachycardia is rapid heartbeat. It is expected in fright or anger (as a result of epinephrine), fever and hyperthyroidism (increased metabolism), anemia (response to increased need for oxygen), and, of course, exercise.

Paroxysmal tachycardia is the occurrence of sudden attacks of rapid heart rate due to some stimulus in the atrium, ventricles, or the nerve-conducting tissue (nodal). Rates of over 200 and up to 300 per minute have been recorded. It needs investigation.

Slow

Carotid sinus reflex causes slowing of pulse, anoxia, and fainting in susceptible people when the carotid sinus in the neck is pressed. A tight collar may initiate a fainting spell.

Low Blood Pressure

Postural hypotension is the reduction of blood pressure when a person stands. Normally the pressure rises to counteract the effects of gravity on the blood. The brain will not be oxygenated adequately if the pressure falls; giddiness and fainting will follow.

The peripheral vessels normally constrict to increase the pressure, and the heart contraction is increased to force the blood up to the brain. In hypotension the blood "puddles" in the veins of the legs and abdomen so that insufficient blood reaches the heart to provide adequate outflow. Adrenal gland exhaustion from stress may be the inciting factor. Pantothenic acid, up to one thousand milligrams a day, and desiccated adrenal gland capsules, might help restore the adrenal gland function.

The wearing of tights or a gravity suit, if they are sufficiently constricting, may prevent the pooling of blood in the dependent areas. Ephedrine sulfate may be helpful. (Dr. Thom says that ephedra can no longer be sold over the counter as teens are abusing it as an "upper.")

Hypertension

Hypertension is elevated blood pressure, uncommon in children, but if it runs in the family, some effort should be made to change the diet and the lifestyle. Its discovery must initiate a full-scale investigation to determine its cause. Very often it will be found that the pressure is normal if the patient is allowed to relax, or the blood pressure is taken at home.

Blood pressure is the measurement (in millimeters of mercury) of the force required to pump blood from the left ventricle of the heart against the resistance of the arteries (systolic or upper value). The diastolic pressure is that pressure sustained by the arterial vessels between heartbeats. The standard for adult systolic pressure is 120 millimeters or so; for the ten-year-old, 100 millimeters. The diastolic pressure is usually 20 to 40 millimeters below the systolic (75 to 80 in an adult; 50 to 70 in a child). Elevation would suggest kidney disease, aortic coarctation, or, rarely, adrenal gland disease.

Those who eat mainly milk products, cabbage, parsnips, radishes, cauliflower, highly salted foods, and little or no vinegar over the years will have a high systolic pressure as they are getting alkaline foods that contain sodium. A high-sodium, low-vinegar diet will increase the systolic pressure.

Those who eat fish, meat, and salads with vinegar dressings will have a low systolic pressure. Vegan vegetarians tend to have the lowest blood pressure of all, because they get little sodium and much potassium. (Potassium lowers the diastolic pressure.) Also, the end product of the metabolism of fruits and vegetables is acetic acid; this removes sodium from the body. Ask any vegan vegetarian if he puts vinegar on his salad. Answer: "No." Then ask what his blood pressure is. Answer: "Low."

Acid foods		**Alkaline foods**	
bread	sweet pototoes	beans (lima and string)	prunes
caffeine	rice	bean sprouts	raisins
corn	squash	cabbage	fresh tomatoes
flours	cooked tomatoes	currants	raw milk
oatmeals	potato	dates	winter squash
peanuts	pasteurized milk	oranges	lettuce
		figs	

If people eat a variety of foods every day, they will tend to have normal blood pressures and little sickness. The lungs, kidneys, liver, and skin will try to balance the acid/base so that the various enzymes can function optimally. Most people in North America are somewhat alkaline, and this tends to push them into hypertension. The body is constantly giving off clues to alert the owner to his/her needs. If a person craves pickles and vinegar, it almost always means his sodium level in the blood is above normal, and his blood pressure may be up. The vinegar tastes sweet to him like apple cider. When he drinks vinegar (one teaspoon in an eight-ounce glass of water), his next urination will test alkaline because he is excreting sodium (an alkali). His systolic blood pressure will be lower in twenty minutes.[152]

DEAFNESS

Hearing loss is a better term, since the word *deafness* suggests a total loss (rare). Congenital hearing loss, usually hereditary or due to intrauterine infection (rubella), must be tested for in the first few months of life. Electronically amplified sound may be used to provide auditory stimulation early in life when it is so important for language development.

Hearing perception may be reduced because of wax impaction, retraction of the eardrum, scarring of the drum, fusion of the ossicles (small bones that carry sound impulse from eardrum to inner ear), fluid behind the eardrum (serous otitis), perforated or bulging eardrum, and calcium deposits on the drum. All these cause **conductive** hearing losses: interference of the sound waves from the outside to the inner ear (nerve and cochlea).

Serous otitis is the most common cause of a conductive hearing loss. It is a serous fluid behind the eardrum and frequently follows otitis media (see Otitis media, Chapter 6). The fluid is sterile because the antibiotics have killed the bacteria, but the fluid cannot escape via the eustachian tubes, due to congestion caused by an allergy or a sensitivity. This fluid becomes thick, retracts the eardrum, and causes the hearing impairment. Retained fluid may have to be drained (myringotomy). Some doctors place a hollow plastic tube in the eardrum. It is left in place for a few weeks to allow the equalization of air pressure to be maintained. These buttons in the eardrum have not been as successful as originally thought. It may cause scarring, calcium deposits, and a permanent perforation. Ears with tubes have higher rates of prolonged fluid, scarring—about 50 percent—and membrane atrophy. There is also an anesthesia risk. The best idea is to control the allergy leading up to the fluid accumulation and improve the immune system.

A chiropractic manipulation can help remove the gluelike substance. The exudate contains a sticky protein matter. When the small eustachian-tube muscular membrane contracts, it can stay stuck together. The manipulation causes a stretch reflex on the eustachian tube; it opens and hearing is restored.

Rules: (1) Have the doctor make the diagnosis of serous otitis; (2) stop any dairy products the child is eating; (3) add vitamin C up to bowel tolerance; as much as three to five grams daily may be necessary. Other supplements include: vitamin A, ten thousand units daily; beta-carotene, twenty thousand units; zinc, B_6, and other essentials as antioxidants and immune system supporters. Homeopathic remedies and cell salts also work. N-acetyl-cysteine helps to thin the mucus.

Neurosensory loss of hearing is due to defects of nerve conduction between the inner ear and the auditory area of the brain. Maternal influenza at the gestational age when the cochlea was forming can cause congenital neurosensory loss. Infections such as mumps or encephalitis at any age may lead to auditory damage. The rubella epidemic some years ago caused severe hearing loss in the children born to mothers who contracted the disease in the early months of their pregnancies.

Infants with normal hearing should be making familiar baby noises such as "da-da" and "ma-ma" by age eleven months. If this is not the case, hearing tests are mandatory.

The eardrum of a child with a sensorineural loss appears normal, in contrast to the eardrum of a child with a conductive loss. The latter is usually thick, dull, retracted, amber-colored, and/or distorted or fixed in some way to suggest a problem.

Children rarely realize or express the fact that they can't hear well. Peculiarities of speech or behavior may be the only clue. Inattention is so common in children that its presence alone is not enough to diagnose a hearing deficit. Some children are so hyperacute in their hearing that they can only tolerate whispers. Since many children become skillful lip readers, parents may need to resort to tricking the child with whispers or watches as testing devices. (Mrs. Spencer Tracy did not realize she had a hearing-impaired daughter until she noticed that her ten-month-old child was looking at her lips instead of her eyes.) By age three or four, most can be tested with the audiogram machine. The child with a hearing problem may only seem bored, inattentive, or slow.

Most school systems have—or should have—arrangements with a capable audiologist to test all children in kindergarten and/or first grade.

Wax

Wax in the ears is a normal situation. The parent's reaction is to tease it out with a cotton-tipped applicator. One may get most of it out, but some is usually pushed farther down into the canal, where it becomes impacted. Adequate examination of the eardrum is impossible. Removal of the wax by the doctor is difficult. Although wax rarely causes deafness, it must be removed so the eardrum can be completely visualized. If the doctor cannot remove it deftly the first time or two with a looped, curettelike scoop, he must wash out the ears. This "ear enema" is frightening to the patient and time-consuming for the doctor; tears, water, and sweat fall together on the floor.

Rules: Don't put anything in the ear smaller than your elbow. Don't use cotton swabs. Chronic, dry wax makers may obtain relief by dropping glycerine or mineral oil in the ear once a week; the wax may not stick to the hairs so tenaciously. Ask the druggist for an ear-wax softening solution. Most of these people just accept the fact they must have the doctor wash out their ears periodically. I know an orchestra leader who comes in for ear cleansing when he has trouble hearing his oboist.

But if the doctor says it's okay, you can syringe the wax out of your child's ears yourself. Instilling a few drops of hydrogen peroxide in the canal prior to washing will speed up removal.

DEFECTIVE VISION

Universal truism: Vision is important for reading. "One in four children may have a vision problem that hampers learning. Children who have trouble seeing or focusing on an object, such as the blackboard, may not notice they have a vision problem and think they're seeing what their peers see. Consequently, children may not be able to tell parents or teachers that they are not seeing clearly. Unfortunately, many of the students who have trouble seeing properly end up being mislabeled as slow learners."[153] Telltale signs: squinting, covering one eye, excessive blinking, dislike of close work, jerky eye movements, short attention span, daydreaming, placing the head close to a book when reading, losing one's place when reading, headaches, nausea, clumsiness, turning or tilting the head, and, of course, avoiding reading.[154]

Refractive error refers to the inability of the lens and cornea to bend the light rays to a clear image focused on the retina. Astigmatism and myopia account for 85 percent of optometrists' clients. Some optometrists believe that these conditions are based on muscle imbalance or tension. There may be a psychosomatic pathway to explain this: "I choose not to see this." The myopic person is comfortable with near vision; far vision is a pain. (One patient, now thirty years old, remembered that when he was thirteen years old, "If I wore glasses, I would not have to play baseball." A middle-aged woman needed hypnosis to recall that her nearsightedness came almost immediately after seeing her younger brother struck and killed by a car. He had always been the unwanted brother, and the accident was a fulfillment of her childhood fantasy, but it was too painful to admit. Her resolution? Myopia. Within a few days of recognizing and coming to grips with the emotional basis of the myopia, her vision went from 20/200 to 20/30.)

Holistic optometrists believe that in myopia the inner muscles of the eyeball become tense—like a clenched fist—due to these unproductive attitudes caused by something the victim does not want to see. An impoverished diet, bad posture, and inadequate reading light will contribute. Genetic factors usually explain myopia under age ten years, but once puberty begins, acquired conditions, especially the role of fear of failure, anger, jealousy—any negative emotion—might allow myopia to develop. Chiropractors know that a neck adjustment can alleviate, and sometimes cure, myopia.

Astigmatism produces a distorted image for the sufferer; all the radial lines on the eye chart are not clearly focused in the retina. The usual spherical cornea may have curvature more like a football. This causes two-line focuses instead of a single-point focus. Minor forms are very common; parts of the viewed object are out of focus or distorted. Eye strain, headaches, and dislike of reading are the possible results of astigmatism. Special cylindrical-type lenses are necessary for clear vision.

Farsightedness (hyperopia) is due to the combination of refracting surfaces of the eye not bending the light rays enough to focus an image on the retina. The image is focused somewhere behind the retina and may be blurred if the focusing part of the eye (crystalline lens) is unable to bring the focus up to the retina. Some farsighted youngsters can see the eye chart perfectly in school vision tests (in reality simple sight screenings) and so are assumed to have an adequate visual system for school. The muscles controlling accommodation are working constantly to make the lens focus on the retina, and the result is fatigue, headache, and disinterest in reading. Most teachers hope the poor student has correctable vision trouble, and glasses will turn the child on to reading. It happens just often enough to make vision testing worthwhile for any suspected problem, especially if the preceding complaints are noted.

Nearsightedness (myopia) is the inability to see objects clearly in the distance because the eye is basically too strong. The combination of the cornea, crystalline lens, and length of the eyeball causes the light rays to be bent too much, creating the optical focus in front of the retina. Concave-type lenses in glasses or contact lenses are obviously necessary. The primary reason for nearsightedness was pointed out in three studies, which all showed that 85 percent of myopia is created from the impact of doing near work. There can be some hereditary tendency, too.[155]

Crossed-eyes, or esotropia, may also be called *squint* or *strabismus.* The eyes turn in, thus two images are transferred from the eyes to the brain. Binocular vision fails to develop since the brain cannot put the two images together. Eventually the brain will choose to use one eye and then the other alternately, or block or "suppress" one of the images altogether. Many times the suppressed eye will lose visual acuity from non use (amblyopia exanopsia). Since these muscles are many times stronger than necessary to move the lightweight eye around, the problem is, in fact, erroneous neurological control. Many esotropias are accommodative. At times an individual will be very farsighted and the gigantic effort of the focusing system causes over-interaction with the pointing muscle of the eye, causing the eye to turn in. This is why the majority of the time surgery is not the answer to this problem. In the case of accommodative esotropia, simple plus lenses—preferably contact lenses—will resolve this. Also, the pull of the muscles can torque the front of the eyeball and the cornea is no longer a section of a perfect sphere; it becomes egg shaped. If overaccommodation is not the problem, then surgery may help the cosmetics, but generally will impede the functional situation.

The eyes are part of the brain; what happens to the orbs will affect the brain, and vice versa. Creeping and crawling are some of the methods now used to get the eyes to team together. The assumption is that there has been some hurt to the midbrain, and the treatment is to improve the nerve connections in the vestibular-ocular-cerebellar loop. Such treatment almost never succeeds if delayed until after age six years. Discovery and correction of this defect is considered mandatory by two years of age to preclude onset of deficient vision in the unused eye. Vision therapy is reported to have a 78 percent improvement rate both in function and cosmetics. In many cases even late diagnosis is not a deterrent for vision therapy if done by a skilled and seasoned developmental optometrist. Many times perceputal sensory therapy, sometimes called perceptual stress therapy, will rapidly relieve the squint condition.

I was saddled with this problem since birth, and despite surgery, patching the good eye, and exercises, my vision ended up at 20/400 in my right eye—the one that gave up. In the last few years I have benefited from the services of optometrists who helped me improve the vision in that eye to 20/200.

This is what I have learned from developmental optometrists. The eyes are connected to everything we do: thinking, feeling, moving, planning, and most of the emotions we experience. The eye exam must be more than simply determining if the child can see the chalkboard. The child must be able to get the whole picture, then sequence that picture, then develop timing and rhythm.

My optometrist, Dr. Roger Tabb, of Portland, Oregon, has told me story after story of children who were called dyslexic, stupid, or emotionally blunted, but after a few short weeks of perceptual sensory training, they were able to read fluently and became cheerful, willing students. One youngster had a sequencing problem and was put into a special-ed class. The boy could read a word in a sentence and then be flummoxed as to the next step; the space between the words was a giant barrier. Dr. Tabb had him catch and throw back a large, soft beach ball as he said the words in a sentence. "The (catch) boy (throw) went (catch) home (throw)." The sequencing, the timing, and the rhythm were all involved, and the boy soon began to read smoothly.

Optometrists know about the interference of low blood sugar and learning, and they understand the interconnectedness of the visual apparatus with all the other nerves and circuits of the brain and the spinal cord. It ties in with what chiropractors can do for patients with learning difficulties.

Wall-eyes, or exotropia, are eyes that turn away from each other. It is a type of squint or strabismus. Surgery is seldom the intelligent answer for this condition. Vision therapy is the leader in creating a functional and cosmetic resolution.

All children should have their visual acuity checked before the age of four or five.
Most pediatricians believe they are doing all they can to evaluate a child's vision if, at the age of five years, the child can see the "tumbling E" at a distance of twenty feet; but this only detects 30 percent of vision disorders. Reading requires the integration of eight different vision skills, and only distance vision is checked by this test. Poor vision will have an impact on the child's athletic ability, musical talents, and self-esteem.

If there is any problem, the pediatrician tends to send the child to an ophthalmologist, an eye specialist trained in the diseases and surgery of the eyes. Let me quote the words of Dr. Larry DeCook, president of the American Optometric Association. In a letter written in April 1995 to the president of the American Academy of Pediatrics, DeCook states: "We are concerned that the guidelines [sent to all pediatricians] appear to indicate that all children who require further evaluation following screening should be examined by ophthalmologists. We find it difficult to understand how a set of national vision screening guidelines can overlook the services of optometrists, who provide the majority of primary eye and vision examinations in the United States for both children and adults . . . it seems inappropriate to recommend initial referrals only to ophthalmologists when surgical or other secondary eye care services will not be needed for the overwhelming majority of children being screened." Optometrists publish the *Optometric Clinical Practice Guideline on Pediatric Eye and Vision Examination.* I am suggesting that if there is any question about a child's vision, the optometrist's office would be the first to visit (see Dyslexia, Chapter 9).

Some infants with a prominent lid fold on the nasal side of the eye may appear to have crossed eyes because the skin covers the medial side of the eyeball. As the bridge of the nose grows, this illusion gradually disappears.

Infants frequently cry in the doctor's office, and visual testing is difficult. Parents should do some home testing. When a light is held about a yard away from the infant's face, the light reflected from the corneas should be symmetrically seen in both pupils. The light reflection is seen as a tiny bright diamond and is a very sensitive test. If the reflected light is noted in the center of the pupil of the right eye but on the outer side of the left pupil, then the left eye is turning in (esotropic). The "cover test" can be used for the older child: He looks at an object with the right eye while the left is covered; the cover is moved to the right eye, and if the left eye does not move to fix on the object, the eye muscles are probably balanced properly. Another test: Slowly move a penlight from a distance of about sixteen inches aimed toward the youngster's nose, keeping the light on the midline. The eyes should be able to track the light within an inch or two of the nose before one of the eyes swings out. This is called the *near point of convergence*.

Another simple test is saccadic fixations. Hold two pencils about fourteen inches apart in a parallel plane to the child's face about a foot from the eyes. Using the eyes only, the child is to look at one pencil and then the other. Notice how easy or difficult this is. If the child has to turn his head or close his eyes to look back and forth, it suggests he will have trouble reading. Treatment? See a developmental optometrist.

Smooth eye movements are as necessary for easy and efficient reading as smooth muscle movements are for great athletes to perform their skills. A penlight moved in an eighteen-inch circle in front of the child—both clockwise and counterclockwise—will allow one to observe the smoothness of a child's tracking ability. If the eye movements are jerky, or he cuts corners, or stops and overshoots to catch up, he is in trouble with future reading skills. Treatment? See a developmental optometrist.

Proper eye development and improved night vision can be aided with bilberry.

TEETH

The teeth are formed from a layer of cells in the mouth epithelium that joins mesodermal cells in the jaws. As some development has begun early in pregnancy (the fifth month), the mother's diet, diseases, and medicine will be reflected in the baby's deciduous (milk) teeth. Tetracycline taken by the mother for some infection will stain the baby's baby teeth that were being calcified at the time of the drug ingestion. They appear dirty, yellow, or green depending on the dose and the length of time the medicine was administered. The same is true for the child's permanent teeth; if possible, he should *not* receive tetracycline in the first six years or so of his life, or the enamel of his permanent teeth will acquire this stain. Some dentists report that bleaching is successful. Too much fluoride will cause mottling of his teeth. There may be a few white patches on the enamel or poorly formed brown enamel if the fluoride was heavy (five parts per million). If severe jaundice was present at birth, bilirubin will be incorporated in the baby teeth. Symmetrically decalcified teeth suggests an infection when those teeth were being formed. It also would indicate that during that period the infection might have done some harm to the developing brain. Some neurological connection might have been destroyed. A developmental specialist should be alerted.

Caries are the decay of the enamel and dentine of the teeth. Acid formed by bacteria in a matrix called plaque, feeding on retained food particles (especially sugar), will create holes in the enamel and eventually in the pulp. Infants allowed to fall asleep with the bottle propped will most certainly develop rampant caries—unless only water is in the bottle. It can happen with breast-feeding, but is less likely. Dentists now speak of plaque control—not just brushing the teeth. The plaque clings to the teeth, usually near the gum line. It is composed of bacteria, sugars, calcium, and other material in a self-perpetuating colony that is resistant to ordinary tooth brushing, like a coral growth. Acids produced lead to caries growth. The teeth must be brushed to rid them of food particles, but dental floss is the real weapon against plaque and calculus. It is best to start the program with instruction from the dental hygienist, who can motivate the patient in its continuation. Poor tooth brushing, sticky candies, and the absence of magnesium in the diet all tend to increase the incidence of this painful problem. A child who is subject to vomiting attacks will suffer an inordinate amount of decay, because the stomach acid will dissolve the surface enamel. The quality, acidity, and amount of saliva has an effect. People exposed to full-spectrum fluorescent light (visible and UV) had one fifth as many caries as those exposed to conventional fluorescent light. Start brushing the baby's teeth as soon as they come in at six months or so. You should keep brushing their teeth for several years until they can be trusted to do so themselves.

Baby or primary teeth will be shed, but if carious, they should be filled, as infected pulp may lead to periapical abscess with gumboil and associated complications.

Calculus is a calciumlike deposit, usually on the lower teeth, that can irritate the gums. Gingivitis is a common sequel to this, so removal is important.

Dentition schedule: The first molars come after the central and lateral incisors. The cuspids fill in the space between the incisors and the molars by about eighteen months. The second molars usually come all at once by age two years or so.

If the first permanent lower incisors have not erupted by age seven, an X ray may be prudent to see if they are there. Occasionally low thyroid function will explain the delay.

An old wives' tale blames roseola on cutting teeth. Roseola is a disease that appears between six months and two years of age, so teething is blamed. It is possible that the act of breaking the gums may provide a portal of entry for the virus, and thus teething appears causally related to the disease.

Infants may be irritable when the teeth are pushing through. Homeopathic and herbal remedies would be appropriate; chewing on a pacifier or rubber ring may be soothing (the pain that feels good.) Sometimes a blue eruption hematoma, a cyst of blood, appears between the crown of a molar and the unbroken gum. It is rarely necessary to cut the gums; the growth force of the tooth is always stronger than the gum tissue through which it is emerging, and the tooth will erupt.

Crowding of primary dentition is obvious by age four. Cranial therapy may preclude later orthodontic care. Babies who have been breast-fed for a year or so rarely have crowded teeth.

Periodic visits to the dentist are important, not only to reinforce good dental care, but also to evaluate the proper time for intervention in jaw malalignment.

Malocclusion is the inability of the teeth to make even contact when the jaws are apposed in biting. The spatial relationship of the jaws may be the chief defect. The upper incisors may be placed forward of the lowers (overbite), or if the lower jaw is prominent, the upper incisors may fit behind the lowers (underbite). These discrepancies are more readily seen in X rays, and if corresponding molars are not making satisfactory contact, top with bottom, some correction is wise. If a few crowns of a few teeth are the only ones making contact, dental disease will result from over- or underuse, and some teeth will surely be lost.

Cosmetic deformity is not the only reason why crooked teeth should be straightened.

Genetic factors and lack of breast-feeding are the chief causes of malocclusion, but they are aggravated by thumb-sucking. "Increased durations of breastfeeding were associated with a decline in the proportion of children with malocclusion."[156] Thumb-sucking is not harmful until the permanent teeth erupt. Corrective measures should be performed before maturity. Clarinet lessons, if prescribed by the orthodontist for the child with prominent lower jaw, are tax deductible. A craniologist should be consulted for an opinion before the orthodontist takes over. Cranial therapy can spread the palate without the loss of teeth.

The first contact the patient has with the *orthodontist* is usually at age eight to ten years when much teeth shedding is occurring. Severe malocclusion problems would require his services in infancy. Banding a child with an overbite at age eight is prophylaxis against tooth trauma. The orthodontist may want some teeth extracted to allow the others to "drift" or spacers may be used to prevent drifting. Most orthodontists are somewhat compulsive in their desire for perfect results; they know teeth will become unaligned if not watched, and that a less than perfect cosmetic result is a bad advertisement. Orthodontists frequently straighten adult teeth that became crowded after the wisdom teeth distorted the alignment. No one is too old or too young for treatment. Motivation of the child is an important consideration in determining the starting date.

Teeth grinding, or bruxism, suggests tension. If nocturnal and persistent, the child should be treated for worms. The physical presence of the worms does not have to be verified because teeth grinding is so common in a wormy child.

CHAPTER 5

Development From Age One Year On

THE TODDLER

After the age of one year, the child becomes a toddler and begins to show a little independence—a sort or preview of what he/she might be like in adolescence. Some behaviors are normal and should be accepted for what they are—testing the environment. For instance, the one-year-old loses his interest in food for eating, but wants to use it to experiment with the effects of gravity. The mother who insists on "finish your plate" teaches her child that dawdling will be rewarded with attention. If she can be reassured he will not starve, she will recognize that the meal is over, and separate child and food. She must pretend it is unimportant.

Children age one to two need constant watching; they demand constant watching; they *want* constant watching. It is as if they get into persistent mischief just to see if someone really cares. It doesn't really matter too much to them, it seems, whether it is good or bad attention, for they *thrive* on attention.

But other behaviors are clearly off base and their cause must be determined. Troublesome children do not seem to get the message that if parents love and feed them, they are supposed to be compliant and cheerful. Children who act up were once thought to have a psychiatric problem: The parents are too strict, too lenient, or inconsistent. In my early practice, if a child was "unmanageable" and if I felt the parents were being "reasonable" and provided "love and limits," I offered the following possibilities: Is this child anemic, hypoglycemic, suffering from a worm infestation or a heavy-metal poisoning? Or is he normal? He is acting like Uncle Ed. Good God! Is it genetic? If a mother brought a child in with unacceptable behavior, I often found it came from the father's side of the family. If the father brought the child in with some oddball trait, I was sure it was from the mother's side.

The parents' job at about this time is to establish some house rules and develop a conscience in their child. (Freud categorized children of this age as "polymorphous perverse.") The trick is to give the child a good self-image without destroying creativity or making the child a simpering wimp. The conscience, or superego, is a set of values the child develops largely through her parents' insistence that she control her impulsiveness; otherwise, she might lose their love. A "nice" (socially acceptable) adult has a built-in sense of social/moral values. If she deviates from this self-control, she feels guilty or depressed. Her internalized "parent" punishes her.

Discipline helps the child internalize impulse control so as he grows, his sense of right and wrong is usually fixed. But children come in all grades of sensitiveness, and a variety of methods is needed to control different children in the same family. One may need only a raised eyebrow to help him recognize a transgression; another may need a "time out" to help him control his impulsiveness—although violence is counterproductive. (See Discipline, Chapter 14.)

Since all children have to go through this civilizing process that is supposed to last a lifetime, their reluctance to be "trained" must be an inborn, genetic trait. Some of this inability to conform to social rules is undoubtedly genetic: "He's just like his father—pigheaded." Every nationality lays claim to these traits: the obstinate Scandinavian, bullheaded German, defiant Scot, indifferent Italian, independent Nigerian, unyielding Pole, and so on.

Discipline is necessary to protect the toddler from self-destruction. Usual no-nos: "Don't run in the street; the car will run over you." "Don't climb up there; you'll fall and crack your head." "Don't eat that medicine, (soap, polish, etc.); you'll kill yourself." "Don't touch the stove; you'll get burned." Variations are endless. A child has to be exposed to a few dangers in the safety of a secure home so he may file the information away for future automatic avoidance—gravity works, fire burns, knives are sharp, and so forth. But if the cortex of the brain is not operative due to low blood sugar or toxic heavy metals, these rules and admonishments will not be recorded in the memory-storage areas.

Here are clues parents tell us that indicate the child is not connected properly and therapy would be indicated: "hard to manage, into everything, clumsy, impulsive, loud, stubborn, punishment has no effect, and he tends to run away." Some attention must be paid to the idea that children who do not "fit in" are not connected properly and the use of neuronal stimulation therapy will be of great benefit (see Cerebral Dysfunction, Chapter 9).

Behavior

Behavior is the observable, overt manifestation of a person's thoughts and feelings. Children usually reflect their moods in a fairly obvious, physical way. Genetic, infectious, anoxic (lack of oxygen), social, traumatic, and environmental factors *all* play a role. A behavior disorder is an action that bothers a child's parents, friends, or others who are significantly affected by his conduct. Some behaviors need investigation. Some need neurological evaluation and therapy. Heavy-metal poisoning might explain antisocial behavior. Sometimes a psychotherapist only needs to get the parents to back off from their rigid child-rearing methods.

Thumb-sucking to one mother may indicate contentment and relaxation; to another parent it suggests that the child is insecure. That parent may feel that if something drastic is not done now, it will become fixed, showing the world that the child came from a "bad" home.

A **hyperactive, impulsive, gabby child** may be completely out of place growing up in a quiet, controlled household where his behavior represents a frustrating disruption that needs strong control measures. He may come to grief because he is unable to internalize the self-control that seems to be the accepted norm in this household. He is labeled "bad" in this environment; he figures, since he is already classified, he might as well act that way. He is more likely to drop out of school ("If you would just sit still, you would do better work"), run away from home ("You are a pest; just get hold of yourself"), and/or take up drug use because he has no success at the acceptable pursuits. The same driven child may be unnoticed in a highly verbal, physically active household.

A **fearful, tense, and anxious** child might easily fall apart in a tense, insecure home. Other children are **rigid, unbending** in their relationships with others or even themselves, and drive on in the quest of perfection. If their goals are not achieved, headaches and stomachaches may develop.

A **wobbly, clinging, floppy, "loosely strung"** toddler may be panic-stricken when handled or moved about. A poorly functioning cerebellar/inner-ear-neural connection may panic the baby as if he were on a broken merry-go-round. The parent of this child will avoid sudden movements. He may grow up to be "delicate," touchy, insecure—not because his parent *wanted* him to be so, but because he insisted that he be handled so. If the father is an athletically oriented mesomorph, his disappointment in this boy may be a subtle but effective aloofness, or he may push him into impossible physical pursuits in which he is bound to fail. The child's anger and frustration can turn into internalizing symptoms (stomachaches, headaches, encopresis [soiling underwear], enuresis [bedwetting], fears, and phobias).

Anxiety and phobias in childhood correlate well with anxiety and depression in adulthood. Nutritional therapies and homeopathy should break the pattern.

The **indulged, overprotected** child, reared in a permissive home (every whim catered to), smothered with love but no limits or control applied, will usually become egocentric (a spoiled brat), disobedient, impudent, and demanding. His mother becomes the slave to every tyrannical whim. If he has not developed a conscience or superego, or any control over his basic drives by age six or seven, he will not be able to do so later on.

Social learning theorists believe that if socially acceptable behavior of a child is rewarded and unacceptable aggression is ignored, the child will learn to control the egocentric drives from his lower-animal brain. This is generally true, but firm limits must also be applied to the child's physical aggression within the context of love. His cerebral hemispheres allow him, if he has time, to evaluate the total situation and compromise the pressures from the environment with the animal demands arising from his body via his hypothalamus.

The Home Environment:

1. In a rejecting home environment, the insults of an inadequate diet, little love, and a paucity of intellectual stimulation, in addition to a rigid, authoritarian (and usually physically aggressive) parent, will almost certainly drive a child to one of the externalizing syndromes (**defiant, vengeful, hostile, rude, or at least negative**).

2. Oral deprivation in the first few months of an infant's life may determine oral habit patterns later on: **obesity** in the endomorphic child, **rumination** in the child who internalizes, high **abdominal pain** in the obsessive child (she can never satisfy her mother), or **anorexia nervosa** in the ectomorphic type.

3. Harsh, punitive methods of enforcing bowel control usually serve only to anger the child, and the resulting **negativism or aggression** may color all his responses to his parents and, as a continuum, to the school and the world.

4. The excessively aggressive adult will, in general, promote **hyperaggression** in a child. This sequence is most consistent if the child is a big, muscular mesomorph anyway, but will almost surely develop if he is an impulse-ridden, hyperactive child. Parents who stimulate their children erotically, or who deprive them emotionally, can count on rearing aggressive adults. **Battered children** frequently grow up to batter their own children; very little guilt may accompany this. However, some children reared in aggressive, hostile environments may learn to completely inhibit their normal aggressive drives.

5. An alcoholic, delinquent **(sociopathic),** hostile father is much more likely to have a child who follows in his footsteps. A genetic influence is suggested, for this is likely to happen whether the father is at home or absent.

6. Family traits of **sociopathy, epilepsy, alcoholism, schizophrenia, and migraine** may allow a child (who might carry similar genes) to be more vulnerable to birth trauma, infection, and a substandard environment.

7. Emotionally handicapped children have a very high rate of learning difficulties **(dyslexia, underachieving)** that suggests associated neurological hurts as another causal factor.

8. If the parents must have autocratic, protective dominance over their children, they may rear **shy boys and inhibited girls.**

15 MONTHS

Toys worth using are a small wagon to fill and dump, small rocking horse, push and pull toys, nesting toys, core with color rings, different shaped boxes, hammer boards, mop, broom, toy phone, teddy bear, dolls, and cars. He can use a cup, but has plenty of spills. She messes in food, often squeezing it as if to kill it before eating it. Most parents try some of the sensitizing foods at this time: wheat, egg, citrus, green vegetables, peaches. He can usually stand with support. She crawls well. He says "mama" and "bye-bye." He can usually walk alone. She is curious and investigates everything; she may poison herself. He needs reward and praise for accomplishment.

These problems usually appear at about this age:

Temper tantrum is a form of communication by which the verbally inadequate fifteen- to eighteen-month-old expresses his anger and frustration. It must be a normal phase of development in social living, because almost all children pass through this period. The child wants to put his finger on the hot stove, his mother says, "That's a no-no!" and the child falls on the floor kicking and screaming.

These episodes will decrease with time if the parents do not "reward" the child for them, with either cuddling and love, or spankings and punishment. The prudent parent will walk into the next room without saying anything. The child may pick himself up, follow the parent, and have another tantrum. The parent should move into the next room. If one gives in and picks up the child for a soothing cuddle, the child thinks, "I've done it; but it takes two room changes."

Boys seem to be more prone to these tantrums, not only because they are innately physical in their responses, but because their speech development is usually slower than it is in girls. As soon as the child learns to swear (he learned it at the neighbors') or imitate "No-no!" he is able to communicate on a higher level than the physical or acting-out level. Self-control cannot be learned until the self-control nerves have matured.

If the temper tantrums continue beyond eighteen months, some communication malfunction is operating. The child does not feel well. Diet? Heavy-metal poisoning? Worms? Anemia? Something is not connected properly.

Accident proneness or awkwardness is a lifestyle with some children. Ill-defined hurts to the nervous system may become obvious to parents at this age. "Mishaps at birth may cause what we generally call 'minimal' brain damage, that makes the child just a little bit different from the others. This kind of child gets abused more often than the one who has a major handicap. Allowances will be made for a child with an obvious problem. The subtle problems are the ones which will get the child into trouble."[157]

Neurological disorganization may be obvious in the hyperactive child who has coordination problems; his inability to curb his motor drives, coupled with his inability to adjust to the sensory messages from his environment, allow him to bang into doors, spill his juice, fall down stairs, slam his fingers in the door, burn himself on the stove. He is not stupid. Some defect in the association pathways of his brain may be responsible. Was he allowed to crawl and creep as an infant before he walked?

The awkward child has a developmental lag. It can be corrected with nervous system stimulation using the crawling/creeping technique that encourages the formations of connections in the midbrain. He needs vestibular stimulation (spinning about in a circle), especially if his awkwardness is coupled with immaturity, explosive temper outbursts, and lack of impulse control. Poor dietary factors (additives, sugar, coloring agents) must be prohibited if the condition comes and goes.

We expect the toddler to be awkward by adult standards, because he falls or bangs into things in his enthusiasm to find out about his environment and to try out his legs. A poorly coordinated child senses his lack of skill and quickly despises any activity that would embarrass him, even though the parents may think he would profit by the training. Therapy would be important before the bad self-image settles in to wreck his life. To a certain extent, a ballerina is born a ballerina.

Breath-holding attacks occur at the time of fright, frustration, injury, temper tantrum, or a spanking. The infant—usually twelve to eighteen months of age—cries two or three times, exhales, holds his breath, turns blue, arches his back, and passes out. He may have some convulsive movements or stiffening of arms and legs. He relaxes in a moment, becomes pale, then resumes normal activity.

It is important to differentiate this from epilepsy. In epilepsy there is no emotionally precipitating factor; usually the child does not cry; the cyanosis accompanies or follows the seizure. The electroencephalogram is normal in the breath-holder; medication is pointless unless the parent "must do something." Attacks may occur daily, weekly, or monthly.

The parents must understand that the breath-holding attacks are innocuous and will cease in a year or so. Studied indifference—a complete turning away by leaving the room—to these attacks seems to be the best method of treating them. Rubbing of the outside of the arms may help to control them.

Headbanging, nodding, or twisting may be evidence of neurosis, tension, epilepsy, or headache; or they may occur in a normal child who has a need to perform this tic for release of energy. If the child seems happy and is eating well, consider it a developmental phase that should pass. Homeopathic remedies are often successful. Obviously there is something wrong. Cranial therapy can quiet this problem.

"The child who wants to rock may have a cerebral spinal fluid partial obstruction. The DeJarnette method for children under two is to lift them by their heels to a slow count to fifteen. A child who was about to have neuro-surgery for an obstruction had this method done for him, and the surgeon said, 'It looks like the problem is clearing up.' No further treatment was necessary; his development has been normal ever since. He was also being breastfed, which stimulates cerebral spinal fluid flow which is necessary for good health."[158]

Example: "We have a three-year-old who beats [bangs] his head. He started at about ten months of age in his crib. He gets on his hands and knees and rocks back and forth into the solid ends of the crib. He used to do it only when we first put him down for the night, and sometimes it would go on for an hour. Then he began to do it in the middle of the night when he wanted to be changed or he needed a bottle. He never seemed to be awake when he was doing this. Our doctor said not to worry. We padded the ends of his crib with two-inch foam and waited for him to out-grow it. He didn't! He pulled the foam down so that he could make good contact with the wood. In a few months he had splintered the wood. We had to tie it together because the screws were not holding.

"He had developed a fingerlike ridge at the area where he was banging himself. It felt hard as bone. Another doctor said he was doing this because he wanted attention. We always gave him plenty. He had us try phenobar-bital, but that knocked him out and he seemed drunk and unsteady during the day, so we quit that.

"We tried not to say anything to him, but when it sounds like your kid is coming through the wall, we are getting nervous that there is something serious going on. And now the ridge is about three fingers wide and a half inch high running from his forehead to the crown of his head. Help."

My findings are that these children—and adults—who need to do some rhythmic act to calm themselves are low in calcium and magnesium. I ask the mothers, "Did you have back and leg aches during the pregnancy with this child?" "Yes," they often answer, as she did in the above case. This mother solved her child's problem with calcium and magnesium, and the ridge disappeared as he grew. The boy loves to drink the pickle juice right out of the jar. He is alkaline.

Nail-biting and **thumb-sucking** are common childhood habits that upset most parents, because they suggest to them that their child is neurotic and they are somehow responsible. The more concerned they are, the more the child seems to continue the habit. Some evidence suggests a familial trait; a mother who struggled with her own nail-biting as a child would be overly concerned when her own flesh and blood does the same thing—almost as a taunt. Sometimes a child will stop nail-biting if fingernail polish is applied to the nails. ("See how pretty!") Most children will quit this habit when their classmates at school taunt them; they will at least wait until they get home.

Facial changes and malocclusion result from persistence of the thumb-sucking habit after the age of five years. The child who must suck his thumb more than twelve hours a day after this age needs a discouraging appliance from the dentist and some counseling from the pediatrician or friendly psychologist. Calcium and magnesium supplements may help. The habit only means the child likes to suck his thumb. Hal Huggins, D.D.S., suggests the use of a loosely applied Ace bandage from armpit to wrist. Then the child bends his elbow to suck, it cuts off the circulation; the cramping discourages sucking. He says they quit in two to seven days. (This should be monitored so circulation will not be stopped completely!)

18 MONTHS

The tuberculosis skin test is often done at this age. He can climb stairs one at a time. She can kick a ball. He says "No" to almost every question; it is a favorite word. She loves to pull a toy or wagon. Children have at least three to five words; girls usually have more words than boys. He scribbles with a crayon. She uses a cup without spilling. The first molar teeth appear now or at least before age two years.

The following concerns usually come up at this age:

Gait disorders: Gait in the normal child varies with age, but once the broad-based, halting steps of early toddling have been mastered, each child develops a painless rhythmic gait of his/her own. Many first steps suggest a neurological defect: An infant may advance one foot and slide the other one into position near it as if she's had a stroke or been in a chain gang. Apparently the nerves to the muscles of the legs develop faster on one side than on the other. This equalizes in three or four weeks.

If the odd gait lasts too long, then a neurological disorganization is the fault. Many of these same children will also have trouble learning to read. Where is the break? The crawling/creeping/vestibular stimulation therapy needs to be tried. "The child can't use his muscles unless the brain knows where the foot is. It is the brain that tells the body how to move, and if it does not know where that body is, it can't move it. The children and adults with whom I worked started to develop better neurological organization because they repeated the movements they should have made as babies."[159]

Genu valgum (knock-knee), if severe enough, may force the child to swing his legs out in a grotesque arc to avoid banging his knees together. A vertical bar the length of the leg with a tight strap about the knee may encourage the growing leg to straighten. (See Legs, this chapter.)

Ill-fitting shoes will make a child limp. Does the limp disappear when the child walks barefoot?

Injured or pulled muscle is the most common cause of a limp. It usually takes ten days to recover normal function. A broken bone is usually too painful to allow normal weight bearing. An incomplete fracture might allow a few days of painful weight bearing. Proteolytic enzymes (which digest protein) will speed recovery, as will homeopathic remedies, such as arnica, rhus tox, and others.

Inflammation such as synovitis will usually allow walking with a limp, but osteomyelitis and septic arthritis are too painful to permit weight bearing. If the child can bear some weight and limps less after the first four days, watchful waiting is in order. If the limp is worse after five days or continues after ten days, it should be investigated. Some children sleep soundly in a position that pinches the nerve that passes over the outside of the knee. Paralysis of the lower leg seems obvious for about an hour after rising. It should be temporary.

One unusual case of leg paralysis was due to pressure on the sciatic nerve in a ten-year-old girl who sat on a cement step reading comics for thirty minutes. She could not stand immediately afterward and noted numbness and tingling below the knee. Complete recovery required nine months.

Muscular dystrophy forces the patient to walk on his toes because his calf muscles are contracted.

Spastic diplegia, usually from a birth injury, would preclude an easy, lithe gait. All variations of this are possible—from slight awkwardness to inability to put one foot in front of another.

Foot drop in a child is a common sign of lead poisoning or postpolio. He has to throw his foot out (like a swimmer in flippers) so his toes clear the floor. The toe hits the floor first, then the heel.

March fracture occurs after vigorous exercise or a prolonged hike. The midshaft of the second metatarsal gives way from this stress. Pain, tenderness, and some swelling are noticed in the midarch. Vitamins C and D will speed healing.

Congenital dislocation of the hip causes a rolling, lurching gait. It is usually diagnosable at birth, but may not be obvious until one year of age when the child takes a few steps. As the head of the femur is not securely locked in the socket, it slides up the side of the pelvic bone. To balance this weakness, the child bends his trunk over to the affected side in order to lift up the opposite foot to step. The hip socket may not have been properly formed if the child did not crawl and creep. In countries where mothers constantly carry their babies about on their backs with their legs separated, this condition is almost unknown. Late treatment would require a body cast.

Flatfoot is the normal appearance of children's feet. They are short, wide, and thick in infancy, and do not begin to look like "feet" until about five or six years of age. The fat pad in the arch is usually present until age three or four; this is accentuated by the knock-kneed appearance at the same age. About 70 percent of children under age four years have flat feet. They will develop an arch if they are genetically destined to do so. The arch of the standing five-year-old should be high enough to insert a finger underneath. Only about 20 percent of the population remain flatfooted all their lives. The army used to reject flat-footed recruits until it was found they had few complaints after long marches. The rocker-bottom foot is apparent at birth, since the head of the talus bone bulges into the arch area. Surgical correction is necessary.

If there is a normal range of motion of ankle and foot joints, and if the child has no pain on walking, the feet probably require no special shoes. The tight Achilles tendon will produce a rigid flatfoot; the foot cannot be dorsiflexed. People who walk with feet everted (externally rotated, opposite of pigeon-toed) will exaggerate a flat-footed tendency, and pain and tenderness will develop in the tendons just above the ankle bone on the inside of the shin. Learning to walk with feet slightly turned in will relieve this.

Shoe salesmen will often insist that parents purchase high-laced stiff shoes with a built-in Thomas heel (where part of the heel extends forward under the arch). These special heels would be necessary if the child complains of pain or tired feet. After a few years of wearing these shoes, the child develops an arch and the assumption is that the shoes have done it. We know, however, that the arch was going to develop anyway. High-laced shoes stay on the feet better, since children are prone to pull shoes off, but soft-soled, light and pliable shoes, moccasins, or tennis shoes are better for growing feet, as they allow greater toe room for growth and exercise. Shoes are only needed for protection from broken glass, snow and ice, nails, worms, and bacteria in the soil. Foot and ankle support is a matter of inborn ligamentous integrity and some muscle education, not stiff shoes. (Witness the novice ice skater: His ankles flop around until his muscles are strong enough; it has nothing to do with how tightly the skates are laced.)

Pronated ankles are usually a family trait, associated with flat feet. The ankles and arches roll inward, and shoes often wear out rapidly on the inside. If pain in arches and calves is associated with this, some arch support in the shoe will help the symptoms, but will not correct the pronation. The support lifts up the arch only while in position; the foot usually slides away from the correction. Some effort to strengthen the foot and calf muscles may provide relief. Running barefoot on wet sand at the beach seems appropriate; or a systematic program of foot exercises using a sponge-rubber-covered board may ease the cramps. (Vimulator by Vitaped Co. is one such device.)

Pigeon-toe is the common turned-in appearance of the feet most easily seen when the child is walking. The feet point toward each other, and the child steps off using the outside of his foot. He may be clumsy and trip frequently.

Most children are somewhat pigeon-toed at birth, since they have held their legs crossed against their abdomen in the confining uterus. If they prefer to sleep prone in the knee-chest position with the buttocks resting on their heels, this turned-in tendency will be aggravated. The tibia (shinbone) will grow spiraling inward (tibial torsion), and the inner borders of the feet will angle inward (metatarsus varus). Parents may not be aware of the problem until their child is toddling, at which time the awkward pigeon-toed gait and instability are obvious.

If parents are aware of the tendency, early exercising and positioning may preclude its development: At each diaper change the feet are angled out; each time the baby is held and cuddled, his feet are turned out against the parent's body in the spread-eagle position; each time he is put to bed his feet are put in the "frog" position (toes turned out). Side- and back-sleeping babies usually have no problem outgrowing this; it only seems to be the ones who sleep prone with their toes turned in.

By the sixth to eighth month of life, if the baby has not begun to sleep in different positions or in the frog position, some bracing during sleep (Denis-Browne splint, shoes glued or riveted to a board with the toes pointing out, or shoes with heels buckled together) must be tried while growth is still rapid. Simply securing the feet together at bedtime may be all that is necessary. The condition must be overcorrected as there is a tendency to return to the inward position. The infant still needs to do the "lizard" exercises (crawling).

The older child is usually fitted with a sturdy shoe, plus a $^3/_{16}$-inch outer sole wedge. When he steps off in walking, this wedge acts as a pivot, and the foot turns outward. Some doctors prescribe a spring cable that runs from a waist belt to a sturdy shoe, and holds the foot turned outward. All these devices will be negated if the child reverts to the knee-chest buttocks-resting-on-the-turned-in-feet sleeping position.

A special reverse-last shoe is used for the inverted foot. (The metatarsus varus, the inner border of the foot, curves in instead of being straight from heel to big toe.) Using it in the first year during rapid growth—and during sleep—will correct this condition easily.

Legs

Genu recurvatum is the condition of hyperextensibility of the knee joint (knee can be bent backward beyond the vertical). If the trait continues into adolescence, the youth should not be allowed to participate in contact sports, as this unstable knee joint is susceptible to injury.

Genu valgum (knock knee) is the normal look of almost all two- to four-year-old children when standing up. At age three the trait is at its peak. When this child stands straight with the knees barely touching, a gap of two to three inches will be noted between the ankle bones, and the arch is virtually nonexistent. Without special shoes this distance will diminish until age six or seven, when the child usually assumes the leg proportions he will retain his whole life. About 60 percent of adults have one to two inches of space between their ankle bones when standing erect with knees just touching. About 20 percent of adults have "perfect" legs—knees and ankles touching easily when at attention. All others are bowlegged. Skilled runners and agile athletes are in these last two groups.

Genu varum (bowlegs). Most children look a little bowlegged when they start to walk. It does not represent rickets, which is rarely seen these days, but is rather a natural curving of the legs. Usually, after the child walks and grows—or by the time he gets beyond two years of age—his legs become more knock-kneed, and he looks flat-footed. Persistence of bowed legs into adulthood is compatible with increased athletic skills.

Grandmother's admonition not to let a baby walk too early is based on her fear of rickets, or soft bones. Nowadays almost all milk (except skim) contains vitamin D, and babies receive supplements of vitamin D along with other vitamins. If a baby has been taking adequate doses of vitamin D, his mild bowlegged appearance is normal. It is frustrating to the baby to be restricted from walking. If she wants to walk early, she should.

TWO YEARS

The child's appetite decreases; serve smaller amounts of food. Let the child ask for more; don't force more food on the child. They can name objects in a picture. Bladder and bowel control may be accomplished at this time—girls sooner than boys, who may take another year. They are able to run. They have sentences of three words. The cuspid or eye and stomach teeth fill in the space between the incisors and the molars between eighteen months and two years. The second molars usually come all at once by two years of age.

Here is the most common and irritating trait of this age:

Whining is a trait peculiar to the two-year-old who is communicating his frustration to his parents. His language skills are rudimentary and he has not learned the value of an appropriate, incisive swear word. He has found that his mother ignores last year's temper tantrum. He also is rewarded by the exasperated look on her face when he whines, so he continues this until boredom or expressive language supervenes. Studied indifference should be the parents' role in coping with this temporary but entirely normal growth phase.

If whining is excessive—more than 55 percent of the time—it might be worthwhile to treat for worms, anemia, search for an infection (ear or bladder), or change the diet, as low blood sugar may cause this.

THREE YEARS

Children have definite food likes and dislikes. This is a good age to have a dental checkup. He can build a tower of several blocks. She knows her name. They know what sex they are. He can turn pages, use scissors, and draw a line. She can name at least one animal in a picture book. He can name at least one color.[160]

Passive-aggressive reaction is the psychiatric term for stubborn, bullheaded, usually silent refusal to cooperate. The child seems to know what behavior his parents are most anxious for him to display, and then seems to delight in not performing it—won't be toilet trained, won't say "How do you do?" or shake hands, or get dressed. The child usually resorts to this rebellion because he feels there are too many pressures on him to produce or perform at some arbitrary standard. He must be allowed some free time and/or be encouraged to verbalize his controlled hostility. He must be allowed to feel successful at something.

The cute, laughing, under-ten-month-old was such a joy to the home, it is hard to believe that he turned into such an aggravation—not eating, not trained, whining, into everything. The parents still love him, of course, because of the earlier programming, but they don't have to like his behavior.

Bowel and bladder control is eagerly sought by parents as a sign of maturity and obedience in their children. It is axiomatic, however, that when full energy is applied to achieve the goal of toilet conformity, success is delayed. The rule then: The older the child, the shorter the training period. Age two years sees the majority of girls happily defecating in the pot. Most boys are willing by age three.

Bladder is the hollow, distensible organ that collects urine from the kidneys. It allows humans to be socially acceptable for long periods of time. Many children have attained early control over their urination needs during the daytime, but this is rare under eighteen months of age. The development of voluntary control of the muscles descends from the neck, to the arms, to the back (the child sits), to the legs (he can stand), and then to the bladder and anal sphincter muscles. The nerves to the bladder and rectal muscles develop *after* the nerves to the leg muscles. **Learning waits on maturation.** Parents should expect some dry periods of two to three hours once walking has been mastered. This is usually after fifteen to eighteen months of age, just at the time when the child is likely to discover negativism as a way of life. He suspects the parent wants something, and the game of spiteful withholding leads to fixed passive aggression. Rapid development of this social function is mainly genetic. But if a two-year-old has not passed beyond his infantile, automatic, involuntary bladder emptying, some investigation of the urinary system is in order.

Possible problems:

1. Narrowing of a part of the urethra may produce a small, weak stream; incomplete emptying of the bladder; straining to void; and, more seriously, back pressure against the kidneys, which could be permanently damaged.

2. Bladder infection or cystitis may go unnoticed in an infant, but cause bladder and kidney damage.

3. A congenitally small bladder cannot distend adequately to hold more than two or three ounces of urine at a time. X-ray techniques can demonstrate this condition.

4. A "nervous" bladder may force urine to be excreted frequently. Magnesium might help this.

5. Some people will pass urine frequently because of a sensitivity to milk, fruit, or chocolate.

When a child is old enough to use the toilet, the flow should be easily audible as it hits the water and should make bubbles. One may have to eavesdrop, as the older child may refuse to urinate for an audience.

Concerned nonchalance is the best method of handling toilet training. Make the pot available; if parents and peers use the toilet, so will the child. As the child grows old enough, use the Tom Sawyer whitewash-the-fence technique. At about age two, when the child says, "I go pee-pee in the toilet," the parent responds, "You can't; it's mine." This may be enough motivation to increase the desire to grow up. After a little bickering, the parent acquiesces, saying, "Okay, but if you wreck my toilet, it's back to the diapers for you." This method may work long enough to establish the habit pattern.

Many mothers have set the goal of going back to work when their children are three years old and in nursery school, but at age two years and eleven months, the indifferent frustrator is still disinterested in toilet cooperation. Nursery schools usually insist on toilet training as one of the entrance requirements, so a few sneaky mothers will try the following: They put the child in used but clean training pants and tell the teacher that he is trained but has a "few" accidents. (Six a day is a few?) At toilet time when everybody eliminates, the previously reluctant one will get the message and use the toilet because his peer group does.

There appears to be a gene for toilet-training time that is as immutable as eye color. Don't try to change this built-in timing device; you will only frustrate yourself and the owner of the clock. Wait until the child says, "Mother, I would like to use the toilet to urinate/defecate now." If you wait long enough, toilet training might take a mere thirty minutes.

Harsh or coercive toilet training may lead to constipation and/or encopresis (soiling the underwear). Some children become completely submissive; their ensuing adult personalities are characterized by parsimony, preciseness, and compulsiveness (over-toilet-trained string saver?). These traits are determined more by the parents' total lifestyle than their attitude toward his bowel functions; it may help to shape his attitude about withholding or producing. In later life he may enjoy the game of setting up tasks for himself and then completing them.

FOUR TO FIVE YEARS

The child's appetite is better. They grow two to three inches each year. They can draw a person. They prefer to play with other children. They can count three objects. She can balance on one foot for ten seconds. He can jump on one foot. She can catch a ball. He can tell a story.

She has learned that if she hurts others, she will lose the love of her parents and/or her new friend. If her nervous system is normal and her parents are balancing praise and love and limits, she will learn self-control of her normal aggressiveness.

FIVE YEARS

This is a good age to get the visual acuity test. They eat three reasonably good meals a day. They can draw a circle and cross. They can ride a tricycle. They often ask "What?"

FIVE TO SIX YEARS

They imitate adult activity. Their favorite word: "Why?" They are interested in the differences between male and female. They can throw a ball. They can name three or four colors.

This age is a great one for testing the limits of the parents' love and acceptance. They seem to know how far to go without getting killed. Noncompliance is an art at this age.

It is also possible that the parent is speaking into the left ear and the child is right-eared. A parent should test the child. (Which ear does he use when on the phone? Ideally we should be right-footed, right-eyed, right-handed, and right eared. Or all left-sided.) It takes a nanosecond for the auditory message to get through the corpus callosum to the association areas where the message can be processed. It could be an auditory delay if you have to remind him all the time. Does he understand?

Dawdling is a passive-aggressive act that drives parents wild, because the harder they scream and cajole, the more skillful becomes the dawdler in his obstructionism. Many children find it results in a great deal of attention with little effort.

When breakfast is on the table and the school bus is coming down the road, dawdling while getting dressed wrecks the morning for the whole family. The child's feeling of self-responsibility would be enhanced by waking him early enough, having breakfast ready, and clearing the path. No coercion is expressed. If he is tardy, *he* has to face the teacher with some fumbling excuse. He was late; he must alter his behavior. The success of this method depends on the child's love for teacher and school. He may dawdle because school is an enemy, or he is academically unsuccessful. He may dawdle because he has low blood sugar in the morning and is a space case. In the latter case, a glass of orange juice about thirty minutes before wake-up call might do the trick. Some have found that getting the child to "bicycle" in bed will get the circulation going; the brain will get some blood flow.

SIX TO SEVEN YEARS

They can dress and undress themselves. They can copy some letters. They can tell a long story. The balance in the brain moves from left to right, and coincides with myelination and linking with the vestibular (balance) apparatus, cerebellum, and corpus callosum. Writing reversals are common until this linkage, and are often associated with lack of the postural reflexes. School starts. If there is any doubt about abilities, it is better to hold a boy back a year. Occasionally a girl can be pushed forward.

These are some of the problems and irritations that may have persisted since infancy that you thought would have disappeared by now:

Encopresis is the repeated soiling of underwear by the passage of small amounts of stool that the child claims he knows nothing about. It is a form of aggression that drives most parents frantic because there is no way to fight it. It is almost exclusively seen in boys, especially hyperactive, disruptive underachievers who are being hounded to sit still and do better. This enforced conformity suggests a passive rebellion—soiling. The treatment is directed at the mind, not the stool, but some effort must be made to determine if the victim is neurologically sound and not constipated from milk intake. A baby is expected to soil his diapers, but if a boy is over three years and not trained, the diagnosis is considered. A boy who has been trained, then develops encopresis after age four to six years, needs remedial steps immediately, as this habit pattern is extremely difficult to dislodge. The parents' punitive measures somehow encourage its continuation.

It may have its origin at toilet-training time when parents were persistently insistent, and the child's immaturity prevented conformity. Frustration leads to anxiety that turns to anger and then to stool withholding. This progression may have been enhanced by the normal appetite loss and excessive milk intake at two or three years, which usually leads to constipation. Retention more than a few days is impossible, and some stool leaks out. The insulted parent reacts in anger, which sets the pattern.

Diet change (stop white foods and milk), adding stool softeners, allowing a ten-minute BM time after breakfast with reward for accomplishment—but no remarks or punishment for failure—will usually allow the child to relax and respond more appropriately to nature's call. Obviously some attention must be directed to improving the atmosphere at school and/or home. Verbal aggression is encouraged as a substitute for his rectal hostility. Pressure to make him achieve must cease. Psychiatric help to alter behavior and mood may be necessary. One should check if the Galant reflex has been retained.

Good habits are routine, often stereotyped practices that parents urge upon a child. It is hoped that good hygiene will become ingrained into the child's lifestyle; he becomes uncomfortable if it is lacking. Bed routine, bathing, teeth brushing, eating proper foods, social niceties, pleasant speech, and concern for others are some of the activities that parents are supposed to "brand" into the child's nervous system. Many compromises are necessary between the parent's ideal of a "nice" child and what the child is willing to conform to. These good habits are usually incorporated into a child's (or the future adult's) daily life more by parental example than by admonishment.

"Bad" habits frequently begin from a physiological need or nervous-energy overflow. Once manifest, they can become fixed as a result of the attention paid to them by a conscientious parent attempting to eliminate them. Night wakefulness, for example, may actually be due to a disease (epilepsy, pinworms, gas, etc.). The mother goes to the bedside and comforts or feeds the child, thus rewarding him for the disturbance. Sedatives, worm medicine, and a diet change may treat the original cause for awakening, but the child has been "taught" to expect some extra attention and will perpetuate the disturbance.

Continuation of undesirable habits suggests that the parents are pushing the child, usually a boy, into activities in which the child sees a limited chance of success. His anxiety and frustration seek some discharge in motor activity: nail-biting, thumb-sucking, tics, restlessness, inability to sleep, bed rocking. Those irritations that continue for a prolonged period suggest that there has been a sensory deficit. The child who did not get enough rocking and cuddling in the first few weeks of life may have to do his own rocking. The treatment is to stop the urgent prodding for perfection, drop the tight schedule, allow him to stare into space occasionally, accept and approve his own accomplishments, albeit below the parents' standards.

Tics are "habit" spasms of muscle groups. They appear to be involuntary, although if the child "really tries," he can reduce the repetitive frequency. Blinking, turning the head, shrugging the shoulders, and wrinkling the forehead are all common. The affected child is frequently tense and perfectionistic; one has the feeling he is trying to control his need to shout, jump, or run, and this bottled-up tension is released in the tic. It is assumed to be a neurotic expression, but some violent tics may be associated with chorea or epileptic equivalents. Tourette's syndrome may be due to some hurt to the nervous system. Magnesium might be helpful. Homeopathic remedies are useful.

Most tics, however, are considered developmental disorders, as they usually appear in boys just starting school. Eighty percent recover completely in eight years. (I watched a tic in one child progress from head turning to shoulder shrugging to body twisting to leg turning before it stopped; it took four years to go from top to bottom.) Neurological development needs to be checked.

If the nervous tics develop after school starts, some investigation needs to be done to see if the child is overgraded. Some find that home schooling is better for some touchy children.

Sleep Problems

Someone said that sleep is our natural state, and that we awaken only to eat and eliminate. Sleep is needed by everyone for varying amounts of time. If deprived of sleep and dream time, humans become mean, irritable, and occasionally psychotic. Anxious people have trouble getting to sleep. The small infant, sans colic, will spend twenty hours a day in sleep; the exhaustion of his rapid growth seems to dictate this.

At one year of age, a child sleeps twelve hours a night and takes a one- to three-hour nap. This pattern is fairly constant until age four to six when he gives up his nap, although he still seems to need it. If his exhausted mother can compromise with a quiet time for an hour or so after lunch, she is doing well. If, however, he happens to sleep during nap time, he will be alert until 10:00 or 11:00 P.M.

REM (rapid-eye-movement) sleep for normal infants is 50 percent of sleep time; by age two years REM is at the adult level of 20 to 25 percent of sleep time. A minimum REM time is a nightly requirement; if this is reduced, a debt accumulates that must be made up in subsequent nights, or the preceding symptoms occur.

A typical young adult drifts down to deep sleep, and in about an hour and a half rises to light sleep and enters REM sleep. After ten to twenty minutes of this, he goes through the cycle again. There are about five cycles (ninety minutes each) during the usual eight-hour sleep period. People who claim they did not sleep a wink may have been in a light sleep with much REM activity.

Enuresis (bed wetting), somnambulism, and night terrors have not been correlated with REM sleep but are associated with arousal from deep sleep. If sleep is not more or less as outlined above, then some damage to the pons may be the problem. A chiropractor must check the top three cervical vertebrae.

Nightmares (scary dreams), somnambulism, and restlessness are common in children. Although emotional tension, family strife, and school problems may be inciting agents, pinworms must also be considered and searched for. Most pediatricians assume that a child with any night problem has worms. A preliminary search for them may be rewarding. It is not necessary to see the worms, but it is nice to know what is being treated. A few days after the treatment has been initiated, the child should sleep restfully again. If there is no improvement, an allergy should be considered. Low blood sugar from a food sensitivity must be considered. If your child is shaking and her pupils are dilated, cuddle and comfort her until the adrenaline is used up. The child reports a scary episode of being chased. The Bach Flower Rescue Remedy that naturopathic doctors use may be helpful here. Rescue Remedy contains cherry plum, clematis, impatiens, rock rose, and star of Bethlehem.

Sleep terrors are the screaming out in the night. The child is flushed and sweating, but not awake. They do not report bad dreams; they have no memory of the event.

A child with somnambulism usually wanders about the house with his eyes open. Most eventually return to bed and remember nothing the following day. If awakened during the act, he may be frightened but is usually just confused.

Sleep rarely comes by parental fiat, but rules are worthwhile as a security aid. An appropriate bedtime should be insisted upon. Consistency and firmness despite protests will help develop self-control and eventual respect for fair parents. Positive influences include vigorous outdoor physical exercise, hot bath, hot supper, quiet, congenial atmosphere, single-bed occupancy, favorite toy, and, if possible, single occupancy in room.

Negative influences include a noisy, unhappy home, multiple occupancy in the room and bed, sedentary activities and television all day, pinworms, allergies, sugar ingestion, separation anxiety, stimulation, and roughhousing immediately before bed. About one in fifteen to twenty children is hyperactive to the point that minimal stimulation precludes relaxation; these children sing, toss about, and find excuses to get out of bed, as if they know that relaxing with their eyes shut will bring sleep. They act as if they're afraid they'll miss something.

Night terrors are not common and occur about an hour into the sleep cycle when deep sleep moves to light sleep. The child cannot be awakened and is thrashing, screaming, and kicking. I have found a connection between night terrors and the ingestion of sugary foods at suppertime.

Won't go to sleep. This seems to be so typical of the two-year-old that it suggests normality. They may stay awake because Mother is home from work. If the usual rituals have been completed *and* all inducements have been exhausted, a sedative about a half hour before bedtime might get the child started. The only trouble is that the usual sedatives that induce sleep in adults have a stimulating effect on most children. The barbiturates are usually worthless. They also have been found to reduce dream (REM) time. Calcium and magnesium might help here. Homeopathic remedies and herbal teas are safe, cheap, and have no hangover effects the next day. Valerian root drops are very effective. If the child has taken a four-hour nap during the day, he will have trouble going to sleep at 7:00 P.M. Shorten the nap to the ninety-minute sleep cycle. Pacifiers may help a baby go to sleep, but if she awakens and cannot find it, she will let you know. A pediatrician I know suggested that a pacifier could be glued to a wrist band—not a necklace—so the child could never lose it. Homeopatlic chamomile is worth a try.

Awakens one to six hours after falling asleep. This is not a habit. The habit is the child's expectation of reward once he has been awakened by his built-in arousal system or worms, gas going sideways, or low blood sugar. The wise parent waits several seconds to see if the child falls back to sleep. (It can happen.) If the cries are louder and more frequent, the parent goes to the child's bed, makes sure that she is not sick or has her foot caught, and return to bed without *cuddling* her, fooling with her, or feeding her. The parent does nothing that could possibly be interpreted as a reward for her wakefulness. She must learn to turn over and go back to sleep as the rest of us do. She may fuss and cry for one to six hours, but she must not be catered to. If the parent finally goes in after three hours, she assumes that the next night she must cry three hours before someone will come. Magnesium is a sleep inducer. (On a high-sodium diet—five thousand milligrams a day—young men slept longer with fewer awakenings than those on a low-salt diet, according to a University of Washington study.)

The older child who cannot drop off to sleep until 9:00 to 11:00 P.M. should be allowed to read in bed with her own night-light, as long as she bothers no one and as long as she awakens refreshed in the morning.

Helpful homeopathic remedies include arsenicum, chamomilla, coffea, ignatia, lycopodium, nux vomica, pulsatilla.

There is some evidence that if infants are allowed to sleep on their stomachs, there is a risk for SIDS. Hal Huggins has also noted that babies sleeping on their backs or who sleep on the Indian cradle board do not need to change position for an hour, while stomach sleepers are more likely to need to move every eight to twelve minutes. He feels the organs of the body are getting oxygen more easily while on the back.[161]

The American Academy of Pediatrics has a brochure on *Sleep Problems in Children,* but not one word about the most common cause of night wakefulness—pinworms!

Posture, if abnormal, suggests disease in bone or muscle. Poor posture, especially if associated with marked swayback (lumbar lordosis), can lead to arthritic changes in the spine. It is also cosmetically undesirable. Muscular fatigue occurs more readily if the spine and pelvis are held in abnormal positions. Pain follows fatigue.

Poor muscle tone is the chief cause of poor posture. The rapid growth during adolescence is more frequently associated with poor muscle tone, especially in the long, slender ectomorph. His chest sags, his spine rounds forward, and the small of his back flattens. Others may develop a marked swayback and tip their pelvis forward. An exercise physiologist or chiropractor would be the best person to monitor the exercises and training this child needs before the problems become fixed.

Scoliosis is the curving of the spine to one side. Its cause is unknown. It is felt that an uncomplicated lateral deviation is due to a muscle weakness like poliomyelitis. The true idiopathic scoliosis is a lateral and a rotational deviation. Not uncommonly, adolescent girls develop this condition during the growth spurt associated with the onset of puberty. It is not painful, and thus may easily be overlooked until the advanced stages. An alert mother may notice, while fixing a skirt for her daughter, that one hip is held noticeably higher than the other; the doctor may find some asymmetry of the girl's back during a routine physical. It is easy to diagnose if one looks for it.

X rays show the extent of the curve. If the girl has not reached her adult height, an elaborate brace (Milwaukee) from chin to hips may partially correct the bend to an acceptable position. Casting may hold it. Some orthopedic surgeons favor use of special metal (Harrington) rods secured to the vertebrae to arrest the process. The chiropractor is the first provider to be consulted. Postural reflexes should be evaluated. It may be that the tonic labyrinthine reflex has been retained from infancy.

Don't forget this item of family business:

Chores are the household duties assigned to children to teach responsibility as well as to make housekeeping a more efficient enterprise (make the bed, feed the pet, do the dishes). The jobs should be considered as part of living together in mutual respect: "You live here. I do this for you, you do this for me." The tasks should be simple enough for the child to understand and accomplish. They should be equally divided among the children. There should be some leeway about time to accomplish them; the child should have some choice of when he wants to do routine tasks.

Each family must decide what philosophy is appropriate for them, at what age an allowance should begin, and how much should be given. A firm commitment has to be made—and understood—by all family members as to when "payday" is, and what chores are required in return. Just because parents can afford to give a lot of spending money to the child who asks for it is no reason to hand it out. The child learns nothing except that his parents are a soft touch.

One clever motivational trick is to offer the child matching funds. For every dollar he earns toward a coveted bike, the parents add a dollar to his earnings. Some families post a list of extra jobs that need to be done, with a scale of payment in accordance with the difficulty and time required for each one. The children in the family can then decide which job they want to do—if any. It is, however, not a good idea to withhold a promised allowance until a child is "nice." It only serves as a barrier, promotes belittling, and sets up a cycle of frustration, anger and hostility. The child finally gives up even thinking about being "nice," because his score card is so hopelessly in the negative.

In spite of rewards and praise, some chores do not get done. A firm, nonnegotiable period of restriction or confinement seems appropriate.

Verbal appreciation of a task well done or commendation for the excellence of a job routinely expected is more important in molding a child's self-respect than money doled out. This positive reinforcement is best done at the dinner table so all may hear.

What a Child Needs

Consistent "no" or "stop it" for doing dangerous things

Safe place to play, use muscles, and run—and have temper tantrums

Chance to scribble and smear without adult supervision

Answers to questions; ask her to name objects

Nighttime rituals: tooth brushing, relaxing bath, story, cuddly animal, favorite blanket, prayers

Love and limits

Honest answers about sex and parts of body

Reassurance or night-light to counter sleep resistance, fear of the dark

Nursery school or constructive social play

Increased periods of separation from parents

Praise for verbal accomplishment and artwork

Chance to dress up and playact

Assumption that he is doing his best in school

Pictures and books about history, as well as "the facts of life"

Sense of belonging in the family

Discussion of her opinions on menus, vacations, etc.

Being read to

Contact with culture: museums, films, plays, zoo, symphony, etc.

Reinforcement for acceptable behavior

Protection from poisons, paints, detergents, medicines (have syrup of ipecac ready)

Some hobby, sport, or job that holds his/her interest

We need to encourage children to retain many childhood traits: sensitivity, curiosity, flexibility, playfulness, creativity, imagination, open-mindedness, and sense of wonder.

The Purpose of Fevers and Infections

People get sick. Some get sick a lot. There must be a reason for sickness. In the past, if a mother brought her child in to my office with yet another infection and asked, "Why?" I would say, "Bad genes from the father's side of the family." Some mothers almost bought that one. I would try to be concerned and sympathetic, but I had no idea why some children were frequently very sick and some breezed right through infancy and childhood without a sniffle, a sneeze, or a hot forehead. Some children can sleep in the cat litter box and never get sick. It doesn't seem fair.

Then our medical literature began to sort things out. We knew that bacteria could be treated with antibiotics, but viruses did not respond. We knew that about 80 percent of infections were due to viruses, and if the parents wanted some treatment for the fever, we had to say something like "I'm sorry, but this is a virus and you will waste your money buying an antibiotic for this one. The fever is a good sign that your child is fighting the disease. The fever is only a symptom of that fight. You will have to wait for a secondary infection, and then I might prescribe something." Some patients left me because that was my policy. There were doctors then, and are still some now, who will prescribe an antibiotic despite the fact that it will not do a thing for the viral infection, and may cause side effects.

We were also discovering that if a child was allergic to something (animals, house dust, grass pollen, certain foods, cow milk), he seemed to be more susceptible to infections—viruses or germs. It was as if the allergy allowed the nasties to invade. So we tried to control the allergens in the child's environment, and it *did* make a difference. Without milk many children did not get repeat ear or bronchial infections. Then some researchers told us that the allergy indicated that there was a defect in the immune system of the frequently ill child. But we did not know how to build that up. I sent a large number of my patients to allergists, and they always found some sort of allergy to something for which they gave weekly shots. That often went on for years.

If my patients developed a secondary infection after a cold—as shown by a green or yellow nasal discharge that seemed to last forever, or a bronchial, ear, or sinus infection—I gave them a series of dead bacterial shots. I also discovered that these shots cut down the need for antibiotics as they helped the children develop their immunity to these secondary bacterial infections. Many needed to be off dairy products for months or years.

Now we understand that protein malnutrition is the most common cause of immune system deficiency. This shows up in children, the elderly, and of course, in the peoples of third-world countries. The poor diet and the low intake of zinc, B_6, iron, and folic acid are the chief reasons. It shows up in those who seem to exist on grains and legumes predominantly. Zinc, B_6, and folic acid are needed for nucleic acid and protein synthesis. Zinc is needed for more than eighty enzymes. If it is low, the thymus will atrophy and the numbers of T-cells will decrease. Thymosin (thymus extract) can increase the number of circulating T-cells of patients with a variety of immunodeficiency diseases. B_6 deficiency will slow antibody production. Without these materials, the immune system cannot mount a normal response.

So the purpose of an illness is to tell the victim that he/she is not eating right, is being subjected to pollutants or allergens, or is under stress of some kind. Mercury/silver amalgam fillings have been shown to hurt the immune system and are related to the development of autoimmunity. The vaccinations that we pile onto children can hurt the immune system. Those with allergies may have impaired nutrient absorption because of bowel wall edema (the leaky gut). Gastrointestinal bleeding due to food sensitivities is a common cause of iron deficiency in children. But do not forget that love, hope, faith, laughter, confidence, and the will to live are important parts of getting well.[162] The body and the mind are connected.

Vitamin A and its provitamin, beta-carotene, are immune stimulants. A deficiency will lead to illnesses, especially those involving the integrity of membrane systems. (A mastoid infection after the measles is an example. Skin infections would suggest low vitamin A intake.) Pantothenic acid is a cortisone precursor, so stress of any kind would exhaust the adrenals. If pantothenic acid is not replenished, the adrenal glands will suffer and viral and bacterial infections will occur. Bioflavonoids work with vitamin C and help to resist the invasion of infections. Copper, molybdenum, selenium, and zinc are vital for immunity.

VIRUSES

Virus is the term given to an ultramicroscopic particle that multiplies inside the body cells and produces various disease states. Specific antiviral agents have not yet proved as effective as have antibiotics against bacterial infections. A specific virus is responsible for a specific disease. Most children have about forty to sixty different virus infections before age seven, at which time they normally have only one or two a year (one or two bad colds a year, one attack of vomiting and diarrhea every year or so, one attack of fever and laryngeal cough every two or three years). Eighty percent of children's infections are "the virus that is going around."

The fever of a virus infection may serve a therapeutic function. As an example, polio virus grows well in tissue culture at 95 degrees F., but poorly at 103 to 104 degrees F. Controlling the fever *too* well may prolong the infection. Acidity inhibits the growth of virus and should be tried, as this maneuver is safe (vinegar or cranberry juice). Ascorbic acid, as well as other available natural therapies (herbs, hydrotherapy, homeopathy), is beneficial in shortening the course and severity of virus diseases. Linus Pauling's research on the use of vitamin C indicated that one thousand milligrams of C a day showed consistent benefit for adults. For a child, that dosage would translate to about five hundred to one thousand milligrams each day, and be increased if the symptoms of a cold appeared. Recent research indicates that if people are deficient in vitamin E and selenium, a virus named Coxsackie could invade a person, and then mutate into a more virulent form that attacks the heart muscle.[163]

There seems to be an irreducible minimum of virus infections (stomach, respiratory flu, and colds) that these children "need" to have for those first few years, until their immune system has "learned" to fight off viruses like an adult. Next to colic and colds, most calls to the doctor are about fevers, and most fevers in children are due to viruses.

Most **viral** infections manifest themselves as fever for seventy-two hours, and when the fever falls, a watery nose, a rash, a strangly, croupy cough, or diarrhea appear, as if the body is trying to slough off the dead virus. The whole disease process lasts seven to ten days. If the child gets worse after the first three days, or the problem lasts longer than the seven days or so, it usually means that some secondary bacterial infection has invaded, and some special attention is necessary. Fever may return, and the clear mucus of the virus turns to a thick, purulent green or yellow mess, indicating a secondary bacterial infection. If the phlegm remains clear and watery, but the symptoms continue without the fever, an allergy is usually the cause of that prolongation.

A high temperature is common in infants with viral illnesses. (I observed 107 degrees in a two-year-old with the "flu"; recovery was prompt without obvious neurological sequelae.)

THINGS YOU SHOULD KNOW ABOUT FEVER

The **temperature** of most normal human bodies is around 98.6 degrees F. when taken rectally. A lower reading of 96 to 97 degrees F. suggests shock, dehydration, or excessive cooling (as in a premature infant in a faulty incubator). It may also be a sign that the temperature is about to shoot up to 103 degrees F. or more.

It is not necessary to subtract a degree from the reading when reporting a fever to the doctor, although 105 degrees F. does sound "less serious" than 106. Depending on the extent of skin capillary dilation, oral, axillary (armpit), or rectal temperature may be the same (if the skin is totally red and hot) or unequal (rectum hot and skin cool). Rectal temperature may be 105, oral 104, and axillary 103. Rectal and oral thermometers can be used interchangeably in these orifices; only aesthetics and hygiene dictate use as labeled. Because of a few scary reports of broken rectal thermometers and perforated recta, it seems wise to use the axillary method until the child is five or six years old, and is cooperatively nonbiting enough to try the oral (under the tongue for thirty seconds—using the digital thermometer—with mouth closed) method. The new skin patch thermometers work well.

The doctor may have the parent evaluate the child's condition by keeping a temperature chart for a few days. A normal child might have 98 degrees F. in the morning on arising and 99 in the evening. A two-degree swing is usually worth investigating (98 to 100, or even 97 to 99) with other tests (blood count, sedimentation rate, X ray, urinalysis). Doctors usually allow full activity the day following an evening temperature of less than 100, although more than 99.5 suggests that a disease is still active. The child's level of interest in food and activity may be more important in evaluating sickness and health than the temperature.

We are trying to switch to centigrade readings, and worldwide science uses this more than Fahrenheit. Try reporting the next fever in centigrade and see how sharp your doctor is.

Fahrenheit		Centigrade
97	Subnormal	36.1
98		36.7
98.60	Normal	37.0
100.00		37.8
102.20	Moderate fever	39.0
104.00	High fever	40.0
105.80	Critical	41.0

Fever is a rise in body temperature due to invasion by infectious organisms or toxins. Some allergies may occasionally elevate the temperature; so may eating meat. High doses of some antibiotics may raise the temperature after the infection is under control. Exhausting exercise, increased environmental temperature, or lesions in the temperature-regulating center of the brain may also produce fever.

A common cause of rectal temperature of 100 to 103 degrees F. on the second to fifth day of life is dehydration, especially in the breast-fed baby receiving little fluid while awaiting his mother's milk to "come in." His kidneys are unable to concentrate urine effectively at this age, so when he excretes large amounts of dilute urine, he loses weight, and his blood becomes concentrated. If a few ounces of water by mouth do not reduce the fever and irritability in an hour, other more serious reasons for the fever must be investigated. Fairly pale urine passed two or three times a day would be a minimal amount to preclude dehydration fever.

A baby born in the winter might be overbundled by conscientious parents, although the room temperature is normal; heavy covering is not needed. A low, even ambient temperature in the immediate crib area of sixty-five to seventy degrees is ideal.

What to Do for a Fever

It would be worthwhile to go through the drill about what to do, as some fevers are a part of growing up and teaching the immune system how to react in the future, but some fevers are serious—usually due to bacteria— and require investigation.

Medical doctors have been taught to "treat" every sickness that comes to their attention. They urge the parents to use fever reducers like Tylenol. (One must remember that acetaminophen is a liver toxin, and more than five doses a day are a stress to the natural antioxidants in the liver.) However, *doctors are supposed to understand that fever is the body's mechanism for destroying viruses and some bacteria.* If we do more than take the edge off the fever to make the child comfortable, we may be prolonging the infection. If, however, home remedies are unable to control the fever and distress, a qualified health facilitator should be consulted. The height of the fever is not as important as the activity level of the child.

The basic natural therapy: It is of little importance to know the name of the disease or whether it is a virus or a bacteria that is invading; the initial treatment with vitamin C is the same. Something is wrong with the immune system. Vitamin C is the easiest, cheapest, and safest first line of defense. Start with one thousand milligrams of C every hour during the waking hours. This would be safe for a child from one year on to seven years of age. For a baby under a year, use five hundred milligrams every hour or so. If the next day the bowel movements have turned sloppy, one would assume that the dose of C is the saturation amount (or the child has intestinal flu); then the dose is reduced to one thousand milligrams every two hours. By the second day, the diagnosis is usually manifest, and the decision to either reduce the dose or continue with the same would be made. If a doctor is consulted and antibiotics are felt necessary, but the patient is better, one could thank the doctor and wait to have the prescription filled until the next day—or not at all.

Here is the protocol that helps to determine if you can safely treat the child at home with (or without) medical advice:

1. Give the child acetaminophen (it is suggested that aspirin not be used, as there is a connection with its use and Reye's syndrome) as an antipyretic, or fever reducer: one grain (sixty milligrams) for every ten pounds of body weight, given every four hours. It takes an hour and a half for a dose to be effective. If the fever is reduced by a degree or two an hour and a half after administration, it implies the disease causing the fever is not

serious, and doing nothing more than giving fluids by mouth, along with vitamin C and an occasional bath with sponging, is all that is necessary. Homeopathic remedies are helpful here. Fever control is just used occasionally to take the edge off the discomfort. The child can be up and around if he feels like it. The antipyretic drug should be administered at least thirty minutes before the sponging so the hypothalamic set point will be lowered. If cold water and no antipyretic is used, sponging is uncomfortable; shivering will occur, which serves to raise the temperature.

2. When the fever of an innocuous infection is reduced, the child will feel better and seem almost normal in moving, smiling, and eating. Germs give off toxins that make a person feel awful. Viruses do not poison the system, so the victim will feel almost normal during the interval when the fever is down.

3. With most virus infections the fever should not last for more than seventy-two hours. If it can be controlled with comfortable baths, and the child can take some nourishment—especially fluids—and move about during the three days of fever, it implies that the child is controlling the infection and/or it is not serious.

Rubbing alcohol mixed with an equal quantity of water is a good fever reducer when spread all over the body and allowed to evaporate. Vaporization removes heat from the body surface; therefore, the skin must be hot to the touch for this treatment to be effective. A comfortably hot bath (96 degrees F.) might be used first to bring the hot blood to the surface. Then the alcohol-water mixture can be applied. Alcohol alone may evaporate too fast and produce uncomfortable coldness, so it is usually diluted with water. (Inhaling too much alcohol might knock the kid out.) The idea is to let the fever continue to act as the stimulus for the body's immune system to do its job; the hydrotherapy is just to make the child comfortable.

For the past one hundred years, chiropractors have been taking care of patients with fevers, either viral or bacterial. Spinal manipulation to the midthoracic spine can dramatically reduce the fever of a virus infection sometimes within fifteen minutes.[164]

Warming-wet-socks treatment: This treatment works beautifully in helping treat infections, and is usually used at bedtime. As it is an immune-stimulating treatment, circulation and white blood cell count are both increased. Soak the child's feet in a hot bath for ten minutes, then wet one pair of cotton socks with cold water. Wring them out, put them on the feet, and immediately cover with a pair of dry wool socks. The wet socks are uncomfortable for only a minute, but by morning the body will have heated up the socks and dried them.

The fact of the sickness, either virus or bacterial, in child or adult, indicates a weakness of the immune response to climatic, emotional, or nutritional stressors. It is an opportunity to review the family lifestyle and correct inappropriate diet, sleep, exercise patterns, and interpersonal relations. Psychoneuroimmunology is at work and must be factored into the equation.

Homeopathic remedies for fever and sickness are useful, safe, cheap, and have no side effects. "Since the symptoms of the sick person represent his curative reaction to the morbific stimulus, the most effective way to cure him will be prescribing the substance which intensifies these curative symptoms."[165] That is the philosophy behind homeopathic therapy. At least this method teaches the body what to do. Like cures like.

Echinacea has been known for centuries in the United States and abroad as an infection fighter. It contains a natural antibiotic, strengthens cell membranes against assault by invading germs, boosts the phagocytes' ability to destroy germs, and increases the production of T-cells.[166] Dr. Daniel Mowrey advises us to take whole, powdered, encapsulated echinacea on a daily basis, both before and during the cold and flu season, and to begin taking a concentrated liquid echinacea extract at the earliest sign that you may be getting sick. (Dr. Thom feels the daily use is unnecessary unless one is coming down with an illness.) A dropperful in the back of the throat works wonders. One might mix it with a little juice, as it tastes terrible. The earlier the better.[167] Zinc lozenges used at the first indication of a sore, scratchy throat might stop a virus. Goldenseal is helpful.

But if the immune system cannot be encouraged to fight a bacterial infection, an antibiotic may be in order.[168] Echinacea is effective against *Candida albicans*, the common yeast infection that often appears after antibiotic use. Acidophilus should be taken with the antibiotics. "There are many other effective herbal remedies for the immune system. See your naturopathic doctor or herbalist for your specific situation."[169]

New and promising research indicates that grape extract powder from certain seeds and skins contains ellagic acid and other disease-fighting antioxidant substances. These substances can help to fight infection, cancer, and heart disease.[170]

Febrile seizure is a generalized seizure that lasts a few minutes at the onset of a fever. Four percent of children have these. They are most common in the one-to-four-year age group, have a family incidence, and are occasionally (2 percent) associated with grand mal epilepsy later. The risk of subsequent seizures, after an initial febrile seizure, peaks between twelve and twenty-four months. Meningitis should be ruled out. Furthermore, a recent report has suggested that phenobarbital prophylaxis for febrile seizures can lower IQ without conferring any protection against seizure recurrence.[171] I would encourage parents with a child who has suffered one of these frightening seizures to increase the daily vitamin C dose and add some echinacea at the first sign of an infection; it might ward off another seizure.

These guidelines might help the parent decide when to call the doctor. Call if any of the following apply:

The child is less than two months old

The fever is more than 40.5C (105 degrees F.)

The child is crying inconsolably

The child is difficult to awaken

The child is confused or delirious

The child had a seizure

The child has a stiff neck

The child has purple spots on the skin

Breathing is difficult

The child is acting very sick

SOME CHILDHOOD VIRAL INFECTIONS AND A FEW CLUES ON HOW TO RECOGNIZE THEM

Chicken pox, or varicella, is the most contagious disease in the world since smallpox disappeared. It is most communicable *before* the rash starts to appear on the skin, so there is not much point in keeping everyone isolated or confined home if the person is not ill, with or without the pox lesions. Chicken pox is a serious illness in an adult, and complications are much more frequent. It is best to have it as a child. Also, the second case of chicken pox in a home is usually more violent than the first.

A slight fever appears and then a small, blistery rash, which breaks out for five days. They look like flea bites, but the lesions in one area of the body will be in different stages of development: some papules just starting, some having become vesicles with a watery head, some turning milky, and the older ones crusting over. The rash spreads from the trunk to arms and legs and face; if the scalp has lesions, this confirms the diagnosis, as humans rarely get flea bites there. Regional lymph nodes will swell; glands on the back of the head (just above where the neck muscles attach to the skull) are characteristically enlarged and tender in chicken pox.

Vitamin C is the treatment of choice, and should be started on the other members of the family, too, as they will surely get it. The basic natural therapy with vitamin C speeds the disease and makes it milder. The last member of the family to get it is usually the sickest. Homeopathics include antimonium, pulsatilla, rhus tox, and sulphur. These remedies should help: aloe vera or comfrey salve, catnip tea, chamomile, yarrow, goldenseal, hops, wet compresses with red raspberry, catnip, peppermint powder in a base of diluted apple cider vinegar.

If the rash spreads to the mouth and down the throat, it is usually associated with a high fever and general misery. Baking soda and oatmeal baths and various lotions to pat on the skin are worth trying. Some children who did not touch their skin still had permanent pits (lack of zinc?), and others who scratched their skin unmercifully did not develop scars.

I say let the child go to school if he is not sick and expose the whole class. Then the majority of the population would be able to get this disease while they are still young. A child with uncomplicated chicken pox does not need to be confined to his bed and may be up and around the house— even to school. I am serious that they should be allowed to go to school. The whole class was exposed before the rash started anyway. However, he is still contagious until the water blisters have dried up.

Adults may get shingles from a child with chicken pox, and vice versa, as it is the same virus. A new vaccine has been formulated that should confirm immunity, but it is questionable whether it produces the permanent immunity that is derived from having the disease itself.

Common cold, or rhinitis or nasopharyngitis, is the most common virus infection of children, because cold symptoms are caused by a wide variety of viruses. It is *always* going around.

Two hundred or more different viruses produce similar symptoms. A child may become immune to one virus, but in three weeks be afflicted by a new—to him—virus. Within one to three days after exposure, the victim develops a headache, a slight fever, malaise, sneezing, and soreness in nose and throat. Within a day or two, the temperature returns to normal and is replaced with a clear, watery nasal discharge with or without a slight, dry tickling cough. These symptoms last five to seven days. If symptoms last longer or fever rises after the third day, a complication has occurred and may need treatment. At the first sign of irritability, whininess, and/or flushed cheeks, the prudent parent will use the basic natural therapy by increasing the daily vitamin C dose to five hundred to one thousand milligrams every few hours, depending on the child's size and bowel tolerance to the C. Homeopathic remedies are appropriate, and when applied early on, can stop the cold in its tracks. Add echinacea and the warming-socks method. Sage tea is helpful for the cough, fenugreek tea to combat mucus, and ginger as a gargle or as a poultice around the throat. Goldenseal and garlic orally will help fight infections.[172]

From the age of two to five years a child has an average of six to eight colds a year. Occasionally anemia and/or allergies will increase susceptibility. Some frequent cold sufferers find that dairy products, sugar, wheat, and/or eggs may trigger an onset. Exposure to cold, damp air, dry winter air, and emotions have all been implicated as causative factors, but proof is lacking; some conditions may allow the virus to multiply, but the virus has to be present to cause the cold. Hand-to-nose transfer is the most common method of passing the virus from one person to another. Frequent hand washing is suggested.

The "snotty-nosed kid" is such a common phenomenon from two to six years of age, we would like to consider the condition normal, except that most parents view it as embarrassing evidence of inadequate care. The mother has perhaps been told that her child is not fed properly, is not getting sufficient vitamins or rest, is allowed to eat candy, is bathed too much or too little, or his socks are wet and dirty. The pediatrician is asked to solve the problem, but all she can do is provide sympathy and treat the secondary infections. The child simply has to have about fifty to a hundred bad colds from birth to age seven, before he acquires enough immunity to settle down to the usual adult frequency of one bad cold a year. Only by strict isolation from others, in a room at 70 degrees F. and 50 percent humidity, can colds be prevented. Under no circumstances should the child with a virus be treated with an antibiotic.

Some swear that as soon as they wore socks to bed, they no longer got sick. Chicken soup can help those who need extra sodium. But for those who have too much sodium, vinegar will help rid the body of that mineral.

Steam, or at least a moisture-laden atmosphere, keeps the respiratory secretions liquid so they will drain more easily. The commercial cold steam vaporizer is safer than the kettle on a hot plate. However, hanging wet sheets and towels about the room is cheaper than a vaporizer. If the humidity is high enough to be effective, the windows should fog up.

Most children are more comfortable in the prone (face down) position if their noses are full of phlegm; otherwise it runs down their throats and produces a tickly cough. An older child might do better on his back with the head somewhat elevated by a blanket roll under the mattress. If pillows are used to elevate the head, foam rubber might be better, if a feather allergy is an irritating factor.

Extra fluids might be urged during the febrile phase, but a regular diet can be resumed during the "drip" stage. Fever is more prominent in the under-six-year-old, but should not last more than seventy-two hours. The drip and snort last about seven days. If the secretions become purulent, a bacteria has become superimposed, and then a decision must be made whether antibiotic therapy would be worthwhile. Extra immune builders (vitamins A, E, and beta-carotene) should first be tried.

Complications of the cold might include: otitis media, sinusitis, purulent rhinitis (bacterial upper respiratory infection [URI]), sinusitis, cervical adenitis, and bronchitis. We are so used to getting medicine for a cold and its complications, we forget the rapid improvement that a visit to the chiropractor can produce. Adjustment of the cervical spine to correct subluxations works something like this: "...subluxation producing nerve irritation which in turn produces muscle spasm. Any mechanism which would block the normal lymphatic drainage system would cause the body to find alternative ways to dispose of the common respiratory pathogens encountered by children every day...Attending muscle spasm could well be the cause for a restriction and stasis of the cervical lymphatics....Cause an increase in lymphatic pressure and swelling of the lymph nodes with a resultant increase in the bacterial invasion of the upper respiratory system. The proper adjustment of the cervical spine will in many cases produce an almost immediate relaxation of the neck musculature. This should then allow the cervical lymphatics to begin to restore normal drainage."[173] Gentle follow-up massage of the neck muscle will continue the improvement.

Nose drops are most effective only if used infrequently—three times a day for two days, then a rest period of a day or so. Patients rapidly develop a resistance to them, and they either don't work at all to shrink the nasal membranes, or if they do work, a rebound tissue swelling produces more congestion than was present originally. A purulent discharge responds poorly to nose drops; a virus rhinitis or allergic drip responds well.

An older child might prefer a homeopathic nasal spray squirted into her nose; for maximum benefit her head should be placed in the upside-down position. A baby with a cold may be very uncomfortable when sucking, and nose drops might allow her to breathe and suck at the same time. Place the baby on her back on top of your thighs with her head hanging over your knees. Two drops of a standard nose-drop solution are placed in each nostril. Clap your hand over her mouth; when she inhales, she will suck the drops back through the nasal passageway. Do this about fifteen minutes prior to feeding for maximum benefit. Oral antihistaminics and decongestants sometimes serve to open up the passageways with less fighting and screaming.

These should help: catnip, chamomile tea, comfrey, fenugreek, valerian tea, white horehound, licorice cough drops, echinacea, slippery elm tea, astragalus.

Croup is a common childhood affliction. It usually appears rather dramatically in the middle of a winter night, when the air outside is clear and cold, and the humidity is low. The air in the house is dry also, and this may trigger the attack.

The child awakens suddenly between midnight and 1 A.M., clawing the air, choking, and "barking." The parents at first think the dog has been frightened until they realize that the racket is coming from the nursery. It is a sudden, scary illness, but after twenty minutes of being upright and inhaling steam in the bathroom with the shower running, the child should be relaxed and quiet. Because most drugstores are closed at this time of night, the best cough syrup is a mixture of equal parts of gin, lemon juice, and honey. For the twenty- to forty-pound child, a teaspoonful is usually adequate to cut and loosen the phlegm and to reduce anxiety for all concerned. Gargling is ineffective as the larynx is below the gargle area. Syrup of ipecac (one teaspoonful) is helpful for laryngeal spasm. These might help: a cold compress on the throat, pitted dates crushed and made into a syrup, vitamin C, garlic crushed with butter and brown sugar, zinc lozenges, marshmallow, hyssop, anise, wild cherry, echinacea tincture, licorice or horehound lozenges, mullein, comfrey, fenugreek, or a tea with red raspberry, slippery elm, and rose hips. Homeopathic aconitum, hepar sulfur, and spongia are an effective triad.[174] Drosera will also help.

Croup is a viral affliction, although allergies and bacteria may play their parts. It almost invariably lasts for three nights. If the steam allows the victim to sleep for an hour or two in between the barking, and there is little or no fever, it is not serious. However, if the croup lasts longer than three days, or if twenty minutes of steam inhalation does not relax your child enough to allow him to sleep, then he needs professional attention. One severe type of croup, almost always accompanied by a temperature of 103 degrees F. or more, is due to bacterial infection (see Epiglottitis, this chapter). Some children develop a croupy sound after they have had a cold for a few days and have developed a secondary bacterial infection. Thick, tenacious material drips down into the windpipe, usually at night. If this is a chronic, recurring condition, it would suggest that the child is allergic to his own bacteria, and perhaps the use of bacterial vaccine will abort further attacks (see Sinusitis, this chapter).

Devil's Grip (pleurodynia) is a virus inflammation of the diaphragm, the large flat muscle (between the lungs and the liver) that draws air into the lungs. It causes pain about the circumference of the lower chest as if the victim were being squeezed. It lasts the usual three to five days, but can be controlled with the basic natural therapy.

Erythema infectiosum, or fifth disease (the fifth form of measles), is a mild virus infection sometimes confused with sunburn, allergy, or German measles. There is little or no fever. Red, apparently sunburned cheeks appear suddenly, and a mottled, pink, reticular or laceworklike rash soon follows on forearms and lower legs. Less rash is noted on the trunk. I have tried this subterfuge: Let the child go to school if he is not sick, and call it an allergic rash.

Gastroenteritis (intestinal flu) is a viral inflammation of the stomach and the small and large bowel, and is the most common infection—next to the common cold—seen in the pediatric age group. It has a characteristic pattern: The periumbilical pain is accompanied by nausea, vomiting, pallor, listlessness, and diarrhea. The pain should come and go. The victim usually feels weak, but without other symptoms between the spasms; then a wave of pain, pallor, and nausea overwhelms her, forcing her to lie down, vomit, or try to expel a stool, which is usually loose.

Vomiting and nausea occur periodically for twenty-four hours, with or without fever. Simultaneously, or on the second day, periumbilical cramps and diarrhea occur that last about a week. A child has not developed sufficient immunity to this virus, so his diarrhea lasts seven days. Most children have this disease about once a year. As they get older and develop immunity, the body is able to shake it off sooner. Adults have this for one day, and it is called twenty-four-hour flu.

If the disease course does not follow this one day of vomiting and seven of diarrhea, a bacterial infection might be suspected (see Bacillary Dysentery, this chapter). With intestinal flu the abdomen is soft between spasms. In conditions requiring surgery, the pain is constant and abdominal palpation is painful. If this "virus that's going around" drags on, it might be that the flu has "stirred up an allergy" to some food that was safe before.

The treatment is fluids containing diluted, suitable salts. Boiled skim milk (twenty minutes seems about right) must be diluted with at least the same quantity of water, or too much sodium will be consumed. Ginger tea, ginger ale, gelatin water, bouillon, and cola drinks are the safest of the fluids. For the older infant, the BRATT diet is used: banana, rice, applesauce, tea, toast. Anything else adds fuel to the fire. The basic natural therapy should be used.

Remedies containing kaolin and pectin may hold the stool together a little, but will not stop the inevitable seven-day course. Whatever is used on the sixth day will be credited with stopping the diarrhea on the seventh. Attention must be paid to hydration if diarrhea is accompanied by fever and vomiting. If the baby can hold up his head, smile occasionally, and urinate two or three times a day, he probably can get by, but responsibility for his care should be shared with a physician. Intravenous fluids might have to be considered.

Gentle chiropractic manipulation to the lumbar spine initiates a parasympathetic response and calms the intestinal tract. For many children, use of colloidal silver and homeopathic tinctures can resolve this uncomfortable mess in just a few hours.[175]

Tourists' diarrhea (la turista) is a mild intestinal disorder lasting a day or two in many people traveling abroad. It usually occurs in the first week of their visit and is ascribed variously to new foods, chemical and biological irritants, and, according to one Mexican physician, "imponderable psychogenic factors." Studies in Mexico, at least, reveal a low incidence of shigella or salmonella. It is noteworthy that the same temporary, non-pathological condition occurs in foreigners visiting the United States.

Herpangina is an acute viral infection with headache, violent sore throat, and high fever (105 degrees F. in infants). Vesicles appear on the soft palate and sides of the throat. After three days of fever, the temperature returns to normal and the patient feels better, but the throat becomes more sore as the vesicles become ulcers. These ulcers heal spontaneously after a week of whining and drooling. The basic natural therapy plus zinc lozenges will shorten the course.

Herpes simplex is a virus that causes a wide variety of skin, eye, mucous-membrane, and nervous-system diseases. Almost every child has had a herpetic infection by the time he is five or six years old, probably associated with teething, which allows the virus to invade the host (see Canker sores, Chapter 14). A homeopathic zinc preparation will cut the duration and severity of the mouth lesions by 40 percent. Strong yarrow tea as a mouth rinse will help. Lysine salve is good, too.

Human Immunodeficiency Virus (HIV) manifests itself with swollen lymph glands, enlargement of liver and spleen, failure to thrive, candidiasis, diarrhea, and central nervous system disease. Pneumonia due to pneumocystis is the most common infection and is the complication that is usually lethal. Chronic herpes simplex infections may occur. As the disease complex progresses, the T lymphocyte count goes down and death is inevitable. Mother-to-infant transmission is the usual way for a child to become infected before or at the time of birth. Only blood, semen, cervical secretions, and human milk have been implicated in the transmission of HIV. Infants born to HIV-positive women usually show a positive test for the antibody at birth because of the transplacental passage of it from the mother, but the infant may not be infected; other tests for infectivity are available.

Most patients with HIV are low in sodium and calcium in the blood.

Traditional Chinese medicine has long known how to fight viruses and build the immune system at the same time.[176] Purified and concentrated allicin from garlic is a mainstay. The treatments for hepatitis are the same ones used for HIV: schizandra, cucumin, salvia, peony, silybum, astralagan, hypericum. They also have herbs to compensate for the side effects of Western medications.

Infectious hepatitis (see Abdominal pain, Chapter 12).

Infectious mononucleosis is an acute viral disease found predominately in adolescents. This illness, with some medical embarrassment, was formerly called the interns-nurses' disease. This "kissing disease" is not strictly confined to lovers, but the young adult seems to be very susceptible. At least close proximity is required for passage.

It sneaks up on the victim. A few days of malaise and anorexia pass before the characteristic swollen neck glands, sore throat, and chills begin. Fever is at its peak (100 degrees to 103 degrees) by the eighth to tenth day, and lethargy, weakness, and headache are common. Jaundice from liver involvement occurs in 10 percent of cases. The spleen is enlarged in 75 percent of victims and is prone to rupture if injured. An exquisite headache is common.

Penicillin is often tried because the symptoms suggest a strep infection. It doesn't work, of course, and often produces a rash.

Intravenous vitamin C at about the one-hundred-gram level (one hundred thousand milligrams), suitably diluted, may control the infection overnight. Some require additional IVs, but oral C at about one-thousand-milligram doses every hour or two will shorten the course of the disease (the basic natural therapy). Complete rest only serves to weaken the muscles and prolongs convalescence. If untreated with C, it will take three weeks for the fever and malaise to subside. Except for some lethargy, the patient is well by the end of the fourth week. High doses of vitamin A for three days (half a million units daily) will shorten the course. Hydrotherapy helps.

"Chronic" mono is now a recognized disease, and may be called chronic fatigue immune deficiency syndrome. An occasional patient will develop a generalized macular (flat) rash and a positive (false) blood test for syphilis that could frighten an unwary adolescent who thought he only kissed his date good night.

Influenza is a virus respiratory infection (the "virus that's going around") that usually occurs in epidemics from December to March. It is especially harmful to very young, weak, or very old victims, and the incidence of secondary bronchopneumonia is greatly increased as a sequel.

It begins suddenly with fever, malaise, chills, muscle aches, and soreness in the larynx and windpipe area. Fever lasts seventy-two hours, and is followed by a week of "choke, cough, and strangle." Phlegm produced is clear or milky; if it turns green or yellow, a secondary bacterial infection has been superimposed, and antibiotics might be considered.

Treatment is the basic natural therapy. Steam, antihistaminics, decongestants, cough remedies (equal parts of gin, lemon juice, and honey), extra fluids, and hot baths cure nothing, but make the patient comfortable while living through the distress. Homeopathic remedies are more helpful: aconitum, bryonia, or rhus tox. Hydrotherapy should be tried.

Several virus types have been found to be responsible for the epidemics that sweep through every winter. Vaccines of these influenza viruses have been developed, and are about 50 to 60 percent beneficial. The major problem is to try to predict which variant will be effective for the next go-around, then try to manufacture enough vaccine to distribute and inject before the epidemic hits. Results are occasionally gratifying in large military installations because absenteeism is reduced, but the doctor in private practice usually hears only the complaints. ("I got your shot, but still got the flu" or "I was sicker from the shot than if I'd had the disease.") Newer, purified vaccines and better predictions might eliminate some of these difficulties. However, science has disappointed us again. Again, the best defense is an adequate immunity due to a healthy lifestyle.

Measles is the name usually applied to the hard, coughing, black, or two-week measles, best referred to as **rubeola.** There are a number of diseases in the measles family: roseola, rubella, rubeola, and fifth disease (erythema infectiosum), and Boston measles are all measles, and are not serious if the child's immune system is operative. Many virus diseases have rashes, and if doctors are unsure, they call it "toxic rash due to the viremia."

Mumps, or epidemic parotitis, is a virus inflammation of the salivary glands. The victim is usually five to eight years old and acquires it from his classmates. Characteristically he has swollen cheeks that fill out the pocket below the earlobe—not to be confused with the swollen glands from tonsillitis, which are high in the neck under the corner of the jawbone. In general, mumps is not a serious infection unless it (a) leads to encephalitis (one in six thousand cases), in which case the patient may be severely incapacitated with a high fever and an exquisite headache; (b) goes to the pancreas, producing a severe stomachache, fever, and vomiting; or (c) finds the testes or ovaries and causes much pain (only in adults). It rarely causes sterility. There is no medical reason why a patient with mumps cannot be ambulatory if he feels well enough. He may select his own diet, but it is true that sour foods such as pickles and lemons may give him some jaw spasm.

The incubation period is about three weeks from the time of exposure. A patient is probably contagious for a day before and five days after the swelling becomes obvious. Once the swelling has subsided enough so that the glands are not visible (but still palpable), the patient is probably not contagious. The parotid glands (curving about the earlobe and extending into the cheeks) are the most likely glands involved, but the submandibular glands (directly under the molars) and the sublingual glands (swelling makes a double chin) may all swell together, creating a grotesque moon face.

(A couple I know, exposed to mumps by their children, got the expensive mumps immune globulin shot, went to Hawaii on their long-planned trip, got severe mumps, and then spent ten days staring at the ceiling of their expensive hotel room, recovered in time to get leied, say "Aloha," and come home.) The basic natural therapy will control the duration and severity of this disease. Homeopathic remedies include apis, belladonna, bryonia, and pulsatilla.

The immunity from the disease is permanent. The immunity from the vaccine is not reliable. Most fatalities from mumps complications occur in the age group over nineteen years, so acquiring mumps as a child seems prudent.

Mumps encephalitis, which occurs in about 10 to 20 percent of patients with mumps, is associated with fever, headache, vomiting, stiff neck and back. It could be confused with polio or other types of encephalitis if there is no parotid gland swelling.

Orchitis is the testicular inflammation that occurs in about one out of four mature males who acquire mumps. It may occur simultaneously with, or shortly after, the parotid swelling. The involved side of the scrotum becomes red, hot, and tender. Fertility may be impaired, but is not usually eliminated, even if the inflammation is bilateral, as it is in about 20 percent of cases. Patients who have been flat on their backs in bed with mumps develop orchitis as frequently as patients who have been ambulatory.

Pharyngitis is an inflammation of the pharynx. Most cases are due to viruses, and are not treatable with antibiotics. The usual seven-day course is shortened with the basic natural therapy.

Poliomyelitis is a viral infection with an affinity for the spinal motor nerve cells. Ninety percent of the adult population are immune to polio. It is assumed they had the disease as a youngster, but it did not invade the nervous system. The disease is infrequently seen now because of better sanitation. The clinical disease dropped off dramatically in the early 1950s just before the drops and shots were begun on a wide scale. Three types of polio virus may all produce paralysis, and immunity to one type does not provide cross-immunity to another. The oral vaccine allows the intestinal-lining cells to develop an immunity, so if the natural virus is swallowed, the immune cells will neutralize its effect before it can invade the circulation and pass to the brain and spinal cord. In the nonimmune patient the virus may cause only a minor cold, headache, and a few muscle aches, or it may cause extensive destruction of the nerves that control muscle use all the way from the palate to the lower limbs. If the virus invades the nerves, symptoms including fever, headache, and stiff neck and back will follow. Muscle pain may be generalized, and weakness soon follows. Anterior tibial muscle (in front between knee and ankle) weakness is common; this causes a foot drop. Most of the residual function returns in four weeks, but improvement will continue over the following two years.

The dreaded bulbar polio results from involvement of the nerves to the palate, tongue, larynx, and diaphragm; swallowing will cause choking and food to return out the nose. The respirator (iron lung) may be needed to assist weak breathing effort.

Sister Kenny used hot, wet wool blankets wrapped about the patient's muscles. The basic natural therapy for infections along with herbs and homeopathic remedies will keep the disease under control.

The polio epidemic of 1949 to 1950 was probably due to the DPT immunizations in 1948 to 1949. It is called provocation polio; the DPT hurt the immune system. The only cases of polio in our country now—about nine a year—are associated with the use of the polio immunization drops.

Reye's syndrome is a virus infection (usually fatal) manifested by fat infiltration occurring in the liver and brain (cerebral edema). The young child appears to have a minor cold, but soon develops vomiting, headache, and lethargy. In a day or two, coma develops and death occurs, apparently from the swollen brain tissue. The course of the illness is rapid. Remedial measures are usually too late to be effective. There is some connection with the use of aspirin. The basic natural therapy (page 158) should preclude the development of this tragedy.

Roseola infantum is an acute febrile, viral illness most commonly seen in the six- to eighteen-month age group. It is second only to influenza as a cause of fever in babies. It is sometimes called teething fever or teething rash. Apparently the baby harbors the virus (possibly in the mouth), and it invades the system when the crown of a tooth breaks through the gum. Its contagious nature is not obvious.

A sudden high fever (104 to 106 degrees F.) may be accompanied by a frightening convulsion. The eyelids may be red-rimmed, but few other symptoms occur; the baby is just hot and fussy. He may clutch his head; he probably has a headache. Fever-reducing medicines and a bath usually bring the fever down temporarily, but it recurs in three hours. When the fever responds, the baby acts almost normally and can be made to smile and eat.

The roseola fever lasts almost exactly seventy-two hours, then disappears rapidly to be replaced with a macular rash, predominantly on the trunk and face and only slightly on the arms and legs. Swollen glands in the back of the head, just above the attachment of the neck muscles, help to diagnose roseola. It is the only disease that has a rash after the fever falls. After the fever drops, many babies will be fussy and irritable until the rash blossoms; then they heave a sigh of relief, smile, and relax.

Examination during the fever reveals no definitive pathology. The throat is usually vermilion—not the blood red of a streptococcal infection. The white blood count is almost always low, even down to three thousand to five thousand cells per cubic millimeter, with a predominance of lymphocytes—a giveaway for a virus.

An occasional, unsure doctor will treat the feverish baby with a penicillin shot at hour sixty. The fever falls at hour seventy-two. When the rash appears at hour eighty, everyone assumes that the rash is due to a penicillin allergy.

The basic natural therapy, plus the wet socks and echinacea, should shorten the course.

Rubella, or "German," "mild," or "three-day measles," may hardly be noticed in a child because there is little or no fever (100 degrees F. or less), a headache, and a rash that rarely itches. A generalized macular rash that suddenly appears is often the first clue that the disease is present. No spots are bigger than a quarter of an inch; on the face they coalesce so that the cheeks appear flushed. The giveaway (if an epidemic does not make one suspicious) is the presence of enlarged lymph nodes on the mastoid bone directly behind the ears. These feel like rubbery peanuts between the skin and the bone, sliding back and forth when palpated. Before the vaccines were generally available, 80 percent of children had the disease by age twelve. Now, in spite of shots, many adolescents and adults are getting rubella. Adults are usually more toxic when infected; joint aches and fevers of 101 degrees F. are common.

The rubella infection in the first three months of pregnancy is the most dangerous time for the fetus; the virus invades the cells while organs are being formed, disrupting normal completion of important tissues. Cataracts, deafness, heart anomalies, and mental deficiency may occur singly or in combination, but anomalies of almost every organ may appear. Many women elect to have an abortion performed if they contract rubella in the first three months of the pregnancy.

Since 1969 a rubella vaccine (live) has been available; it might be effective in protecting the susceptible. If a girl does not get rubella naturally by the time she is in her early teens, it makes some sense to have her immunized with the rubella vaccine, but one should investigate homeopathic immunization first.

Rubeola, or "hard," "two-week," "coughing," or "black" measles, has largely disappeared from infants and children in the past twenty years, because many children are now immunized against it at fifteen months of age. As if to mock the manufacturers, the disease is now common amongst teenagers. It appears that the immunity supposedly provided by the vaccine is not perfect nor permanent. It suggests that we should let our children get the disease naturally, but make it milder with the basic natural therapy. Homeopathic sulfur and pulsatilla are helpful for the measles case.

Rubeola begins with a fever (the virus is invading) about ten days after exposure. When the fever drops, a dry cough develops, then sore, watery, red-rimmed eyes become increasingly bothersome. The fever then recurs and rises daily until the fourth day when it may reach 103 to 105 degrees F. The cough is especially persistent but still dry. The watery nose (often bloody), red eyes (light-sensitive), and redness inside the mouth make the patient uncomfortable. Swollen glands are noted on the back of the head. A few white spots (Koplik's spots) may be seen inside the cheeks. Finally, at the height of the fever, the cough becomes worse and the rash appears. Pink macules about one-fourth inch in size begin at the hairline, spread to the face, and sweep down over the body. This takes about twenty-four hours. Symptoms do not abate until after the rash has arrived at the toes. The next day the fever is down, the cough loosens, and the rash begins to fade. Four days of getting worse, then four days of getting better is the pattern. The patient is contagious throughout this time.

Because rubeola is a respiratory infection, the incidence of a secondary bacterial such as bronchitis, pneumonia, and otitis is high. Not infrequently the virus invades the nervous system, and encephalitis symptoms predominate. The viremia may depress the platelets, and hemorrhages appear in the rash (black measles). Cortisone may be indicated for this complication. The basic natural therapy (see page 158) will keep the disease from being too serious. Large doses of vitamin A can also help to prevent ear, lung, and mastoid complications.

The eyes are light-sensitive (photophobia), so a darkened room will make the patient more comfortable, but light does not damage the eyes.

Since most adults have had this disease by age six or seven years, and thus have developed immunity, a newborn baby will be immune by passive transfer of the mother's immune globulins via the placenta. After age four months he becomes susceptible. The live measles vaccine is routinely given at age fifteen months. If an unimmunized child is exposed to measles, he can be given a dose of gamma globulin just sufficient to allow him to have a modified case. He gets the disease, but in a mild form; the immunity he develops is enough to protect him permanently.

The vaccine is not as effective as the pharmaceutical companies would lead us to believe. Getting the disease naturally while under the influence of the basic natural therapy or gamma globulin is still the best way to provide permanent immunity.

You may not want to know about this rare disease caused by a virus:

Rabies, or hydrophobia, is an almost uniformly fatal viral disease of the nervous system. The virus is inoculated into the victim by a rabid cat, dog, bat, fox, skunk, or other wild animal (but apparently not by members of the rodent family). The virus travels by way of the nerves to the brain, where an encephalitis is produced. This causes extreme excitement, anxiety, hyperactivity, pain, and finally exhaustion, coma, and death. The spasm of the throat muscles gives it the name *hydrophobia* (fear of water). Soon restlessness, excitability, and then terror overcome the patient.

Because of the fatal outcome, people bitten by rabid animals should receive the hyperimmune serum followed by rabies vaccine. Surveillance of the suspected animal is most important. A dog who has bitten a human must be quarantined; if the animal dies and the characteristic negri bodies are found in its brain at autopsy, the bitten person must be given the vaccine. Bats may be carriers. Bat bites demand treatment without delay, as waiting for the demise of the bat is fruitless. Domestic animals are an unlikely source of the disease because of the inoculation most states now require. But the biting animal should not be destroyed; it is important that it be kept alive so that behavior may be observed.

Apparently chipmunks, rats, mice, and gerbils are unable to carry the virus, so their bites need only local treatment. A rabies death occurred in our town a few years ago in a boy who had been bitten by a dog in Spain. Before the diagnosis was established, he had, of course, spread the virus about the hospital. Twenty-two hospital personnel ended up receiving the vaccine as a precaution.

Protozoan diseases are due to parasites that invade the host through bites (malaria), ingestion (giardiasis), or the placenta (toxoplasmosis). They are destructive, chronic, and difficult to eradicate completely.

Giardiasis is the intestinal upset manifested by weakness, cramps, and diarrhea assumed to be due to the protozoa *Giardia lamblia*. It is transmitted from person to person by flies and unwashed food. Just brushing your teeth in "clear" spring water may allow one to get this. It is not a clear-cut pathological agent, as many children have it in their stools, but have no symptoms. Child-care centers may spread this parasite if hand washing rules are not followed.

Spirochetal Diseases

Lyme disease usually begins as a rash at the site of a recent tick bite. Various symptoms follow for a period of weeks or months: fever, malaise, headaches, arthralgia. Antibiotic treatment with doxycycline or amoxicillin is helpful.

Rickettsial diseases are those illnesses due to organisms smaller than bacteria and larger than viruses. Like viruses, they require the living cell for growth.

Cat scratch disease is considered a rickettsial infection resulting from a minor scratch from a cat who harbors the infectious material in his claws. After two or three weeks the nearby lymph nodes swell, become tender, and the victim develops a low-grade fever. If the hand is scratched, the armpit glands swell; if the leg, the groin glands may enlarge to one-inch size. The basic natural therapy might shorten the three-month disease course.

BACTERIAL INFECTIONS

Sir William Osler: "The patient who takes medicine must recover twice. Once from the disease and once from the medicine."

Bacterial infections are caused by germs, and are usually characterized by the formation of pus (skin abscesses, sties, pyelonephritis, tonsillitis, sinusitis, meningitis, osteomyelitis). One hundred years ago Louis Pasteur was able to associate a particular disease with a particular bacterium. This somewhat limited approach focused on the idea of finding a specific remedy for a specific disease. A contemporary of Pasteur, Antoine Bechamp, developed the idea that disease is not caused by the invasion of these newly discovered microorganisms, but by changes in the body's cells, the "territory." The body deteriorates first, then the bacteria grow in this fertile soil.

Somehow modern allopathic medicine has become locked into the Pasteur idea that the invading bacteria are the cause of the illness. We have now become aware that the promise of a safe antibiotic to kill every invading germ is pie in the sky. Who would have thought all those little microscopic bacteria have become smart enough to mutate into superbugs? When Sir Alexander Fleming noted that a feeble penicillium mold could inactivate bacterial growth in the culture dish, everyone was sure we had the answer to pneumonia, strep throat, osteomyelitis, syphilis, meningitis, and even acne and postnasal drip. We had some answers for a while, but they are not good enough now.

Why Do We Get Sick?

Is there a lesson we are not learning? Yes! An infection indicates that something has changed your territory, your immune system. The body is alerting its owner to some flaw in his lifestyle. Look on sickness as an opportunity. The illness should act as a motivation to change. If the immune defenses are strong enough, the microbes cannot invade and colonize.

Allergies, sensitivities, viruses, improper diet, acid/base imbalance, pollutants, and stressors will drag a body down, impair the immune system, and allow a nasty bacterial infection to invade. Sinus infection is secondary to a nasal allergy or a milk sensitivity. A bladder infection may occur from improper toilet habits or food sensitivities. Bathing too much or not enough might irritate the skin sufficiently to allow a skin infection.

The acid/base balance of the body is critical to the maintenance of health. Apple cider vinegar (acetic acid) consumed daily might discourage bacterial infections, because bacteria do not live well in an acid environment.[177] Gargling and swallowing salt (sodium chloride, one teaspoonful in a glass of water) at the time of the bacterial invasion can slow the infection; sodium chloride was used before refrigeration to prevent the putrefaction of meat. If the sodium level in the blood is low, adding salt to the diet might help a child's body fight off infections.

Antibiotics do not help build the immune system; they do not teach the body anything. "No antibiotic can be said to have proven successful in truly eradicating any infectious disease in modern times."[178] Bacterial diseases are still around; we cannot eradicate them from the planet, but if you are deathly sick from the invasion of some nasty bug, antibiotics are a godsend. Just pray that the germ you have is not resistant to the antibiotics the doctor prescribes.

If you are not too sick or feverish, a day or two using the basic natural therapy might be tried first to test your body's ability to fight the infection. Three days of a fever is enough time for the body to mobilize its defenses and develop as much immunity from this particular invasion as is possible. More exposure to this bacteria would be a stressor and of little benefit to the immune processes. A purulent mucus draining from the nose, or noted in the sputum after coughing, means that bacteria are present and could be treated. It is to be remembered that "the antibiotics destroy the bacterial cell wall, thus killing the bacteria, but liberating its toxic contents. In contrast, cells of the immune system engulf intact bacteria, removing them safely from the body."[179]

Severe infections—pyelonephritis, pneumonia—might best be treated with antibiotics upon recognition, and the patient may be ambulatory in just a few days. For overwhelming infections—meningitis, endocarditis, septicemia, osteomyelitis, liver abscess—hospitalization seems mandatory. Repeated serious bacterial infections suggest the need to test the immune system. Some need gamma globulin shots every few weeks.

Antibiotics have their place, but the patient may develop an allergy to the medicine, and frequently develops a yeast infection (candidiasis) following antibiotic use. Yeast infections can weaken the immune system, making the victim more susceptible to another infection; a repeat course of antibiotics will renew the yeast infection again with even more devastating results. Yeast infection can even cause autism. Yeast overgrowth in the intestines can cause food sensitivities, as well as malabsorption.

In addition, many bacteria have become resistant to the antibiotics. "There may be a time down the road when eighty percent of infections will be resistant to all known antibiotics."[180] In the early 1940s just one million units of penicillin was enough to eradicate the strep that caused scarlet fever. And it worked in just eight to twelve hours. A miracle. Now, however, it takes a million units twice daily for ten days to do the same thing.

There seems to be a survival of the fittest among bacteria; the hardy ones learn how to become resistant to antibiotics. Hospitalized children who suffered from serious *H. influenza* infections were twice as likely to have been treated with antibiotics in the month preceding their hospitalization. These germs are smart, but with the right supports (a healthy diet, adequate fluids, hydrotherapy, homeopathy), the smarter, educated body can handle most of them. What is your doctor's approach to the treatment of infections?

Not Too Serious Bacterial Infections You Might Treat at Home for a While

Bronchitis is an infection of the bronchial tubes, usually of bacterial origin. The victim has a hard cough and may raise purulent material. It tends to be triggered by a cold and may be mild or severe. If a person has repeated bronchial infections, a milk or inhalation allergy must be considered. Some have bronchitis because they are allergic to their own bacteria.

Most people use vitamin C at the first sign of the burning in the larynx area, but if the disease progresses and becomes more chesty, they switch to large doses of vitamin A (two hundred thousand units daily for four days for a child). Frequently vitamin C works on the problems from the neck up, while vitamin A works on the inflammations from the windpipe on down into the chest. These should also help: garlic, lobelia, mullein, cowslip, fenugreek, Irish moss. Bronchial infections can be improved with the use of proteolytic enzymes. (These will help digest infectious material.)[181]

Asthmatic bronchitis is common in children whose bronchial tubes frequently overreact to infection with an increase in mucus secretion and spasm. The characteristic expiratory wheeze plus a fever of 100 to 101 degrees F. following a cold or influenza is the giveaway.

The pus created as a result of this invasion inflames the tubing into the lungs, increasing the cough and fever. Wheezing on exhalation, accompanied by shortness of breath, is easily audible to the parent if the child's open mouth is held close to the adult's ear. The wheeze is usually accompanied by rales (the sound of dropping sand on metal), which is the noise produced by exhaled air bubbling through the pus-laden tubes. Treatment with antibiotics (and perhaps epinephrine) is required if, after a few days, the vitamin C and A are not enough. The child who has this affliction more than two or three times a year is a candidate for an allergy workup.

Conjunctivitis, or surface infection of the conjunctivae, creates inflammation and a yellow or green purulent exudate that may glue the eyelids together. An antibiotic ointment is appropriate.

Cystitis is a bladder inflammation that usually causes urinary burning, urgency, and frequency, but rarely fever or stomachache. It is most common in immature females, and is rare in males, so it is assumed that the bacteria migrate up the urethra from the germ-laden vaginal and/or anal area into the bladder. A bubble bath may lead to cystitis; sensitivity to the soap sets up an irritation and infection follows. The usual bacterium responsible is *Escherichia coli*, the common intestinal germ. Urinalysis will reveal pus cells and usually albumin.

If a male develops cystitis, he probably has some abnormality of urinary tubular structure that creates urinary stasis and, like stagnant water, encourages germ growth. But urinary tract infections in male or female lead to pus moving up the ureters and damaging the kidneys.

Pus cells and bacteria must be present to diagnose cystitis. If no pus is found, an allergy (to citrus, chocolate, milk, etc.) may be operative. Since bacteria have difficulty living and multiplying in acid urine, acidifying with ascorbic acid or cranberry juice makes perfect sense. Cranberry (sold as a capsule now) has been found to prevent bacteria from clinging to and colonizing on the walls of the urinary tract. Safe and cheap. The basic natural therapy is usually enough to control most cystitis infections. Herbs, homeopathic remedies, and teas will help: uva ursi, corn silk, echinacea, goldenseal, marshmallow tea. Colloidal silver can control some cystitis infections.

Urologists recommend antibiotic prophylaxis to preclude kidney invasion by bacteria. They do an X ray while the patient is voiding a radiopaque dye to see if urine runs up the ureters. Whatever the method, monitoring for infection is mandatory.

Otitis media, or middle-ear infection in the space just behind the eardrum, is probably the most common bacterial infection affecting children. Eighty percent of children have at least one ear infection under the age of three years, and one third have had more than one episode. Ten million children are treated for this condition every year. The eustachian tube, which allows for the equalization of the air pressure between the middle ear and the pharynx, acts as a pathway for bacteria.

The story starts with an ordinary cold that follows the usual drippy nose, sneeze, and irritability routine. On the third to fifth day, the child becomes more irritable and/or begins to scream as if stabbed. He may indicate his ear; a baby may refuse to suck on his bottle or the breast as the negative pressure in his nasopharynx pulls on the inflamed drum. Fever of 101 to 103 degrees F. usually suggests pus under pressure behind the eardrum, in which case he may be more sick and miserable than in pain. Usually there is a purulent discharge from the nose. An occasional child will be only slightly uncomfortable, then have sticky yellow pus pouring from his ear the next morning. This means that the eardrum burst as a result of the pressure of the pus that built up behind it.

The standard treatment by medical doctors is to prescribe an antibiotic that the child is to take daily for ten days. Most doctors feel treatment is indicated in almost all cases. The absence or disappearance of pain does *not* mean no treatment is necessary. Lancing the eardrum (myringotomy) might also be done. An abscessed otitis media responds faster if the drum is lanced and the pus evacuated. It takes at least eight hours for the medicine to be absorbed, find, and kill the germs sufficiently to reduce the inflammation and relieve the pain. If the child is still uncomfortable after twelve hours, she is on the wrong antibiotic and/or the drum needs lancing. The child is to be seen on the tenth day of the medication to determine the extent of healing and whether medicine should be continued or changed.

Decongestants, phlegm driers, membrane shrinkers, and/or antihistaminics are usually given simultaneously to allow the eustachian tubes to remain open. (These remedies are not very effective.) Myringotomy is done less often nowadays since antibiotics seem effective. The doctor rechecks the ear and usually says something like, "There may be some fluid left behind the eardrum, but the infection seems resolved. Don't let him get another cold. It'll go right back to his ear. If the fluid remains, we will have small tubes placed into the eardrum to equalize the pressure, promote drainage, and maintain adequate hearing."

If not treated, the infection can lead to hearing loss and/or perforation, scarring, mastoid inflammation, lateral sinus thrombosis, Bell's palsy, or meningitis. In patients who have been successfully treated, a secretion may yet remain behind the eardrum (serous otitis).

The preceding three paragraphs of advice have evolved over the last five decades since antibiotics were invented and used for every infection. However, it has been discovered that 80 percent of ear infections did not need to be treated with an antibiotic in the first place.[182] So you might want to ask your doctor what will happen if you don't take the drug. If a child is treated for an ear infection with an antibiotic within the first day or two of the onset of symptoms, he is much more likely to get another ear infection within a month. Treated children were two to six times more likely to have another ear infection within the next six weeks as compared with children treated with placebos.[183, 184] The underlying problem is an immune system weakened by diet, stress, food allergy, or inadequate early treatment of a minor cold or infection. We now know that if a patient is allowed to mobilize his own immune system with diet changes, warming-wet-sock treatments, mullein ear drops, the basic natural therapy, and some appropriate homeopathic remedy, he may not get sick for another year—in contrast to the recurrence if only antibiotics have been used. If the infection invades the mastoid bone or gets into the meninges, then use the antibiotics. Once the body learns how to fight off these infections because the immune system has been primed, repeated ear invasions are rare.

Homeopathic remedies include aconite (for the sudden pain), belladonna (for the high fever with flushed face), chamomilla, and pulsatilla or mercurius (for the thick pus from the nose). The ear drops contain olive oil, mullein flower, and garlic; the drops are put into the ear canal four times a day during the painful time. A cotton plug is put in the canal to confine the drops. Dry heat from a lamp about six inches from the ear may be helpful for five minutes four times a day. Or apply a hot water bottle or moist hot cloth to the ear for ten to fifteen minutes, three to four times a day.

Naturopathic doctors suggest lymphatic massage. Use gentle, slow, and rhythmical sweeps with your fingers from below the ear down to the collarbone. Then hold at the clavicle for a few seconds. This encourages the drainage of congested lymph nodes and vessels.

Bottle-fed babies have five to eight times the number of ear infections as do breast-fed babies. Even in the breast-fed ones, if the mother is drinking cow milk, enough of the cow milk protein will enter the baby to encourage an infection.[185] In 1994 a well-documented study of 104 children with recurrent serous otitis media revealed a high incidence of food sensitivities and food allergies among them.[186] There was a significant statistical association between food allergy and serous otitis media in 78 percent of the patients. (Usual offenders: cow milk—most common, then wheat, egg white, peanut, soy, corn, orange, tomato, and chicken.) When the foods were stopped, the ear problems cleared. When the reacting foods were reintroduced, the fluid returned to the middle ear.

Keeping the feet warm or wearing ear coverings will not prevent ear infections; the germs crawl up the eustachian tubes on the *inside*—*not* the outside. Blowing the nose may blow bacteria through these tunnels to the middle-ear space. It is supposed to be better to let the nose drip or to snuff up the material and spit it out (ugh!).

Prophylactic sulfa or penicillin have led to the emergence of resistant strains of bacteria and allergies to the medicine. A trial of a few shots of a bacterial vaccine may be helpful in teaching the body how to fight off infection (see Sinusitis, this chapter). Frequent infections may alert the doctor to check the patient's immune globulin level.

Tonsil and adenoid tissue normally enlarges until age five or six. Repeated ear infections are more likely due to food sensitivities and not to the size of those lymph tissues. Some recent research indicates that tonsil and adenoid removal may actually hurt the immune system (see Tonsillectomy and Adenoidectomy, Chapter 7). Doctors who use cranial therapy can help control ear infections.

Children who had repeated courses of antibiotics were 50 percent more likely to have developmental delays than children who did not get the antibiotics. The children with developmental delays were more likely to have had adverse reactions to the immunizations, and many of them had tubes placed in their ears for serous otitis.[187]

"Sixty-nine percent of children being evaluated for school failure who were receiving medication for hyperactivity gave a history of greater than ten ear infections. By contrast, only twenty percent of non-hyperactive children had more than ten infections."[188] The repeated courses of antibiotics allow the yeast to grow in the gut. This yeast causes alterations in the intestinal flora that allow for the absorption of food antigens. These go to the brain and promote hyperactivity and learning problems.[189]

Otitis external, or swimmer's ear, is any inflammation or infection in the ear canal (from the ear hole down to the eardrum). Virus, allergy, fungus, or bacteria may be primary, secondary, or all involved simultaneously. Swimmer's ear occurs because the retained water macerates the canal skin and wax (cerumen). This debris provides a good media in which germs grow; it is dark, wet, and warm. An unpleasant odor is usually due to the growth of *Pseudomonas* and *E. coli* germs, or mold and fungi like that growing in dirty socks. The ear-canal orifice is smaller than usual, the pain is aggravated by movement of the ear, and local lymph nodes are swollen (in contrast to otitis media).

Swabbing with alcohol on a fine wick of cotton after showers and swimming might prevent a recurrence. It is not uncommon for a baby to have itchy, smelly ears. If he likes to have his ears scratched, and the ear hole smells like dirty socks, he surely has some infected debris in the canal. Cleansing followed by appropriate drops should clear this up. Dr. Steven Davis has had success with the use of colloidal silver drops into the ear canal. It has a calming and germicidal effect.

Scarlet fever is a streptococcal sore throat or tonsillitis (or pharyngitis if tonsils are absent) which is accompanied by a red, generalized rash resembling sunburn. There is usually a pallor around the lips. The incubation period is short, taking but two to four days for transmission from one person to another. Fever, headache, vomiting, and weakness are followed in a day or two by the rash. The throat and tonsils are swollen and a deep blood-red color, often hemorrhagic. With a viral infection, the throat is usually more vermilion or pink. The glands in the neck just under the curve of the jawbone become swollen and tender. Hyponasal speech is common, in contrast to the hoarseness of croup or the sore trachea accompanying the flu. A strawberry tongue is associated. A week after the fever subsides, the skin about the fingers and toes will peel off as if sunburned. Although vitamin C is helpful in the treatment, most doctors will insist on penicillin or erythromycin for a full ten days.

Sinusitis is a frequent complication of the cold, but more common in the older age group when the sinuses are more fully developed. The symptoms are those of any collection of pus in an enclosed space: fever, headache (usually over the involved sinus—for example, a sore cheek indicates that the maxillary sinus is involved), purulent nasal discharge, and elevated white blood count.

Chronic sinusitis is more commonly due to obstructive lesions like a deviated septum, or inhalation or bacterial allergies. Many people develop sinusitis because of a milk allergy. The swollen tissues caused by the allergic reaction plug up the sinus cavities and allow bacteria to grow.

Many people are relieved of this chronic problem after receiving a series of bacteria (their own or a stock solution) injections. If every cold ends with a purulent discharge and responsible allergies have been controlled, a few shots of this dead bacteria vaccine may cure the sticky mess by "teaching" the sufferer resistance to bacterial invasion. They are valuable for some "zonkers" (people who make that terrible throat-clearing noise) and helpful for sufferers of asthmatic bronchitis.

The basic natural therapy would help the tired immune system. Pycnogenol is helpful. Proteolytic enzymes will help break up the pus.

Tonsillitis is an inflammation of the tonsils, either viral or bacterial. Viral throat infections superficially resemble a strep throat, but are not as blood-red. Eighty percent or more have been found to be viral even though the tonsils and adjacent tissues are reddened (or vermilioned). The parents may elect to do either of the following:

1. Treat the child with the basic, natural therapy for seventy-two hours and see what course the disease takes. If hoarseness, a watery, runny nose, and a cough develop after the seventy-two hours of fever, they may call it "that virus that's going around." When a child is asked where his throat hurts, and he points to his larynx, chances are that it's the virus. If he points up high into his open mouth and sounds hyponasal, or if his palate is immobile, he is more likely to have a bacterial tonsillitis, and therefore *could* be treated with an antibiotic.

2. Request an examination, a throat culture, and a white blood count. If the throat culture grows a pathogenic streptococcus and the white count is elevated, a full ten days of penicillin is the standard allopathic treatment. But the basic natural therapy (see page 158) might do the job as well. This latter case is a strep, but three days of supportive care prior to antibiotics seems to allow the body enough time to develop some strep antibodies against the next invasion. Penicillin used too early in the disease may preclude any antibody development. With natural therapies the disease is controlled and the patient's immune system has been primed for the next onslaught. Repeated tonsil infections, viral or bacterial, suggest a milk (or other food) sensitivity as the inciting agent.

Chiropractors will manipulate the cervical spine and encourage lymph drainage in the neck. Colloidal silver sprayed into the throat will speed healing.

You Should Have Help from a Health Care Provider for These:

The following infections would make the victim very toxic, possibly in shock, with severe stomachaches and usually foul-smelling diarrhea and persistent vomiting:

Appendicitis (see Pain, Abdominal, Chapter 12).

Bacillary dysentery is a more dramatic, fulminating form of intestinal inflammation than intestinal flu (see Gastroenteritis, this chapter).

Cholera may be mild, but one out of twenty infected people will have a painless, voluminous, watery diarrhea—characterized "rice water"—that rapidly causes dehydration.

Food poisoning is the nonspecific term applied to a variety of food-borne toxins, bacteria, viruses, or parasites. Usually some deviation from good, clean food management is responsible.

Botulism is a severe, frequently fatal disease resulting from the ingestion of the poison produced by the *Clostridium botulinum* germ. Seventy-five percent of the cases are due to home-canned food, obviously inadequately prepared. The disease may appear as an intestinal upset and then progress to muscle paralysis, double vision, trouble swallowing and talking, respiratory paralysis (possibly requiring an iron lung), and death.

Clostridium perfrigens is widespread in the feces of humans and animals. Adequate cooking is the common sense control measure. In one study one hundred people were served at a banquet. The four who did not eat the chicken salad had no symptoms. Of the ninety-six who did, seventy-five became ill twelve to fifteen hours later with cramps and diarrhea, but no fever. The duration of the symptoms was eight to twelve hours; severe but short-lived.

Salmonella infections are transmitted from another person or animal, or may grow and remain for long periods of time in meat, milk, and eggs. Pet turtles may have the disease (who can tell?) and spread it to the household. It is the most common cause of food poisoning. A recent outbreak affected nine thousand people before it was controlled.

Staphylococcal food poisoning accounts for 25 percent of food poisoning cases, and is caused by a toxin produced by some strains of the staphylococcus. The bacteria grow in custards, ham, beef, fish, chicken, and salads improperly prepared and allowed to stand without refrigeration before consumption.

The following diseases cause prolonged fever and prostration:

Brucellosis, undulant fever, also know as or Bang's disease, is transmitted to man from domestic animals, most notably the cow and the pig. The symptoms appear suddenly with chills, fever, malaise, cough. Sometimes it appears with only lassitude suggesting a psychological problem.

Cavernous sinus thrombosis is the occlusion of veins deep inside the head, usually due to an infected clot that has spread from the nose, eyes, teeth, or upper lip. A pimple in the nose may release bacteria into the veins inside the skull. This infected, thrombosed clot causes fever, chills, headaches, swollen lids, and blindness. Immediate antibiotic treatment is necessary.

Tularemia, or rabbit fever, is a bacterial disease transmitted from animals to humans by ticks, fleas, or lice. Hunters, sheep shearers, or animal handlers are the chief victims. A small sore develops at the skin site where the bacteria have entered; the local lymph nodes enlarge and may become abscessed. Antibiotics are the treatment.

Typhoid fever is a bacterial infection whose predominant symptoms include fever, headache, prostration, and suppression of white-cell response. Adequate sanitation has suppressed its spread, but isolated, explosive epidemics still appear. Inadequately controlled water supplies and overtaxed sewage facilities in "health" resorts can allow one carrier to infect scores of innocent vacationers. The health department must continue constant surveillance of public water supplies and known carriers, who must not be cooks or food handlers (as was Typhoid Mary, who left a string of victims in her wake). The ingested typhoid bacteria invade the blood stream through the intestinal wall and multiply in the liver, spleen, and lymph tissue. A blood culture grows the causative bacillus in the first week of fever, when a blood agglutination test is usually positive.

(I remember a patient, age eight years, who seemed to have the "flu." He had a couple of loose stools accompanied by a high fever and seemed more knocked out than usual, but his white count was only five thousand. That low count suggested a virus, like intestinal flu. After about five days of this, we ordered agglutination tests for everything the lab could do. The lab technician was so excited when she called, she stammered: "Has h-h-he had any typhoid shots recently? Well, his t-t-titer is still positive when diluted four thousand times!" Chloramphenicol cured him, and we subsequently found typhoid germs in the well at his grandmother's house, where he had visited two weeks prior to his fever.)

The following diseases cause a persistent cough or respiratory symptoms that are inadequately controlled with cough remedies:

Cystic fibrosis is an inherited disease characterized by chronic lung infection and intestinal malabsorption. Afflicted children have repeated attacks of bronchitis, often due to resistant bacteria; frequent large, greasy, foul-smelling stools; wasted, malnourished bodies—especially buttocks—and shortened life expectancy. CF is inherited and affects about one child in two thousand.

The pulmonary complications are due to the lack of normal mucus production in the bronchial tubes. This chronic pulmonary infection leads to hypertension of the pulmonary blood vessels and pressure on the right side of the heart. Antibiotics are lifesaving, but resistant strains of *Staphylococcus* and *Pseudomonas* have appeared. Most doctors use antibiotics intermittently, or only if fever and an acute infection are present. Low selenium may be a contributing factor.

Diphtheria is very rare. The victim has a severe sore throat and extreme prostration. A thick, dirty membrane grows into the windpipe, causing obstruction to breathing (black diphtheria). It produces a powerful toxin can damage the heart muscle. This disease had almost disappeared by the time the DPT shots were started.

Epiglottitis is an inflammation of the epiglottis (the area just above the larynx) and is a severe form of bacterial croup. The child may become dusky (slightly cyanotic) and make a loud noise on *both* inspiration and expiration. He usually has a high fever and an elevated white blood count. His chest heaves in and out, he is anxious and restless from fighting for air, his pulse is elevated above 160 beats per minute, and respirations are over 50 to 60 per minute. The child will respond to oxygen, a mist tent, and antibiotics in the hospital, but the disease may progress so rapidly that a tracheotomy (airway surgically made through the trachea at the base of the neck) may have to be done while awaiting improvement.

Whooping cough or pertussis is a bacterial respiratory infection that typically lasts six weeks. Two weeks of dry, irritating, usually nocturnal cough without fever are followed by two weeks of whooping. The child coughs, coughs, coughs in spasms until all his breath is exhaled; he then inhales suddenly and deeply with a characteristic "whoop." He may become cyanotic. He may cough so hard that he breaks capillaries in the skin of his face (petechiae) or in the sclerae (subconjunctival hemorrhages). Vomiting may be a problem severe enough to cause dehydration, weight loss, or malnutrition. Secondary otitis media or bronchitis are common complications. In the last two weeks of the disease the cough reverts to the dry, irritating cough of the initial stage. In the last few decades the disease has become less serious whether the child has had the shots or not.

An elevated white blood cell count (twenty thousand per cubic millimeters or more), predominantly lymphocytic, is found.

DPT vaccine immunizations (diphtheria/pertussis/tetanus) have not been as effective as promised to protect children from this awful disease. Indeed, some children seem more susceptible to the diseases these shots were designed to control (see Immunizations, Chapter 7).

These diseases produce severe headache, prostration, and often a stiff neck and back:

Meningitis is a severe, rapidly progressive, frequently fatal infection of the meninges. It is a bacterial infection of the surface lining of the brain, usually considered to be blood-borne. Bacteria are carried from the nose or throat to the brain, where they create a usually characteristic set of symptoms: high fever, coma, and a stiff neck and back. Upon examination, pus is found in the spinal fluid. Antibiotics, if given early enough, are usually curative, and if the infection is not too overwhelming, the patient can usually be saved. One type, due to the meningococcus, is considered to be contagious; the others, because the infection is quite well locked up inside the brain, are not.

The meningococcus type is often found in school dormitories or army or navy barracks where many people live together. Some strains are now becoming quite resistant. It is rapidly overwhelming, sudden in onset, and sometimes fatal before diagnosis can be made and treatment instituted.

The newborn infant with this may only vomit, become irritable, and change his sleeping habits. He may have no fever. He may be limp instead of stiff. His fontanel (soft spot) is frequently full or tense.

It takes twenty-four hours for the antibiotic to be absorbed, arrive at the meninges, and kill enough bacteria to make a difference. Nursing care, intravenous fluid, and oxygen are all directed toward holding the patient together until the antibiotic becomes effective.

The following diseases produce fever and pain in some area:

Osteomyelitis is an infection of the bone. The infection must be blood-borne as there has been no portal of entry. The pus that forms eats away at the bone and the marrow. Huge doses of the appropriate antibiotic are indicated.

Peritonitis may be secondary to a rupture of the appendix or other intestinal area, or from a penetrating wound to the abdomen. The germs that leak out from the burst organ set up an intense reaction as the peritoneal area tries to wall it off.

Peritonsillar abscess, or "quinsy," is a rare sequel of tonsillitis. The streptococcal bacteria invade the tissues behind the tonsils; pus collects. Surgical drainage is required—we hope with sufficient anesthesia.

Pneumonia is a lung infection usually due to bacteria, but viruses, fungi, allergies, dry winter air, smog, low levels of gamma globulin, and aspirated matter (kerosene, food, dust) may allow the invasion of the

germs. (A patient once got a staphylococcus pneumonia after he ate chocolate. He was allergic to chocolate; it gave him a pimple on his lip. Staphylococcus grew in the pimple; those germs were inhaled into his lungs
where they continued to grow.)

The usual story starts with a dry cough. On the second to fifth day,
sometimes associated with a purulent nasal discharge, a shaking chill and
a 104 to 106 degrees F. temperature occur. Convulsions, cyanosis, and
prostration may be present. A dry, muffled cough (the infection is below the
cough reflex) is common in pneumonia and bronchopneumonia. Tylenol
usually has little effect on the fever, so the doctor cannot call it "that virus
that is going around."

Grunting respirations, shortness of breath, lack of response to Tylenol,
and a high white blood count would just about give away the diagnosis of
pneumonia even without an X ray. Doctors used to love this disease; it's
what they save antibiotics for. We can usually guarantee that in about ten
hours fever will fall, breathing becomes easier, cough loosens or lessens,
and the child can play or eat or at least act better. (I told a boy with pneumonia that he would start to feel better eight hours after the shot I gave him
at 7:00 P.M. He set his alarm for 3:00 A.M. and called me because he said he
was still sick. I responded with, "From *now on,* you'll feel better." Now I say
ten hours.)

If the response is adequate, i.e., the germ is not resistant to the antibiotic, the treatment can usually be continued orally for a week or so. The
dreaded staphylococcus is often resistant to the usual antibiotics. In this
case culture of the sputum and sensitivity studies are mandatory. The basic
natural therapy (see page 158) should be used along with the antibiotic.

Pyelonephritis (pyelitis) is a kidney infection due to a germ, usually associated with some obstruction, albeit minor, to the flow of urine. Like germs
in stagnant water, the bacteria are not flushed out completely or rapidly
enough to prevent them from multiplying in the bladder or the kidney. As it
is more frequently seen in females, it is assumed that the bacteria multiply in
the urine, migrate up the ureters, and invade the kidney substance.

The infection is usually ushered in with a violent chill, headache, and
stomach or backache, followed by a high fever. If antifever medicines plus
a hot bath are ineffective in reducing the high fever, it should alert the
physician to seek a bacterial infection (otitis media, tonsillitis, pneumonia,
or pyelitis). A chill and a fever in a female almost always means a kidney

infection. The urine has elevated amounts of albumin and is loaded with pus (white blood cells). If a urine specimen is not available, an elevated white blood count would show that bacteria have invaded (twenty thousand WBC per cubic millimeter). A wet cloth diaper can be wrung out and the specimen will reveal a few pus cells (mixed with soap granules and cotton fibers); a plastic bag can be affixed to the perineal area and a teaspoon of urine may find its way into this. A culture usually reveals the *E. coli* bacterium, thus suggesting that the infection came from fecal contamination.

Treatment with an antibiotic or a sulfa drug almost always reduces the fever within twenty-four hours. The basic natural therapy will help.

Teaching a girl to wipe her anus from front to back after bowel movements is a parental duty as it will discourage germ migration. Drinking apple and cranberry juice has been helpful in promoting an acid urine that discourages bacterial growth. A few patients will remain free of bladder and kidney infections if they do not drink milk, or orange and tomato juice. (One patient would develop 104 degrees F. of fever and back pain the day after she drank any amount of milk or had a piece of cheese!) Some occult allergic mechanism makes the outlet tube opening (urethra) swell up, precluding the complete emptying of the bladder, and the full-blown infection follows. A urologist should outline a plan of urinary infection control.

Rheumatic fever is an inflammation of a variety of body tissues: joints (arthritis), skin (rashes), brain (chorea), and, most important, the heart and its valves. It is always preceded by a streptococcal infection, and is seen most often in the seven- to ten-year-old. Freckle-faced redheads are more susceptible. The patient recovers from the initial sore throat, but within two to four weeks he begins to run a fever, develops migratory joint aches (ankles, wrists, knees, and elbows, with or without redness and swelling) and a rapid heart rate disproportionate to the temperature elevation, and, less frequently, begins to make involuntary, purposeless movements (chorea or Saint Vitus' dance). Nodules form about his joints or in his scalp, and he may blossom with a rash (erythema marginatum) of irregularly curved lines over the trunk.

Heart murmurs are heard, the blood shows some anemia, the sedimentation rate and streptococcal antibodies are elevated. The chest X ray usually shows some heart enlargement, and the electrocardiogram may show changes. The throat culture is usually positive for the beta hemolytic strep if the triggering strep throat was fairly recent and/or untreated.

It is estimated that about 3 to 5 percent of untreated strep throats will lead to rheumatic fever, but only one tenth of that number will do so if adequately treated (with ten full days of penicillin). Penicillin is usually given to be sure the strep has been eradicated from the throat. Bed rest until the sedimentation rate is normal seems sensible, but most children will get bored and "cheat" when they begin to feel better. The exact etiology of this disease is obscure; the most plausible theory is that the streptococcal infection stimulates the body to manufacture antistrep antibodies, which then attack some antigen in the heart, joints, and skin.

Many children escape permanent heart damage with the first attack of rheumatic fever. It is very important to protect them from streptococcal infection so that further attacks of rheumatic fever will be prevented. Some doctors will treat their patients with years of regular doses of penicillin, which will almost always prevent the streptococcal infection that precedes rheumatic fever. At the same time it would be prudent to build the child's immune system with large doses of vitamins C, A, and beta-carotene. Glutathione would be helpful.

Not every murmur means rheumatic fever, and not every rheumatic fever victim is handicapped. Doctors may do much harm by restricting the activity of a child because he has a murmur. If the scarring is severe enough to compromise the blood flow, the child will become weak and short of breath while active, and he will limit his own activity automatically.

In the last decade rheumatic fever has made a comeback from the preceding low infectious rate. It may be that the bacteria has developed a resistance to penicillin, or some toxin is interfering with the children's immune systems.

Septic arthritis is a rare bacterial infection in a joint space. Large doses of antibiotics for two or three weeks are needed to prevent damage to the joint lining.

Tetanus, or lockjaw, is a severe, painful, frequently fatal disease (60 percent mortality rate), due to a toxin produced by a germ, *Clostridium tetani,* that enters the body through a break in the skin. A puncture wound by a rusty nail or a crushing wound is a more likely portal of entry. The germ does better in deep wounds, as it grows in the absence of oxygen. Within a week or so after the invasion of the germ, the patient notices muscle stiffness, especially of the neck and back. He has difficulty opening his jaw. Headache, chills, and sweating are followed by convulsions triggered by slight stimuli. The mouth is drawn into a fixed grin, the head is pulled back, and the back arched. The patient becomes fearful. He may die of respiratory complications or uncontrolled seizures.

Newborn babies may develop tetanus through the contaminated umbilical stump. (In some areas of the world where sanitation is at a minimum, the delivery is climaxed by using a shoelace to tie off the umbilical cord!) Tetanus antitoxin neutralizes the toxin.

Prevention by active immunity takes the worry out of contaminated wounds. Some doctors now elect *not* to give the DPT shots because they are not safe or effective, but will give just the tetanus (T) part of the DPT (see Immunizations, Chapter 7). They will follow up with the T to the two-year-old and the five-year-old booster. A routine booster of tetanus every ten years is more than adequate. (This applies to adults as well.) If a few years have gone by since the last booster and the patient receives a significant puncture wound, he should have a tetanus booster within forty-eight hours. The wound should be washed thoroughly with soap, water, and a brush, despite the child's objections. Homeopathics are helpful in the treatment of this devastating disease.

That so few cases of tetanus have developed in our army is a miracle, considering the number of soldiers and the number of dirty wounds. I understand that the few soldiers who got lockjaw during WWII had somehow escaped the tetanus shot when they were inducted.

The following infection may cause only a low-grade fever and fatigue:

Tuberculosis is a bacterial infection due to the tubercle bacillus. Much time and expense devoted to quarantining cases practically wiped it out in the 1980s, but it is having a comeback. It is usually acquired by inhaling the bacteria exhaled from the tuberculous cavity in the lung of a diseased victim. The newly exposed victim may be able to trap and wall off the bacteria if his immune system is working well, so that adjacent tissue is not destroyed. At the height of this reaction, an X ray of the lungs may reveal a small shadow at the periphery of the lungs plus an enlarged lymph node close to the main bronchus (called a primary complex). About six weeks after this initial contact, the body forms a sensitivity to bacillus and the skin test becomes positive.

If not walled off and calcified, the original contaminated area may spread to new patches of lung, or bacteria may be carried to other organs of the body. TB is usually diagnosed by the positive skin test. Positive reactors are X rayed to determine the extent of the disease. All contacts are similarly investigated.

Treatment is instituted for:

1. All children under five years of age with positive skin tests;

2. All children and adolescents who have demonstrated a recent tuberculin skin test change from negative to positive;

3. All who have been in recent contact with an open case (contagious or usually cavity-containing adult) regardless of the skin test response.

CHAPTER 7

Possible Concerns

These May Interfere with a Healthy Life

ASPARTAME, UNNATURALLY SWEET

If you hit your head and you get a headache, you have learned not to hit your head. It makes sense. Your body is saying, "Try not to do that anymore." Knives are sharp; if you cut yourself, you bleed. It is the way things are. Gravity works. Water is wet. But if you get symptoms, and they don't make sense, you should consider a sensitivity. Your body is trying to tell you in the only way it knows how. "Stop and think a minute," it is saying. "What happened immediately before those symptoms appeared? What am I doing now that is different from when I had no _____ ?" (Fill in the blank with *headache, confusion, memory loss, dizziness, blindness, tremors, bloody nose, sneezing, muscle aches, gas, rash, insomnia, depression,* etc.) If you smoke and get a cough, your body is sending a signal. If you stop drinking coffee and get a headache, does that mean you should drink a cup every three hours? Well, no.

If your youngster has started to imbibe a couple of diet drinks every day or so and now seems "different," does it mean anything or are you being paranoid? I have largely given up coffee, which I used to crave (read: *be addicted to*), and find no joy in diet drinks, so I don't know what symptoms my body would use to signal that I am sensitive to aspartame.

Dr. Paul Toft, a chiropractor practicing in Minnesota, told me of his inappropriate depression; there was no reason for his sadness. He heard of the risks of taking aspartame (ASP) while watching a television show. He was smart enough to stop eating anything with ASP in it, and in a few weeks he became symptom-free. (Television can be valuable.)

The Food and Drug Administration (FDA) gets more calls related to the reactions to aspartame (Equal, NutraSweet) than anything else in the marketplace. It is being consumed by two hundred million persons because it is in over five thousand products. That agency, however, refuses to remove it, as these stories are just "anecdotes," and do not represent any scientific study. They claim that aspartame has been tested for reactions more than anything else they've had to survey. According to the FDA, animal and human tests conducted since the 1970s indicated that it was a safe sweetener. It has been termed a food additive—not a drug—and any reactions need not be reported to a federal agency, nor is continued safety monitoring required by law.

The Centers for Disease Control (CDC) reports receiving many letters with complaints of untoward effects from the use of aspartame. Here is a quote from the National Soft Drink Association: "There have been hundreds of reports suggesting a possible relationship between consumption of NutraSweet and subsequent symptoms including headaches, aberrational behavior, and slurred speech."

FDA Commissioner Arthur Hull Hayes, Jr., was appointed head of the FDA in 1981, and despite a flood of questions about the safety of aspartame for human consumption, he approved its use in dry foods in that same year. *Science Times* reported in 1985 that he had approved of the product based on studies that were "scientifically lacking in design and execution." Note this follow-up: Hayes was hired as senior medical consultant for Burson-Marsteller, the public relations firm retained by G. D. Searle, the pharmaceutical firm that introduced NutraSweet.

How did all this happen? A researcher happened to lick his fingers after mixing up some chemicals that he was working on for a control of stomach maladies. It was very sweet (160 times as sweet as sugar with virtually no calories). What a find for weight-conscious Americans who need the sweet fix but do not want the calories. Aspartame contains:

- Phenylalanine (50 percent), a neurotoxin that will cause seizures in susceptible persons; its toxic effects are cumulative and may not show up in short-term testing; it lowers or blocks the production of serotonin, thus causing craving for carbohydrates, increase in PMS symptoms, insomnia, mood swings, aberrant behaviors, and depression;

- Aspartic acid (40 percent), which can cause brain damage in the developing brain; has caused holes in the brains of laboratory animals;

- Methyl ester (10 percent), which becomes free methyl alcohol, a poison itself, and which is metabolized into formaldehyde (embalming fluid), formic acid (ant sting venom), and DKP (a brain tumor agent).

They all have adverse effects, but not everyone is affected equally. Therein lies the problem: If everyone who ingested the stuff got a headache, the FDA would have pulled it off the Generally Regarded As Safe list (GRAS). Since all those people are on Equal or NutraSweet from all those food and soft drink products, prescriptions, and over-the-counter drugs, more reports should be noted. Susceptibility seems to be a partial reason.

Headache is the most common symptom reported, but there are seventy others including nausea, vertigo, insomnia, numbness of extremities, blurred vision, blindness, memory loss, slurred speech, suicidal depression, personality changes, hyperactivity in adults and children, seizures, rashes, anxiety, muscle and joint pain, loss of energy, menstrual cramps, tachycardia, hearing loss, weight gain, and death (five of the latter). Anything can do anything.

Sensitive people would more likely notice the connection between ingestion and symptoms. Some do not notice anything until they stop, and then they feel better. Mary Nash Stoddard of the Aspartame Consumer Safety Network (P.O. Box 780634, Dallas, TX 75378) has received reports from pilots who have noticed the connection of aspartame use and near misses in their flying machines. The FAA does not officially recognize aspartame reactions. Many pilots have lost their certificates to fly when they reported to their flight doctors that they cannot see or have had seizures—obviously a contraindication to piloting a plane. Mary has received over six hundred pilot-related calls from 1988 to 1995.

Are you riding in a car driven by an aspartame user? "Accidents underscore the need for further inquiry into . . . . driver error: confusion and aberrant behavior caused by products containing aspartame."[190] Dr. H. J. Roberts further notes, "To my knowledge no extensive trials on humans were done or published prior to approval of aspartame. I have data on more than 630 patients and correspondents with reactions attributed to aspartame-containing products, some life-threatening. Over 123 individuals experienced seizures."[191]

In a recent letter to the *JAMA (Journal of the American Medical Association)*, Roberts writes: "I recommend that this synthetic supplement be removed as an 'imminent public health hazard.' Two other possible aspartame-related problems are of concern: the acceleration of Alzheimer's disease and brain cancer. The latter was demonstrated in several animal studies long *before* the arbitrary approval of aspartame for human use."[192]

Researcher Diana Dow Edwards (Brooklyn, S.U.N.Y.) discovered that aspartame ingestion caused birth defects. NutraSweet yanked her funding.

Whom can we trust? I thought these government agencies were supposed to protect the innocent public. Does money mean that much to some people that they would jeopardize our health? How many employees of Searle drink the stuff?

FLUORIDE: IS IT GOOD FOR US?

Fluoride may be a nutritionally important mineral for teeth and bones. "It is also well established in biochemistry that fluoride is a very potent enzyme poison. Its anti-enzyme activity does much to explain why fluoride is a carcinogen—it enhances the cancer-causing potential of other substances."[193] In 1993 the United States National Research Council pointed out that "Fluoride is no longer considered an essential factor for human growth and development"[194] This was a follow-up of their statement in 1971: "That in itself is no indication of fluorine essentiality, inasmuch as caries incidence depends on many factors, and many persons with perfectly sound dentition have had only minimal exposure to fluoride."[195]

From John Yiamouyiannis, Ph.D., the world's leading fluoride researcher, "The question remains: Does fluoride reduce tooth decay? The answer is contained in the largest study on fluoridation and tooth decay ever done in the United States.[196] In this study of over 39,000 children, ages five to seventeen years, from 84 areas throughout the United States, it was shown fluoridation did not reduce the decay of permanent teeth. It did show that fluoridation apparently interfered with the eruption of baby teeth and, as a result, reduced the decay rate of the baby teeth of five-year-olds by about 40 percent. However, as the number of erupted baby teeth among children living in fluoridated areas caught up with the number of erupted teeth among their counterparts in nonfluoridated areas, so did the decay rates of their baby teeth. Among six- and seven-year olds, there was only an 18 percent and 11 percent reduction in the decay of baby teeth of children living in fluoridated areas. Among eight-year-olds, there was no reduction."

Poisoning of the teeth by fluoride is called *dental fluorosis*. Dr. Yiamouyiannis continues, "Fluorosis has been reported in eight to 51 percent of the children living in fluoridated areas in the United States, and while four studies published in the *Journal of the American Medical Association* have shown that fluoridation leads to increased hip fracture rates, not a single case of a person with fluoride deficiency (poor bones, poor teeth, poor health, poor anything) has ever been found." [197, 198]

Fluoridation as a public health measure was considered after a low cavity rate was discovered by Dr. George Heard in the people living in Deaf Smith County, Texas. The researchers who came to Texas at Dr. Heard's request attributed the low decay rates to fluoride (2.6 milligrams/liter) in the drinking water. But the water that seeps through the strata in Deaf Smith County also contains calcium (fifty-one milligrams per liter), magnesium (forty-seven milligrams), sodium (ninety-two milligrams), chloride (thirty-four milligrams), sulfate (one hundred thirty-seven milligrams), nitrates (five milligrams), and other minerals. The water has a hardness factor of 321. I got this information from the chief engineer of the city of Hereford, Texas, the county seat of Deaf Smith County. For his part, Dr. Heard felt it was the good diet, especially the consumption of fresh dairy products from the area, not the fluoride in the water, that was responsible for the low tooth decay rate in Deaf Smith County. [199]

Teeth, like bone, need calcium, a protein matrix, magnesium, phosphate, and many trace minerals to make them tough and last a lifetime. A study twenty years ago in New Zealand showed that molybdenum was related to a reduced rate of decayed/missing/filled children's teeth in that country. Strontium and boron have also been linked to reduced tooth decay rates. [200] A key factor, of course, is the sugar intake of the average U.S. citizen: one hundred pounds per year. But it is not just the sugar passing over the teeth that allows the bacteria to eat away at the enamel. Other causes are obviously operating, such as heredity, diet, toothbrushing, not flossing, vomiting, amount of saliva, acidity of mouth. The type of bacteria in the mouth will contribute to the state of the enamel. The key mineral for the protection of teeth and the integrity of bones is magnesium, not fluoride.

Decades ago medical doctors used fluoride to suppress thyroid activity in patients with hyperthyroidism. The FL-ion replaces the iodine-ion and the thyroxin hormone becomes useless. Fluoride depresses metabolic activity. Is it possible that the FL-ion is now contributing to the incidence of chronic fatigue syndrome, which is such a popular diagnosis today?

According to the handbook *Clinical Toxicology of Commercial Products* (1984) fluoride is more poisonous than lead, and just slightly less poisonous than arsenic. It severely truncates the immune system, leads to bone cancer, and has a number of other known harmful effects—information that has been withheld from the public by the very people who are supposed to lead us to good health. It can cause nausea and vomiting, weakness, unusual excitement, skin rashes, sores in the mouth and on the lips, and pain and aching of bones. Many European countries have outlawed fluoridation of water supplies because of its known dangers.

Consider the following facts and their sources, and ask yourself why you have not previously been made aware of them.

- *Physicians' Desk Reference:* "Dental fluorosis [mottling] may result.... In hypersensitive individuals, fluorides occasionally cause skin eruptions such as atopic dermatitis, eczema, or urticaria. Gastric distress, headaches, and weakness have also been reported. These hypersensitive reactions usually disappear promptly after discontinuation of the fluoride."

- *Canadian Dental Association:* "Fluoride supplements should *not* be recommended for children less than three years old."

- *New England Journal of Medicine:* On March 22, 1990, an article reported fluoride treatment of osteoporosis caused increased hip fractures and bone fragility.

- *National Institute of Environmental Health,* 1993: "In cultured human and rodent cells, the weight of the evidence leads to the conclusion that fluoride exposure results in increased chromosome aberrations, i.e., genetic damage."

- *National Cancer Institute:* Dr. Dean Burk, former chief chemist, reported that ten thousand or more fluoride-linked, cancer-caused deaths occur yearly in the United States.

- *National Cancer Institute, New Jersey Department of Health, and Safe-Water Foundation* all found incidences of osteosarcoma, a type of bone cancer, far higher in young men exposed to fluoridated water compared to those who were not.

- A New Zealand study involving sixty thousand twelve- to thirteen-year-old children showed no difference in tooth decay whether the children were getting fluoride or not. Additionally, fluorosis was also found in the fluoridated areas.

Despite all these negative studies, the American Academy of Pediatrics still recommends daily fluoride supplementation: none for the first six months of life, 0.25 parts per million (ppm) for the six-month-old to the three-year-old, 0.5 ppm for the three- to six-year-old, and 1.0 ppm for the six- to sixteen-year-olds.

There is no difference in the decay rate in non-fluoridated area as in fluoridated ones. This is true all over the world.

The constant use of fluoridated water takes its toll on human health. Dental fluorosis (early fluoride poisoning) first appears as a chalky white area on the tooth. In advanced cases, teeth become yellow, brown, or black, and the tips may break off. If a child is poorly nourished, it only takes as little as 0.4 ppm of fluoride to produce dental fluorosis.

In 1985 Japanese researchers proved that only 0.2 ppm is capable of weakening the immune system. Fluoride has been shown to transform normal cells into cancer cells.

Over the last few years, court cases have shown that fluoride is a threat to the public health as it leads to cancer, brittle bones, wrinkled skin, arthritis, and torn ligaments. It may also cause genetic damage. In animal studies, water fluoridated at 1 ppm had increased tumor growth rates by 25 percent.

Topical fluoride is practically ineffective in reducing tooth decay.[201] A family-sized seven-ounce tube of fluoridated toothpaste contains enough fluoride to kill a child weighing less than twenty pounds. Fluoridated toothpaste has been shown to cause acne around the mouth.

"Relief from this poison must come via the legislative process. And there is no question that the legislature does have the legal authority to forbid the addition of fluoride to public water supplies,"[202] says Dr. Yiamouyiannis. "With truth as an ally, it's a lot easier to win. The truth is, fluoridation is chronically poisoning millions."

Dr. Richard Foulkes feels that there has been incalculable harm done to the environment. He wonders if the decrease in the salmon population might be due to this very toxic chemical running through the fish. Tons of fluoride are used, and the children who are supposed to profit from its use receive about one percent of the total output.[203]

IMMUNIZATIONS: THREAT OR MENACE?

Immunization is the artificial development of disease resistance achieved by forcing the body to respond to inoculation with dead or attenuated germs, viruses, and toxins. The body responds with its immune mechanisms, producing "memory" antibodies. When the system is next challenged with the actual disease germs or viruses, the already alert white cells and immune globulins are able to resist immediately without having to go through the "learning" process. In the unimmunized child—so goes the logic—the delay in the initial sensitizing process required to mobilize these defenses may be lethal; therefore the baby shots are usually begun in the first two or three months of life before some friendly neighborhood carrier breathes on the susceptible infant. Forty years of experimenting with the immune systems of humans (and animals) have proven that Mother Nature does it better. The immunity derived from most vaccinations is not complete and is temporary at best. And for many it is very dangerous, even lethal. The term *immunization* gives one a false sense of security; better to call them shots and drop the term *vaccines*.

The body has tremendous potential for keeping us well if modern medicine and diet are not rude to it. Immunization shots act as stressors to the immune system, and allow the invasion of the very diseases from which the shots were designed to protect us. The development of the child's immune system largely takes place naturally between birth and ten years of age.

Dr. Randall Neustaedter suggests that parents, when faced with the decision to allow their child to be vaccinated, do the following:

1. Get information about the vaccines;

2. Decide which vaccines you do or don't want;

3. If you decide to vaccinate your child, choose the right time.[204]

The following is the schedule of immunizations currently recommended by the American Academy of Pediatrics:[205]

Birth	HBV (hepatitis B vaccine) (see Newborn, Chapter 2)
One to two months	HBV
Two and four months	DPT (diphtheria, pertussis, tetanus) Hib (Haemophilus influenza bacteria) OPV (oral polio vaccine)
Six months	DPT, Hib
Six to eighteen months	HBV, OPV
Twelve to fifteen months	Hib, MMR (measles, mumps, rubella)
Fifteen to eighteen months	DPT
Four to six years	DPT, OPV
Eleven to twelve years	MMR
Fourteen to sixteen years	DT

That's a lot of shots.

Diphtheria/whooping cough/tetanus (DPT).

Diphtheria is extremely rare now. (Dr. Mendelsohn reports, "During a 1969 outbreak of diphtheria in Chicago, four of the sixteen victims had been fully immunized against the disease."[206])

Pertussis (whooping cough) is still seen in those who have had all the shots. This is odd, since three shots will produce an antibody response in 95 percent. But the rise in the antibody titer is only a part of the body's immune response; other parts of the immune system (cellular response) have not been activated. In addition, the whooping cough germs in the vaccine cause alarming reactions. In 1995 Dr. Anthony Fauci, director of the National Institute of Allergy and Infectious Diseases, said that the vaccine has controlled the disease in the United States for many years, safely and effectively. Really? Where has he been?

Whooping cough is not as severe as it was just a few decades ago. The children are sick, but the degree of illness depends upon the immune system they are carrying around. Many of the children had the complete series and even a booster at eighteen months, and they still got whooping cough. The statistics reveal that the incidence and the severity of whooping cough was decreasing in the 1930s, before the widespread use of the pertussis vaccine. The statistics from an outbreak in Cincinnati in 1993 showed that most of the children who came down with pertussis had had their complete series of shots and the booster.[207] (82 percent of those seven to seventy-one months old had received at least three doses of DPT vaccine.)

In the United Kingdom, since 1970, more than two hundred thousdand cases of whooping cough have occurred in fully vaccinated children.[208] Many families refused the immunizations because of the reactions. Since the decline in pertussis immunizations, England and Sweden have noted fewer hospital admissions and death rates from whooping cough. The U.S. is number twenty on the infant mortality list in the world. Is "unconscionable" the right term?

In Australia half of the population is immunized and half is not; the incidence of the diseases is the same in each group. Dr. Archie Kalokerinos wrote a book delineating his experiences with the Australian government's vaccine program to improve the health of the Aborigines. Every other child he immunized died within a few days of the DPT shots. Dr. Kalokerinos's recourse was to administer, at his own expense, one hundred milligrams of vitamin C per month of age per day to each of his patients receiving the vaccine. (The six-month-old would get six hundred milligrams, the one to two-year-old received a thousand milligrams of C, and the two-year-old received two grams, and so on until age ten, after which the dose stayed at ten grams daily.) Result: No child died when on his regimen. He became convinced that sudden infant death syndrome (SIDS) was related to the DPT shots.[209]

However, the American Academy of Pediatrics says that SIDS is most common in the second to sixth month of age, so the connection of the DPT and SIDS is not causal, but coincidental. But in the 1970s, the authorities in Japan suggested that there might be a connection and told the health authorities to give the DPT shots at age two instead. Result: SIDS disappeared in Japan.[210] But the incidence of other invasive bacterial infections rose significantly after age two years. (There goes the immune system again.)

Tetanus may follow a dirty puncture wound. It is a serious disease, and hits about one hundred people in the United States each year. The fatality rate of those under fifty is but 5 percent. Most of the victims are over fifty years of age, as most of the elderly have no circulating antibody to the tetanus toxin. The tetanus toxoid may be the more the logical approach to childhood immunizations. Think about this plan: Start the tetanus shot after your child is twelve months old—when he is walking around in the barnyard, and before he steps on the manure fork. (A booster at two years, five years, and every ten years throughout life makes sense.) Dr. Dick Thom feels as I do: "Because the tetanus germ is implanted into the body via a puncture, it follows that the tetanus shot makes some sense, as it is administered via a puncture shot."

Live poliomyelitis vaccine (oral polio vaccine, OPV) combining all three polio viruses is usually given orally along with the infant DPT shots. It is an attenuated virus and provides a mild or subliminal (unrecognized) disease in the intestinal-tract lining. If the "real thing" comes along later, the cells of the intestine are able to recognize it as an enemy, and destroy it before it invades the system. Randall again states, "All cases of paralytic polio in this country since 1979 were either caused by the oral vaccine or contracted in a foreign country during travel. During the period 1980–85, fifty-five cases of paralytic polio were reported."[211] He believes, "Since the risk of acquiring polio is near zero if a child is not immunized, it seems unjustifiable to risk polio from the live vaccine." He suggests another choice: Give the child the shot of the dead polio vaccine first. This provides a lowered level of antibody production, but more reactions. Then give the live polio drops at eighteen months.

It is interesting to note that although the Salk vaccine was credited with halting the United States polio epidemic in the late 1940s, the epidemic of polio in Europe ended at the same time without the benefit of the vaccine.

Haemophilus influenza bacteria vaccine (Hib). Because this bacteria can cause meningitis, otitis media, pneumonia, epiglottitis, and other serious infections, it has been thought that a vaccine administered to children would help to prevent these serious and sometimes fatal diseases. Ampicillin was formerly the drug of choice, but 40 percent of haemophilus is resistant to this drug. The shot is given early (two, four, and six months of age) to protect the susceptible infants, as the peak incidence of meningitis occurs in infants six to seven months of age. "The incidence of invasive disease caused by *H. influenzae* type b has declined dramatically since introduction of conjugate vaccination in the United States."[212] (American Academy of Pediatrics *Red Book*.) But life-threatening infection from Hib may still arise despite the Hib shot.[213] There was sharp decline in the incidence *before* the vaccine was licensed. Apparently these vaccines do not immunize—they sensitize and cause an increase in the recipient's susceptibility to infectious diseases.

The Hib was licensed in 1985. Centers for Disease Control researchers attributed the 90 percent decline in Hib to decreased transmission; however, Dr. Michael Osterholm found that 41 percent of Hib cases occurred in vaccinated children. Children were much more likely to get the disease if they had received the vaccine.[214] Whom do you believe?

The vaccine seems to impair the child's immune system. In addition there are serious reactions from the vaccine itself: convulsions, allergic reactions, and one fatality within four hours of the shot. Dr. Julie Milstien reports that there were sixty-three cases of proven H influenzai type b invasive disease that occurred soon after immunization with the vaccine that was supposed to prevent that same disease.[215] It makes one wonder about safety and efficacy.

Measles, mumps, and rubella vaccine (MMR). This three-in-one shot is usually given after twelve to fifteen months of age since the passive transfer of a mother's immunity to her baby may interfere with the MMR's ability to develop antibodies against these diseases in her baby. Since the vaccine for measles was licensed in 1963, there has been a decline in the incidence in young children. It is about 96 percent effective in raising the antibody titer, but that is apparently not enough as cases of hard measles (rubeola) are appearing in adolescents for the first time since 1965. Sixty to 90 percent of measles cases are occurring in fully immunized youngsters, and these cases cause more complications in the older age groups; the shots appear to be only delaying the disease.

Before the advent of the measles vaccine, 95 percent of the population over the age of fifteen was immune to measles, because practically everyone had contracted the disease. Now more and more adults are contracting hard measles (rubeola); it is a serious disease in adults. In states with comprehensive immunization requirements (kindergarten through twelfth grade), between 61 and 90 percent of measles cases occur in persons who were appropriately vaccinated (Markowitz, et al, 1989, quoted by Sam Pinkerton).

Or worse. Neustaedter quotes Dr. Richard Moskowitz: "It is not difficult to imagine that introducing the virus directly into the blood would continue to provoke an antibody response for a considerable period of time. Antibodies begin to be produced in large quantities against the cells themselves, and frank auto-immune phenomena of necrosis and tissue destruction supervene."[216] This might help to explain the relationship of postvaccine autism in those immunized against rubella; the antibody titer against the rubella virus often becomes astronomical.

D. L. Levy points out the long-term possibilities. "Despite short-term success in eliminating the disease, long-range projections demonstrate that the proportion of susceptibles in the year 2050 may be greater than in the prevaccine era. The susceptibility to sustain endemicity in a closed population is about six percent, which may allow for new epidemics in adults in the coming years."[217] What's next? A booster every five years?

The **mumps** vaccine was licensed in 1967. For the next two decades the incidence of mumps went down, but by 1987 the incidence went back up again. The disease has shifted to the older age groups, who are more susceptible now and are more likely to suffer from its complications. The solution the vaccine manufacturers give to this waning immunity is to give a booster shot of everything every five to ten years. Line up.

The **chicken pox** vaccine has just been released for use (1995). I would not trust it. Most vaccines are only protective for just a few years, if at all. The children who grow up without protection will be extremely ill when they get it as adults. It is a miserable, dangerous disease for adults and those with a truncated immune system. With the basic natural therapy, the disease can be controlled in children and they will be forever immune.

Conclusion: The shots do not provide complete protection like the immunity one gets from the disease itself. Use of the basic natural therapy (see page 158) during the body's struggle with the disease will assuage the virulence of the disease, and will still allow for complete and permanent immunity. Dr. Bernard Dixon writes in the *New Scientist* (July 5, 1979) that the World Health Organization concedes that the most effective type of immunization is good nutrition. The suffering third-world children have nutritional deficiencies, not vaccine deficiencies.

The American Academy of Pediatrics (AAP) states firmly: "In the United States, immunization has sharply curtailed, or practically eliminated, diphtheria, pertussis, tetanus, measles, mumps, rubella, poliomyelitis, and Haemophilus influenzae type b disease." That organization does not seem to be aware that these diseases were almost completely eliminated by the time the vaccines became available, and the diseases are still reported. A 90 percent decline in death rates from infectious disease occurred before vaccinations commenced. The *Red Book* again (p. 29): "Although modern immunizing agents are generally considered safe and effective, they are neither completely safe nor completely effective."

The AAP *1994 Red Book* clearly states that parents are to be informed of the risks and benefits of these vaccinations. "Questions should be encouraged so that the information is understood and coercion is avoided." The National Childhood Vaccine Injury Act of 1986 includes requirements for notifying parents about benefits and risks. Providing the appropriate vaccine information became mandatory in 1992. The funds have been exhausted, so the rules for vaccine injury compensation have become more rigid. "As of March 10, 1995, the only adverse events presumed to be associated with DPT vaccination are anaphylaxis occurring within four hours and encephalitis occurring within 72 hours of the DPT shot."[218] All other symptoms of brain injury will not be compensated. The academy feels that any reactions are usually mild to moderate in severity with no permanent sequelae, and only rarely is a reaction permanent. This seems well and good as long as it is not your child.

In the United States from 1990 to 1993, the FDA counted a total of fifty thousand adverse reactions following vaccination. The FDA admitted that this number represented only 10 percent of the real total, because most doctors were refusing to report vaccine injuries. In 1994 the Centers for Disease Control and Prevention in Atlanta, Georgia, monitored the status of half a million children who had received the DPT and the MMR shots. Thirty-four major side effects were reported, including asthma, blood disorders, diabetes, neurological disorders (polio, meningitis, and hearing loss), and the most upsetting of all, seizures. The rate of seizures increased three times above the norm within the first few days after the shots.

About 10 percent of babies suffer from persistent, piercing crying spells the day after receiving the DPT injection. These infants may have fever and drowsiness after the shot. The nervous system can be hurt from these shots; encephalitis may manifest subtly without fever and with minimal findings. Damage may not show until weeks or months later. The package insert from the vaccine supplier Connaught states, "In a large, case-control study in England, children two to thirty-five months of age with serious, acute neurologic disorders such as encephalopathy or complicated convulsions were more likely to have received DPT in the seven days preceding onset."

The Connaught Company (a DPT manufacturer) package insert (which doctors probably do not read to their patients' parents) also states, "Sudden Infant Death Syndrome (SIDS) has occurred in infants following administration of DPT." They quickly follow that statement with the point that there is no causal connection. The Centers for Disease Control has this to say (1992): "Every vaccine has risks as well as benefits. A few people may get sick. Very rarely, OPV causes polio. There is a very rare chance that other serious problems or even death could occur. The DPT shot: less often a child may have a convulsion, usually from high fever or shock collapse.... rarely brain damage that lasts for the child's life has been reported...."

A summary: "(1) Vaccines have immediate, sometimes drastic, side effects. (2) Vaccines have unknown, long-term side effects which may include post-encephalitis brain damage. (3) Vaccine efficacy may decrease over time, making children susceptible to the viral diseases as adults when the diseases are more serious."[219]

What is happening: Once an immune mechanism in the body becomes committed to a specific antigen (the bacteria or virus), it becomes incapable of responding to other challenges. The vaccines may be using up a large percent of the body's immune capacity, and the immunity they provide is apparently incomplete and temporary. Immunizations reduce the reserve immune capacity: immunologic bankrupcy. "Natural immunity in the healthy person is based on a series of body defenses. When the vaccines are injected directly into the body they bypass the outer defenses of the body."[220] Apparently all parts of the immune defense system need to be stimulated to provide permanent immunity. "In a study done on the effects on the helper/suppressor ratio (lymphocyte subsets) of routine tetanus immunization in eleven healthy adults, it was found that there was a significant though temporary drop of T-helper cells in four of the eleven subjects."[221] If that happens to healthy adults, what about the effects of the routine immunizations on infants with their immature immune systems?

There are two subclasses of T-helper cells circulating in the body. One is a "memory" cell, which is permanently committed to a former antigenic challenge, whether virus, bacteria, toxin, or vaccine. Those cells cannot respond to new challenges. The other cell is a "naive" cell, which acts as a reservoir for new invasive challenges. The massive influx of antigenic stimuli in the form of vaccines into the child's immature immune system could force many naive cells to become memory cells, using up the naive ones, and causing an imbalance in the immune system. Asthma, frequent infections, autoimmune diseases, and chronic fatigue could follow.[222]

When a child recovers from a disease, he becomes permanently immune to that particular disease, and only a small part of his immune system's capacity has been committed. In developing natural immunity by actually having the disease, only tiny amounts of antigenic material are usually sufficient to induce immunity, leaving the reserve capacity of the immune system relatively unaffected.

Ear infections are much more common in vaccinated children. Autism has appeared within a few weeks of the MMR shot. (Cindy Goldenberg describes her son's struggle with autism after he received the MMR vaccine at thirteen months.[223]) Chronic, degenerative diseases have been reported to follow vaccination: multiple sclerosis, asthma (six times more frequent in children receiving the pertussis vaccine than those not receiving it.[224]), increased blood pressure, ADD (which has increased in the past twenty to thirty years), increased rate of personality and behavioral changes, auto-immune diseases, allergies, and cancer have occurred since immunizations have been initiated, and the dramatic rise in violent behavior since the 1960s could, in part, be related to the mass immunization program forced upon our children.[225] The nervous system is especially vulnerable to a damaged immune system. A large U.S. military base was shut down because of an epidemic of meningitis; the stricken soldiers were healthy, but freshly vaccinated, recruits.[226]

Ronald G. Lanfranchi, D.C., Ph.D., of New York City, has a suggestion: "Conduct a twenty- to thirty-year study of matched groups of vaccinated versus non-vaccinated in which all problems would be recorded and compared." He continues, "If the government is going to force us to put known toxins into our children, they have a tremendous responsibility to be absolutely sure of the outcome." Let the parents decide if they want their children immunized, as is done in Australia.

Here is a caveat from my friend Dr. Bruce West: "Once all girls are vaccinated, and they grow up and have their own kids, where will their kids get their natural immunity?" He answered his own question with: "This nightmare is already upon us with measles. In 1990 there were ninety deaths from measles. Almost half of these occurred in appropriately vaccinated children. According to the National Vaccine Information Center, the main reason for the increase in measles was that vaccinated mothers were unable to pass on protective antibodies to their infants."[227]

Why must all these vaccines be thrown at children during infancy? The immature immune system is already struggling to handle a few, simple cold viruses.

If these vaccinations are so safe and effective, why must they be made compulsory? If they were safe and effective, I would think people would be knocking on the doctors' doors for them. Forcing the shots on the public seems odd, given that the dangers and ineffectiveness of the vaccines have been well documented in prestigious medical and scientific journals. Studies have shown no difference in incidence or severity of whooping cough between the vaccinated and the unvaccinated children. The fatality rate of those children suffering from whooping cough under one year of age increases if they have had the vaccine; that would indicate the truncated immune system. In studies done on children in day-care facilities, it has been documented that these children were both more likely to be vaccinated and at a higher risk of contracting invasive bacterial infections. (This argues for the use of daily vitamin C as an immune booster for children in day care.) Epidemics of whooping cough occur every three to four years whether children have been immunized or not.

The idea of freedom of choice for parents seems to be the logical resolution of this dilemma. But if you decide to have your child get the shots, at least give the child one thousand milligrams of vitamin C, five hundred milligrams of calcium, and a hundred milligrams of B$_6$ the day before, the day of, and the day after the shot to help hold the child's immune system together during that stressful time.

It appears to me that we should let Mother Nature have her way with our children; that is, let them have these inevitable childhood diseases, but only if the children have the immune systems strong enough to breeze right through them and gain permanent, complete immunity. The greatest gift you can give to your child is a healthy immune system.

BUT IT TASTES SO GOOD

Junk Food Wrecks the Brain. We had always thought it was just that foods were impoverished from being grown on depleted topsoil, or there was too much sugar added, or that the vitamins and minerals had been removed to prolong shelflife. Now we find out that some nasties have been added, some by accident, and some on purpose to keep the bugs from eating the foods until they get to market. In a study reported in the *Archives of Environmental Health* in 1982, Thatcher and colleagues found high levels of cadmium in hair samples from children who had been eating large amounts of refined carbohydrates: "The higher the proportion of the diet attributable to junk food, the higher the amount of cadmium in their hair." Tests scores on the children showed a negative effect on learning skills. You would think that if the foods were so processed and purified, there would be less heavy metals. In whole wheat there is a distinct ratio between zinc and cadmium, and the zinc keeps the cadmium in check so that it does not exert a toxic effect. However, in the refining of the grain, the zinc is lost, but the cadmium remains. The cadmium is a toxic threat, because there is no longer the buffering action of the zinc. Violent youths have high amounts of lead and cadmium in their hair.

"The persistent toxicity of lead was seen to result in significant and serious impairment of academic success, specifically a sevenfold increase in failure to graduate from high school, lower class standing, greater absenteeism, impairment of reading skills sufficiently extensive to be labelled reading disability, and deficits in vocabulary, fine motor skills, reaction time, and hand-eye coordination."[228]

Pesticides and herbicides are in our foods. Each manufacturer and food producer believes that the amount is not sufficient to poison anyone because they are following government guidelines for their particular chemical. No one seems to be aware that these biocides (means "kills life") are additive and they may not hurt the unwary until twenty years have elapsed between exposure and disease (cancer, allergy, asthma, lupus, chronic fatigue, nervous and endocrine system dysfunction, and birth defects).

Acute organophosphate toxicity may simulate the flu or the "crud" that is going around. The symptoms of headache, nausea, and irritability only show that something has invaded the body. But any symptom means that the body's detoxification processes (the liver mainly) have been overloaded. It could mean that the immune system has been truncated by vaccines, stress, parents' tobacco smoke, nitrates and heavy-metal poisoning, and only a little whiff of some herbicide cloud on the neighbor's field would be enough to allow immune failure. Pesticides are widely used in the United States to improve crop yields, but public health is at risk from this practice. In addition, many farmers only use nitrates, potassium, and phosphates as soil additives, without regard for some of the trace minerals, such as molybdenum, chromium, selenium, and zinc so important for the detoxification system. The Delaney Clause—an amendment to the Federal Food, Drug, and Cosmetic Act that calls for zero cancer-causing pesticide residues in processed foods—does not regulate raw food such as meat, fruit, vegetables, and dairy products. Despite that amendment, pesticide use has increased from five hundred million pounds (in 1959) to more than one billion pounds per year in our country in 1990. The Environmental Protection Agency estimates that 270 pesticides are used on food crops, and sometimes more than one pesticide is used.

Children are at special risk because of rapid growth and their consumption of high amounts of fruits and juices per pound of weight. According to the booklet *Pesticides and Children,* more than 80 percent of supermarket fruit and vegetable samples (tested from 1990 to 1992) contained more than one carcinogenic pesticide.[229] The consumption of fruits and vegetables by the average one-year-old is two to seven times greater than the national mean. In addition, "10 percent of community water system wells and 4 percent of domestic wells contained one or more pesticides. In the Midwest and Louisiana, eleven million people drink herbicide-contaminated water. Children are exposed to 'cides on pets, at school, at home, and especially if they live on a farm. They get hit from multiple sites."

If you can smell it, you are ingesting it, and it is having some effect on you. (I was aware of an infant who began to have seizures because of out-gassing from the formaldehyde of a new mobile home, plus kerosene from a lamp. Anticonvulsive medications stopped the seizures, if he was given a dose strong enough to put him to sleep. The parents moved to an older, chemical-free home and the seizures slowed. They increased again when he was two and ate some pesticide-laced watermelon from Northern California in 1990. Blood tests showed he was very alkaline. Vinegar ingestion helped to decrease the frequency of the seizures.) "Organophosphates and carbamates interfere with the normal function of the nervous system by blocking the action of cholinesterase, an enzyme essential for degrading the neurotransmitter acetylcholine. Acute poisoning by the compounds can cause diarrhea, muscle twitching, visual disturbances, hypertension, mood swings, respiratory distress, and death."[230] The combined dose of insecticides can easily exceed the EPA's safe dose for these organophosphates. "Safe tolerance levels are set on the assumption that only one residue occurs at a time on a serving, but much of the food we eat actually has multiple residues of pesticides, " stated Philip Landrigan, M.D., M.Sc.[231]

"Depending on the dose, some pesticides can cause a range of adverse effects on human health including cancer, acute and chronic injury to the nervous system, lung damage, reproductive dysfunction, and possibly dysfunction of the endocrine and immune systems. The committee found that foods eaten by infants and children are underrepresented in surveys of commodity residues."[232]

Pollutants may cause depression at exposure levels about 1/10 to 1/100 of those that produce overt symptoms of clinical poisoning.[233] Research has shown that very small amounts of organophosphate pesticide can stimulate inflammatory responses in mast cells and basophils, the cells responsible for initiating allergic reactions.[234]

The cancers that have been prevalent in farm workers have now begun to affect the general population. Brain and nervous tissue tumors and acute lymphocytic leukemia in children have increased more than 25 percent from the 1970s to the 1990s. There are reasons for these increases. In the 1970s alar was found to be carcinogenic, but growers continued to use alar to make fruits ripen simultaneously and also to prolong their shelflife. Finally the alar alert in 1986 encouraged consumers to avoid apples and their juices and sauces. But it was not until 1989 that the EPA announced that alar was probably carcinogenic. Finally the manufacturer halted sales of alar in the United States. (It is still sold and used overseas. Do you buy overseas-grown apples?)

"Exposures to carcinogenic pesticides in food occur disproportionately during infancy and childhood. For instance, by age six the average American child has accumulated about thirty-five percent of the allowable life-time cancer risk from captan, a fungicide used frequently on apples, grapes, and peaches and considered a probable human carcinogen."[235] There doesn't seem to be any good news about the use of 'cides on growing foods. Reports show that the bugs become resistant to the pesticides, and the growers have to change to more toxic ones. It is similar to the growing resistance of bacteria to the various antibiotics. Eco-agriculture, as encouraged by Acres, USA,[236] is showing the way to healthy crops and a nil use of 'cides.

Look for "certified organically grown" foods at your grocery store. If you do not find them, ask the manager to get them. Greater demand for pesticide-free foods will encourage farmers to change to eco-farming. Have you noticed that dogs prefer to drink water in the toilet bowl after flushing? Their sensitive noses tell them that the chlorine is dangerous to their health. (The flushing discharges the chlorine into the air.) Chlorine can affect us if we shower too long; we have washed off the natural oils, and the chlorinated chemicals can be absorbed through the naked, unprotected skin.

Our drinking water poses health risks from pollutants such as bacteria, viruses, lead, pesticides, radon, and radioactive waste. Dr. J. Gordon Millichap writes about these pollutants in his book and suggests ways to minimize exposure.[237] "Enteric viruses may be present in drinking water without signs of bacterial pollution." One third of all bottled water sold in the United States is actually taken from a public water system. Polluted river sources that have been chlorinated carry the highest risk of cancer. Glass bottles for water are safer. The use of aluminum and iron salts, sulfates, and polymers in the purification of water may introduce hazards. Mercury is discharged into rivers and lakes from industrial sources. The amount of mercury found in fish may be three thousand times the original concentration in the contaminated water. "Chlorinated hydrocarbon insecticides are the most ubiquitous and persistent pesticides in the environment."[238]

So what are we supposed to do until the Department of Agriculture and the farmers decide to stop this crazy, unnatural, inappropriate, counterproductive, dangerous pesticide use?

• Improve your and your child's liver-detoxifying abilities. One phase of liver detoxification is through cytochrome P450 mixed-function oxidase, a group of enzymes. These enzymes metabolize the invading chemicals that find their way into our bodies via the skin, the lungs, and the intestines by an oxidation process or by a biotransformation method. The liver then converts them by conjugation into products that are excreted via the bile or through the urine. These foreign chemicals cannot be detoxified unless nutrition is adequate at least; the more toxins entering the body, the more the nutrients are required. Dr. Jeffrey Bland, in a study of 350 children with a variety of neurological problems, found that they were getting more toxins from the gut and were less able to detoxify them in the liver. This impacted their brain chemistry. When the gut mucosa is disturbed, holes are created that allow passage of various substances that put a burden upon the liver. The liver attempts to detoxify these substances, but the by-products of this process create superoxide, hydroxyl radicals, and hydrogen peroxide. These substances cause oxidative stress to the brain, the heart, and the kidneys. These substances can interfere with the ability of the brain to detoxify its own neurotransmitters. Too much or too little of these NTs will alter brain function. There is as much as a thirtyfold difference in the range of detoxification abilities in people. Dr. Bland raises the question, "Is it because intermediary compounds have not been correctly produced, detoxified, and excreted?"

When Bland analyzed the 350 children for glutathione levels, he found many were very low in blood glutathione. They could not make it or they were under high oxidative stress, causing the depletion. He feels that if children have sustained brain-stem, cortical, or midbrain injuries, oxidants were affecting their brain chemistries. Many of these neurologically damaged children have shallow breathing, low activity, compressed chests, poor posture, and low oxygen use. The low oxygen tension is paradoxically the time when the brain is under oxidative stress. The treatment for the chemically sensitive people, those hurt by the pesticides, and the damaged children left to lie huddled up in hospital beds: vitamins C and E, bio-flavonoids, coenzyme Q10, selenium, and zinc. The grape-seed powder has antioxidant properties.[239] The children need to move about, to breathe. Neurodevelopmental training seems appropriate also.

• Try to eat certified organic food, as raw as possible. Try not to eat packaged, processed food. Eat foods that will rot, but eat them before they do rot. Avoid monosodium glutamate, aspartame, red and yellow food dyes, sulfites, nitrites, BHA, BHT—if you can.

A POISON IN YOUR HEAD

Mercury/Silver Amalgam Fillings. Ever since Dr. Weston Price documented the absence of decay in the teeth of tribal people because of their wholesome diet, I have become convinced that even one cavity in one tooth indicates that the victim is already nutritionally flawed. God and Mother Nature intended our permanent teeth to be permanent, or they would have given us another set to erupt at age forty-five years or so. Dr. Price found his subjects had beautiful teeth—uncrowded and free of holes. "Store-bought food gives us store-bought teeth."

We are all stuck with some cavities due to our mother's diet when she was carrying us, and the goodies she gave us if we finished our supper. We may be down to an irreducible minimum of the decayed/missing/filled (DMF) rate. Nutritional supplements can only do so much. So we have to have cavities filled.

In the last few decades, people have begun to question the safety of the silver/mercury amalgam fillings. The American Dental Association has taken the firm stand that, since this mixture has been used extensively for more than 150 years and they have heard so few complaints, it must be safe. Despite that reassurance, many people have had their amalgams removed and replaced with gold or composite fillings. "The United States Public Health Service considers mercury exposure from dental amalgam to present a risk to patients, and renders all previous position of USPHS and its agencies obsolete and invalid."[240]

Hal Huggins, D.D.S., advocates the removal of mercury from the body. After all, he says, it is a very poisonous substance, and over time, the mercury is released from the filling and the body stores it. Although his case histories are largely anecdotal, he has seen near miracles when patients have the mercury dug out and replaced with some inert substance. He has seen anxiety, multiple sclerosis, arthritis, dementia, and whatever clear up after these replacements. But we had all thought the stuff was safely tucked away inside the enamel cusps. How could it get out?

Experiments on humans and animals have shown that the mercury half of the amalgam mixture slowly erodes away and becomes airborne, traveling from the mouth into the lungs and to the kidneys and brain, predominantly. It can be found all over the body and becomes covalently bound to cell proteins—maybe not much, but just enough to do something to some people. Not everyone is affected, obviously.

However:

• In 1986 Lars Friberg was the lead author on a major scientific paper demonstrating a direct correlation between the number and size of amalgam dental fillings and the amount of mercury contamination in the brain (*Bio-Probe Newsletter,* Sept. 1994).

• Dr. Alfred Zamm, M.D., quoted in the *Bio-Probe Newsletter* says, "The chemically intolerant and the mercury intolerant are, in fact, one group."[241]

• "There are now three animal studies and one human autopsy study clearly demonstating the transfer of dental amalgam mercury from the fillings of pregnant females into the fetal brain tissue." (This from the *Bio-Probe Newsletter,* Sept. 1995, referring to a research article.[242])

• The total mercury concentrations in the liver, kidneys, and brains of 108 children and forty-five fetuses correlated with the number of dental amalgam fillings of the mother. The infants had died suddenly and most were diagnosed with sudden infant death syndrome. These concentrations demonstrate the transfer of mercury from the fillings of the mothers to the tissues of their babies.[243]

• Christer Malmstrom, D.D.S., of Sweden: "Our results show that amalgam dental fillings expose children to considerable amounts of mercury."[244] In February 1994, the government of Sweden publicly announced the final timetable for the ban on the use of mercury/silver amalgam as a dental filling material. The ban took effect in July of 1995 for children and will take effect in 1997 for adults.

There does not seem to be any safe level of mercury in the body. It can affect any tissue of the body, but the immune system is particularly vulnerable; it is a favorite target of mercury. There is good evidence that low-level exposure to mercury vapor has adverse effects on the immune system of genetically susceptible animals.[245] Dental amalgam and dental nickel alloys can adversely affect the quantity of T-lymphocytes.[246] T-lymphocytes are part of the immune system. Silver dental fillings provoke an increase in mercury and antibiotic-resistant bacteria in the mouths and intestines of primates.[247] Dental amalgam is a greater source of mercury exposure for humans than any other nonoccupational source, including food.

Now, that makes sense. The patient who needs fillings is either nutrient-deficient or has a truncated immune system, or he wouldn't have the cavities in the first place. I'm sure the mercury poisoning is happening to everyone with mercury amalgam fillings, but the symptoms only show up in those with nutrient insufficiencies or genetic weaknesses. Mercury disables enzyme function. The neuron degeneration found in the brain-stem tissue of some SIDS infants might also contain mercury those infants got from the mother during the pregnancy. Just enough—along with other factors—to hurt the respiratory center there.

A few of the more common symptoms related to mercury intoxication are fatigue, allergy, depression, dizziness, headaches, vision problems, and rashes.

Remember how we thought that lead in paint and gasoline was safe, that DDT and asbestos caused no harm to humans, and tobacco was a fun recreational smoke? When a presenter was criticized for not giving both sides to the amalgam controversy, he replied, "We did not ignore the good news—there was none."

It is worthy to note that at least six European countries strictly regulate amalgam; it is not allowed to enter the water supplies. Mercury is a serious environmental pollutant. Is it really safe to allow it in our heads?

IF IT AIN'T BROKE, DON'T FIX IT

Tonsillectomy is the surgical removal of the tonsils. The risk of the operation must be weighed against the risk of leaving them in. Despite technical advances, a few deaths from this operation are reported each year. Reaction to the anesthesia, bleeding, and aspiration of blood or tonsillar tissue into the lungs still occur.

The size of the tonsils is one reason for their removal, as it is normal for them to grow larger—along with the adenoids and other lymph tissues—up until five or six years of age. After this age they shrink, and of course, as the body gets bigger around them, they look smaller. If, however, tonsils are chronically infected, and every cold or sore throat ends with swollen anterior neck nodes (just under the corner of the jawbone) and requires antibiotics, removal seems justified. The most compelling reason for removal of the tonsils is that they are so big and pendulous that they flop down into the child's throat, occluding his airway when he lies on his back.

It is often difficult for the doctor and the child's parents to arrive at some reasonable compromise about the operation. The parents must be told that the operation will not stop colds (look to allergies instead), that the child will still get sore throats, and that age seven seems to have some curative "magic" to it. A trial of no dairy products for a month or two might preclude the need for tonsil removal. Many children have been put on the waiting list for a "T & A" at age five. But when it was their turn at age seven to go under the knife, the need for the surgery had disappeared (not the child; the indications). Be sure to ask questions. Can we wait? Will the operation help?

The average child has about six to eight respiratory infections a year until age six. When he is seven years old, he should react like an adult—one sore throat, one attack of influenza, one cold, and one bout of intestinal flu a year. If he exceeds this arbitrary optimum (mine), then he should have his immune system boosted with the usual basic natural therapy (see Chapter 6) before his tonsils and adenoids are removed. Even an allergy workup would be worthwhile before the T & A. After tonsils are removed, some decrease in sore throats should be anticipated, and the chronically swollen anterior cervical nodes should decrease in size.

But think about this quote from Dr. Robert S. Mendelsohn: "In pre-paid group practices where surgeons are paid a steady salary not tied to how many operations they perform, hysterectomies and tonsillectomies occur only about one-third as often as in fee-for-service situations."[248]

It is common to see children who had suffered from chronically infected tonsils and adenoids become cheerful, energetic, and ravenous eaters after the removal of these offending tissues. The improved appetite must indicate that the child feels better or can at least swallow more easily. (I sometimes wonder if he eats more after his surgery because he kept hearing his mother say he would once he had the operation. He may figure that if he doesn't, he might have to go through the operation again!)

Adenoidectomy. Adenoids are blobs of lymph tissue found just behind and above the soft palate, attached to the back wall of the pharynx. They are similar to the tonsils in structure and function. Although they cannot be seen ordinarily, they are assumed to be swollen and/or infected whenever the tonsils are. Normally enlarged from age four to six years, they create hyponasal speech and may occlude the opening of the eustachian tubes, which allow for the equalization of air pressure in the inner ear. The location of enlarged adenoids explains why children snore and breathe through their mouths. But repeated ear infections and/or hearing impairment are not necessarily due to the enlarged adenoids, and removal of the adenoids will not usually affect the incidence of ear infections. Adenoids should not be removed just because they're there. There is a risk to adenoidectomy.

Nasal allergy due to house dust, bacterial allergy, and food allergy must be controlled or eliminated first. The most common inciting agent for the production of ear infections is a sensitivity to dairy products. The most likely clue that a milk sensitivity is present is the audible clue called "zonking" caused by postnasal drip. It appears that this mucus, produced by the milk sensitivity, makes the adenoids swell like a sponge. This phlegm—not the adenoid tissue—is also responsible for plugging the eustachian tube and allowing the germs to grow in the middle ear (otitis media).

Removing the adenoids will not stop the milk sensitivity. Treating every ear infection with antibiotics does not allow the child to develop his immune system. All doctors have seen the pathetic child with nasal symptoms who had his adenoids removed, only to become saddled with asthma or bronchitis—as if his adenoids were protecting his lungs.

The adenoids are rarely removed from a child who has a short palate, as she may develop hypernasal speech because the palate is not long enough to reach the pharyngeal wall without the adenoids to bridge the gap. This is especially true of the child with a repaired cleft palate. Rule of thumb: The farther away the trouble is from the tonsils and adenoids, the less likely their removal will do any good.

CHAPTER 8

The Nervous System

The nervous system is the network that allows for communication between one part of the body and another. If the eyes detect an oncoming car, that message goes to the motor part of the brain that activates the legs to get going. In response to various incoming stimuli, the neurons respond at either a faster or slower rate.

The brain and spinal cord compose the central nervous system. The peripheral nervous system includes: (1) the sensory nerves, which transmit messages to the central nervous system; (2) the motor nerves, which carry impulses out to the glands and muscles; and (3) the autonomic nervous system. This latter is not considered under direct voluntary control; it allows the body to prepare for fight (rapid heart, extra adrenaline), for flight (blood diverted from intestines to muscles of legs), for foraging (increased intestinal activity, saliva, and digestive enzymes), and for finding a place for feces (when a stool has moved to the lower rectum).

THE CEREBRAL CORTEX

The cerebral cortex is the thinking, conscious, and social (conscience) part of the central nervous system. Consciousness consists of the combined rhythmical firing of the billions of neurons in the nervous system. Many motor responses of the human organism can short-circuit the cortex, because an inciting incident, for example, needs a rapid, reflex response, not a thought-out action. A finger is burned and the hand is pulled away reflexively; the "thinking" part of the brain is not called into use. An angry crowd reacting during a ball game is operating on the collective animal brain of all the participants. A soldier in the heat of battle is functioning via his lower, subcortical brain.

A state of equilibrium exists between the environment and the various nerve-conduction pathways of the sense organs to the cortex of the brain. Our perception of the world depends on this baseline input. If our eyes tell our brain that the horizon is on a tilt, the cortex sends the appropriate nerve impulses to the muscles to shift the body until the perception of the world is level again.

If the conductivity of the nerve cells in the sensory areas of the brain is altered, a false message or dysperception occurs. Things or people may appear larger or smaller or unfamiliar enough to be menacing. The anxiety that follows these unfamiliar impressions will lead to withdrawal or approach (or attack), hyper- or hypoactivity, depression, or somatic symptoms. The panic that may overtake an LSD user on a bad "trip" is the result of a chemical dysperception-induced sensory input. ("That telephone pole is coming right at me!")

Like the simplest of living organisms, humans spend their lives either avoiding or approaching the environment. This yes-or-no, on-or-off, left-or-right, come-or-go is easily noted in the single-celled organism, but because of the complicated mixture of nerve connections and chemicals, the human is able to modify her involvement with the world. She can qualify her response with "maybe" or "later" or a "yes" today, but a "no" tomorrow. As a child grows, she learns by imitation and a reward system that she can use to get what she wants and still not lose her friends, parents, and peers.

All conscious learning takes place in the cerebral cortex part of the brain, but the body is the communication path between the environment and the nervous system. The sensory pathways transmit information to specific (primary) areas in the cortex; those messages then go to nearby association areas that give meaning to or interpret what has been seen, heard, or felt. The temporal lobes receive auditory sensation. They also store memories of past events and the emotions associated with those events. These association areas allow us to hear music, not sound. Sensation is innate, but perception is learned.

Dark and light colors are noted in the visual sensation area at the back part of the cerebral cortex. Something is seen, and the visual perception area just forward of that area receives these impulses and tells us we are looking at a house. If it is our home, emotions are brought to the conscious level. What we are looking at now has meaning; secondary areas are being stimulated. These are all interconnected to the auditory areas (from the temporal lobe) and the tactile areas from the sensory cortex farther forward.

These perceptions must occur at a certain stage of the development of the nervous system or they will never be incorporated as a permanently stored memory in the association areas. Opportunities for spontaneous learning must come in the first few years of a child's life. Heat, cold, color, texture, and the touch and sight of a round ball are all stored simultaneously in the appropriate association areas. The smell, touch, sight, and sound of the baby's mother are all perceived as "good" in the cerebral association areas. The infant has learned that his mother is to be trusted and obeyed. We hope.

Much of humankind's behavior is learned, in contrast to the animals whose behavior is mostly innate or inborn. Through experience, a person learns to modify his/her behavior. Early motor behavior is generally innate but not necessarily present at birth (ability to walk, talk, think). When the cerebral hemispheres mature (nerve fibers develop a myelin sheath) these potentials become observable abilities; the latent becomes manifest. **Learning waits on maturation** is a basic neurological concept. Learning (teaching?) cannot be too early or too late; the neural pathways must be stimulated during the period they are meant to develop, or their ability to function is lost. But this loss does not have to be forever: Constantly used pathways of neuron connections become more efficient as they are being myelinated. The connections between nerves become more numerous and sophisticated.

Each child develops these capacities for learning at a predetermined, genetically controlled rate. (One child may walk well at ten months, another not until eighteen months; both may be normal.) Rote memory of a three-year-old child is but a show-off gimmick used by proud parents, but usable, meaningful learning of the information must await the development of the nearby associative pathways. Intuitive parents know how to stimulate their child appropriately so she may learn about the world in an atmosphere of mutual trust. Pushing a child beyond her capacity produces anger, frustration, and/or depression.

God, Mother Nature, and/or evolution placed the neocortex on top of the old, animal brain to facilitate human development. The old brain (with its built-in responses for aggression, sex, pleasure, and displeasure) was not eliminated in the developmental processes because of the proximal positioning of the centers for breathing, heartbeat, temperature control, and hunger. We need to be aggressive and sexual every once in a while, but in a more socially acceptable way than that of the impulsive animal.

The cortex with its innate ability to allow humane responses to give an individual pleasure should be strong enough to control the animal brain (the emotional or limbic system). This is the object of parenting: Reward the child for positive acts and he may grow up to become a responsible, social human being. However, a number of forces can sabotage this master plan.

Two factors alter the ability of the cerebral cortex to make a valid decision compatible with the human response:

1. The cortex receives too many stimuli or the stimuli are too intense or painful:

   (a) The screening device fails;

   (b) The environment presents too many sensations.

2. The cortex is unable to handle normal stimuli because it is suffering from chemical imbalances that interfere with impulse transmission along the nerves:

   (a) Low blood glucose;

   (b) Amino acid, mineral, or enzyme defects;

   (c) Drug reaction, infection, anoxic or traumatic insult. This may lead to convulsions, mental retardation, spastic diplegia (stiff, weak legs), and memory defects.

One function of the limbic system interposed between the spinal cord and the cortex is to act as a filtering device to modulate the incoming messages that come from all the sense organs. In general this action has an inhibitory effect and tends to screen out extraneous stimuli; otherwise, we would have to notice every heartbeat, gas pain, dog barking, and leaf falling. It could drive us nuts.

And, indeed, some people do notice their environment too acutely. The pituitary sends messages to the adrenals to either fight or flee. It was a good and necessary neural loop response when you were in the jungle looking for supper. Nowadays we are sending too many stimulating messages to our adrenals based on some comparatively feeble stressors. Why do we need to call out our best chemicals, when the only exciting thing in our environment is the threat of rain, a dirty diaper, or a frown? Does a wrinkle in your underwear distract you enough that you have to tear off your pants? A fun game to one person might be a calamity to another.

Perception is the key to the variations in responses of these different types of people. We have more nerves that serve to dampen or inhibit incoming stimuli than we have nerves that tell us about our environment. If the limbic system screening mechanism is working well, it will allow emergencies to get through so that we can run or fight; in other words, to stay alive—an important human function.

As the infant grows, he incorporates memories about his environment into his cortex: Gravity works, a full stomach is pleasurable, some things are sharp, some are soft and comfy, and his parents smile and show love when he does certain things. The reward system, deep in the thalamus in the lower brain, is a powerful memory reinforcer that gives enough pleasure to the child that he pursues those activities again and again to relive the pleasurable feelings. Since childhood memories, reinforced by pleasure or pain, remain locked into the cortical, subcortical, and limbic memory systems all through one's life, it is easy to understand why adult psychopathology can have its origins in traumatic childhood events. (I read of a woman who thought of death whenever she had an orgasm. This unpleasant feeling was finally resolved when she was able to resurrect from her unconscious the memory of falling on and killing her pet canary while masturbating as a child.)

It is obvious we must protect the cortex—it's really our only hope of a comfortable existence. The brain is the busiest organ humans have. It must be nourished while growing both prenatally and postbirth. It is the part of our bodies that is the most vulnerable to energy deprivation. It must have a constant supply of nutriments day and night since it has no storage capacity for glucose. The child's brain has two to three times the energy requirements of the adult's. The liver and the muscles store glycogen so they can function for up to a day, but the brain will lose its ability to function in just a few minutes if deprived of oxygen and sugar. The brain requires 25 percent of the blood supply from the heart. If the energy supply falls, the cortex simply does not perform, and any number of cognitive, memory, and motor skills will shut down. When the cortex slips, the animal (reptilian), emotional, limbic brain takes over, and the input from the environment might elicit only mean, impulsive, aggressive, surly responses (the hibernating bear syndrome). The child who ate a doughnut and a soft drink for breakfast may be hit with falling blood sugar during the first-period class at school. Drowsiness, spaciness, poor academic performance, and noncommunication may be his lot. The teacher needs to teach the cortex; the limbic system cannot be educated.

Characteristics of Those with Cortex Injuries

Many of the injuries to the **cortex,** like cerebral palsy, are obvious, but a damaged cortex will have trouble processing information. The cortex is in charge of dominance, right or left. If there is no dominance, the person is slow to decide. If there is mixed dominance, there will be stress. The corpus callosum (a large bundle of nerves that communicates between the two sides of the cortex) is slow sending messages to the other side. This person cannot process information fast enough. This will depress him. Fine motor coordination is poor, language skills are immature, he has trouble expressing himself, his gait is usually clumsy, he has trouble doing more than one thing at a time, he has poor symbol recognition, and creativity is reduced.

Psychotherapy deals with the cortex. Talk therapy can help a patient feel better about himself, but it will not heal the breaks in the cortical part of the nervous system; it cannot fill those holes. A hurt to the nervous system (anoxia, fever, trauma, vaccinations, deprivation, low-protein diet) may not reveal itself at the time it occurs, but later it becomes manifest when the involved area is supposed to mature (become myelinated) and become serviceable. Subtle disorders in behavior or learning will then show up and frustrate child, parent, and teacher. Reeducation using the developmental approach (neural stimulation: crawling, creeping, vestibular stimulation), psychiatric help, behavior modification, vitamins, minerals, and drugs may all be necessary. It is best to treat the brain—not just the behavior.

THE MIDBRAIN

The midbrain includes the limbic system, the thalamus, the hypothalamus, the basal ganglia, and the cerebellum. These are all the areas between the pons (below) and the cerebral cortex (above). They have to do with instinct and metabolic functions. In here are the organization centers of sensory, motor, and autonomic functions. The postural reflexes have their origin at this level and emerge in the first few months of life. Their function is twofold: to store the actions of the earlier reflexes and to put information into the brain that is needed for creeping and later bipedal function, which helps to separate us functionally from lower animals.

Characteristics of Those with Midbrain Injuries

With midbrain injuries, in addition to the difficulties in filtering out and prioritizing incoming stimuli, the child is more likely to be hyperactive, distractible, fidgety with a short attention span, poor memory, bossy (in an effort to control the world around him), easily provoked, and ticklish. He often displays explosive temper: the limbic rage. He may have low blood pressure, and feels the need to move to elevate his blood pressure to get sugar to the brain. He may complain about his clothes as he notices things too easily. Hot and cold are extremes to him. The midbrain has control over balance and vestibular function, so these persons are often clumsy and accident-prone. They may have trouble climbing, catching a ball, or enjoying a swing. They are also lacking in depth perception. They usually avoid play activity and sports. Articulation in speech may be affected. The midbrain has the control of many hormonal and autonomic functions, so these children may have trouble with allergies, environmental sensitivities, immunity, fatigue, addictions, temperature regulation, and digestive and urinary control problems. They are often finicky eaters. They may wet the bed. Walleye is due to a midbrain hurt. Learning disabilities are due to hurts in this section—not the cortex. Midbrain injured children respond to creeping, that is, moving on hands and knees.

Here are a few of the conditions, along with hyperactivity and academic difficulties, that Florence Scott, R.N., has found to be associated with pons and midbrain hurts: antisocial (insufficient conscience, lying, cheating, stealing, no sense of guilt, no empathy); difficulty in family and peer relations; feeling of not belonging; drug and alcohol abuse; lack of common sense. It suggests that if nutritional, toxic, and metabolic problems cannot change a person, neural therapy would be appropriate.

"He is so smart, he couldn't be brain-damaged!" It is obvious that psychotherapy will have little to do with improving the mental status of those whose injury is at the pons or midbrain level.

Crawling on the belly and creeping on the hands and knees are often the best remedy. It is best done for five to ten minutes daily, seven days a week. These exercises stimulate the formation of new dendrite and axon branches of nerves that have failed to be stimulated at the appropriate time during infancy. Experts in the field of development know at what stage in the growing child certain brain connections are made. By having the child—or adult—recapitulate the movements that would have been normal at that stage of development, new connections around the nonfunctioning areas can be made.

The Limbic System

The limbic system consists of a number of nerve centers; it is the emotional part of the brain. Centers in this area store potentials for whole acts of behavioral responses: fear, rage, sexual drive, feelings of well-being, and other organized, integrated emotional responses. These responses are all set to go, and only need the proper stimulation. These behavior centers, when stimulated by electrodes, will cause subjects to engage in certain specific activities. If the cortex is inoperative (from hypoglycemia or heavy metal poisoning), these areas take over and appear to be responsible for antisocial acts, e.g., inappropriate aggression, stubborn noncompliance, sexual assaultiveness, and limbic rages. Too much limbic system stimulation, and too little cortical control, equals one obnoxious child.

Certain types of psychomotor epilepsy could be explained by a similar mechanism; an irritable focus in or near one of these areas might "take over" the victim, much to his surprise and to the concern of his family.

The fibers in this limbic screening system release norepinephrine (basically a stimulant related to adrenaline) at the synaptic end (junction with another nerve fiber) of the axon. This appears to be the reason why stimulants have an inhibitory effect on this system, and also helps to explain the paradoxical calming effect of dextroamphetamine and methylphenidate (Ritalin) on many hyperactive children. Stimulants mollify the incoming stimuli so the cortex can attend to one sensory input at a time.

Insults to the nervous system of hyperactive children due to problems during the mother's pregnancy (e.g., anoxia) have usually been blamed for distractibility and impulsiveness, but recent studies indicate that other factors, such as genetic tendencies (thus chemical and enzymatic) and a poor diet, might prevent the filtering system from blocking out extraneous and overwhelming internal and external stimuli.

The function of the limbic system's filtering neurons can be enhanced by the use of magnesium and the B vitamins, B_6 being the most important. Vitamin C and pantothenic acid are the precursors for the adrenal hormones. Magnesium seems to shut the door to a few incoming stimuli. If touchy children are treated with magnesium, they will become less ticklish and less distractible. They can relax and fall asleep more easily.

The Thalamus

The thalamus is a relay station between the cortex, cerebellum, basal ganglia, and the reticular activating system.

The Hypothalamus

The hypothalamus, below the thalamus, is a small area at the base of the brain (just above and connected to the pituitary gland). It has both nerve and chemical control over the pituitary. The hypothalamus acts as a thermostat in body-temperature regulation; it affects blood pressure, sleep, eating, and drinking. Lesions of the hypothalamus have been responsible for the following: precocious puberty, somnolence, obesity, convulsions, and, of course, diabetes insipidus.

When stimulated, other parts of the hypothalamus provide pleasure, so it is rewarding to repeat the acts that reproduce these pleasurable feelings. (Eating when hungry leads to pleasurable satiety, so an animal learns to eat to avoid the displeasure of hunger.) If the neurons in the satiety center of the hypothalamus are stimulated, the animal stops eating; if the neurons are destroyed, the animal develops a voracious appetite and becomes grossly obese. (I have a patient who was afflicted at age two with severe epiglottitis requiring a tracheotomy. Since then he has become enormously overweight and maddeningly stubborn. I assume the lack of oxygen destroyed some hypothalamic center that has to do with recognizing satiety.)

THE PONS

The pons is the next level down from the hypothalamus and has connections to the **cerebellum,** which governs movement, making actions initiated in the cortex smooth and coordinated. The cerebellum regulates postural reflexes and muscle tone, as it receives feedback messages from the muscles. Although far from the eyes, it is an important part of the eye/ear/vestibular/cerebellar loop that is so important for reading. The cerebellum matches sensory input to cortical intent.

Both vision and hearing are dependent upon the **vestibular apparatus.** Signals from the vestibular system pass along the vestibular nerve to the cerebellum. The latter coordinates information from the inner ear with other parts of the body. The cerebellum grows and matures (becomes myelinated) between birth and about fifteen months of life. If a child has delayed vestibular function, he will be slow in all gross motor patterns requiring coordination of both sides of the body: that is, posture, eye-hand coordination and fine motor control. The cerebellum is important for the transition between primitive and postural reflexes.

Characteristics of Those with Pons Injuries

"A dysfunction of the pons may create in a person an inability to take in information from the world around him."[249] He doesn't seem to be in touch. Inattention, so common in the hyperactive child, may represent a pons problem, and not a hearing or visual dysfunction. He cannot trust others; he may become a hermit. He may have diminished pain perception, as cuts and bruises go unnoticed. He may abuse others to invite retaliation; he needs to be hurt or hit just to know where his body is. He has difficulty bonding to parents or classmates. He has persistent anxiety because many things seem threatening, but he may appear to be unafraid (like a stunt-man). He responds only to firm, direct stimuli. He has trouble reading horizontal lines. Crossed eyes are a pons injury. Pons-injured children will respond to crawling therapy, i.e., crawling on the belly.

Vestibular stimulation can improve coordination, attention, balance, speed of learning, and auditory discrimination. Spinning, or rapid circular motion like a merry-go-round, will stimulate the nerves involved with the ocular-vestibular-cerebellar loop and improve the ability to learn. The Institutes for Neuro-Physiological Psychology in Chester, England, have found that a slow spin for the complete 360-degree circle on a chair for a minute is the most helpful. If it is an infant, it can be held in the lap of an adult, and the chair spun for a few one-minute turns. This improves balance and motor activity dramatically.[250] This is called neurodevelopment stimulation and apparently increases the neuron connections through that loop so important for learning and coordination.

Some developmental researchers and teachers have them spin like a heliocopter until they get dizzy, then stand with their eyes closed, which is when the vestibular stimulation takes place. This is repeated several times—up to five minutes total. Some teachers have found this vestibular stimulation helps learning. The teacher will get the children to stand and turn for a couple of minutes, and then they can focus their attention better. Vestibular stimulation has been shown to facilitate learning in developmentally delayed preschoolers. Ninety seconds of vestibular stimulation prior to language training allowed the children to acquire the skills more quickly.[251]

If this vestibular stimulation causes nausea, the movements are slowed. They can start with slow rolling on the floor, until this no longer causes dizziness. Nausea occurs when there is a mismatch between the eyes and the information from the proprioceptors of the body. Use a swing, snow saucer, merry-go-round, hammock, rolling on the floor, rocking chair, swivel chair, or minitrampoline. Move rapidly and stop abruptly. Aim for fifteen seconds.

THE MEDULLA

The medulla is located at the top of the spinal cord and is vital for survival, as nerves here send messages to the diaphragm (basic breathing) and the heart (basic heartbeat). Injuries here are incompatible with life.

REFLEXES

Reflexes are like road maps to the brain. In the last three decades, research has shown that newborn babies possess certain primitive reflexes mediated by the brain stem that are necessary for moving through the birth canal, and for sucking from and clinging to the mother. These early reflexes should disappear (or be stored) in the first few weeks or months of life. If, however, they continue past the first few months of life, they are considered aberrant and will actively hinder the development of later skills. Diagnosis: **neurodevelopment delay.** This is the basic reason for the continuation or appearance of many conditions noted above: in general, a poorly organized person.

But all is not lost. We know that if nerve cells die, they are dead and will not regenerate as skin cells do when cut. But other nearby nerve cells, if properly stimulated, can extend their axons and dendrites to make new connections and take over the function of the destroyed nerves. This proven method of stimulating the brain has produced amazing results in cases thought to be hopeless.

The diagnosis of brain damage used to be a devastating one, because it created images of finality. But the brain is highly plastic. Every time we stimulate the brain, **nerve growth factors** are created in the area of stimulation, which increases the proliferation of dendrites. It has been found that chemical markers guide the axons to exactly where they need to go. Nerve pathways may have been interrupted by some hurt, but by recapitulating the movements the baby would have been making at that time of trauma, the connections of the axons and dendrites can reconnect to the part of the brain where uninterrupted information would initially have put them.

"We know, for instance, that during the period of creeping on hands and knees, the cerebellum becomes myelinated. The cerebellum is part of the ocular-vestibular-cerebellar loop, which controls the movement the eyes need for smooth reading."[252] Dr. Arnold Gesell said, "The floor is the gym of the infant."

SPINAL CORD

The spinal cord is the portion of the central nervous system contained within the vertebral column. Injuries to the spinal cord are usually due to falls or diving injuries; fractures of the vertebrae are usually associated. Paralysis of all function below the level of injury is common, and little return of function can be expected. (New neurosurgical techniques of injecting nerve growth factor at the break are showing some promising results!)

Neurological reorganization improves the function of the central nervous system. It may involve patterning. There is a pattern for each of the stages in the developmental profile. These patterns are sets of movements done repeatedly to trigger a reflex. This is the stimulation that activates the axons and dendrites to grow and connect over the breaks or hurts to the nervous system. These patterns tell the central nervous system what to do and in what way. Crawling and creeping are the second component of the therapy. The therapist diagnoses at what level the nervous system has been stopped in its maturation. Then the sensory stimulation is begun at that level, whether pons or midbrain.

THE NEUROBIOCHEMISTRY OF BEHAVIOR

Research has indicated that every communication system of the body has a feedback control that limits its action:

- ACTH (adrenocorticotrophic hormone) from the pituitary gland stimulates the adrenal cortex to produce its hormones; these, in turn, have an inhibitory effect upon the production of ACTH.

- When the level of glucose rises in the blood, the beta cells of the pancreas release insulin, which serves to lower the blood glucose level by transporting glucose into the liver and muscles as glycogen and into fat tissues.

- Nerve cells themselves secrete chemicals, e.g., norepinephrine and serotonin. These chemicals have a rate-limiting effect on their own precursors.

- In a similar way a feedback mechanism is constantly operating between the body and its environment. Environmental messages impinge upon the brain via receptors in the skin, eyes, ears, muscles, mouth, and nose. The brain must readjust to the change by telling the muscles to withdraw, ignore, or approach. Pain or pleasure is the determining factor when the brain makes a value judgment.

For the brain to function optimally it needs the proper connections and maximum nutrition. Here are some possibilities to consider if your child is not as perfect as you would like—or at least standard.

Stress means different things to different people. It is obvious that some people can handle stress and others cannot. It is basically a sensory overload due to improper limbic system filtering, or a malfunctioning cortex, or both.

Hay fever, for instance, is the result of an environmental pollen overload that impinges on the nasal mucosa inadequately protected by cortisone from the adrenal glands. There may be many reasons for this: (1) The adrenal glands are exhausted because they have not been adequately supplied with enzyme precursors (vitamin C and pantothenic acid); or (2) these glands have been overstimulated by some psychic stress due to an overload of the cortical-pituitary-adrenal hookup; or (3) low blood sugar has forced these glands to devote their secretion to the maintenance of an adequate blood sugar level; or (4) all of the above. Hence, hay fever could very well be produced by emotional causes, and not just by pollen overload.

An autistic child who seems to be run entirely by internal stimuli (as shown by his stereotypical, rhythmic behavior, his lack of eye contact, and his paucity of affective facial expression) has found his environment unbearably overwhelming. He is making his own stimuli to crowd out what he perceives as a frightening world. Vitamin B_6 and magnesium can help him adjust to the environment. It is no surprise to learn that about one third of alcoholics are schizophrenic when sober; alcohol must be screening out a hostile world.

Some effort must be initiated early in life to identify the infant or child who demonstrates any evidence of an overreaction to stress. These irritable, overresponding approachers, and these miserable, depressed, shy, scared withdrawers, must be made more comfortable early in life. If nothing is done to get the pressure off them, they will learn that the world is a threat. They will either continually fight us or withdraw from us as a way of life. These responses cause the environment (other people) to treat them as social misfits, so they become locked into this behavioral fix. The cortex-environment feedback loop, once established, is difficult to interrupt. When these children, who were probably hurt in their midbrain in fetal or early infant life, are treated with developmental stimulation via the visual-auditory-vestibular loop, the nerve networks are stimulated to grow and replace what has been lost.

The exciting, hopeful part of all this is that many "psychiatric" symptoms due to life's problems are remedial, but until now we have all been taught that everything was psychogenic—the result of bad parenting. This explanation created depression and guilt in the victim's caretakers, but little improvement in his behavior.

The brain cannot have a rash or a cramp. It can only respond with changes in thought, feeling, or behavior. These nervous system functions are basically chemically mediated. By altering the chemicals in the brain, we can change the way the brain perceives and responds to stressors by fortifying the enzyme systems that are responsive to those stressors. (I am assuming that we have also made an effort to eliminate the stressors.)

We can all accept the fact that our genes are responsible for the enzymes that make the chemicals that influence our bodies. Is it too big a step to say that hyperactivity is due to the fact that the victim does not have enough norepinephrine in his limbic system? The dual approach of nutrition and neurological stimulation has been helpful for these children who have been classified as incorrigible. Without this, they become the throwaway children.

We know that enzymes are put together by minute amounts of amino acids, vitamins, and minerals, plus an energy source, usually glucose. If a gross deficiency of these essential chemical ingredients leads to death, and conversely an adequate supply creates health, there is a whole range in between, a continuum, in which an increased deficiency will result in the appearance of an increasing number of symptoms. The appearance of symptoms is the body's way to alert its owner that something is amiss. There is a tilt. Symptoms are an opportunity to motivate one to search for the cause: Are they a neurological defect or a chemical slip?

If only our environment could supply everything we need! Then the daily stressors of gravity, poor lighting, low blood sugar, heat, cold, noise, tough teachers, and thoughtless peers could all be "character-building" or "a challenge." When we are exhausted, they become depressing put-downs instead. We now have tests to determine what has gone wrong. Deficiencies can be pinpointed. Poisons that prevent the enzymes from functioning optimally can be measured. Methods eliminating such problems exist.

Sleep disorders may also respond. Allergy victims may be awakened by a full nose or a tight, wheezy chest in the middle of the night, because they ran out of cortisone, which was used up because of adrenal exhaustion due to low blood sugar (ice cream at bedtime?). Control: vitamin C and pantothenic acid plus a protein snack at bedtime to prevent the nocturnal blood sugar drop. (A vitamin injection given to a young man eliminated his 4:00 A.M. nose-blowing session virtually overnight.)

Calcium has a beneficial effect on sleep induction. Because of its known action on cell wall permeability and enzyme activation, an insufficient amount may prevent the release of neurochemicals needed for appropriately timed sleep.

Tryptophan, an amino acid, is found in beef and other protein-rich foods. It is a precursor of serotonin, a neurochemical. The increased amount of insulin produced following a rich carbohydrate meal tends to lower the amounts of other amino acids relative to tryptophan; hence, more tryptophan is available to enter the brain and become serotonin. (It is known that cats, at least, when deprived of tryptophan have insomnia.) A steak, a potato, and a rich dessert may cause drowsiness—not because the stomach is full, but rather because of the extra tryptophan. In some insomniacs, ingesting one gram of tryptophan induced sleep more quickly. Corticosteroids induce the breakdown of tryptophan—less corticosteroids, more tryptophan. Corticosteroids are at their lowest level in the evening; perhaps more tryptophan is available in the evening to induce sleep.

If stress releases cortisol and tryptophan is metabolized thereby, perhaps the decrease in serotonin during stress is related to the decrease in available tryptophan. Depression, some forms of hyperactivity, and some psychotic states are associated with decreased amounts of serotonin in the brain. Therefore, stress, with its associated excessive excretion of adrenal cortical hormone, may prevent the body from providing the brain with enough tryptophan to allow an optimum supply of serotonin. Depression and insomnia could follow. Who doesn't get depressed if sleep is interrupted?

The above intertwining chemical phenomena are mentioned to show that the biochemical and neurological feedback mechanisms are enormously complicated. It shows how difficult it is for a doctor to prescribe for a patient with an allergy, a neurosis, a pain, a depression, or a psychosis without upsetting some other enzyme/chemical system. Cortisone therapy for asthma or arthritis can lead to a psychosis or stomach ulcers! If the doctor would listen to the patient telling him what the patient's body is telling the patient, the doctor would be able to move up the chemical chain a couple of links and be more permanently helpful and produce fewer side effects along the way.

Natural, biodegradable treatments can make our physiology function for us so that we can end up with a better body, inside of which we could live quite comfortably. We can better relate to our environment. We can develop a body sense. Our dysfunction could be a loss of neurons from some long-forgotten hurt, a nutrient deficiency, or a distortion of the acid/base balance.

The psychiatrist should nourish his patients right along with psychotherapy and tranquilizers.

The allergist should refuse to treat patients if they eat sugar and white flour; he should insist his patients get vitamin C and pantothenic acid right along with the desensitizing shots.

The pediatrician should insist that all his patients nibble on small amounts of protein and complex carbohydrates. He needs to have his patients take acidophilus when he treats them with antibiotics. He should walk into schools, axe down the candy machines, and get protein snacks into all the classrooms.

Delinquents, criminals, and alcoholics should all have five-hour glucose tolerance tests and have their hair tested for heavy-metal poisoning. Stephen Schoenthaler has told us that if prisoners are fed whole, natural foods, violent acts within the prison system are reduced 80 percent.

Pregnant women should be encouraged to nibble on protein and be given extra vitamins and glutamic acid from the moment of conception— and for years before, if possible.

Inadequate enzyme functioning is due to faulty genes, which become manifest when there are environmental influences. If the proper chemicals are not produced by the body, the cortex does not experience the world correctly. The following rather common behavior categories might help one recognize oneself or members of the family. Manipulation of the diet could be done simultaneously with developmental stimulation, behavior modification, or whatever other environmental changes may be necessary to reduce stress and cheer up the body. The aim is to return the metabolism to homeostasis.

• The colicky baby is noticing either his environment or his stomach too acutely. The doctor perceives touchy, sensitive people who may be causing the distress. He prescribes a sedative for the baby and a tranquilizer for the parents.

Try this: Assume the baby has an allergy to cow milk and an inadequate limbic-system filtering mechanism. To do: Change the milk (but don't stop nursing), stop flavored vitamins and all solids being given to the baby, provide vitamin C (up to one hundred milligrams a day per month of age), and use some vitamin B_6 (twenty-five milligrams per day) and pantothenic acid (one hundred milligrams two or three times a day). Some swear by the benefits of B_{12} injections. B_{12} promotes the integrity of the intestinal lining, so it might block the leaky gut.

• Suggestions for the two-year-old who fights going to bed, has multiple allergies, repeated ear and chest infections, won't eat, looks tired, whines all the time, and has circles under his eyes: The parents are told they are making him nervous.

To do: Assume he does not feel well. Check for anemia, stop all dairy products, remove the feather pillow and the cat with whom he sleeps. Clean out his room, have him sleep on a hypoallergenic mattress on the floor, give him some iron drops, and stop the sugar and the white flour. Let him nibble on little bits of good food, like chicken, cooked peas, old-fashioned peanut butter, fruit, and berries.

• What about the touchy, goosey, afraid-of-everything, cannot-relax-and-sleep child who may think the world is too close to him?

To do: Organize a structured, scheduled environment with definite activities. Redecorate his room with soft blues, browns, and greens, and as few objects as possible short of making the room look sterile. Allow him to attend to one thing at a time. Let him rock and suck or hold a blanket to his ear for as long as he wants to or needs to. If the child rocks himself, he is telling you that he needs vestibular stimulation. You need to rock him. You can spin around with him, taking a whole minute to make a 360-degree turn in the dark. Then stop for five seconds. Then spin slowly back the other way. This should be done two or three times a day. This is to imitate the vestibular stimulation he would have experienced in his mother's womb. Five hundred milligrams of magnesium a day can help.

• How about the withdrawn, unhappy, sullen, won't-do-anything, has-no-friends, and avoids-eye-contact child who perceives the world as a threat, as if there are too many demands upon him?

To do: Assume he is being bombarded with too many incoming stimuli and/or has low blood sugar and/or has some abnormal brain waves. Change the diet. Give him gentle massage. Let him do the nibbling on protein snacks. He needs vestibular stimulation as outlined in the preceding example. Show acceptance. If you don't get through to him, an EEG might help discover the cause. A hair analysis might reveal some heavy-metal toxins. If a child can be labeled a Jekyll-and-Hyde type of person, it usually means that his blood sugar is bouncing up and down because of his diet.

• The hyperactive boy who is cheerful and busy at home, where he can run with the dog, is scolded in class because he cannot sit still. He seems bright but cannot put anything on paper. He may have an auditory dysfunction. Auditory and vestibular stimulation might help. The vestibular system is closely connected to auditory and visual processing. Check hearing, visual, and tactile input.

• Another one: The nonreader is not just a brat, but may be unable to decode the ink spots on the page.

To do: If he doesn't turn on to the academic world right away with a better diet and perhaps even some stimulant medication, he needs the help of a reading therapist. A developmental optometrist may be the first stop on his way to academic success. A craniologist is another choice. Be sure to check hearing, vision, and neurological development.

• And then there is the bed-wetter or the child with encopresis. Rather than displaying nonverbal urethral and anal aggression, he truly may not be able to respond to the messages coming from his body up to his brain.

To do: Diet and medicine may allow him to develop socially acceptable habits, but check his neurological development.

• There is one of these in every neighborhood: The mean kid who is lying, cheating, lighting fires, constantly fighting, and "borrowing" things may have a conscience, but cannot use it because of faulty cerebral connections or low blood sugar, heavy-metal poisoning, or an odd EEG. He must be helped nutritionally and medically before he is labeled a delinquent. EEG biofeedback may help, but check hearing, vision, and neurological development.

• What can be done for the clumsy, accident-prone, hates-sports child?

To do: Do not push him into activities that will embarrass him, or he will hate himself more than he does already. He needs some exercise, but it must be noncompetitive. Nature-study walks, tree planting, rock gathering, or butterfly or stamp collections could get him moving. His neurological function must be checked. Something is not connected. Vestibular training would be helpful. Again, check hearing, vision, and neurological development.

In all of the preceding scenarios the child should be checked for vision problems, hearing problems, and vestibular function. If there are problems in any of these areas, they may be improved with a developmental approach.

It is obvious that all the body functions are interdependent. When one merely swallows a glass of water, seventeen thousand reactions take place in the body. To attempt to correct a metabolic imbalance in the body, several things have to happen at the same time. The acid/base balance must be made optimum. The ratios of the minerals, one to another, are more important than the absolute levels of each. The body cannot do its job if there are deficiencies.

Research chemist Jeffrey Bland, Ph.D., points out the importance of the intestines and the liver in protecting the brain from toxic insults from the environment, as well as from the internal milieu.[253] Chronic and acute mental problems are related to the accumulation of metabolic, neuroactive toxins in the body (see Junk Food, Chapter 7). One of the more than five hundred functions of the liver is to detoxify these chemicals that we have swallowed or the body has manufactured. Bland has found that "even in apparently healthy people, hundreds of substances that originate from the bacterial action in the gut can escape across the gastrointestinal mucosal border, and all of these substances must be detoxified by the liver." When the gut becomes leaky (see Leaky Gut, Chapter 11) more toxins are delivered to the liver, and if that huge organ is not up to par, these metabolically active substances move around the body and may end up in the brain. So the prevention and therapy of brain disease starts with the intestines. He clearly shows the connection between "neuronal biochemistry, detoxification mechanisms, overall toxic load on the body, and cognitive and emotional function." Impaired metabolism will lead to the buildup of toxins; these will alter brain chemistry and cause disorders of what the brain is responsible for: thoughts, feelings, and actions.

"It is possible that organophosphate exposure may be another etiologic factor in the production of minimal brain dysfunction syndrome so frequently demonstrated in our younger population."[254] One hundred organophosphate-poisoned subjects exhibited persistent intellectual and motor impairments nine years after the initial poisoning episode.[255]

It is very complicated, but there are simple and sometimes easy ways to correct the distortions and bring the body and the brain into homeostatic balance. The diet is a good place to start....

For everybody: broccoli, Brussels sprouts, kale, cabbage, cauliflower, soybean products, green onions.[256, 257]

CHAPTER 9

Brain Damage and Cerebral Dysfunction

The Following Hurts to the Nervous System Are Obvious:

BRAIN DAMAGE

Cerebral palsy affects about a million people in the United States. Twenty-five percent are severe enough to be bedridden, and usually succumb to some infection before age five. Half are seen by neurologists and orthopedic surgeons who perform tendon operations or prescribe physiotherapy. But this treats only the symptoms and signs, not the causes. The whole child must be considered. Sensorimotor and developmental therapy can do wonders. Developmental optometrists and chiropractors can be very helpful in the care of these children.

Research indicates that if pregnant women receive magnesium during their pregnancies, their babies were less likely to develop cerebral palsy. Cerebral palsy occurred in 7 percent of low-birthweight infants whose mothers received magnesium, but in 18 percent of those whose mothers did not.[258]

Mental retardation is intellectual impairment sufficient to slow learning ability. All degrees are seen, from mild (common) to severe (rare). It usually becomes manifest when the child is slow at arriving at developmental landmarks. If undetected in the preschool years, it will then come to light when formal schooling is attempted. The child cannot cope with reading and simple arithmetic, and then social and emotional problems are added to his burden. Memory, reasoning, and abstract thought are usually equally reduced.

241

Affected children frequently have other associated neurological problems such as seizures, and clumsiness, as well as speech, hearing, and visual disorders.

Poverty, poor diet, and an unstimulating environment are contributing forces.

The hopeful note is that innovative educational techniques, if applied during the first year, can improve intellectual function. Some examples of known problems associated with mental retardation are as follows:

Genetically determined: phenylketonuria, galactosemia, lipidoses.

Maternal infections: rubella, syphilis, toxoplasmosis, cytomegalic inclusion disease.

Chemical and metabolic: X ray to pregnant mother, low thyroid (cretinism), hyperbilirubinemia, toxemia, maternal drug ingestion.

Birth-related: prematurity, anoxia, cerebral trauma, hypoglycemia.

After birth: trauma, infection, severe anemia or protein deficiency, lead poisoning, deprivation.

By far the majority of patients with mental retardation have no suspicious history of infection or trauma to bring the problem to the attention of parent or doctor until some observation at about ten or eleven months of age makes the diagnosis possible. ("He doesn't sit up well." "He doesn't care when I leave the room." "He doesn't do anything.") If the test profile shows great abilities in one area (e.g., verbal) and very poor in another (e.g., math), a specific learning disability can be addressed. Overall low levels tend to indicate a metabolic or genetic problem.

If correctable conditions have been addressed (anemia, cretinism, environmental deprivation, low-protein diet, hearing and speech defects, phenylketonuria, subdural hematoma), some management plan must be organized for long-term therapy. Neurological development therapy may be helpful. The parents must be supported and encouraged. Guilt is the common parental reaction to the realization that their child is retarded. ("I didn't take my vitamins when I was pregnant.") Parents should seek the counsel of a sympathetic doctor. Most find that joining the National Association for Retarded Children is the best thing they ever did. They are relieved to share the problem, are kept aware of research in the field, and are able to anticipate problems by communication with other parents. Early intervention helps the child and the parents.

CEREBRAL DYSFUNCTION

Cerebral dysfunction is the term applied to children who are unable to learn or behave in a fashion considered normal for their age. They seem normal, but fail to benefit from the classroom education. The problem may be psychological, neurological, nutritional, toxic, or genetic, or could it be the way we teach them in school? Different observers have different opinions depending on their training.

ADD (Attention Deficit Disorder), With and Without Hyperactivity

Hyperactivity is a form of cerebral dysfunction. It is the term used to describe excessive motor activity not appropriate for a child's age or for the situation. To qualify for the diagnosis of ADD with Hyperactivity, the following major traits must be present (a child can have ADD and not be hyperactive):

Hyperactivity; Distractibility; Impulsivity

The Therapeutic Category

Some doctors prefer to limit the cerebral dysfunction diagnosis to the child who responds to the amphetamine drugs—hence, a therapeutic category. It took about twenty years for therapists to figure out that the stimulant did not operate at the cognitive (cortical) level. Drugs like Ritalin serve to slow the synaptic reuptake of norepinephrine in the limbic system, the screening device that keeps the world at a safe distance. Ritalin also serves to increase the cerebral blood flow in critical areas. If a child with a learning problem does not respond to this drug the first day, he would be excluded from that doctor's diagnostic category.

The Behavior Modification Failure Category

A psychologist might use the term *cerebral dysfunction* for a child with normal or above-average abilities, but who shows marked variability in skills that cannot be accounted for by environmental events. At a conference in Florida in 1972, Drs. Klein and Klein said that the basic problem was "a diminished sensitivity to reinforcement." This means the child's behavior is not modified by rewards or punishment. These children don't get it. They are not paying attention; something is in the way. The brain's thousand points of light are not lit up. Of course, behavior modification will not work because the problem is located in the pons or the midbrain. Behavior modification only works on the cortex, where reasoning and judgment are housed.

The Undisciplined Child Category

A teacher might use the term *cerebral dysfunction* for any child who is disruptive in the classroom because of distractibility or a short-attention span, or who has dyslexia. The child is placed in the special education class; his peers label him "retardo." He gets a bad self-image. It is sometimes assumed that the child was not properly disciplined at home.

The Difficult to Raise Category

A parent would use the term *cerebral dysfunction* for a child who is hyperactive, a racehorse, accident-prone, hostile, or just difficult to live with despite adequate childrearing techniques—love and limits. Counseling to change negative parental attitudes, and to arrange a more concrete, routinized environment as compensation for the child's poor control, may be necessary.

Hurt to the Nervous System Category

A neurodevelopmental delay specialist might find the child has had a hurt to the midbrain and needs neurological stimulation to bypass that brain hurt. When the syndrome was first analyzed by Dr. Charles Bradley in 1937 and stimulants were suggested as a control, it was felt the children so touched were hurt at birth from lack of oxygen, premature birth, or some bilirubin insult.

Inadequate Nutrition Category

Many children have food sensitivities, vitamin and mineral deficiencies, heavy-metal poisonings, allergies, and problems from malabsorption. They do not feel well, and are unable to focus their attention on school work.

Cerebral dysfunction is a catchall diagnosis for a variety of conditions that don't fit elsewhere. It is not like diagnosing and treating pneumonia. The point here is that these children can be helped with a variety of techniques—and may need all approaches including a developmental approach, a nutritious diet, extra vitamins and minerals, behavior modification, neuro-biofeedback, psychological therapy, search for heavy-metal poisonings, homeopathic remedies, and even drugs. The assumption is made that some part of the nervous system is not working. There are diagnostic tests to discover the break.

Along with the excessive motor activity, distractibility and impulsivity are present.

Distractibility is usually associated with a short attention span and hyperactivity. If the five- to six-year-old cannot focus her attention on a story or project for more than a few minutes at a time, and is constantly moving from one area to another, she is distractible. The child is best diagnosed by a kindergarten teacher who has a few other children with whom to compare. The "problem child" is usually a boy, suggesting genetic influences. If someone drops a pencil or sneezes on the other side of the room, he is the first one there to investigate. He is **unable to disregard unimportant stimuli.** He would be served best if put into a special, small class with few distractions. If his mother sends him to another room to get the shoes he forgot the third trip ago, he calls out in fifteen minutes, "What am I doing in here?" He was sidetracked by a few attractions along the way, or he may not have heard everything she said because of an auditory delay. She was talking into the wrong ear. The doctor notices that these children are so touchy that it is hard to examine them: The otoscope light bothers their eardrums, the stethoscope is too cold, and the hernia check may have to be postponed. Too many nerve endings.

Impulsivity describes a level of immaturity expected in a normal one- to three-year-old child. Such behavior is less frequent after this age as self-control becomes somewhat built-in, due in part to the development of control centers in the brain and a little discipline from Mom and Dad. But some thoughtful investigators are finding that many reasonably normal children become hyperactive and disruptive because they are forced to sit in the boring classroom. They learn better in other situations.

The recent book by Thomas Armstrong, Ph.D., points out that the preceding symptoms "are sufficiently global as to be likely to result from any of a wide number of potential causes. These children have a different style of thinking, attending, and behaving, but it's the broader social and educational influences that create the disorder, not the children."[259] He feels ADD is not a clear-cut disease, but is a phenomenon that results from cultural standards that insist on rigid, compliant, conformist behavior. Society needs to be protected from these children. They are labeled deviant; they don't fit in. Instead of accepting these different children and trying to educate them with alternative methods, we give them Ritalin, their straitjacket. (This is the strong conviction of the home-schooling advocates.)

Diagnosing the ADD Child

The reading specialist, the developmental therapist, or psychologist may observe the child:

Is unable to locate sound source; confuses *p* and *q*, *b* and *d*; reversing *was* and *saw*, *dog* and *god*; is dyslexic; has visuo-sensory conceptual disorder; has impaired spatial relationship; has eye-hand coordination confusion; cannot distinguish right from left; loses place on page; has no proprioception; has no idea where his body is unless he moves; has poor figure-ground perception; has a scatter of IQ test results. He probably has faulty development in his sense of equilibrium due to a break in the eye/ear/vestibular/cerebellar loop. It might be delayed development. A developmental approach would restore the necessary connections.[260] Slight insults to the brain are usually not detectable by a psychological evaluation or examination by a skilled neurologist. Probably 75 percent of us have some hurt or dysfunction somewhere in our nervous system. Indeed, the victim of some malfunction of his nervous system is more likely to *develop* psychological symptoms due to his frustrations and his feelings of inferiority.

The parent and the doctor may have observed:

Hyperactivity in the womb; some oxygen deprivation before, at, or after delivery; difficult delivery; premature, overdue, or postmature birth; smallness for age, or second of twins; pneumonia or bronchitis requiring oxygen in the hospital; colicky, fussy, demanding behavior; refusal to be cuddled; squirminess; need to prop bottle; ease of stimulation; ticklish; sleep resistance (light or restless sleeper); accident-prone; excessive climbing, falling, and swallowing poisons; more than the average number of ear infections, use of antibiotics, candidiasis (69 percent of children being evaluated for school failure who were receiving medication for hyperactivity, gave a history of greater than ten ear infections[261]); loves animals, especially dogs and horses; constantly asking questions; constant movement, inability to sit still, even to eat or watch television without rocking or fiddling with something; constant nibbling; loves sweets; eager, enthusiastic, and stimulating qualities that make the child nice to know but awful to live with.

The diagnosis is made comparatively. The parents living with a hyperactive child may not realize their child is hyperactive until they have another more placid, "normal" child. Or they may only realize that the child is hyperactive after the teacher complains that he will not sit still, be quiet, or finish his work. He is hyperactive and disruptive only when forced to follow the classroom rules.

The teacher notices:

Overactivity; frequent trips to bathroom or fountain; too much talking that is loud and out of turn; disruptive effect on class; restlessness; fidgeting; foot-tapping; annoyance to other children; inability to keep his hands to himself; ticklish; knowledge and interest in everyone else's work but failure to finish own; difficulty with arithmetic and spelling; failure in "self-control"; popularity (class clown) but over-responsiveness with laughing or crying; immaturity; daydreaming; underachieving.

Where or What Is the Pathology?

Some of these children have had some history of injury or sickness that could have hurt them (sickness during pregnancy, difficult delivery, prematurity, cord about the neck, whooping cough, pneumonia, vaccination reaction, asthmatic bronchitis, concussion, high fever plus convulsions, meningitis). A strong genetic factor may be present. The hurt is thought to be in the limbic system which acts as a screening device to keep extraneous stimuli from impinging on the cortex (see The Nervous System, Chapter 8). Brain research indicates that many of these hyper kids are not getting enough energy to the frontal lobes where thinking is done.

In addition to the rather obvious disruptive behavior, these children are sometimes afflicted with dyslexia. Other neurological signs, such as clumsiness, poor balance, loud talk, slobbering, and delay in tying or buttoning skills may be present. Visual and hearing deficits must be tested for and ruled out.

Therapy for ADD

Parents want something done right away, and the doctor knows that Ritalin will work in just an hour. Teachers need to have a calm classroom so that they can teach, and seem to know which children would profit by medication like Ritalin or an amphetamine. It is not cheating to put the child on a drug temporarily as long as these other suggestions are followed to find out and treat the cause—the break in the nervous system. If the Ritalin does calm him down, you at least know that he has a deficiency of the neurotransmitter in his limbic system that should screen out unimportant stimuli. It does work in 60 percent of the cases, but there are side effects. "If the medicine works, then the child needed it" seems to be the criterion for using the drug. What it really means is that the child does not have enough norepinephrine in his limbic system.

Basic and appropriate measures would be to have him checked by a developmental optometrist, a developmental therapist, and a reading therapist, and to get a routine physical and a chemical screen to find levels of the blood components.

Depending on the results of these exams and lab tests, the parents should do the following:

1. Three weeks of a no-dairy, no-wheat, no-eggs diet. This would be of most benefit for the child who had ear infections and circles under his eyes.

2. If the child is ticklish and notices everything, he is probably low in magnesium; five hundred milligrams a day of this safe mineral should calm the child down in just ten days. Most of these children are low in calcium, magnesium, B_6, and some amino and essential fatty acids.

3. If the teacher says he is okay in the morning, but a terror in the afternoon, he is eating something for lunch that is stimulating him (sugar, additives?). The ones with mood swings (Jekyll-and-Hyde behavior) are usually sensitive to sugar, dairy foods, wheat, corn, or soy.

4. If he seems sullen and has headaches, a hair test might show a heavy-metal toxicity. Test for anemia and treat for pinworms.

5. Since his inability to disregard unimportant stimuli may mean he has a hurt in the pons area of his brain, he would profit from developmental stimulation therapy along with the preceding suggestions. The following homeopathic remedies for hyperactive children are suggested: argenticum nitricum, calcium phosphate, chamomilla, kali bromatum, lycopodium, medorrhinum, stramonium, tuberculinum.[262]

Counseling to alleviate psychological blocks and negative parental attitudes may be necessary. Diagnostic tests for reading disability and education on a close one-to-one basis would be ideal. Self-confidence, a good self-image, and immediate rewards for attainable goals are important in working with these children, who easily become depressed or hostile because of their inability to succeed. As an aside, hyperactivity is inversely related to serotonin levels in the platelets in the blood; the more hyperactive a child is, the lower are his serotonin levels. Vitamin B$_6$ in large doses will increase the serotonin levels.

One authority believes that this type of child does not know where his body is unless he moves. Vestibular stimulation along with crawling, creeping, and jogging may give his nervous system the information that he somehow missed as an infant. A good massage every day will help.

Homeopathic remedies can be dramatic. These herbs should have a calming effect: red clover, catnip, lobelia, valerian, chamomile, lady slipper, mistletoe, hops, skullcap. (Gaia Herbs of Harvard, Massachusetts, has one called Melissa Supreme. It contains lemon balm, chamomile, passion flowers, skullcap, wild oat, gotu kola, and glycerite.)

I discovered that the usual child brought to me for some classroom control is a blond, blue-eyed boy who often has relatives with diabetes, alcoholism, or obesity. He is very ticklish, and his behavior varies from pleasant and compliant to wild and mischievous. I take them all off milk, sugar, junk food, and additives. "Children who have taken more than twenty cycles of antibiotics in their lifetime are over 50 percent more likely to suffer developmental delays."[263] I add magnesium, calcium, and B$_6$. I get them to nibble, eating small amounts frequently. If the parents follow this routine and I choose the clients, I get a 60 to 80 percent control of the "deviant" behavior.

Hyper behavior is on a continuum from barely noticeable to off-the-wall spinning as soon as the child arrives in the home or the classroom. I am sure that a small percent require the drug so that good behavior can be reinforced and unacceptable behavior can be extinguished. We also know that some are hyper because they are anxiety-ridden or cannot read. Many of them are depressed.

Other Related Conditions

Handedness preference is genetically determined. Dr. Robert Block, pediatrician, says that all children are ambidextrous until age three or four. Then they start to show a preference. The majority of people are right-handed, but recent investigations indicate an increasing number (up to 30 percent) of children preferring the left hand; this is probably due to their parents' general awareness that attempts to change dominant left-handedness can cause frustration, stuttering, and learning problems. The breadth of the thumbnails is a clue: The right thumbnail is broader in a person who is genetically right-handed. If the person with a broader right thumbnail prefers to use his *left* hand, it may suggest that he has suffered some neurological impairment to the left side of his brain, from whence emanates the control of the right side of the body. Left cerebral dominance means the person is right-eyed, -eared, -handed, and -footed. Attempts to change dominance, once established, are frustrating to the child and about as difficult as changing blue eyes to brown.

Dyslexia is a specific reading disability; there is no known cause. (Dr. Nina Haddock of Ramona, California, suggests that the simple expression "reading need" might take the onus of permanence off of the affliction.) By the narrowest definition, primary dyslexia applies only to children who have at least average intelligence, have no measurable psychological, physical, or neurological fault, and have not been deprived at home or at school. About 10 percent of the population have this to some extent. They are usually males, and their fathers have had similar problems; this is the genetic type. It is due to a central brain problem rather than to any pathology of the eye itself. Most children with severe eye problems become readers despite their visual handicap; there is more to reading than seeing. It requires a complex neurological pathway involving hearing, vestibular sense, ability to perceive (recognizing the difference between a *b* and a *d*), and remembering the associated sounds. These children with the genetic form of dyslexia can be helped with developmental therapy.

Dr. Albert Galaburda of Boston feels that dyslexics cannot break down words into basic sounds. He said, "The role of vision in dyslexia has been ignored mainly because ophthalmologists could find no difference between the eyes of good readers and bad readers." Dyslexia researcher Dr. Drake Duane of Arizona State University states, "The nervous systems of those who are dyslexic are atypical." Something is wrong with the structure or the connections in the cerebral nervous system. This is why I could not get these patients to read, even with the best of diets and vitamins. The brain distributes language processing over many areas; learning is a function of the entire central nervous system. Researchers have found different speeds of processing of incoming language and visual stimuli. "One of the main functions of the brain is to coordinate information received through the sense organs and to translate this raw data from the senses into meaning—a process we know as perception."[264] So states Faulkner, an expert on dyslexia. Poor readers have a lack of eye-hand coordination, poor figure-ground perception, a lack of accurate sense of position in space, and distorted spatial relationships.

Most of these children have vestibular problems. Neurodevelopmental training can allow these children to coordinate what they see and hear. Then they can learn to read. Many of their primitive reflexes had been retained. How the child processes what is coming into the retina and on back to the brain for organization can also be helped by optometic therapy, preferably by someone who uses perceptual sensory training (see Defective Vision, Chapter 4). Developmental optometrists may use vestibular stimulation on a trampoline to encourage the growth of the dendrites in the nervous system to bridge the gap from some former hurt.

Conceptualization of speech occurs in the left cerebral hemisphere as a part of the intertwining of auditory and visual association areas. (The right cerebral hemisphere area is involved with spatial relations.) The victim of dyslexia may be unable to use his association areas to give meaning to the word he is "seeing."

Learning disorder means about the same: some neurological problem that precludes adequate progress. It includes mental retardation, sensory impairment, short attention span, poor memory, deficient conceptualization, and distractibility. About three fourths of infants in whom learning problems later developed had suffered some considerable trauma before or during birth.[265] Some simply went to school before they were ready for reading. Girls can usually learn to read at age five and a half, but boys should probably wait until six and a half, or even seven, before they start the first grade. (A Gesell study found that early eruption of teeth was correlated with academic ability: The earlier the loss of the incisors and the eruption of the six-year molars, the higher were the scholastic abilities.)

No specific test can detect children who are destined to do poorly in school, but the kindergarten teacher would be suspicious, and the first-grade teacher would know. If behavior modification techniques and/or medication do not route the child into normal class advancement, he becomes more disruptive because he is angry and frustrated. Inability to read at grade level must be investigated next. Remedial reading is the next step, and if success is early, he may yet keep up with his class. Maintaining a satisfactory self-image is all-important. Early identification is the cornerstone of treatment; the further behind the child is academically, the more difficult is the remedy.

Nothing is wrong except they are unable to relate the printed word with its appropriate sound. (The Japanese claim dyslexia is unknown to them, as there is a specific sound for each character.) They may become disruptive and distractible, and have a short attention span secondary to the reading difficulty. Failure and frustration push these children into an antisocial subculture where they find peer group acceptance. Those children with subtle learning problems get abused by teachers, parents, and classmates.[266]

The cerebellum and the vestibular systems are involved, and these can be fixed with developmental therapy.

Early childhood clues that dyslexia may develop: delayed speech, marked stuttering, cluttering (see Communication Disorders, this chapter), poor self-expression. After the first grade the dyslexic child shows poor memory for printed (in contrast to spoken) words, spelling is bizarre, handwriting is atrocious (sports skills may be excellent), and there is difficulty with time and up-down concepts.

The problem becomes obvious by the first half of the second grade; a thorough investigation must be made by this time and appropriate remedial measures taken. Many children cannot learn to read if the look-and-say method is employed. The phonic method (sounding out) is used as remediation; it should be the primary method. Most schools have remedial reading programs successful with the first or second grader who has a developmental lag in reading skills. The severely dyslexic victim is unreachable via the usual visual pathways, so auditory and kinesthetic (touch) methods must be used. The teacher's expertise and enthusiasm are all-important.[267]

Education is rooted in reading ability, so the child who cannot read becomes frustrated by his embarrassment, hates school, and develops antisocial and/or psychological symptoms. Every effort must be made to bolster his ego and give him success as quickly as possible. Fire setting and vandalism directed at schools are often the end result of school failure.

Also, "Dietary deficiencies are hampering neural function in these children."[268]

Developmental optometrists are skilled in dealing with these children. Auditory specialists should be part of the team. Many of these children have retained some of the primitive reflexes. The therapy attempts to override those primitive ones and recapitulate normal development.

OTHER THERAPIES FOR THE LEARNING-DISABLED AND THE HYPERACTIVE CHILD

My approach of no milk and no sugar worked on many of my blue-eyed blonds and the green-eyed redheads who had a family history of sugar problems and who were sensitive to dairy, but it did not work on all. Dr.

Benjamin Feingold provided insights into a child's maladaptive behavior when he discovered that sensitivities to certain dyes, additives, aspirin, and related salicylate foods caused the brain to go on "tilt." He opened the door to interest in anything that might cause a child's brain to misfire: lead and mercury poisoning, aspartame reactions, fluorescent lights, parasites, tough teachers, and pressure from unaligned cranial bones. Cranial-sacral therapy can be dramatic with many of these children if diet and the supplements have proven to be ineffective.[269] These are quotes from the medical literature assembled by Doctor's Data of West Chicago, Illinois: "Hair cadmium and lead were significantly correlated with both intelligence scores and school achievement scores."[270] "Increases in arsenic and the interaction of arsenic with lead were significantly related to decreased reading and spelling achievement."[271] "Slightly increased levels of mercury in hair have been associated with decreases in academic ability."[272] There are more.

Neurodevelopmental Therapy. Now, due to the seminal work of Florence Scott, R.N., of Oregon, we have been able to bring order out of chaos. As a young nurse assigned to paralyzed victims of stroke and diving accidents, she was able to stimulate the regrowth of nerve fibers—but, of course, not the nerve cells themselves. These axons and dendrites were able to bypass the nonfunctioning nerves and make new connections. She translated that information (neurological healing) to the reconnection of nerve departments in children diagnosed as brain-damaged.

A hurt to the nervous system produced a developmental delay: The infants and children did not arrive at their normal stages of development at a reasonable time. She noted that most of the children retained many primary reflexes long after these reflexes should have been stored or replaced with the postural relexes or the more mature ones emanating from the cortex.

She found that if she could reintroduce the child (or adult) to the activities that were functioning at the level of the hurt, she could stimulate nerve fibers to work around the defect. She asks, "Where are the breaks in neurological development?" Start at the bottom and stimulate the brain by use; the axons and dendrites will regenerate and reorganize. The newborn is at the medulla level: sucking, breathing, digesting, and defecating. By one year the infant is at the cortex level. The parts of the brain are there, but not usable until the nerves are myelinated (have their insulation).

Scott and her trainees teach the parents what to do after she has determined at what level of the nervous system lies the break. She has these hurt children crawl on their bellies like a lizard for five minutes twice a day for as long as it takes—months, sometimes—if she thinks the damage was at the pons level of the brain. Then, creeping exercises are performed if the problem is felt to be at the midbrain level. Vestibular stimulation is appropriate for the hyper child with reading problems. Goddard states, "Stimulation of the postural reflexes through specific physical exercises can encourage the development of more mature patterns of response and will also suppress underlying reflex activity. Balance and coordination will improve. One must inhibit retained primitive reflexes as these impede the processing of information in the brain."[273]

If a teacher is having a tough time with a noncooperative pupil, she could get the child to do the creeping and crawling around the classroom as if the child were on an obstacle course. It is not punishment; it is a game, but one with therapeutic results. A teacher might find that a child can be helped with spinning about: "Go outside and do your vestibulars."

COMMUNICATION DISORDERS

This is the general term used to encompass defects of hearing, vision, perception, cognition, speech, or learning.

Speech. Since meaningful speech is dependent upon adequate hearing, early assessment of gross hearing in infancy should be a part of the early examination of the child (by six months). A child should have a few intelligible words by two years of age. A child should be able to speak at least one or two sentences by age three, be able to pronounce initial consonants by age two or three. If things seem amiss, an exhaustive evaluation of the auditory apparatus must be made, as development of communication relies heavily on ability to hear (see Deafness, Chapter 4).

Lack of early speech, beyond the babbling in the first few months, usually means a sensorineural defect (inner-ear, cochlear, or auditory nerve malfunction). It is vitally important that the babbling and syllabic repetitions the infant makes be reinforced by imitations from the adults in the environment. A reflex speech pattern is established early, and communication is enhanced. If a baby says "da-da," and no one responds with a smile and a "da-da," he may stop saying it and remain silent for lack of a reward.

Stuttering is nonfluency in speech, and is considered abnormal after age five. It is so common for the two- to four-year-old to try to imitate the fluent parent that he becomes trapped, as if he shifted into neutral with the motor running. His thought comes out like this: "I...I...I...I...go...go... go...to...Grandma's." If the "helpful" listeners try to slow him down or have him repeat the sentence correctly, he becomes involved in the *mechanism* of the idea, and his nonfluency is enforced. (Ask a musician or an athlete to analyze his technique. He just "does it." To pick it apart makes him slow and clumsy.) Dominance training would help this situation.

When their child stutters, parents must discipline themselves to avoid comment. They must look on it as a normal developmental stage in the child's progress, just as standing and falling must precede walking. Most children sail through this if they are *not* told it is wrong. A very few with psychological and/or neurological problems will remain fixed at this immature level. Help is needed if improvement is not shown by the fifth birthday.

Cluttering is a speech imbalance frequently seen in a hyperactive, impulsive, outgoing child. He talks rapidly, but repetitions, hesitations, and incomplete sentences are frequent. Dyslexia is commonly associated with cluttering. Something is not working. At least check the eardrums.

Echolalia is the seemingly mechanical repetition of words or syllables. The small child just learning to talk will say "ba" in imitation of hearing someone else say it. The child may originate the conversation by making a random babbling sound that the eager parent praises. Thus, if the child says "da," the father may interpret it as the forerunner of "daddy," and repeat it to the child, who in turn repeats it in a circular kind of communication. The three-year-old may respond by repeating the last word or two of a sentence. This is a normal part of the process of learning to talk. Vestibular stimulation is indicated for this child if echolalia continues beyond this age.

Convulsions, seizures, and epilepsy are periodic attacks of involuntary movements, thoughts, or feelings, with or without an alteration of the consciousness. Children have a low threshold for seizures; conditions like fever, electrolyte imbalances, and other stressors may result in a seizure. If the condition is labeled epilepsy: (1) seizures are recurrent, (2) they are usually the same, and (3) the patient is relatively normal between attacks.

Recent evidence indicates that only about 40 percent are controllable, not curable. There is no epileptic personality. The IQ range of the epileptic child has the same distribution as the normal population.

The brain-wave test, or electroencephalogram (EEG), may be a useful tool in aiding diagnosis, but is not infallible, as some seizures have their origin deep in the brain, too remote for the test to reveal. (Conversely, 15 percent of "normal" children have abnormal EEGs.)

Seizures due to birth anoxia, meningitis, metabolic disorders (alkalinity), hypoglycemia, PKU disease, congenital syphilis, rubella, toxoplasmosis, and other problems are more likely to be associated with mental retarda-tion or the hyperactive syndrome.

Tonic-clonic seizure (formerly called grand mal) is the more common type. (One third of seizures in children are of this type.) Usually an aura (noise, lights, pain) or some strange symptom (stomachache or headache, irritability) gives warning of the explosion to come. The victim suddenly stiffens, cries out, falls, and his eyes roll up. Initial pallor is replaced by flushing, then cyanosis as he holds his breath. After thirty seconds of |stiffness, the body is overcome by a series of powerful, jerking, rhythmic movements that may go on for some minutes. Urine is usually forced out of the bladder by the straining. Sleep is the usual rule after this exhaust-ing exercise. Some headache and mental confusion are present after awakening.

It may be a manifestation of stress due to a high fever, head trauma, tox-icity, lack of oxygen from breath holding, low blood sodium, or low blood sugar (hypoglycemia). A brain lesion must be ruled out with the EEG and the MRI (Magnetic Resonance Imaging) tests. Half the children with one of these frightening episodes will not have another, which brings up the dilemma: Should this be treated? Many of these children are somewhat alkaline as demonstrated by the blood test.[274]

Absence seizure (formerly called petit mal) occurs in about 4 percent of children with epilepsy. These seizures commonly begin about the age of five years, and there is a family connection. The child momentarily loses consciousness and seems to stare vacantly into space, then resumes the pre-seizure activity. She does not fall, has no memory of the lapse, and is fre-quently accused of inattention or daydreaming. She may have many attacks a day. The EEG shows a typical pattern. Although control is sometimes dif-ficult, some may outgrow the problem by adolescence. Hyperventilation (overbreathing) may bring on an absence attack. These attacks must be dif-ferentiated from partial complex seizures and daydreaming, and structural brain lesions.

Myoclonic seizures are fast, repetitive movements of a muscle group. These jerky movements are not accompanied by a loss of consciousness. They are often associated with some degenerative disease and mental retardation.

Psychomotor attacks may vary from a minor emotional outburst with-out adequate environmental stimulus, to a complicated body action, which, although coordinated, is purposeless (e.g., plucking at clothes, chewing, swallowing, or rubbing hands). Some loss of posture is usually associated with the attack, and there may be hyperactivity before the spell and drowsiness afterward. Sudden unexplained outbursts of violence, aggression, or running away may be classified as psychomotor. The EEG may show that the temporal-lobe area is the focus.

Epileptic equivalent is the name given to any one of a variety of otherwise inexplicable symptoms that may be the result of abortive seizures. Headaches suggesting migraine, stomachaches (abdominal epilepsy) followed by pallor and somnolence, automatic purposeless acts, and sudden, explosive, impulsive attacks may all appear to be psychogenic in origin, but might well be set off by an irritable electrical focus somewhere in the brain. Tourette's syndrome and limbic rages may fit into this category. Fainting attacks without a reasonable environmental stimulus, or unaccompanied by hypoglycemia or anemia, should be investigated.

The majority of grand mal seizures have EEG abnormalities. Psychic strain, fatigue, loss of sleep, or biochemical or infectious agents may precipitate a spell. There are documented cases of grand mal seizures being triggered by certain kinds of music or patterns of light. A two-year-old boy discovered that if he looked through the mesh of the back screen door during April and May at about nine or ten in the morning he would have an exciting—to him—grand mal seizure. It was a visually induced seizure. He got some sadomasochistic high out of the seizures and used to run to the back door every sunny day in the spring. Drugs were worthless. The doctors fitted him with glasses with polarized lenses so the light pattern was changed. No more seizures. One woman has seizures when she hears the voice of a particular television talk-show hostess; her voice sets off abnormal electrical discharges in the brain as detected by the EEG. Treatment: She turns off the television when that woman comes on. How many of us have friends, clients, or relatives whom we cannot stand? Their voices are like fingernails running down the chalkboard. How many of us have cousins who give us a headache, nauseate us, and put us in a trancelike state? Better not visit them; you might have a fit. Some people will have seizures while playing video games on the television monitor.

The workup might include a physical and neurological examination, X ray of skull, urinalysis, blood tests for sugar, acid/base balance, calcium, urea, EEG, and possible spinal tap.

The care of the patient during the seizure involves protecting him from harm. Turning him to the side position to prevent secretions from running down his windpipe and loosening his clothing are all that is necessary. Most patients have bitten their tongues at the onset of the spell, so jamming a stick in the mouth is unnecessary and may only do more harm (break teeth). If the seizure does not stop after a few minutes the patient would benefit by being given some oxygen and perhaps an injection of an anticonvulsant. "More children are hurt, or killed, from overtreatment of seizures than from the seizures themselves."[275]

Most neurologists feel that the surly attitude of some epileptics is due to the attitude of society toward them rather than any inherent neurological nastiness. The Epilepsy League is fighting mightily in an uphill battle to dispel some medieval old wives' tales, but they have a long way to go.

Treatment involves the use of drugs that are increased in dosage until control is effective. An effort should be made to normalize the blood chemistry, as blood tests show most epileptics are somewhat alkaline. Sometimes all they need are some inexpensive acidifiers, like vinegar. If the sodium in the blood is above the mean, and the patient loves vinegar and pickles, he may respond to a teaspoon of apple cider vinegar in a glass of water three times a day. Seizures are a good example of how the chemistry of the body can affect the nervous system in a very dramatic way. Apparently there is a deficiency in the activity of the sodium/potassium adenosine-triphosphatase-membrane pump in the tiny area on the neuron where the seizure begins. It is called an *irritable focus*.

In the last few decades, however, nutrient excesses and deficiencies have proven to be inciting agents to seizures. Hypoglycemia is one cause. (Ninety percent of people with seizures have periodic low blood sugar. This has been known since 1934.) "Electrolyte balance is disturbed and there is a tendency to alkalosis."[276] There is a high percentage of subnormal glucose tolerance tests in epilepsy.[277] Magnesium deficiency is especially common in those with epilepsy. Tetany and convulsions were first shown to occur in magnesium-deficient rats in 1932. In one trial of thirty epileptic patients, 450 milligrams of magnesium daily successfully controlled seizures in all of them.[278] Nerve fibers are influenced by the concentration and ratios of the calcium and the magnesium; they both affect the sodium and potassium permeabilities of the nerve cell wall.

Epileptic patients had significantly lower selenium levels than any group except those with cancer.[279] Manganese may be low in those with epilepsy, whereas serum copper, lead, and mercury may be high. Folic acid, vitamin D, taurine, and B_6 may help control convulsions. The neurotransmitter GABA (gamma-amino-butyric acid) has a calming or inhibitory effect on the nervous system. B_6 is necessary for the synthesis of GABA.

A high-fat diet can be remarkably effective.[280] Bacon, heavy cream, and only enough protein to sustain growth is the diet. Results were good in many who had no control over seizures.

These might help: black cohosh, lobelia, valerian tincture, ginkgo, skullcap, lady slipper.

Tetany is the increased irritability of muscles, usually from a lower-than-normal amount of calcium and/or magnesium in the blood, or higher-than-normal amount of sodium and/or potassium. Alkalosis may be a contributing factor.

Electroencephalogram, or EEG or brain-wave test, is the record of amplified electrical waves that arise from the surface of the brain. It is helpful, but not specific, in diagnosing convulsive disorders, blood clots on the brain, tumors, and other lesions. A high percentage of children have abnormal EEGs associated with an impulsive, explosive, destructive personality (the Terrible-Tempered Mr. Bang).

Dr. Matthew J. Fleischman of Eugene, Oregon, has been using an EEG biofeedback technique to help people develop better focusing techniques. It is a self-regulation of attention without drugs. It helps people regain control of their wandering attention. Close to one thousand universities around the country are using this method.

Hypoglycemia means low blood sugar. Glucose levels in the blood normally rise and fall depending on food intake, exercise, stress, insulin secretion, thyroid function, adrenaline release, fever, and other factors. It is normally at its lowest ebb after nocturnal fasting, and rises in response to meals three times a day. The level rises higher and more rapidly after a sugary or high-carbohydrate meal and rises more slowly but is more sustained after a protein meal. Functional hypoglycemia is the oversecretion of insulin by the pancreas in response to a rapid rise in blood sugar. The blood sugar plummets too rapidly and/or too low below the level necessary to maintain well-being.

The metabolism of the brain is completely dependent on oxygen and glucose; therefore, hypoglycemia first gives rise to symptoms referable to the nervous system.

A new baby might have cold, clammy skin, twitches, eye rolling, drowsiness, or poor feeding or sucking. Hypoglycemia may lead to brain damage and mental retardation, so diagnosis and therapy should not be delayed when the preceding symptoms are noted.[281] Hypoglycemia in the newborn is due to the baby's attempt, in utero, to provide insulin for his diabetic mother (the baby produces extra insulin in response to his mother's hyperglycemia). Immediate oral sugar is the emergency treatment of the hypoglycemia attack.

Children or adults with reactive hypoglycemia (rapid fall of blood glucose two to three hours after a sugary meal) should be provided with three protein or complex carbohydrate servings a day. Garlic pearls three times a day are helpful. When the blood sugar drops, some notice drowsiness. Some become hyperactive. Many are spacey or depressed. A few are mean or appear stupid. Teachers notice that they cannot teach their pupils for the week after Easter or Christmas vacation, and especially after Halloween.

A ten-year-old girl who recently suffered the agonies of her parents' divorce had become mean and vindictive after the breakup, which was as amicable as the parents could make it. The parents had tried to explain everything, but this usually cheerful, open, friendly youngster had become a terrible-tempered Ms. Bang, flying off the handle after minor provocations. The psychologist in charge of the case figured that the girl had not been able to "blow off steam." Part of the story was her huge mood swings. She would be pleasant and compliant, then for some insignificant stressor, she would blow her top. A regular Jekyll-and-Hyde person. We all need a little psychotherapeutic help occasionally, but to deny the laws of chemistry is to cheat the client. Any stressor forces the body to lose calcium, magnesium, potassium, and the B complex vitamins. The blood sugar tends to plummet. With the proper diet and supplements, she became her former cheerful, compliant self. Most people do not eat well after any loss, and these nutrients may not be resupplied for the body's use.

Try this little test: Ask your child to take the garbage out first thing in the morning before breakfast. Ask him/her to do it the following day *after* breakfast. Note the response: On an empty stomach you are likely to be confronted by an angry child with a knife drawn. After a full stomach— when the social part of the brain becomes operative—you will more likely hear, "Okay, whatever you say!"

I have heard of a businessman who takes clients out for breakfast. He serves them a Danish with coffee and sugar while he eats fruit and low-fat sausage or a soft-cooked egg. He can get almost anything he wants from his guest in about forty-five minutes.

I tend to get depressed during the Christmas holidays. A psychiatrist would tell me that it is because my mother has long since died, and that holidays bring back old memories of supportive things I never told her when she was alive. The real reason I am dull, pouty, and mute is that I am eating tons of cookies left on our doorstep by well-meaning friends and relatives.

Researchers found that "blood sugar levels fell significantly further in the children than in the adults. The children's adrenaline levels rose twice as high as the adults' and remained elevated during the five hours of scientific observation."[282]

Licorice root helps to normalize blood sugar levels.

A doctor who is asked to see a child with "peculiar symptoms" may be tempted to overutilize the laboratory. We used to get X rays, kidney studies, calcium, and sugar levels in the hope that something would show up. A baby with convulsions may not need extensive testing, but should at least have a fasting blood-sugar test. If the convulsions are due to hypoglycemia, he will surely be brain-damaged if the condition is not corrected immediately. (A patient I knew with a blood sugar level of twenty to thirty milligrams per one hundred milliliters of blood at age three months had to have seven-eighths of his pancreas removed before his seizures stopped. The investigation, however, was not made early enough to prevent brain damage. His IQ ended up at about fifty.)

Eighty percent of the people who telephone me by mistake have not eaten a proper meal. All this fits with the following typo from the Concord, N.H., *Monitor* (the printer probably had a sugary breakfast): "She will work with physicians at the hospital to treat patients with acute and chronic lunch problems."

Glucose tolerance test is a method of assaying the body's ability to absorb, transport, use, store, and excrete a specific amount of glucose taken orally. After ingestion, blood glucose levels are determined at half-hour, hour, two-, three-, four-, five-, and six-hour intervals. The test is valuable in detecting equivocal cases of diabetes, renal glycosuria, and hypoglycemia.

Motion sickness is a common problem of all age groups. It is an uncontrollable attack of nausea, vomiting, pallor, cold sweat, and weakness that persists in some people for the duration of a car, boat, train, or plane ride.

True vertigo is due to the reflex action of the hypersensitive vestibular (balancing) apparatus in the inner ear. It's a sign that the messages received from the body (proprioceptors) do not coincide with the messages from the eyes. It happens in the car, when the frame of the car remains stable in relation to the eyes, but the body experiences the changes in gravity as the car sways. The vagus nerve gets stimulated and tells the stomach to empty. Vestibular stimulation may be the best treatment. It may be controlled by the calming action of antihistaminics or by the use of antivomiting tranquilizers. It is best to administer the drug about one half hour before departure.

Light-headedness, giddiness, weakness, or dizziness is suggested if the child lists and falls to one side as if drunk. This condition is due to temporary cerebral hypoxia (decreased blood flow). Anemia, intestinal cramps or flu, low blood sugar (hypoglycemia), hyperventilation, sudden standing after lying down (postural hypotension; may mean poor adrenal gland function), toxins from inhaling chemicals (sick building syndrome), or a shot in the doctor's office without crying may all produce a light-headed feeling (see Fainting Spells, Chapter 15). Hunger should be thought of. Allergic disturbances may produce vertigo or light-headedness, and improve with allergic control (tomatoes, citrus, wheat, milk).

Motion sickness can be controlled with ginger (two five-hundred-milligram capsules about an hour before traveling, acupressure bracelets, ginger tea, or ginger candy). Cocculus and gelsemium can be helpful. Swallowing one teaspoon of onion juice with one teaspoon of honey might stop the dizziness.[283]

If vertigo occurs in a child, it is usually due to inflammation or edema of the inner ear (labyrinthitis) and adjacent balance-control structures. Otitis media is noted, and the vertigo disappears after treatment or discontinuation of milk ingestion.

CHAPTER 10

Things You Thought You Would Never Have to Deal With

AGGRESSIVE REACTIONS

Aggressive reactions include anger, defiance, disobedience, delinquency, and arson. With the help of his parents, the growing child learns what he can and cannot do or have. If it is impossible for him to control his anger by channeling or expressing it—not suppressing it—by age six years, then something has gone wrong either psychologically, nutritionally, or neurologically. He is fixed at an immature level of development. Physically he is six, but emotionally he still acts like a two-year-old. The kindergarten teacher is best able to detect this infantile behavior because he has the rest of the class with whom to compare him.

The workup for a child with these attributes would include a hair analysis for heavy-metal toxicity, evaluation of the diet, search for pesticides in home or environment (flea collars, pest strips, louse shampoos, lawns treated with organophosphates), and neurodevelopmental analysis. Psychological counseling should be a part of the program. If drugs are used to control behavior, they should only be for a short period of time.

Oppositional defiant disorder (ODD) is one category of behavioral disturbances. This one has a pattern of negativism, hostility, disobedience, and outright defiance, and shows up before age eight years. These children are hostile and negative: arguing with adults, temper tantrums, noncompli-

263

ance, and inability to compromise. There is often a family history of similar problems; these children have been subjected to inconsistent punishment or neglectful child care. Psychiatric care or family therapy is suggested.

Conduct disorder is the other category and includes four groups: aggressive reactions, nonaggressive conduct (deliberate destruction of another person's property), deceitfulness (lying, breaking promises, shoplifting), and violation of rules (running away overnight, staying out late). Many children with these problems have a family history of similar conduct, have a drug problem, and often have a learning disorder.[284]

ANOREXIA NERVOSA

Anorexia nervosa is a fairly rare but potentially serious emotional disturbance, usually found in adolescent girls, as only 10 percent of those with anorexia nervosa are boys. Severe restriction of food intake, coupled with alarming weight loss, triggers the parents to be punitive at mealtime—which only seems to make the victim more determined to waste away. Logic is of no help. Psychiatric aid is needed. Early, conflictful parent-child relationships and/or schizoid traits seem to be the norm. The father may have set up the problem by his remark, "If you could just lose about ten pounds, you would be perfect." The girl can never live up to the father's ideal of perfection. Once the girl has gone through a few meals of eating a tablespoon of cottage cheese and a lettuce leaf, she notices that some attention has been paid to her.

"Finish your dinner, dear," her mother prods. The anorexic girl finds that this is a way of gaining control.

Her father takes up the gauntlet. "Listen to your mother. It's good for you. Eat it," he demands with clenched teeth. She eats less and locks herself in her room. Then, because of the meager diet, she becomes deficient in the B vitamins and zinc. These deficiencies cause food to taste terrible, which helps her continue the impoverishment.

What has started as an adolescent game has become a nutritional deficiency and a psychiatric nightmare. A zinc solution dropped on her tongue will taste like water, a positive diagnosis of zinc deficiency. A person with adequate stores of zinc finds the drops are very offensive. The amazing thing is that the semistarved girl will start to eat when the zinc therapy has been used for a couple of weeks. Although psychiatric help is advised, zinc therapy for these people may be all that is necessary. Zinc-deprived people have impaired concentration, irritability, antagonism, and nasty temper tantrums. Their sense of taste and smell disappear, and food may taste like excrement. No wonder they won't eat.

Overcontrol is the theme of most of these families. If the young lady feels she cannot escape, she will show her drive for freedom and power with a passive-aggressive act: anorexia.[285]

ANXIETY

In 1924 Dr. Searle Harris reported in the *Journal of the American Medical Association* that many of his patients had panic attacks, nervousness, feelings of doom, weakness, and insomnia. He found that the following were usually the basis of their "psychosomatic" complaints:

1. Deficiencies or inactivation of any of the more than forty vitamins, minerals, amino acids, and essential fatty acids that the brain needs to function; the body cannot make something out of nothing;

2. The presence of toxic metals;

3. Hypoglycemia;

4. Food sensitivities and environmental allergies, plus adrenal gland insufficiency.[286]

Francis Pottenger, in his *Pottenger's Cats,* reminds us that the quality of nutrition in childhood correlates with the ability to handle stress as an adult.[287]

Anxiety is the conscious awareness of the symptoms of fear—rapid heartbeat, shortness of breath, chest pain, nausea, tightness in the muscles, flushing of skin, sweaty palms, tremors, crying, and a feeling of impending doom—without certain knowledge of the cause.

Anxiety is a leftover emotion from a more primitive era when people frequently met extreme physical threats. Anxiety was more useful then. When a caveman met a ferocious beast, he needed these physical aspects. The sight of the beast is registered in the temporal lobe of the brain, which remembers that these animals are dangerous. The temporal lobe quickly sends a message to the hypothalamus, the master control area for the endocrine glands. In the split second that the hypothlamus finds out about the danger, it sends a message to the pituitary, which produces hormones that increase the blood sugar and speed up the metabolism. The adrenal glands are also alerted and secrete cortisone and adrenaline—flight or fight are the choices.

Just a decade ago psychiatric theory assumed that anxiety was due to some psychic block smoldering just under the surface. Parental oversolicitude? Conflict in the home? Does the home prize outward tranquillity and control? All true, but new evidence indicates that biochemical factors are playing a big role: "Up until about five years ago, if you talked about the neurochemical basis of anxiety, people would laugh at you."[288] Now many psychiatrists are controlling their patients' anxieties with biological therapies. Almost everyone can benefit from understanding the chemical factors that help create anxiety and the nutritional factors that will help end it.

That adrenaline release allowed our ancestors to survive. Now we have far fewer immediate physical threats. But people still have this same strong, physical anxiety reaction, even though most modern threats and stressors are largely symbolic. For example, trying to finish homework by bedtime evokes the same essential physical responses as trying to kill a saber-toothed tiger. However, the body no longer needs this extreme physical reaction, because homework simply does not require a monumental "flight" or "fight." Consequently, we are often in a state of fearful anticipation because we are filled with unused adrenaline coursing through our arteries to those tense muscles. "The fight or flight emergency response is inappropriate to today's social stresses," says Harvard's Dr. Herbert Benson.[289]

But the nervous system is there, waiting to be used. The glands, with their hormones, and the brain areas are ready. In some children, though, these physical defense systems seem to be, in effect, too "ready," too "tightly wired." In these children the anxiety reaction is too easy to trigger. These are the chronic worriers, who are fearful and anxious, who have a low threshold for stress, who have complex phobias, and who have constant anxiety. They are labeled "neurotics."

Telling these children to "take it easy, relax" doesn't work. Specific nutrients, dietary change, desensitization techniques, breathing techniques, and exercise programs combined with psychological counseling are the therapies that help patients.

In the 1930s Hans Selye became aware that when an animal perceives a stressful situation, a General Adaptive Syndrome is activated: cortisol and adrenaline are released from the adrenal glands, lymphocytes are released from the spleen and lymph nodes, and if prolonged, hemorrhages and ulcers appear in the stomach lining. We animals can handle short-term stressors, but if the stressors are chronic, and if the diet is inadequate to replace the lost nutrients, disease will overcome us. Loss of autonomy is the worst stress of all. What chance does a child have in a house full of rage on a diet of Twinkies ?

But many children feel anxious and tense without a stressor (tiger) in their environment. That is a dysperception. Even without a scary object to fight or run away from, they still become nervous or edgy. In these people it is so easy to set off the fight/flight response that any minor stress can provoke strong physical feelings of anxiety and nervousness—at least a rapid heart and sweaty palms. Life provides an abundance of minor stressors. Of course, we know there are stimulus seekers who put themselves into stressful situations: telling lies, stealing cookies, cheating. Are they addicted to excitement? They are the "adrenaline junkies."

Hyperactivity is connected to the same chemical loop. When I examined eight thousand hyperactive children who were unable to settle down in the classroom, most of them were ticklish, sensitive, had a short attention span, and were **unable to disregard unimportant stimuli.** That last feature is what got them into trouble with the teacher and prevented them from finishing their work (see Limbic System, Chapter 8).

More than 90 percent of people with hypoglycemia report feelings of nervousness, and at least 60 percent noted anxiety as a prominent symptom. Hypoglycemia will cause B complex vitamins and magnesium to run out of the body; these are the very nutrients we need to stay calm.

Caffeine can cause nervousness and headaches when one tries to withdraw from a five-cup-a-day habit. Two to three cups of coffee doubles the amount of epinephrine floating about in the blood stream. Same with caffeine in soft drinks. (Is it acting like Ritalin?)

The treatment is to help these people disregard some of this incoming stimuli. Magnesium (five hundred milligrams daily), calcium (one thousand milligrams daily), niacin (produces an uncomfortable flush, so start with a low dose, fifty to one hundred milligrams daily and try to build up to five hundred milligrams), vitamin C (one thousand to five thousand milligrams daily, depending on age and bowel tolerance), B_6, and thiamine improve the screening device and can calm anxiety.[290] These harmless nutrients encourage the manufacture of antianxiety neurotransmitters. Other neuroregulators of special importance are prostaglandins derived from fatty acids. Gamma-amino-butyric acid (GABA) is an important neurotransmitter in the brain and has the property of inhibiting the transmission of impulses over the nerve network. Its primary effect is to calm the brain's function by limiting its activity. An anxious person has too many of the wrong chemicals and too few of the right ones. Valerian, skullcap, passion flower, and myrrh are calming agents. Homeopathic remedies for the anxiety often seen in children include aconite, calcium carbonate, gelsemium, lycopodium, and silicea.[291]

No caffeine, alcohol, white flour, or sugar of course. Eat small amounts every two to four hours to maintain the blood sugar. Check the blood test for chemical imbalances.[292]

AUTISM

Autism is early childhood withdrawal. There is a reluctance of the infant or child to engage in social interaction, e.g., smiling, and responding when fed, held, or entertained. The child relates to humans as if they were inanimate pieces of furniture. The child indulges in routine, stereotypical mannerisms, such as hand waving and rocking. He is initially classified as mentally retarded or deaf because of his immature and indifferent social behavior. But when testing is successful, abilities may be found to be higher than suspected, albeit deficient. Various strange withdrawal signs are found, along with his desire to maintain a pathological, monotonous sameness in his surroundings.

Treatment is generally unrewarding, but possible. Dr. Bernard Rimland of San Diego has found that these children are more likely to respond to the use of vitamin B_6 (two hundred and fifty to seven hundred and fifty milligrams, or eight milligrams of B_6 per pound of weight) and three hundred milligrams of magnesium along with the other vitamins and minerals. Rimland quotes a study by French professor Gilbert LeLord: Ninety-one children were treated with the B_6 and the magnesium. Fourteen percent improved markedly, 33 percent improved, 42 percent showed no improvement, and the remainder became worse. Vestibular stimulation has helped to improve the eye contact. *The Ultimate Stranger: The Autistic Child*, by Carl Delacato is valuable reading. Cranial therapy has slowed some of the head banging. Some of these children need to be institutionalized because of their unpredictable outbursts or severe intellectual retardation. Behavior modification—reward for social interaction—is part of the therapy. A postvaccination encephalitis can trigger autism (see Immunizations, Chapter 7). Dimethylglycine (one hundred and twenty-five milligrams per day) has proven helpful; large doses seem safe. Antifungal medications may be curative if the symptoms developed after heavy antibiotic use.[293]

BEDWETTING

Bedwetting or enuresis is the persistence of nocturnal wetting; 8 percent of girls wet the bed after age four years, and 15 percent of boys after age five. The cause is unknown in the vast majority of cases, but a hereditary tendency is usually present. Scientists studied four hundred families and found a genetic marker in 90 percent of families. These children often have a small bladder capacity and a penchant for deep sleep.

These children should be checked for: (1) anomalies of the urethra, bladder, and ureters; (2) urinary infection; (3) diabetes; (4) sensitivities to milk, citrus juices, or chocolate. Poor school performance, unhealthy environmental attitudes, and other emotional disturbances may be causative, but many feel these are secondary to the concern over the wetting.

Genetic susceptibility plus some nutritional factor or stress allows the problem to become manifest. Chiropractors have found that a number of patients have a subluxation between cervical vertebrae number one and two. Sometimes a pelvic adjustment is necessary. (A Wisconsin chiropractor told me that the most common cause of bedwetting is that the child has fallen backward off the turnip truck and landed flat on his/her lower back. The pelvic adjustment gets the lower back and the wetting under control.) Some evidence indicates that the infantile spinal Galant reflex is still present and must be inhibited. The child wants to control it, but nothing short of sleeping on the toilet will keep the bed dry.

A routine urinalysis is the minimum workup. If oddities are suspected, a specialist (urologist) is needed to determine the size and efficiency of the bladder and kidneys. Watching the child urinate will often tell about urological health. Without straining, the stream should be forceful, making bubbles in the toilet bowl. The stream size is important.

If no anomalies or infections are found, one must consider a sensitivity. It is as if the bladder is sneezing. Anything can do it, but is usually some milk or juice: chocolate, orange, tomato, pineapple, or peach. The sensitizing food or drink, rather than the volume of urine, seems to irritate the bladder to empty at undesirable times. It is worth trying. Eliminate milk, ice cream, and cottage cheese from the diet for a week or ten days. If he stays dry, milk is the culprit, and without it, his bedwetting is cured. "You may have to eliminate foods to which a person is sensitive for a long time before you can see a positive change. It was sixteen weeks in the case of one girl."[294]

After a child passes the age of six or seven, he usually becomes embarrassed about his condition, especially when he finds that he cannot spend the night with friends or go on camping trips. The child may get neurotic or feel inferior as a result of the bedwetting. "Passive or urethral aggression" is the psychiatrist's term. The bed is equated with the mother, as it is soft and warm. The child is paying the mother back for some real or imagined put-down. He is "taking a leak on her." This is hard to believe knowing how deeply these children sleep.

The child, a deep sleeper, usually has a small or "immature" bladder. It is not able to store all the urine that has accumulated during the night. His bladder sends a message to the spinal cord saying it is full; however, no message from the spinal cord gets to the social part of the brain that knows it is unacceptable to urinate in bed. The social awareness part of the brain is asleep and unable to respond to the message of the full bladder. The spinal cord does not have any social awareness, so without the brain telling it what to do, it acts on its own authority. It sends back the message to the bladder: "Dump it!"

Almost all children outgrow the condition when they fully mature. Their muscle strength is greater, their bladder capacity has increased, and they may not be sleeping as deeply as they did in their childhood, so they become more aware of the full-bladder impulses that tell the sleeping brain to find a toilet.

Awakening the child and taking him to the toilet between 11:00 P.M. and midnight may keep the bed dry, but the bladder doesn't "learn" anything. The brain must help out.

Old-fashioned methods—strapping objects to the back (so the child cannot sleep supine; pressure on the kidneys?), eating salty nuts or raisins at bedtime (the raisins are supposed to turn to grapes during the night to soak up the fluid), or sleeping with head lower than feet—may work by preventing sound sleep and allowing the victim to be more aware of bladder distention and find a toilet.

Devices that ring bells at the first bit of wetting usually serve to awaken the family, who must then arouse the child. The method does work, though, on the conditioned-reflex principle. There is a correlation between dyslexia and bedwetting. If a developmental program is instituted, bedwetting can disappear. Some studies indicate that enuretics as a group have a higher-than-normal incidence of abnormal EEGs.

A logical training regimen can help if the child is at least seven years old and motivated. During the day he can be rewarded for holding his urine instead of passing it at the first urge. He should also learn to stop and start the stream a few times during urination. These exercises can stretch his bladder capacity and develop voluntary brain control over the sphincter muscle that holds urine in the bladder. Five hundred milligrams of magnesium at bedtime might allow the bladder to stretch enough to hold the required ten ounces. Adjustments by the chiropractor can be dramatic. Because low blood sugar and the resultant deep sleep is a factor in bed-wetting, the child should eat a protein snack at bedtime and have no sugary goodies.

A recent treatment involves the use of desmopressin acetate as a nasal spray. Its main therapy is for those with diabetes insipidus. A four- to eight-week trial is reasonably safe, and modestly effective, in children age six years or older. Homeopathy and herbal medicines will also help with this condition.

The family's attitude should be a casual and relaxed approach. If he has been dry for some time and then develops this trait, one should look for physical problems, diseases, and, more important, school pressures or other emotional difficulties that may have cropped up.

DEPRESSION

Depression in children is the result of the loss of some love object. The depth or quality of the reaction may seem inappropriate by adult standards but should be respected by the family members. Some children are, by temperament, more easily upset, sensitive, or depressed than others in the family because of their nature, or because they are low in some nutrient. Children who have been taught to control hostile feelings completely will more easily turn these feelings toward themselves, and their guilt will devastate them into depressive reactions more readily. Sometimes a child will make depressive statements such as "No one likes me" or "I'm stupid," and he automatically gets a reassuring statement from the parents. The child receives this as "They need for me to be happy." But he might find it more useful to learn that ups and downs are part of the life game. He should be listened to and allowed to think of his own way out; it may be less reinforcing of the depressing comments.

Therapy using the nutriments in the Anxiety section would be helpful. Nutritional therapies are well-researched and nontoxic, and have no side effects.

The administration of tryptophan (forms serotonin) alone accounted for the recovery of seven of eleven patients hospitalized for depression. For tryptophan to be utilized properly, most people take it with extra B_6 and C, cofactors in the synthesis of serotonin. It has been found that people who have committed suicide tended to have a deficiency in their ability to use serotonin.[295] In some, just using phenylalanine was enough to control depression in twelve of twenty hospitalized patients.[296] Phenylalanine improved 95 percent of 370 depressed patients.[297] The amino acid tyrosine was also shown to be an effective antidepressant.[298]

These antidepressent nutrients are found in foods, but not usually in sufficient enough amounts to be therapeutic for the depressed child. Amino acid powders can make up the difference. Blood tests determine which neurotransmitter precursors are inadequate. The treatment is then more accurate. Amino acids are of limited use without the appropriate vitamins and minerals, all in a milieu of the proper acid/base balance.

Low levels of zinc, B_6, and manganese in the body will allow susceptible children to become depressed. Depressed patients were found to have low folic acid levels.[299] Too much histamine, the substance liberated in the allergy reaction, can lead to depression. If the histamine level is lowered by methionine and calcium, the depression is relieved. High copper in the blood and brain can lead to depression, and sometimes paranoia. Vitamin C, zinc, and manganese will help get rid of the copper load. (Look for copper pipes; it competes with zinc for entrance into the body. We need both, but in the proper ratio.) Exposure to lead, cadmium, mercury, and arsenic should be tested for with a hair mineral analysis.

Depressed children tend to have a "malabsorption syndrome," a general failure of the body to properly utilize nutrients, including those the brain needs. "Many people are not digesting and absorbing food properly, so they do not receive the nutritional precursors needed by the brain. Often, this failure is not of sufficient severity to be recognized by the family doctor. Food allergies and sensitivities contribute to malabsorption of needed nutrients."[300]

When people felt terrible despite eating good and nourishing foods, I would inject them with vitamins and minerals intramuscularly and intravenously, with startling and sometimes unexpected success. They would report a feeling of well-being, of better sleep, of less gas, more cheerfulness, and buoyancy. They had been taking the vitamins and minerals by mouth, but got no benefit until I injected the same ones into their bodies, bypassing the inefficient intestinal tract. For a variety of reasons, the intestinal lining was not working, and it needed those nutrients to form the enzymes in the cells of the intestines that do the digesting and absorbing. But they could not absorb them because the lining cells did not have the proper nutrients. A catch-22: They could not get well because they were sick. After a few shots that transported the nutrients to the digesting cells via the circulatory system, they were able to carry on—like priming the pump. B_{12} by injection seems to be the most important one of the B vitamins to improve intestinal absorption.

Homeopathic remedies for sadness in children might include aurum, ignatia, natrum muriaticum, phosphoric acid, and pulsatilla. These can be helpful to improve digestion and mood: oats, ginkgo, gotu kola, dong quai, borage, basil, skullcap, hops, suma, Saint-John's-wort.[301]

Balancing the body chemistry, especially the acid/base metabolism, can control many disease entities. If the patient it alkaline, they get an acidic diet. If acidic, they receive an alkaline producing diet.[302]

PARASITES AND WORMS

Our hunting-and-gathering ancestors did not have the parasitic infections that we do because they kept moving to new locations. Most parasites have an intermediate host, like snails, earth, or other animals. But now, because of antibiotics, day care, foreign travel, immigration, water contamination, low fiber consumption, bottle-feeding, and diet changes, it is estimated that 30 to 50 percent of our population harbors some kind of parasite. Apparently antibiotic use alters the balance of intestinal organisms. Parasites prevent absorption of necessary nutrients from swallowed food. Sickness follows and more antibiotics are prescribed, leading to more distortion of the intestinal milieu.

Pinworms are the most common cause of night wakefulness in children. (One of my four-month-old patients acquired worms from his four-year-old sister, who was "helpful" in feeding and changing him. The mother thought her baby had colic, but one day when she was changing his diaper, he happened to discharge a stool with a great number of quarter-inch white, crawly, squirming worms. Both children were treated with the appropriate medicine, and both were soon cheerful and happy again.)

In infant girls, these small worms may wiggle forward into the vaginal opening, up through the uterus, out the fallopian tubes and into the peritoneal cavity. Worms can obstruct the appendix, causing appendicitis.

The pinworm's life cycle: The pregnant female worms come out at night to lay their microscopic eggs around the anal opening. Each female may lay several hundred (thousands?). This causes intense, unignorable itching; the child usually scratches this area, picking up a number of eggs underneath his fingernails. Despite daily baths and clean fingernails, he will still harbor some eggs under his nails. Then when he handles books, toys, or athletic equipment, he leaves some of these eggs behind. Another child may pick up these toys and, of course, transmit the eggs from his hand to his mouth. It does not take more than two eggs (one male, one female) to start a new cycle in a new child. When these eggs get to the colon, they hatch, male meets female, female gets pregnant, and lays her eggs outside the anal opening. Again the itch, and again the cycle is repeated.

The cardinal symptom of worms is night wakefulness. If a child is wakeful at night and not sick with a sore throat, ear infection, or gas attack, he may have worms. Other worm symptoms to check for are stomachache, teeth grinding, dark circles under the eyes, and an itchy, burning sensation around the anal opening. Most afflicted children are also irritable and tense because they have not been sleeping properly. They cry easily, are grouchy, fussy, and often mean, suggesting a behavior problem. Most remedies are now quite effective, and within seventy-two hours after the proper dose, the sufferer should have been relieved of enough of his internal population to show noticeable improvement. Homeopathic remedies and Chinese herbs are safe and effective.

If the sticky side of transparent tape is pushed against the anal area first thing in the morning, it will pick up enough of the eggs so they can be seen under the microscope. If the child has worm symptoms and has not had adequate treatment for them for a few months, he should be treated on the assumption that he has them again. The treatment will not hurt him in any case. One dose is given by mouth and repeated in ten days. It only kills the adult worms, so the repeat dose is needed to kill those that have developed from the eggs present ten days previously. Side effects from the medicine are rare, and no enemas are necessary. Natural remedies including garlic and black walnut are available from naturopathic physicians.

The following items should dispel some old wives' tales:

1. Worms are found in all strata of society.

2. Sitting on cold cement does not cause worms.

3. Neither does eating candy.

4. A huge appetite is not a symptom of worms.

5. A child who picks his nose does not do so because he has worms. But the child who picks his nose or sucks his thumb is more likely to ingest some worm eggs because he always has his hand at his face.

Some authorities feel that upward of 60 percent of all children have them at one time or another. Anybody with worms was automatically considered to be of a lower social order and obviously did not bathe regularly. Even today, the general public does not hear about worms, because when a horrified mother discovers that *her* child has them, she seldom broadcasts the news.

I have developed a new theory (perhaps based mainly on the fact that my own children had worms periodically): Children have worms because they have friends. If a child does not socialize too well, he may not have any friends from whom to get worms. So I would say, if your child gets worms frequently, he may be just relating to his peers. (If he **never** gets worms, he either has antisocial tendencies or uninfected classmates.) Pinworms are really a social disease among children. If the whole world could be treated at one time, we might be able to get rid of these pesky creatures once and for all.

Because of the stigma, most mothers treat their children in secrecy, without letting school or neighbors know what they are doing. Parents often called me at 1:00 A.M. asking me to do something. They often whispered, because they did not want the neighbors to hear that "The children have worms." Because the drugstores were not open, I had them give the child a garlic enema. That was enough to smoke out the worms for a while. Thus, by the time a mother has her child free of worms, those defunct worms' grandchildren are incubating in her neighbor's child, who in a couple of weeks will be ready to give his worm eggs back to their original donor.

Nightmares are common because the worms irritate the child, so that he is more likely to dream, and of course, he does not dream about worms. He will dream about the last thing he remembers—usually the horror show he watched on television. Television gets blamed for a lot of symptoms that are really due to worms.

PHOBIAS

School phobia is a form of anxiety that affects about one in twenty kids. In primary school children it is ordinarily a separation anxiety that the child has transferred to the school; it looms as the obvious villain in the plot to wreck his daily routine. He senses that his home is about to break up (parental hostility, impending divorce, etc.), and it might happen *today*, while he is away at school.

It could also mean that the child had a sugary breakfast, then a wave of adrenaline hit him because his blood sugar happened to be low the minute he stepped over the school threshold.

School phobia occurs more frequently in girls. The cure rate is high. Some hate school because there is a big dog between home and school. As in most psychological problems, one theory of causation is too simplistic. A child may hate school—not fear it—because he is unsuccessful due to some neurological impairment or dyslexia; he would prefer to avoid another day of "You could do better if you tried." Another child may be depressed, uncomfortable, or preoccupied because of a stressful home and need to absent himself from an environment that is unsupportive. Nutrition and psychotherapy could solve this one.

Visual or vestibular problems may trigger an attack. This may come from the poorly innervated midbrain, and is called *neuronal disorganization*.

URINARY DIFFICULTIES

It is important that a parent occasionally observe the boy's urinary stream. He usually cannot micturate for the doctor on command. A fine, misty, high-pressure spray that must be forced out by tensing abdominal muscles suggests a stricture, and operative intervention is required to preclude bladder and kidney damage. If this stricture is discovered early in infancy at the time the ammoniacal ulcer (at the boy's meatal opening) is bleeding and about to heal and contract, the use of an antibiotic eye ointment may heal the ulcer as it maintains the normal opening. The eye ointment tube (one-eighth-ounce size) has a pointed dispensing end that can easily be inserted a few millimeters into the urethra; the inserted ointment and the stretching action of the conical end of the tube prevent the ultimate narrowing that occurs if the ulcer is untreated.

The girl has her problems, but not from ammonia. The short urethra in the female empties into the moist, dark, germ-laden area between the lips (labia) of the vaginal opening. Her anatomy thus makes her susceptible to ascending bladder and kidney infections. Not all females are susceptible, so other factors such as tight underwear, wiping the anus from back to front (instead of from front to back), insufficient fluids, faulty voiding habits, and alkaline urine (germs grow better in alkaline urine than in acid urine) all play a role.

CHAPTER 11

Allergies and Sensitivities

Dr. William Rea calls sensitivities the "twentieth-century illness" because of their recent origin: "This condition is the result of the body's reaction to a myriad of substances that have become a part of our environment, especially chemicals. These cause the breakdown of our immune and enzyme detoxification system, making our bodies develop sensitivities to any number of agents found in the everyday environment, and resulting in acute and chronic illness. It is estimated that as much as 60 percent of all human illness is at least partly the result of these hidden food, chemical, and inhalant sensitivities."[303]

A case in point: A woman had a large amalgam filling placed during her pregnancy. Her child had eczema from the time of birth. This child received amalgam fillings at the age of three, and at age five years developed asthma just four months after the placement of two deep amalgam fillings. She always had headaches and had double vision from ages seven to ten. After removal of all her fillings and their replacement with composites during adolescence, her allergies disappeared.[304]

ALLERGIES

Allergy is a broad term, loosely applied to any physiological reaction that cannot be explained by infection, injury, or tumor growth. If a patient has gas after drinking milk, he has what we call a sensitivity, although a lack of the lactase enzyme may be at fault. The term *allergy* should really be limited to eczema, allergic rhinitis (hay fever), bronchial asthma, drug reactions, serum sickness, and contact dermatitis. These true allergies can be detected by a blood test, called the IgE. In contrast to true allergies, *sensitivities* are not considered valid by most allergists, as there is no reliable (to them) method of testing for them except by a patient's subjective evaluation. In general, if a person has some odd symptom, it is a sensitivity. It is called anecdotal, and is subject to doubt.

The allergic patient's symptoms are highly individual, and characteristically change with time from one organ system to another. The baby who has had eczema will frequently develop hay fever at age seven years, especially in May, when playing ball in the grass. Asthma may supervene when he gets a dog or cat at age twelve. Other factors are usually related to the allergic symptoms and may even be blamed because they seem to be the inciting agent: infection, emotional factors, temperature changes, and chemical irritants. The history of the patient's allergic background is the most important part of the diagnostic detective work. The family background is important, too, since about 60 percent of allergic people have a positive family history of allergy.

Are there any advantages to having an allergy? Allergy is an altered bodily reactivity to an antigen in response to a first exposure. It is also an exaggerated reaction to substances or situations that are without comparable effect on the average individual (*Webster's Collegiate Dictionary*). If a human gets cut, he bleeds; that is not an allergy, as we all do it. Bleeding tells you to do something to stop it. It is a clue. A sneeze is a clue that you are inhaling something to which you are allergic. You move to another location, vaccum better, or get rid of the cat. So there is some benefit to allergic symptoms. But why doesn't everyone sneeze when they mow the lawn? What is the point of an allergy? Why did Mother Nature give us this ability to react to our environment? What is she trying to tell us?

One answer might be that Mother Nature wanted all mothers to nurse their babies. In a study of more than three hundred allergy-prone children who were carefully observed from birth through age fifteen years, more than 50 percent of the the children fed cow milk or soy milk developed allergies, whereas only 28 percent of the breast-fed children developed allergies. Children from allergy-prone families are more likely to develop allergies, but nursing the baby will avoid or at least postpone the development of the allergies.[305]

I get postnasal drip after I drink milk or eat a piece of cheese. Is my body warning me that I should go easy on the dairy because if I eat too much, I will get asthma, become anemic, develop Crohn's disease, constipation, or appendicitis? Or does it mean that I should investigate my genetic inheritance, my lifestyle, or my supplement intake?

We know that a disease is an opportunity to find out what is wrong with a person's lifestyle, diet, exercise program, habits, or companions. But an allergy? It seems so silly to be allergic to strawberries, corn, seafood, wheat, or soy. What is the body trying to tell us about ourselves? I could easily get the impression that becoming allergic to eggs, pork, or milk may be God's method of punishing us for eating one of His creatures. But why not everyone? One explanation is that we are being punished for introducing foods into a baby's diet in that critical first year when all she was supposed to be getting was mother's milk, straight from the breast.

Once inside the circulation, the various immunity-control mechanisms recognize these incompletely broken down substances, assume they are bacteria or something dangerous, and produce antibodies against them, so that if they ever return, they will be attacked. A patient of mine was fed egg at three months to increase her iron intake; she promptly developed hives. When egg was reintroduced at nine months, she reacted with angioedema (swollen lips), cramps, and diarrhea. Egg at eighteen months caused anaphylactic shock, with pallor and a collapse on the floor. I am convinced if the egg had initially been served after her first birthday, she would not have developed the allergy at all.

As a result of Hans Selye's research on the adrenals in the 1930s, the importance of cortisone as a modifier of stressful situations has achieved such renown that synthetic cortisone is now used as an antiallergen and antiinflammatory drug. It is used and overused for asthma, eczema, hay fever, poison oak reactions, autoimmune diseases, and inflammatory arthritis. We now know that if stressors are perceived by the body, the pituitary will stimulate the adrenal cortex to squirt out cortisone to handle the increased needs of the body. The adrenals will react with increased cortisone production when the blood sugar falls, and we all are aware of how our rotten, sugary diet will produce hypoglycemia. If the adrenals can get exhausted from thoughts, fears, depressions, and food, it could be that allergies are the body's clever way of getting our attention.

If you are sneezing from house dust, scratching (the itch that rashes) from milk ingestion, wheezing from the dog, throwing up when you eat soybeans, or having cramps after corn, stop and recognize that your adrenals are being stomped upon. What rebuilds the adrenals?

We all know that vitamin C and pantothenic acid are the chief precursors for cortisone. Allergic people should take more than the rest of us "normal" people: One to five thousand milligrams a day of C would be the dose with which to start. Pantothenic acid (PA) is usually recommended at the five-hundred- to one-thousand-milligram level. I have a patient who had to take four thousand milligrams daily before she got relief from hay fever during her allergic season, and experienced no side effects from the PA. We know that B_{12} can improve the filtering mechanics of the intestinal lining and thus prevent the absorption of some sensitizing foods. Magnesium can relax the tense muscles in the bronchial tubes in asthma. "The herbal approach to the control of hay fever is to drink one to three cups of fenugreek tea daily beginning one to two months before the season. Sage tea dries up excess mucus."[306] Dr. Thom suggests nettle tea. Vitamin E can act as an antihistaminic. Many swear by the use of bee pollen, burdock, goldenseal, marshmallow, lobelia, stinging nettles, and ma huang.

More women are breast-feeding their children, thank God. Why, then, are allergies more prevalent? The incidence of asthma was but 0.5 percent in 1919 in the United States. In 1994 it rose to 8 percent of the population. Asthma incidence has increased threefold in the past twenty years. The Centers for Disease Control report that one in twenty people in our country have asthma. The asthma rate for individuals of all ages rose 42 percent from 1982 to 1992. Autoimmune diseases, in which the body becomes sensitive to parts of itself, have doubled in that time. We know that heredity plays a role in the tendency to have allergies.

I would like to propose that the increased inhaling of polluted air and the ingestion of nutritionally impoverished foods have been the factors to damage our collective adrenal glands. Dr. Harold Buttram points out that the research of Kathleen Rodgers, Ph.D., at the University of Southern California Medical School in Los Angeles helps to explain the increased rate of allergies and sensitivities. She demonstrated that as little as $1/700$th of the toxic dose of an organophosphate pesticide could stimulate inflammatory responses by a certain class of immune cells. These pesticides are found in all food, air, and water, and may be playing a role in the increased incidence of allergic problems.[307]

A very significant rise in allergies can also be attributed to the increased number and frequency of immunization shots, which are changing the way our bodies react to everything that is out there. Our immune mechanisms are so busy figuring out what to do about those vaccines that there are few unprogrammed parts of the immunity left for ordinary colds, flu, and allergy control.

Recommendations for my pediatric friends: Nurse from your mother for three or four years. Don't eat any solids until you are over one year of age. Don't let anyone give you immunization shots. Take vitamin C and pantothenic acid daily. Don't let anyone upset you. Find work that has nothing to do with pesticides or pollutants. Run naked through the woods eating bark, leaves, and berries.

Allergies are telling you that you must change your lifestyle.

Asthma occurs when the bronchial tubes fill with mucus and go into spasm, due to the irritating effect of some inhaled or ingested pollen, bacteria, pollutant, or food. It is more likely to be found in people who are on the alkaline side of the acid/base scale. The incidence has risen sharply, probably due to the increase in pollutants in the air and food. Medical researchers at the University of California at Irvine have found that children are six times more vulnerable to pollution than adults.[308] Wheezing showed up in only 3 percent of six-year-olds who had been breast-fed. Nine percent of bottle-fed children had wheezing attacks at age six. Eleven percent of recurrent wheezing among six-year-olds studied was attributed to lack of breast-feeding.[309, 310] Asthma is more common among children whose mothers smoked during pregnancy; children who live with smoking adults; babies born to mothers age twenty years or younger; babies born weighing less than 2,500 grams; and children who live in small homes with large families. (From Michael Sly, M.D., at Children's National Medical Center in Washington, D.C. As few as five cigarettes a day smoked by the parent caused a subsequent increase in frequency of asthma.)

Asthma produces a characteristic wheeze (more on expiration, less on inspiration) that is easily detected by having the victim breathe into the observer's ear. This is a reasonably serious condition, and the doctor's advice should be sought. In most children, asthma is usually triggered by some infection, or when an infection is superimposed on an inhalation allergy. A large percentage of children can be helped if parents will do some careful detective work and elimination tests. If asthma occurs fairly constantly in the first year of life, milk is the most likely offender. Goat milk may be curative.

If asthma always follows a cold and a fever of 100 degrees F. or so, and a purulent discharge is present, a bacterial allergy is likely. This victim may respond to infection control as well as to a series of dead-bacteria injections (either a stock solution or one made up from the patient's own mucous secretions; see Sinusitis, Chapter 6).

If wheezing occurs only in early spring, tree and grass pollen may be the culprit; if in spring and summer, grass pollens; in summer and fall, weeds. (Many midwesterners and easterners come to Oregon between August and October to escape ragweed.) Only plants that launch quantities of their pollen into the air, such as ragweed, give hay fever sufferers any real trouble. Goldenrod, despite its wicked reputation, is pollinated by insects, and will not usually provoke an allergy unless brought into the sensitive person's immediate presence. If the wheezing lasts all winter, house dust and mold spores may be the cause. Most of the sufferers usually have watery eyes and some nasal itch symptoms. If the inhalants cannot be avoided, a program of desensitization will control the symptoms in 70 to 80 percent of cases.

If symptoms occur when near cats, dogs, furniture, wool rugs and blankets, feather pillows, etc., these must be eliminated. Dr. Alan Gaby says, "In seventy-five percent of childhood asthmatics and about forty percent of adult asthmatics, unrecognized food allergy is a contributing factor. Most likely offenders: dairy products, peanuts, chocolate, corn, wheat, citrus, eggs, pork, or fish. Yellow dye no. 5 is thought to trigger asthma in as many as one hundred thousand Americans."[311] Some are mildly sensitive to all those foods, but have no symptoms unless some emotional trauma occurs—school difficulties, loss of a parent, or tension at home, for example. Some can control asthma if they control hypoglycemia. Many asthmatic children have low amounts of hydrochloric acid secreted in their stomachs. This might account for low absorption of magnesium, which needs to be acidified. Or the protein in the diet was not being digested thoroughly. Betaine hydrochloride would be useful here.[312] Some people will develop a severe attack of asthma after ingesting aspirin.

ALLERGY CHECKLIST

Most Common Inhalants Causing Nasal or Lung Trouble

House dust: usually a mixture of molds, spores, fur, cottonseed; animal hair or dander from cats, dogs, and birds; pollens from trees in spring, grass in spring and summer, ragweed in summer and fall; chemical irritants such as sprays, deodorants, cleansers; horse and pig hair that may be in the upholstery.

All surroundings should be as free as possible from dusts of all kinds. Most people cannot control the dust conditions under which they work or spend their daytime hours, but everyone can, to a large extent, eliminate dust from the bedroom, where they spend one-third of their lives. The following simple instructions describe the preparation and maintenance of a dust-free sleeping room for those with perennial nasal congestion and/or nocturnal cough and/or asthma:

Clean the Room Thoroughly

1. Remove all furniture, rugs, curtains, and draperies from the room. Empty all closets.

2. Clean the walls, ceiling, and floors. Scrub the woodwork and floors in the bedroom and closets. Wet-mop the floors.

Keep the Room Free from Dust

1. Any flues that open into the room should be sealed. If you have hot-air heating, seal the opening with oilcloth and adhesive tape and use an electric heater. If this is not practical, then place a common screen (like dampened cheesecloth) over the hot-air outlet behind the grating and change the screen frequently. Change furnace filters frequently.

2. The furniture that has been removed from the room should be thoroughly cleaned before it is returned. The room should contain a minimum amount of furniture and furnishings. A wood or metal chair may be used (not upholstered). Use plain rag rugs and plain light curtains (both of which must be washed at least once a week).

3. The room must be cleaned daily, and given a thorough and complete cleaning once a week. Clean the floor, furniture, tops of doors, window frames, sills, etc., with a damp cloth or oil mop. (The oil used should have no odor; if there is an odor, the child

may be sensitive to it.) Air the room thoroughly. Then close the doors and windows until the child is ready to occupy the room.

4. Keep the doors and windows of this room closed as much as possible, especially when the room is not occupied. Use this room for sleeping only. Dress and undress in another room.

Bedding Is Important

1. Scrub the bed. Scrub the bedspring.

2. Box spring, mattress, and pillows must be encased in dust-proof coverings. These are impervious to dust and keep the child from coming in contact with the harmful allergens that are present in all bedding material. Several cotton sheets may act as a barrier between the mattress and the child. Hypoallergenic mattresses are available.

3. Be sure to clean the bed and encase the pillows, box spring, and mattress outside of the bedroom before they are returned to the room.

4. Do not use any kind of mattress pad. Sheets and blankets should be laundered weekly.

5. If there are two beds in the room, both of them must be treated as described above.

General Suggestions

1. Care must be taken to keep down the dust throughout the entire house. Go over all floors and furniture with a vacuum cleaner at frequent intervals—once daily if possible. Following this, the house should be aired thoroughly. Cleaning must be done while the child is away from the house. Use a damp or oiled cloth to avoid raising dust. How about a central vacuum system?

2. Pets, birds, and animals must be kept out of the house. Cats and dogs should be particularly discouraged. A difficult decision must be faced by a family who finds their child has become allergic to the dog or cat. Some people put up with allergic symptoms rather than "lose" the animal. Keeping the animal in the garage and maintaining a strictly "sterile" room, plus adding an electronic air-filtering machine (tax deductible), might be a suitable compromise.

3. Avoid cosmetics, perfumes, insect sprays, or powders, and odoriferous substances such as camphor, tar, etc.

4. The child should not go into any room while it is being cleaned. He should be careful not to handle objects that are covered with dust, such as books, boxes, or clothing that have been stored on shelves or in cupboards over a long period of time. He should be kept away from attics and closets.

5. Keep out of the room all toys that accumulate dust. Use only unstuffed, washable toys.

6. Keep bedroom door closed. Attach a flap at the bottom.

Most parents compromise with the preceding suggestions. If a few things are done and the symptoms disappear, that would seem sufficient. If trouble returns, the remaining items might be done. If improvement is not obvious in a few weeks, a consultation with an allergist would be the next step. Skin tests may pinpoint the offending inhalant. (If molds give a big skin reaction, some relief may occur by drying out a basement or putting plastic over bare earth under the house.)

The nutritional approach to the control of asthma is through the use of the following, individually or all together: Magnesium at about the five-hundred-milligram level seems to be the most important one to add (Julian Whitaker, M.D., author of health books, says, "When there is a magnesium deficiency, there is increased histamine release from the cells, causing constriction of the bronchioles"); vitamin B_6 at about the fifty-milligram level daily; vitamin C, at least one thousand milligrams daily; cayenne pepper, quercetin, omega-3 essential fatty acids, and, of course, garlic. Eating more vegetables, which are loaded with vitamins C, E, and other antioxidants, can help prevent asthma.[313]

It has been found that 60 percent of children and 40 percent of adults become asthma-free when given shots of B_{12}. (Three cubic centimeters of B_{12} intramuscularly every day for ten days for the adults, and one to two cubic centimeters daily for the child, depending on size and age.)[314] Magnesium relaxes the bronchial tubes. Vitamin B_6 (one hundred to three hundred milligrams daily) will alleviate mild to moderate asthma if taken with the magnesium. Most asthmatic people are somewhat alkaline and need acidification. That can be done with vinegar if the blood sodium is up. Ammonium chloride will acidify a person if he is alkaline and the nitrogen elements in the blood are low. Vitamin C is ascorbic acid and should also help. One increases the dose daily until some sloppy bowel movements are produced, and then the dose is lowered to a subdiarrhea dose daily. Sulfites will trigger asthma in some sensitive people.

These may help: comfrey, licorice, onions, garlic, slippery elm, lobelia, capsicum, ma huang, gingko, and alfalfa.

Eczema is a word that means itchy, scaly, weeping dermatitis. Most infants with eczema (3 percent of all children in 1945, and now 10 percent) have the atopic variety, which means hereditary allergic background. Urban pollution may be a triggering event. Eighty percent of people with eczema, or atopic dermatitis, have relatives with hay fever or asthma; their children with eczema may acquire these conditions as they grow.

The familial tendency to develop asthma, hay fever, or atopic dermatitis affects 20 percent of the population (inherited as a simple dominant gene). These atopic people form increased amounts of immune proteins, including immunoglobulin E, in response to ingested and inhaled antigens. Atopic disorders are disorders of immune and tissue response, aggravated by the environment as well as ingested and inhaled allergens.

The dermatitis is usually found on the checks and the flexor surfaces of the knees and elbows. These areas periodically become eroded, weepy, and secondarily infected because of the constant scratching.

Psychological factors are important triggering agents in the older child or adult. Ingestion of certain foods may aggravate the basic condition. (Milk, wheat, egg, citrus, and tomato are usually responsible, but coffee and soda pop can do it, also.) Most dermatologists believe that there is no nutritional reason to develop atopic dermatitis. They also believe that only 5 percent of atopic people have food allergies. But maybe they have food sensitivities, or poor absorption. (The adopted baby mentioned in the section on breast-feeding was soon cleared of eczema with breast milk. Was it an allergy to the cow, or was it the gamma-linolenic acid in the breast milk?)

Atopic skin is inherently dry and itchy, and the itch-scratch-itch cycle is readily established. It is the itch that rashes. These people are very intolerant to wool or rough-textured fabrics. Atopic skin is basically dry, and the horny layer is thicker than normal. Retained sweat is irritating; atopics are worse in a hot, humid environment. Skin blood vessels of atopics respond abnormally. Skin of flexor areas of elbows and knees retains greater than normal warmth; skin temperature at night is warmer; atopic victims more often dig at their skin during the night.

Skin tests for food allergies are only about 25 percent accurate. One trouble is that the skin of these people is so sensitive, even just scratching it will often cause it to flare up. The electroacupuncture according to Voll (EAV) testing would be helpful.

Rules:

1. Infrequent bathing with a minimum of soap. Bathing dries the skin. Water cleansing after a messy bowel movement, and soap and water cleansing of the hands if they are filthy, are allowed. Bathing with an acid soap may be safe if the water is treated with an oil and emulsifier. This oily film may encourage the retention of water in the dry skin. Soap-and-water shampoo is allowed if the body is protected. The skin will be hydrated with the bathwater, but the moisturizer, like petroleum jelly, must be applied within three minutes of the bath to hold the moisture in.

2. The entire skin surface is cleansed at least twice a day with Cetaphil 19 or Wibi 19 lotion. It is rubbed in until it foams and then gently wiped off with a soft cloth, leaving a lotion film. It may be reapplied to particularly dry or itchy areas several times a day.

3. Some dermatologists feel that oily or greasy lubricants are taboo, but they may soften the skin by preventing the escape of moisture. Petroleum jelly after the bath is safe. Bag balm (used for the cow's udder) might be helpful. Dr. Thom says that ointments with chamomile or peppermint oil will reduce the need to scratch.

4. Inflamed or pruritic areas of the eczema are treated with a steroid preparation (cortisone ointment) several times daily only as a last resort. (Cortisone eventually causes atrophy of the skin.) Calendula cream is safe and rarely sensitizes the skin. The parents should begin to apply cortisone sparingly but frequently (three or four times a day) to a new lesion as soon as it is noticed. Early treatment shortens the duration.

5. If any evidence of secondary infection is present, medical doctors will prescribe a course of seven to ten days of systemic antibiotic treatment (usually erythromycin). This can lead to a yeast infection (candidiasis). Vitamin C on a daily basis might just keep the immune system alert to bacterial invasion. It is safe and cheap. (The dose is one hundred milligrams of vitamin C per month of

age per day. If there is an infection flare-up, the C would be pushed to ten times that daily, prophylactic dose.) Potential allergic sensitizers such as topical antihistamines and anesthetics should not be used on atopic skin. The routine use of topical antibiotics in atopic dermatitis is not necessary. Since topical antibiotics are potential allergens, they should be used infrequently for short periods of time.

Early effective therapy of active lesions is essential. The parents must be educated in how to handle flare-ups as soon as they begin.

6. Antihistamines may be helpful for nighttime sedation and for the antipruritic effect, since much scratching is done at night. Evening primrose oil or flaxseed oil orally has been helpful as it may add needed oil to the skin.

Only soft cotton clothing should be worn next to the skin; it should be well rinsed and free of starch. No wool, fur, or other napped or scratchy fabric should come in direct contact with the skin. Atopic children should be underclothed. Graduated exposure to sunlight is beneficial, as is swimming, if precautions are taken to prevent overdrying.

These children usually outgrow the worst of their eczema at eighteen to twenty months, but just as the parents are beginning to relax about skin care and diet, the problem may move to the nose and lungs; hay fever and asthma frequently follow. Half the children who have atopic eczema will develop some respiratory allergy in later childhood, and they usually have strongly positive skin test responses.

Desensitizing vaccine shots are helpful at this time, although they seem to be almost worthless for eczema. If some infectious trigger mechanism seems to play a role in causation (i.e., each bacterial upper respiratory infection makes the eczema worse), the use of a bacterial vaccine may be beneficial.

It is assumed that the immune system and the adrenal glands are not functioning properly in these people with genetically dry skin. The nutritional supports are vitamin C (the preceding rule no. 5), pantothenic acid (a cortisone precursor), and the essential fatty acids. Zinc and beta-carotene are helpful adjuncts to therapy. Homeopathy remedies can be a godsend. A German study of atopic eczema patients showed that with the preceding therapies, the addition of lactobacilli to the diet helped to normalize the gut flora, and relieve the itching.

These should help: echinacea, black currant oil, Saint-John's-wort, chaparral bath, burdock, chickweed, heartsease ointment or cream, blue-berry leaf, hawthorn berry, licorice.

The Eczema Association for Science and Education is in Portland, Oregon; (503) 228-4430.

Hay fever is allergic rhinitis. It is a profuse, watery discharge from the nose and eyes accompanied by sneezing and an uncontrollable drive to rub, pick, or otherwise fool with the nose and eyes. (Your eyes shut auto-matically when you sneeze so your eyeballs will not come out of the sock-ets.) The irritation may involve the throat and produce a burning sensation, postnasal drip, a dry cough, throat clearing, and a characteristic "zonking" sound. The nasal mucosa is a pale or bluish color in contrast to the redness accompanying a cold or bacterial infection. A smear of this mucus is full of eosinophils, the hallmark of allergy. Circles under the eyes suggest allergy, but are usually associated with a food sensitivity. A crease near the end of the nose where it has been bent from rubbing indicates hay fever.

The pollens (grass, animal danders, house dust, and molds) in the air irritate the membranes of the allergic sufferer, histamine is released, capil-laries dilate, and serum leaks into the mucosa. The glands secrete mucus to protect the lining.

Avoidance of the offenders is the best treatment. Vitamin C and pan-tothenic acid in large doses are both safe and inexpensive. Bioflavonoids, quercetin, pycnogenols, and freeze-dried stinging nettles (urtica) will help. Allium cepa (onion) is the homeopathic remedy.

Hives, or welts, are the signal that the body has taken in some allergen, usu-ally a food. The skin rash is red, swollen, and itchy; the eruptions are of an irregular size and shape, and occasionally have a bleached center. In only about 20 percent of the cases is an obvious food the inciting agent. Hives are assumed to be the result of histamine release from mast cells in the body. Hives, there-fore, may follow any inciting agent: cold, heat, fever, emotion, virus infections.

Frequently a parent reports that the child has hives, and there has been nothing new in the diet to explain it. Careful questioning may reveal a dol-lop of ketchup on last night's meat loaf or one chocolate-chip cookie. It is possible that the cow who gave the milk the child drank might have eaten something unusual (like thistles) or was given penicillin for mastitis, and the child happens to be sensitive to one of those. Most people get a flush from the ingestion of niacin, which releases histamine from the basophils; check the label on the vitamin bottle.

The child is usually not sick, only fussy and irritable, often scratching himself to the point of bleeding. Antihistaminics are indicated but are not curative, as the hives constantly move from one area to another, usually for a week. It seems to take that long for the irritant to be excreted.

Homeopathic apis, urtica, rhus tox, and others should help.

Cold hives is the unique sensitivity to cold only, usually from the sudden change rather than the degree of coldness. The chilled skin becomes swollen and red. (I knew a girl who drank her cola at room temperature to prevent her hand from swelling to ugly proportions.)

Solar hives break out on the exposed areas of the skin when sunlight hits them. Vitamin B_6 can control them, but some people need three hundred milligrams injected twice daily for the duration of the summer.

Food allergy is a fairly common condition in infancy, probably because so many foods are given too early to the baby, with his immature digestive system designed to digest breast milk exclusively. Probably everyone is sensitive to at least one food. Only about 5 percent of babies show an *allergy* to cow milk by the skin tests and the IgE blood test. But at least 50 percent of infants have become *sensitive* to cow milk. Sensitivity to cow milk or other foods cannot be measured except by the symptoms, muscle testing, and electroacupuncture testing. Some allergists do not believe in the possibility of food sensitivities, so if the skin and IgE tests are negative, they may tell the parents that it is okay to give cow milk to the baby.

Cookies and teething biscuits—containing wheat—may produce distressing gas and diarrhea. It may be an inborn error of metabolism (gluten-enzyme lack) and not an allergy. If an infant is sensitive to one food, he *seems* to be more likely to develop other food sensitivities. For this reason, egg, wheat, chocolate, fish, citrus, tomatoes, peaches, green vegetables, and pork are best introduced to the diet only after the first year. Diet elimination is more helpful in determining a food sensitivity than skin testing. Some foods will bother children only when in combination. Wheat may be okay, but wheat cereal with milk may cause a blowup.

The red circle of inflammation around the anal opening is usually due to a food or medicine reaction. If a mysterious rash appears on the body and is accompanied by this perianal rash, it suggests that some food or drug consumed in the previous twenty-four hours is responsible.

Many behavior problems in children (and adults) have been laid directly to allergies or sensitivities. Many surly, crabby children have become cheerful and pleasant after desensitization and/or food eliminations. Some children do well if their food is laced with digestive enzymes that break the foods down into their nonsensitizing parts.

Even children with electroencephalographic abnormalities may be improved by the withdrawal of offending foods. Grand and petit mal attacks have been relieved in some. Hyperkinetic behavior, insomnia, restlessness, irritability, bedwetting, fever, headaches, oversensitiveness, crassness, fatigue, salivation, chilliness, hypotension, tearing, negativism, unreasonableness, shyness, quickness to anger, suspiciousness, numbness, tingling, and tremors are but a few of the conditions that have improved after the offending foods have been eliminated. Dr. Marshall Mandell found that 92 percent of hospitalized schizophrenic patients were allergic to one or more common sustances. A rule: If a symptom doesn't make sense, think of sensitivities. The body is trying to tell the owner of the body that something is wrong. Pay attention!

When surly, crabby children are placed in a hospital for a few days for study and to give the parents a rest, the children may turn out to be compliant and cheerful. It was assumed by the hospital staff that this "parentectomy" was therapeutic; the parents must be the cause of the psychological problem. The more likely cause is that the child has been removed from a leaky gas stove, formaldehyde-laden carpets, cleaning solvents, etc. Some people get better when they get sick and cannot eat. When they begin their usual diet, they revert to their former nasty personality.

An allergic patient had an opening in his skull from an earlier operation. The patient's brain would swell and expand out of the surgical hole, pushing up the overlying scalp whenever the patient ate something to which he was allergic.[315]

Homeopathic remedies such as chamomilla, bryonia, colocynthis, and magnesia phosphorica are sometimes dramatic, but each requires some study to know which is the most appropriate for that particular child.[316]

Tension-fatigue syndrome is a food-sensitivity-induced combination of dull, generalized headache; ill-defined, recurrent periumbilical abdominal pain; leg aches (growing pains); violaceous half circles under eyes, which are usually associated with pallor and unhappy appearance; tiredness and fatigue; nervous tension; stuffy nose, usually associated with coughing, sneezing, bronchitis, and zonking.[317] Some personal or family history of atopy can usually be elicited. The most common offending foods are those mentioned in the preceding section on food allergies.

No skin test is reliable in determining the offender, so a diet-elimination program must be adhered to rigidly: no dairy products (most imitation milks have some milk protein in them) are to be ingested for a minimum of three to four weeks. Dr. Dick Thom says it may take six weeks. If no improvement is noted, the other possible offenders are similarly dropped from the diet. The electroacupuncture according to Voll (EAV) testing done by naturopathic physicians is reliable in determining sensitivities.[318] This long-term approach must be followed because at least five allergy-induced, long-lasting chemicals may have been elaborated by the body's allergic response, and it takes a few weeks for them to be metabolized and eliminated.

Gastrointestinal allergy or sensitivity is a term loosely applied to the inflammation of the intestines following ingestion of specific foods, and is related to the tension-fatigue syndrome. Lactase deficiency, gluten-induced enteropathy (celiac disease), and cystic fibrosis may appear to be allergies, but are the result of enzyme deficiencies. An intestinal wheat allergy in a baby might disappear when he is two only to reappear as a nasal allergy to grass pollens when he is three.

Conditions variously related to food allergies include cheilitis (cracks at the corners of the mouth from contact), angioedema of lips and palate, stomatitis (mouth inflammation), recurrent canker sores (herpes virus triggered by an allergy), hay fever, asthma, edema, spasm of throat, hoarseness, nausea, dyspepsia (indigestion), vomiting, cramping, fullness, gas, diarrhea, constipation, mucus in stool, and pruritus ani (itchy anus).

Response to the food may be immediate—sometimes even before the food is swallowed. The whole protein is more likely to be involved in this reaction; fish, seafoods, berries, nuts, and egg whites are the common allergens.

A delayed response to ingested foods occurs after a few hours or up to a day or so. Wheat, corn, milk, eggs, beef, pork, white potato, oranges, chocolate, and legumes are more likely to cause delayed reactions as some breakdown product of the food protein is the usual offender. Children often absorb food proteins before they are completely digested; this is supposed to account for the greater frequency of food allergies in the younger age group. Skin tests are not reliable if the body reaction stems from food breakdown products.

Confusion in establishing the diagnosis is related to the following:

1. Cooked foods may be safe but raw ones dangerous. (Toast is okay; bread is bad.)

2. Quantity is a factor. (Two strawberries are okay; six cause hives.)

3. Cumulative effect. (Daily bacon; gas on Sunday.)

4. Concomitant effect. (Milk okay; milk and wheat result in gas.)

An elimination diet must be adhered to for six weeks; choices are made from the safe list. If symptoms are gone, then add one new food every four days.

FOOD ALLERGY CHECKLIST

Foods Most Likely to Cause Trouble

Milk	Pork
Cottage cheese	Green vegetables
Ice cream	Citrus fruits and tomatoes
Chocolate	Vitamins (with binders and fillers)
Wheat	Spices
Corn	Garlic
Fish	Onions
Eggs	Nuts
Berries (especially strawberries)	Applesauce
Caffeine in soft drinks and coffee	

Safest Foods

Wild game: deer, elk, buffalo	Pear sauce
Lamb; free-range chicken	Bananas
Rice	Pears
Barley	Yellow vegetables
	Zucchini

Some sufferers from food sensitivities find that taking intestinal digestive enzymes will control the problems. Pancreatin is one. Dr. Lawrence A. Plumlee reports that Michael L. McCann, M.D., at Kaiser Permanente, Cleveland, Ohio, has found that twenty-five to fifty thousand units of protease before eating allergic foods prevented or reduced food reaction in more than 90 percent of patients. These enzymes are responsible for breaking down the proteins into their nonallergic components (amino acids), thus these cheap capsules assuaged the sensitivities.

Geography tongue is a benign condition in which the usual papillae on the surface have been lost temporarily; the papillae at the edge of these areas give the tongue the appearance of a map. South America one day may be Africa the next. It is most usually due to a food sensitivity.

Antigens are protein substances that stimulate the body to produce antibodies against them. Their surface regions have antigenic properties, called *allergens* (liver extract, horse serum). Injections of a stock solution of the usual respiratory bacteria (antigens) will significantly cut down on secondary infections (see Sinusitis, Chapter 6).

Antibodies are synthesized by the body in response to an antigen. They respond specifically to that antigen when it is reintroduced into the body. This combination of antibody and antigen then initiates a further host reaction: the release of mediators. Histamine is one. These protein antibodies are called immunoglobulins: IgA, IgM, IgG, and IgE. IgE is the chief reactive carrier.

Atopy is the constitutional and familial susceptibility to immediate allergic reactions. This type of sensitivity is seen in 20 percent of the population. Atopic reactions include asthma, hives, hay fever, and eczema. When atopic individuals are desensitized, a new antibody, called a *blocking antibody*, is formed, whose action is to increase the threshold of tolerance to injected allergens.

Delayed hypersensitivity is the general name for the positive response to skin testing of a variety of bacterial, viral, fungal, and parasitic diseases. If the tested person has had the disease for which he is being tested, his skin will develop a red, itchy swelling in forty-eight to seventy-two hours. If a person shows a positive reaction to a tuberculosis skin test, it means that the body has become sensitized to the complex proteins of the TB organism. It indicates a cellular immunity. It is a reliable diagnostic aid to detect previous infection of tuberculosis, histoplasmosis, cat scratch disease, brucellosis, coccidioidomycosis, and trichinosis.

Desensitization is the reduction of a patient's response to a foreign substance. Desensitizing someone to grass pollens or house dust is usually accomplished by injections of the offending material. Aqueous injections of grass pollens are given once or twice a week in increasing doses just short of local and systemic reactions. It may take two or three years.

Hypersensitivity is the response of the body to the antibody-antigen reaction.

1. Autoimmunity is a form of hypersensitivity in which the antigen is native to the host (rheumatic fever, thyroiditis).

2. Anaphylaxis or immediate hypersensitivity occurs within minutes of a repeated antigen exposure. It is a violent allergic response to a substance, i.e., penicillin, seafood, bee venom. The victim goes into shock, the blood pressure falls, pulse is rapid and weak, and pallor and cyanosis appear. Treatment is epinephrine injection, possibly the use of cortisone, oxygen, and treatment for shock.

3. Serum sickness is a hypersensitivity, a milder form of the anaphylactic reaction. It usually appears a week or two after the ingestion of some sensitizing substance. Hives (urticaria) and angioedema are usually the hallmark of serum sickness. Eyelids, lips, and tongue are swollen and itchy. Hives appear at pressure areas (on the feet where shoes rub and at the belt line). Swollen, tender joints are typical. Angioedema is sudden swelling, usually of the eyelids, lips, or ears, that is most often assumed to be an allergic response to a drug, food, or insect bite. The sudden, alarming swelling may suggest an infection (abscess or cellulitis), but the absence of pain will rule out a bacterial etiology.

Leaky gut syndrome is a condition of damaged intestinal lining through which incompletely digested foods, toxins, bacteria, fungi, and other antigens move into the circulation of the body. The gut epithelium is the active transport of nutrients from the lumen of the intestines to the circulation and the rest of the body, but unwanted and unneeded particles may cross over into the body as well. "Bacteria and yeast in the intestinal tract attack unabsorbed food, in the process creating harmful compounds, many of which pass into the circulation and are small enough to cross the blood-brain barrier and enter the brain cells."[319] If the liver is unable to handle the load, these foreign products will migrate to other tissues of the body (joints, kidneys, heart, brain) and cause symptoms, mischief, and sometimes a disease like asthma, arthritis, etc. The gut with its attached liver and other digestive organs is basic to the health of the body. Nutrients and energy foods are swallowed and we assume that the gut will sort everything out, absorbing what is good and useful, and eliminating the undesirable stuff. Many ingested foods and medicines can injure the gut lining and make it hyperpermeable. Then the liver has to detoxify what has moved from the intestinal tract into the circulation. If you cannot get well despite eating good foods and swallowing supplements, it may be your inefficient gut.

Chemical sensitivity, joint aches, headaches, and food allergies may be due to the leaky gut. Gas, bloating, abdominal pain, indigestion, and alternating constipation and diarrhea are symptoms that your intestines are under stress. Your gut is trying to tell you something. These are a few of the things that can hurt the lining of the intestines to make it hyperpermeable: some bacteria, protozoa, yeasts (like candida), parasites, antibiotics, processed foods, alcohol, sugar, caffeine, foods to which a person has become sensitive (because they were introduced in the first few months of life), ibuprofen, aspirin, and anything that is not a pure food.[320]

If one suspects the child has the problem, one must prohibit the ingestion of candy and other junk food, and add digestive enzymes and acidophilus bacteria to provide a more normal gut flora. Aloe vera gel, flax teas, antioxidants, bioflavonoids, and other nutrients will all help.[321] Part of the investigation is to have food sensitivity studies done and a stool exam for parasites and their eggs. Giardia can cause this.

Enzymes only act on the surface of foods, so the idea of "Fletcherizing" foods in the mouth (chewing foods thirty times, or until they are a soup in the mouth), especially starches, will improve digestion and allow for more complete absorption of the nutrients eaten. We are what we absorb, not just what we eat. If food is not chewed well, it puts an extra burden on the starch-digesting enzymes in the small bowel: "A great strain is placed on the pancreas from the excessive intake of refined carbohydrates. Poor eating habits decrease the amount of enzymes produced by the pancreas and contribute to the onset of diabetes and food allergies."[322]

CHAPTER 12

Pain

ABDOMEN

The region between the lower rib edges and the pelvic and pubic bones contains the liver (upper right), the spleen (upper left), stomach (upper central), kidneys with adrenal glands (upper left and right toward the back), and the small and large bowel (all areas), with the appendix in the lower right region. The bladder is in the central lower area.

All parents, spouses, brothers, sisters, and friends should practice palpating their own, their children's, their siblings', and their loved ones' abdomens occasionally to become familiar with the normal feel of the abdomen and its contents. The doctor always palpates the abdomen as a part of the routine examination, but a swollen organ or tumor mass may develop silently and require immediate investigation long before the yearly checkup. During bathtime, a parent has a good opportunity to do this home checkup. Under the pretense of tickling or playing "get you," the parent can practice a little preventive medicine without alarming the child or producing unwanted navel-gazing hypochondriasis. If the parent can develop a sense of where things are, and learn the meaning of various signs and symptoms, a diagnosis of an abdominal problem can be made more quickly and accurately. Parents need to know if something is seriously wrong, or if it is only a little gas going sideways.

Generalized Abdominal Pain

This can happen at any age. Most abdominal diseases begin with unlocalized abdominal pain. After several minutes or an hour or two, the pain settles at one area, most commonly around the navel. Recurrent abdominal pain (RAP) occurs in 15 percent of children. There is no obvious pathology, but eventually the condition turns out to be a food sensitivity, gas stretching the intestines, a type of migraine or epilepsy, or some vague "emotional" disorder. Fifty percent of the parents had similar complaints. Migraine occurs in 10 percent of parents of children with RAP. One third of the mothers had nausea and vomiting, fatigue, and headaches while pregnant with the suffering child. Twenty percent had some natal complication (stress). Twenty percent of the infants had colic (milk sensitivity?). One third of the children were written off as having emotional disorders, and according to the 1980 *Pediatric Yearbook,* the emotional category included: maladjustment, restlessness, defiance, jealousy, enuresis, tics, eating problems, school problems, anxiety states, and compulsive neuroses. Most of the children with RAP were high-strung and intelligent, but timid and apprehensive (need magnesium?). If your child seems to fall into this RAP category, see if tension fatigue syndrome, food sensitivity, worms, gas, or irritable bowel is a more precise diagnosis—or one of the following:

Mesenteric lymphadenitis is the inflammation and swelling of the lymph nodes in the abdomen. The mesenteric glands in the supporting tissue between the intestines and the back abdominal wall become involved secondary to a throat infection. It may mimic appendicitis since the white blood cell count is elevated. Surgery is the only way to differentiate these conditions, and although finding a normal appendix produces some embarrassment for the surgeon, he must not wait if appendicitis is a consideration.

But usually the child is not too sick, and his temperature, when taken rectally, is no more than 99.5 degrees F., so the parents assume that he is a neurotic, a goof-off, or a hypochondriac. The doctor can find nothing in the examination to suggest disease (the affected glands are too deep to palpate), and the blood count may be normal. However, the lethargy, appetite loss, and circles under the eyes would put the diagnosis into the organic rather than the psychological column (especially if he comes in from play to lie down). The story is common in the four- to six-year-olds, who are especially prone to infections and swollen lymph tissue anyway.

Tension-fatigue syndrome should be ruled out first. If an infection is considered, a trial of vitamin C daily for ten days (five to ten grams daily) would be the safest and most appropriate method of controlling this difficult-to-diagnose condition. If the proper therapy has been tried, it will relieve the dull, achy fullness the child experiences, his color and appetite will improve, and the parents may feel some guilt because they had assumed their sick child was faking the whole thing.

Central, Midabdominal, or Periumbilical Pain

This usually means that the disease is confined to the small intestines. Intestinal flu is the first consideration. Pains caused by colic or food allergy are also likely to be located here.

Gas attacks are localized to the navel, the spasm comes and goes, and the abdomen is usually only slightly tender to palpation. Gas may be produced by the action of gas-forming bacteria (clostridia). As everyone knows, bean products produce a large amount of gas (carbon dioxide and hydrogen—don't light a match). Flatulence from certain foods is common and evil-smelling (see Food Allergy Checklist, Chapter 11). Gases may be absorbed from the colon and exhaled from the lungs, producing a foul breath. Most gas comes from swallowed air, but a close second is due to the faulty digestion of junk food. Eighty percent of swallowed air is nitrogen, which is poorly absorbed into the bloodstream and must travel through the intestines to be eliminated as gas. Carbon dioxide, oxygen, and methane will be absorbed and exhaled in the lungs.

Air swallowers may be helped by exhaling before swallowing. Belching aids may prevent the gas from passing from the stomach to bowel. (One tablespoon of apple cider vinegar in a small glass of water is a belch aid.) Some people have gas because of too much acid; others because of too little acid. Digestive enzymes should help digest the foods down to their basic simple carbohydrates, amino acids, and fatty acids.

Lower Right Abdominal Pain

Appendicitis is an inflammation of the appendix, which, in most people, is found in the lower right area of the abdomen. If the parents and siblings have palpated each other's abdomens for months, then it would be easy to detect the spasm in the lower right side of the abdomen when appendicitis strikes.

It can occur at any age. It tends to run in families, perhaps because they are all on a low-fiber diet. A bit of dried-up fecal material acts as a cork to the opening of the appendix. I have seen it occur in twins within a few months of each other. It is almost never seen in third-world people who are eating raw, unprocessed foods. Constipation seems to be the precursor. Modern, low-roughage diets lead to appendicitis, diverticulitis, gall bladder trouble, hemorrhoids, heart attacks, and a variety of modern diseases. In countries where the people have small bowel movements, the hospitals are large. In countries where the people have large bowel movements, the hospitals are small.

Appendicitis can fool a trained observer, as it may start around the navel and then move to the lower right side. If the inflammation is great enough, the appendix abscesses and ruptures, causing peritonitis. The trick is to diagnose appendicitis while the appendix is still intact, and get the surgeon to remove the dirty thing. Good rules to remember are: (1) Appendicitis pain feels like the worst gas pain one has ever had, but it does *not* go away; and (2) If one has a good bowel movement and the pain does not go away, it is probably appendicitis. A skilled doctor's evaluation of the abdominal muscle spasm compared with other areas of the abdomen is mandatory. Lower right muscle guarding, plus a rectal temperature of 99.5 degrees to 101 degrees F., plus an elevated white blood count of twelve to sixteen thousand, plus tenderness on the right side by rectal palpation, is classical for appendicitis.

If an inflamed appendix is suspected, the use of laxatives, sedatives, enemas, painkillers, or hot or cold applications is extremely dangerous.

Upper Right Abdominal Pain

This pain is associated with liver and gallbladder diseases.

Gall bladder disease. The gall bladder is the storage sack for bile. It is tucked under the liver in the upper right side of the abdomen. It is rarely a problem in children.

The liver is responsible for at least five hundred separate, important functions. It stores glucose as glycogen and reconverts it to glucose to maintain the blood sugar at a fairly constant level. It stores protein. It is responsible for fat metabolism. Urea, albumin, and clotting factor precursors are formed in the liver. Vitamins A and D are stored in the liver. The newborn baby's liver stores the iron it has received from the mother; this is gradually depleted by six months of age. The liver can also detoxify a number of medicines and poisons, as well as make bile.

Hepatitis is a virus inflammation of the liver. A dull, constant ache or fullness in this area is chiefly found in hepatitis—a viral illness, usually accompanied by a yellow tint to the whites of the eyes (sclera) and, if severe enough, to the skin.

Two types are recognized. Infectious hepatitis (IH) is passed from person to person, mainly by the oral route, and takes about a month to manifest itself after exposure. Serum hepatitis (SH) is passed by the injection of contaminated blood fluids or needles; the virus is carried by the bloodstream to the liver. The liver shows destruction of cells and inflammation throughout. New cells regenerate, fortunately, in the majority of cases.

The patient usually feels as if he has stomach flu because the initial symptoms are nausea, vomiting, stomachache, fever, and occasionally diarrhea. The stomachache is usually high up under the right rib edge and is dull and constant. After a few days of sickness, the patient begins to feel a little better, only to notice that his eyeballs are yellow. Jaundice and a tender liver in an otherwise healthy child almost surely mean IH. The urine becomes deeply yellow because of the bile that backs up into the circulation. The stools may be light in color. It is estimated that for every one patient with obvious IH (jaundice and tender liver), nine patients have a mild case that is assumed to be flu.

The patient should be allowed to be active after the fever and weakness have diminished. If he feels okay, he should be up.

The contagious period with IH is probably the two weeks preceding the height of the illness (fever, tender liver, jaundice). Food handlers, teachers, and children are usually allowed to return to their jobs or school three weeks after the onset of symptoms, although the virus can still be recovered from their stools.

This viral infection can be treated with vitamin C, silimarin, rest, and a reasonably adequate diet. Small amounts of food taken frequently may sneak by the nausea. Patients are usually away from school or play for three weeks and may be "out of sorts" for a month afterward.

SH patients are not contagious, as no virus can be demonstrated in the stools. Many health authorities are recommending the hepatitis B shot during the newborn stage on the assumption the child will become a prostitute, an active homosexual, or an intravenous drug user!

Upper Left Abdominal Pain

Fullness or distress at or under the rib edge suggests spleen enlargement (found in 50 percent of infectious mononucleosis victims) or gas in the large bowel or colitis. If pain is referred to the shoulder (shoulder-strap pain), the disease or injury is affecting the diaphragm.

Upper Middle Abdominal Pain

Gastric and duodenal ulcers. Burning, distress, or fullness in the area between the navel and the rib edge that is relieved by food and/or antacids is the cardinal symptom of an ulcer or at least hyperacidity. The time-honored view that the distress is caused by frustration or unresolved anger may be true, but does not indicate that an ulcer is burning a hole in the intestinal lining.

It has now been proven that a bacteria, *Heliobacter pylori*, is the causative agent in the formation of the usual peptic ulcer in the duodenum. Half the world's population is affected with this; many have no symptoms. It has to do with uncooked foods and unsterile water. The incidence in the developed countries is decreasing. There are about a half million new cases reported per year around the world. The cure rate approaches 90 percent when the patients are given an antibiotic like erythromycin or tetracycline along with metronidazole plus a bismuth compound for ten days.

Lower Left Abdominal Pain

The lower left abdominal area may be painful, tender, or bloated if constipation or pinworms are present. Gas in the colon resulting from the ingestion of irritating foods (milk, corn, onions, cabbage, garlic, beans) may produce severe, cramping pains; usually these irritants first create pain in the umbilical area, and *then* in the lower left area. A bowel movement provides temporary relief because the painful distention is relieved.

Irritable colon describes bowel-movement irregularities (hard, small pellets or loose, big, sloppy stools) associated with abdominal cramps in an overachieving, driving, success-oriented child. The child grows, eats, and sleeps well, but his stools may be big, loose, and frequent for a day. These episodes alternate with constipation.

This condition is a collection of little-understood bowel problems that include food allergies (especially to milk and wheat), abdominal seizures (abnormal EEG), and psychosomatic predispositions—the parents have the same thing. Could there be a gene for stomachache? Some authorities believe that these people have not lost the Galant reflex (see Reflexes, Chapter 4).

Attacks may be triggered by respiratory infections, teething (always a safe bet), eating chilled foods, and emotional crises in a child whose parents have gastrointestinal "weaknesses." It is a benign, self-limited condition, beginning in infancy and disappearing at age three years, perhaps coinciding with toilet training and the parent's boredom with stool gazing.

The child may have had colic or a milk intolerance as a baby; the mother was forced to be concerned and eventually taught the child to report every twinge. His recital at breakfast is rewarded by a day in bed, so his hypochondriasis is reinforced.

However, it is amazing how a pale, weak, whiny child can be transformed into a happy, outgoing, pink-cheeked athlete when milk or wheat or corn is eliminated from the diet. Not *every* obscure symptom is psychosomatic.

These might help: magnesium, potassium, calcium, goldenseal and myrrh tea, slippery elm, comfrey root, mullein, aloe vera gel, pokeroot.

Constipation (see Chapter 3).

Lower Mid-Abdominal Pain

This usually means a bladder infection—almost exclusively found in the female. Burning and frequency of urination accompany the pain, and a urinalysis reveals pus cells (see chapter 6).

HEADACHES

Headaches in children are more likely to indicate an organic disease than tension, worry, or neurosis. Most commonly it is associated with fevers of viral origin. Usually the child is unable to describe the type (throbbing, steady, dull, sharp) or severity of the pain until he is over eight years old. The parents can only infer a headache in a young child by his undue lethargy, furrowed brow, scalp rubbing, or ear pulling.

Distended blood vessels or distorted meninges are the chief reasons for the pain. A headache aggravated by activity and relieved by rest is an example of a vascular headache. A brain tumor or blood clot would stretch the meninges and cause pain. A migraine headache in a child is usually associated with vomiting to the point that the head pain is almost forgotten; the pain may be all over the head and not just on one side as is typical in the adult.

A similar headache associated with abnormal brain waves is called an *epileptic equivalent* (see Chapter 9). It comes on suddenly and is associated with pallor. The giveaway would be the child's falling asleep afterward, as if the nervous system were exhausted. Food sensitivities are a frequent cause of headaches. The most common allergenic foods include chocolate, corn, pork, milk, nuts, fish, and eggs. Dr. Seymour Diamond of the National Headache Foundation says, "In people susceptible to headaches, foods containing preservatives such as monosodium glutamate (MSG), amino acids, such as tyramine, or nitrates seem to have a direct effect on blood vessels in the head, causing them to expand, thereby resulting in an attack." A good plan is for the parent to make a diet calendar, listing all the foods consumed in the previous three to twelve hours before the headache. After three or four headaches, it should be obvious that one (or more) food is always included— if indeed it is an allergic headache. ("He has a chocolate bar every day after school, and by supper he is pale, has sunken eyes and a crushing headache.")

Eye strain can cause headaches, usually frontal, but a child with a refractive error usually avoids reading to avoid the headache. Sinus trouble, in order to be severe enough to cause a headache, will usually give other clues: purulent nasal discharge, fever, and tenderness to bone pressure at the sinus site. Tension headache is supposed to be due to the neck muscles pulling on the scalp at the back of the head. Headache may also be due to neuritis or neuralgia of the sensory nerves of the scalp. The pain is sudden and radiates along the pathway of the nerve; the skin supplied by this nerve is usually extra sensitive. A common neuralgia pain is due to irritation of one of the cervical (neck) nerves supplying the back side of the head. Tension of the back neck muscles aggravates the neuralgia and a vicious circle begins. A chiropractor would take care of this one.

A careful history taking is the most important diagnostic aid in headache evaluation, but eye examination (choked disk and refractive errors), skull X ray, EEG, blood-sugar examination, blood pressure check and urinalysis (hypertension due to kidney disease), and spinal-fluid examination may be necessary.

For people prone to headaches of a vascular nature, daily exercise can release the endorphins that are the body's own morphinelike substance.

Migraine is a severe headache caused by the dilation of blood vessels to the scalp and outer membranes (dura) of the brain. Ten to twenty million people in the United States are affected. Sixteen percent of women and 9 percent of men suffer from this disorder. The incidence of chronic migraine grew nearly 60 percent in the single decade from 1980 to 1989 (from a lecture by William Meggs, M.D., Ph.D., in April 1994). More than half of migraine patients can tell that an attack is coming on because of symptoms that occur hours to days before the attack. A period of visual sensations (spots, zigzag lines, flashing lights) may precede the actual headache. Strange feelings of numbness or tingling may occur on the face or arm on one side of the body. These subjective symptoms are assumed to be due to the constriction of the vessels that supply blood to the sensory areas of the brain. After this spasm, relaxation of these vessels results in a pounding, incapacitating headache associated with flushing of the skin on the same side. Exertion aggravates the pain, and the victim prefers to lie quietly in the dark, hoping blessed sleep may come. The pain may last for hours or days.

In few other diseases of the nervous system do the influences of psychology, genetics, and organic pathology so intertwine as in migraine. Most authorities note the familial incidence (70 percent have a positive family history of sick headaches); higher incidence in females with rigid personalities and high personal standards of performance (the attacks are frequently triggered by a frustrating situation in which anger and hostility would be an appropriate outlet, but an unbending conscience will not permit this release—even verbally); a high percentage of brain-wave abnormalities; and a high rate of allergic manifestations in the history. (In one British study, 90 percent of the migraine headaches were triggered by a food sensitivity.[323] Although a migraine "personality" is described, anyone can have such a headache, even if all the preceding predisposing factors are absent. In a group of ninety-nine children with frequent migraine headaches, 85 percent were relieved of their headaches if kept on a hypoallergenic diet. When trigger foods were added back one at a time to the diet, the culprits were identified. Most common foods in descending order of frequency: cow milk, egg, chocolate, orange, wheat, benzoic acid [a preservative often in sodas], tomato, tartrazine [yellow dye no. 5], rye, fish, pork, beef, corn, and soy.[324])

Caffeine, ergotamine (combined in Cafergot), antihistamines, tranquilizers, and antiemetics constitute the medical treatment. Children may respond better to phenobarbital and/or Dilantin. Calcium, magnesium, and feverfew, along with specific homeopathics, are recommended by naturopathic doctors.[325] One clever trick is for the victim to rebreathe his own expired air during the aura that usually precedes the headache. It should take about ten to twenty minutes (*Therapaeia,* May 1982).

"Pure salmon oil in a capsule three times a day will generally relieve migraine sufferers. With one a day for children we find significant reduction of the migraine, even to the point that the parents think that the child is cured."[326]

Cyclic vomiting may be the childhood equivalent of migraine. It is the periodic, recurrent attack of violent emeses. At first it appears to be only an attack or two of gastroenteritis (intestinal flu), but when the attacks occur every few weeks and are not followed by diarrhea, some nervous-system disorder is possible. The attacks seem to be triggered by some emotion-charged event. As these children grow, the vomiting becomes less prominent, and headaches increase in intensity. There is a family history of this, usually on the mother's side.

These children are unable to mobilize sugar from glycogen. Under stress, they burn up fat for energy and become acidotic, which induces vomiting. Ketones are found in the urine for a few hours prior to vomiting, so a suspicious parent might test the urine for them. If ketones are present, a sugary drink may abort an attack. Treatment after the attack begins consists of antiemetic suppositories.

If a child has headaches severe enough to incapacitate him during exciting play, migraine should be considered. If headaches are frequent, a diet elimination should be tried first to rule out the possibility of an allergy. Common offenders: chocolate, milk, corn, nuts, wheat, eggs, citrus, fish. If improvement occurs with aspirin and caffeine and/or ergotamine, it would suggest that the headaches are due to dilated cerebral blood vessels.

CHEST PAIN

Heartburn is the sensation of burning (occasionally described as heat, fullness, gas, distress) at the lower end of the sternum (breastbone). There is almost never anything wrong with the heart. It is assumed that stomach acid is being regurgitated up into the esophagus to create the sensation; in this situation the victim usually describes a mobile pain that moves up the chest into the throat. It may or may not be associated with stomach contents rolling up into the throat (on bending or lying down). If liquid antacids relieve it, acid is assumed to be the offender. Food allergies (milk, pork, chocolate, and others) may produce the sensation.

Rib syndrome is a painful area of the chest, appearing in active children usually between six and twelve years of age. The sore spot is about two inches to the right or the left of the sternum (breastbone). It is usually just a dull ache in the rib at that point, but it may be a sharp, stabbing pain that stops the child's activity. It is thought to be due to an irritation or inflammation where the bony rib joins the cartilage. It heals in time without treatment. Tenderness of the rib from firm pressure would suggest the rib syndrome; the treatment is reassurance, along with extra calcium and vitamin D.

MUSCLE, BONE, AND JOINT PAIN

Juvenile rheumatoid arthritis is a severe, progressive, crippling disease indirectly related to rheumatic fever. It appears to be one of the diseases in which the body's immune mechanisms overreact. The joints swell and become painfully stiff. Because of disuse, the adjacent muscles atrophy, thus exaggerating the problem. Nutrition and physiotherapy are instilling motion and hope, if treatment is begun early.

The chief problem is making an accurate diagnosis, for the onset of the disease (more frequent in girls at age four or five years) may be sneaky— with vague joint aches and irritability—or it may come as a violent 106 degree F. temperature that rages for days or weeks without any other clues.

The joint inflammation (knee, wrist, and cervical spine most frequently) comes and goes for many years. About half the treated patients recover

completely at puberty with no residual deformity. Some develop permanent deformities before the disease quiets down. About one third go on to
adult rheumatoid arthritis. Vitamins C, E, pantothenic acid, and beta-
carotene should help.

Synovitis is a traumatic inflammation of the hip joint, a common cause
of a limp in a child. Pain may be about the hip, thigh, or knee. The inciting injury may have been ignored in the excitement of play. Occasionally a
tonsil infection is associated. It is difficult to abduct (turn out) the thigh at
the hip because of the painful spasm. Some avoidance of weight bearing is
worthwhile, albeit impossible with some age groups. Traction may be necessary. The limp should be almost gone in seven to ten days; if not, coxa
plana (see below) must be considered.

Hip: Coxa plana or **Perthes' disease (slipped epiphysis)** mainly affects
males between five and ten years of age. It is more likely seen in the heavy
child, so weight bearing has been assumed to cause this slipping of the growing head of the femur. He might have suffered an almost forgotten injury a few
weeks before he develops symptoms. A dull ache in the groin and/or pain and
stiffness in the inner side of the thigh and knee are relieved by rest. A limp
soon develops. As the epiphysis slips off the neck of the femur (thighbone)
due to the shearing force of the body weight, the pain and limp increase.
X rays reveal that the epiphysis at the head of the femur is undergoing destruction (aseptic necrosis); the calcium fragments and finally reossifies. This takes
two years or more to run the cycle. No cause has been found. Surgery using
nails or pins to hold the epiphysis in place during growth is one treatment.
Avoidance of weight bearing is essential until evidence of complete reossifica-
tion of the epiphysis appears in the X ray (two to three years). Failure to
adhere to this no-weight-bearing rule will usually result in a permanent limp,
shorter leg, muscle atrophy, limitations of hip motion, and arthritic changes.
This is no easy task for the parents of a lively five- to ten-year-old boy! Extra
nutrition with calcium, plus vitamins C and D, are important.

Cramps, or charley horse, muscle spasm, or growing pains, are usually
nocturnal. They may be confused with rheumatic fever arthralgia, but are
not migratory. They typically appear in a healthy, active child who, after a
day of heavy exercise, falls exhausted into bed. In about an hour he/she
awakens with a scream and clutches shin, calf, instep, or behind the knee.
Heat, massage, and aspirin allow him/her to sleep again in about an hour.
Hypoglycemia explains many cramps.

Local accumulation of lactic acid following exercise, plus a temporary
reduction of calcium, seem to be the underlying factors in producing the

painful muscle spasm. There is a familial tendency. Acidifiers like ammonium chloride or betaine hydrochloride will make the calcium and magnesium more soluble and relieve the spasms. Low potassium may be associated with this.

Another explanation: When the body gets low in calcium, it can borrow from the bones. When the body gets low in magnesium, it must borrow it from the muscles. As magnesium disappears from the muscles, calcium tends to replace it. The muscles will become tense, tighten, and cramp. (Calcium stimulates muscle to contract; magnesium loosens up the muscles.) Some people need calcium; others need magnesium.

Vitamin D in doses of one thousand units per day for a week should prevent the attacks for several weeks. Treatment might be necessary again if the pain recurs. Some find that zinc supplements may help. Vitamin E (tocopherol, fifty units four times a day) may also be curative because it improves glycogen storage in the muscles. Riboflavin has helped some athletes with cramps.

Myositis is a muscle infection or inflammation. Viruses (coxsackie), bacteria (streptococcus, staphylococcus with abscess formation), fungi (actinomycosis), and parasites (trichina) may all invade the muscle and create pain, spasm, fever, and swelling.

Traumatic myositis is a deep muscle bruise with hemorrhage. If severe enough, muscle tissue can be damaged and replaced with fibrosis (scar), with some loss of size and strength. Occasionally the blood ossifies and a dense calcium deposit appears (for example, Horseback Rider's bone in the inner thigh muscles). Enzyme therapy has provided some miraculous cures.

Epiphysitis is an inflammation of the growing end of some bones and appears at specific ages, depending on the bone involved.

Heel: Sever's disease is an inflammation of the heel bone where the epiphysis attaches. It is usually seen in the rapidly growing athlete, so is assumed to be due to the pull of the Achilles tendon on this nonfused plate of bone. The sufferer has a dull ache in the heel, which disappears with rest. A doughnut of sponge rubber under the heel may soften the pain.

Shin: Osgood-Schlatter's disease is an irritation of the upper growing end of the tibia (shinbone) about an inch below the bottom end of the kneecap. Local pain and swelling in this area in a twelve- to fourteen-year-old youth is diagnostic. It is aggravated by running, kicking, and kneeling. Symptoms last about a year. Athletes are often involved, and to get them back into the game, chiropractors have found that electrical stimulation will resolve this problem more quickly than immobilization. Calcium and magnesium supplements are helpful.

Spine: Scheuermann's disease (juvenile epiphysitis of the spine) develops at puberty with vague pains most commonly in the lower thoracic spine. Early examination is usually not revealing, but over the subsequent months a gradual rounding of the midback occurs. The vertebral bodies become wedge-shaped, allowing the spine to flex forward. Treatment is most effective, if early.

Tennis elbow is common in those whose occupation requires frequent rotational movement of the forearm (carpenters, tennis players, screwball pitchers). It begins as a dull ache at the outside of the elbow, which progresses to a weakness of grasp. It is assumed that some muscle fibers have been torn loose, and continued activity precludes healing. Treatment is rest (by splinting) and heat; enzyme therapy is helpful. Acidifiers will help as these people are usually alkaline.

Ankle strain usually occurs when the weight of the body is imposed on the turned-in, flexed foot. The ligaments extending from the outer anklebone to the side of the foot are torn. Pain, swelling, and, after a few days, a bruise are noted. If most of the fibers are intact, a few days of rest are sufficient to restore painless, normal function. Poor neurological organization may account for poor posture and frequent ankle strains.

Chiropractors know that in this type of injury the cuboid bone in the foot has slipped out of position. In ten seconds this can be put back into its proper position. The patient is able to walk immediately with minimal tenderness. The chiropractor is a valid teammate in injuries and many infections.

Occasionally a hairline fracture occurs in one of the supporting foot bones; without proper immobilization it may undergo degeneration. Vitamin C and proteolytic enzymes help speed the healing.

Allergic arthritis, or at least joint aches related to certain food ingestion, is fairly common but should not lead to permanent disability. I assume an internal "hive" or some type of tissue swelling in the joint lining accounts for the symptoms that might last a day or two. Citrus, tomato, chocolate, milk, pork, nuts, fish, or seasonings are the likely offending agents.

Traumatic arthritis, as the name suggests, is the pain and swelling in a joint that follows an injury—most commonly in the knee.

If a joint is injured to the point of swelling, pain, and limitation of motion, then rest and support are indicated. Vitamin C in large doses and hourly ingestion of proteolytic enzymes are now standard. Cold applications in the first twelve hours are worthwhile to control swelling. Thereafter heat, gentle and intermittent, may encourage the swelling to resolve itself more quickly. Excessive, constant, and deep heat (diathermy and ultrasound) may be dan-

gerous if used early, as it may *increase* the swelling. Deep heat is more beneficial for old injuries. Use of the joint prior to healing only causes further
injury and may produce more internal scarring. No one seems to have any
guidelines to indicate whether the victim needs orthopedic attendance for a
sprain on the first day, or whether he should wait until seven days go by and
face the usual, "You should have called last week." However, persistent and
severe pain with motion or when bearing weight on the joint usually brings
the normally alert patient to the doctor in the first three days.

Back pain is not unusual in children. Persistent pain, not associated
with some obvious trauma, suggests a congenital weakness of the spine
(spina bifida, lumbosacral asymmetry, spondylolisthesis). Ill-advised exercises, once thought to strengthen and increase the flexibility of the back,
are now known to be dangerous. Touching the toes with the knees straight
creates a leverage on the bodies of the vertebrae many times the weight of
the exerciser. The intervertebral disks may suffer if the exercise is vigorous
and prolonged. Chiropractors are better trained to diagnose and treat back
pain than medically trained doctors.

Consider this study: Those with a previous injury were more likely to
have backaches; volleyball seemed to increase the risk of having a backache; the prevalence of backache was over 50 percent among those who
spent more than one hour a day watching television; children who carried
their satchels by hand had more backaches than those who carried supplies
in backpacks.[327]

Torticollis or wry neck (see Torticollis, Chapter 2, for congenital form)
may occur following an injury that causes a fracture of one of the cervical
vertebrae. Careful transport to the hospital is necessary to avoid accidental
spinal cord injury.

One common form follows rotating the head to look backward. The
patient notes a sharp, painful snap and his neck becomes locked in a
turned, cocked position. After X rays have ruled out a fracture, this subluxation (or partial dislocation) is reduced with traction. Anesthesia is suggested. Chiropractors are helpful.

A frequent pediatric wry neck occurs after exposure to a cold draft or a
minor respiratory infection. No injury can be elicited. The child is comfortable
when lying still, but complains of pain and cocks his head to the affected side
when standing. To turn his head, he moves his whole body. A massive, continuous and hot wet pack—like a horse collar—relieves the distress of this
muscle inflammation; it is possibly a myositis due to a virus. It lasts three days.

CHAPTER 13

Skin

In the following description of skin diseases, terms are used that should become familiar to the reader. However, the dermatologist still has to see most skin lesions because of the difficulty of describing lesions over the phone. (Dermatologists might be considered to be psychics.)

Macule is a flat, small, not palpable change of color (freckles, vitiligo, first-degree burns, roseola, stork bites).

Patch is a large macule (Mongolian spots, sunburn, nevus flammeous).

Papule is an elevation the size of a pea or less; it is visible and palpable (most moles).

Nodule is a large rounded papule (some drug eruptions).

Plaque is a flat nodule.

Vesicle is an elevation the size of a pea or less but containing clear fluid (chicken pox, herpes simplex and herpes zoster, contact dermatitis).

Bulla is a large vesicle (poison oak, second-degree burn).

Blister is a term used for both vesicle and bulla.

Pustule is a pus-filled elevation smaller than a pea (acne, iodide drug reaction, folliculitis, chocolate dermatitis).

Furuncle is a large pustule.

Abscess and carbuncle are big furuncles.

Wheal or hive is a solid elevation as small as a matchhead or as big as a palm (insect bites, angioedema).

Oozing is seen when serum exudes from broken skin (broken second-degree bulla, atopic eczema, impetigo, abrasion).

Crusting or scabbing is the coagulation of blood and serum on the surface of denuded skin (healing chicken pox, abraded skin).

Scaling is the visible exfoliation of the skin (pityriasis).

Ulceration is a deep loss of skin.

Pigmentation refers to an increase in melanin (suntan, moles).

Scarring is the replacement of lost tissue by connective tissue.

Abscess is a boil. It hurts and is red, hot, and turgid with pus. It usually results from a break in the skin with the simultaneous introduction of contaminated material. Possible causes could be a bite from an insect or another child, a cat scratch, or a sliver. Boils on the buttocks, however, may follow the ingestion of chocolate. Continuous hot packs help the body's defenses wall off the infection, kill the trapped bacteria, and allow the absorption of debris, or the rupture and discharge of retained (formerly called "laudable") pus.

Three layers are essential for an effective hot pack. First, add one teaspoon of table or Epsom salt to one quart of hot water. Saturate a small towel or washcloth in this solution and place it over the abscess. Cover completely with a plastic sheet to keep out all air and retain heat. (If convenient, add a hot-water bottle next.) Over all this place a large, dry bath towel or beach towel, and secure it to the adjacent area. Let this remain for twenty-four hours; it should not be changed. The redness and tenderness should have decreased. A dry dressing may be put on the area between hot-pack treatments. If improvement is not noted in a day or so, your doctor may advise internal antibiotics and/or surgical incision and drainage. Five to ten grams of vitamin C daily may help to control the spread of the infection. Beta-carotene, zinc, and vitamin A should help reduce the recurrences.

If pimples, furuncles, boils, sties, or pustules persist or recur, they suggest that the victim or a family member is a carrier of the staphylococcal bacteria. An allergy to chocolate? It at least means the victim's immune system is not up to par. Control methods include daily showers and the possible use of staphylococcal vaccine injections to bolster the patient's immunity. Putting a dollop of antibiotic ointment up everyone's nose to kill the source of infection may only serve to cause a sensitivity.

Acne is the curse of adolescence. At an age when a youth is having problems enough with his image, his grades, his budding sexuality, his parents, and his rebellion, he is saddled with pimples, blackheads, and greasy skin in the most conspicuous places.

Fifteen percent of adolescents have no problem at all. Another 15 percent have deep pustules and cysts; they need specialized care to minimize scarring. Extra zinc and vitamin A are helpful to minimize the problem. Many have found that Retin-A has been their best control.

The remaining majority must content themselves with a washcloth, soap, and water (used frequently but not too vigorously), sunlamp treatments, various drying and peeling ointments recommended by friends and druggists, and occasionally intermittent ingestion of vitamin A. The aim of all treatment is to allow the oil glands to discharge their secretions before they dry and plug up (resulting in blackheads) or become infected (pimples to pustules to abscesses to scars). Benzoyl peroxide is still the standard treatment, as it kills bacteria and unplugs the oil glands.

Rubbing alcohol will act as a grease dissolver and cleanser for the oily adolescent skin. Its drying effect may allow the oil glands to discharge their secretions more easily, thus precluding blackhead and pimple formation. After a washcloth and soap-and-water washing of face, shoulders, and chest, an alcohol-saturated cotton ball should be rubbed vigorously over the acne-bearing skin to cleanse and dry it further. Hydrogen peroxide works, too, but will lighten the hair if you are not careful.

If calendula soap and water plus alcohol cleansing are ineffective in the control, exposure to sunlight or ultraviolet light therapy (just enough to produce a pink flush and slight peeling) is the next step. Topical remedies are available.

Dermatologists believe that chocolate, coffee, cola drinks, and greasy foods have little effect on acne, but most people know these can trigger a crop of pimples. Whole milk and high butterfat ingestion can be inciting agents. If the elimination of dairy products for a month does not improve the skin, milk may be reintroduced. Skim milk is preferable, in any case. Increasing the ingestion of raw vegetables, whole grains, plus drinking plenty of water, along with carrot and citrus juices, will help with control. Dr. Steven Davis says, "Most adolescent acne is due to a toxic effect of the liver. Doing liver purges will have a significant healing effect."[328] Check herbal remedies for this method.

Helpful: Vitamins A, C, E, B complex, with emphasis on niacin, which increases skin circulation. Zinc, chromium, and selenium improve the skin. Try these: red clover, alfalfa, goldenseal, burdock root, chaparral, echinacea, Oregon grape, sassafras.

George Reed of Houston, Texas, writes this: "Most acne problems arise from an imbalance in the vitamin A/vitamin D ratio."

Intermittent use of tetracycline (in the lowest dose possible) to effect control seems to be safe. It often leads to candidiasis, however.

If these modalities are ineffective, a dermatologist might want to try cryotherapy (cold treatment) or intracystic injection of cortisone drugs.

Ammoniacal diaper results from the conversion of urea to ammonia by bacterial action in the diaper. The skin of many babies' buttocks is extremely sensitive to this chemical, thus blisters and ulcers may form. A boy may develop a meatal ulcer just inside the urethral opening of his penis, which, on healing, may lead to a stenosis (narrowing). Obstruction to urinary flow may result in bladder and kidney damage. (This is one argument against circumcision; the foreskin protects the meatal orifice.)

Ammoniacal diaper is usually obvious in the morning after an all-night sleep. The strong ammonia smell is due to bacterial action that changes the urea in the urine to ammonia. Boiling and bleaching the diapers are of no benefit. Some attempt must be made to: (1) destroy the bacteria that live in the diaper; and (2) counteract the ammonia. The diapers can be soaked in various bacteriocidal solutions, or they can be put out in the sunshine or exposed to ultraviolet light. When the bacteria are eliminated, no ammonia will form. Pouring an ounce of vinegar in the second of two double night-time diapers (so that the vinegar doesn't actually touch the baby's skin) will acidify the urine and neutralize the ammonia. Or pour vinegar into the final rinse of the washing cycle. Using diaper-service diapers may be the only way to stop it. Apple or cranberry juice, the amino acid methionine, or vitamin C can be given in the child's supper to acidify the urine. Protecting the skin with heavy ointments, and the reduction of fluid intake, are of secondary importance. Adding extra water to the child's diet will not wash the ammonia out and only serves to make the condition worse.

Fluid components in the diet to which the baby is sensitive (citrus, tomato, etc.) might cause redness and scaling on areas where the urine contacts the skin. Solids in the diet (peaches, eggs, apricots, chocolate, etc.) are more likely to cause a circumanal redness *between* the buttocks where the diaper does *not* touch. Poorly rinsed diapers containing soap remnants will cause red, rough skin everywhere the diapers touch. Double rinsing should solve this one. A rash at the belt line and upper thighs would come from contact with the edge of the rubber or plastic diaper liner. A bright red rash common in the first few weeks is caused by a yeast, candida, which grows well in this area because it is dark, warm, and wet there.

One dermatologist told me that diaper rashes are (1) caused by diapers; (2) aggravated by diapers; or (3) not caused by diapers. In societies where diapers are not used, there are no diaper rashes.

Blepharitis (eyelid rash) is the red, scaly, slightly thickened margin of the eyelids often associated with seborrheic dermatitis, dandruff cradle cap, and acne. Greasy skin seems to be chronic with these people. Some crusting and matting of the eyelashes may occur. It is aggravated by dairy-product ingestion and pollen allergies. A low-fat diet is suggested. It may clear up when dandruff is eliminated; a keratolytic ointment on the scalp may help. The use of B_6 in doses of fifty to one hundred milligrams a day may speed the clearing.

Canker sores, or aphthous ulcers, usually occur singly on the lips or gums. They are painful and last about a week. They are assumed to be a virus infection, but are triggered by stress, sunshine, or menses, or ingestion of chocolate, walnuts, or citrus. Local treatment of these pesky sores includes cortisone ointment, sodium bicarbonate, antihistaminics, and tincture of benzoin; most of these are ineffective, however. Lysine ointment will shorten the course. The homeopathic remedy rhus tox, if used when one notices the first tingle of the oncoming sore, may help stop the progress. L-Lysine, five hundred milligrams daily, has been effective for some. Pantothenic acid, at five hundred milligrams twice a day, will shorten the course for others. Both of these latter remedies must be taken as soon as the victim notices that initial twinge. Dr. H. D. Mintun, of Walnut Creek, California, supplies us with this bit of therapy: Purchase an aerosol container of engine-starting fluid (diethyl ether) and observe safety instructions (explosive). When the sore is on its way, "the patient takes a cotton-tipped applicator, places it at the orifice in the head of the aerosol can, releases some of the ether to soak the cotton, and applies this to the painful area six to ten times daily." There is immediate relief, the eruption is slowed, and the lesion regresses faster. It might even prevent future eruptions. Dr. Thom: "An ointment with melissa has been shown to reduce the course of herpes, and aloe vera has been approved by the FDA." A homeopathic zinc preparation should help.

Carotenemia is the appearance of the pigment carotene in the blood to a level that allows staining of the skin. It is only noticed in the thick layers (palms, soles, and nose) and never in the whites of the eyes (in contrast to jaundice, where bile pigment is the coloring agent). This harmless condition appears after the large ingestion of carrots, squash, and sweet potato. The pigment is dissipated after age two unless these yellow foods are given in abundance.

Cheilosis is the fissuring and cracking at the mouth corners due to vitamin B deficiency. This is usually complicated by a yeast infection (moniliasis) that must be treated, along with improving the diet with cereals and meats.

Contact dermatitis is due to an allergy in 20 percent of cases, and in the other 80 percent, it is due to an irritant. The rash is usually red, itchy, and slightly raised, but may become papular, vesicular, and/or scaly. Secondary infection (pustules, impetigo) may develop if scratching of the surface has occurred.

Plastic, hair sprays, soap (especially bubble bath), earrings, nylon clothing or socks, shoe dyes, permanent-press clothing, rubber diaper liners, safety pins, tape, toilet seats, metal rings, and eyeglass frames are all frequent causes of contact dermatitis. Dishpan hands is common because the skin is exposed to wet water, and then to dry air. It will show up first in the web spaces between fingers, and under rings. Chapping of the lips is similar, as this area is wet and dry, alternately. People with atopic tendencies must go into dry work. Petroleum jelly is the safest to use on the skin. It is put on right after bathing and then cotton gloves are used. Alternating with aloe vera will help the skin heal.

Rubberized or plastic mattress covers can cause an extensive rash on a baby despite intervening cotton sheeting. A red neck rash is usually due to a plastic bib. Most baby oils have perfumes that can irritate a baby's skin. Neomycin in antibiotic ointments may sensitize the skin and make a treated sore look more inflamed than before treatment. Pacifiers may cause a mouth rash; teething powders may make the gums red. Colored toilet paper may create a red perianal rash. Retained laundry soap may produce a diaper rash, and so forth.

The detective work that the dermatologist must perform in determining the cause of some of these rashes is prodigious. Dermatologists may have to make house calls (!) to solve their cases.

Poison ivy or **oak contact rash** is an allergic response due to exposure to the oil on the leaf of the *Rhus toxicodendron* plant. It begins as reddened, itchy, burning patches of skin on exposed areas after contact with the plant. It appears in new areas for five days as the skin progresses to edema and blister formation.

The sting, itch, and burn are intolerable to some, and scratching may lead to impetigo. Lotions with local anesthetics and internal antihistamines are of limited value. If the patient cannot sleep, systemic (oral or intramuscular) cortisone is very effective; it works better if given before blisters form. Homeopathic remedies may help stop the problem in just a few hours (rhus tox; anacardium). Naturopathic physician Tori Hudson steeps dried calendula and grindelia in water to make a soothing tea solution. Soak a piece of cotton gauze in the tea and apply it to the area. Drinking the tea will enhance the healing. Or combine grindelia and sassafras into a tincture.

It is important that the susceptible, exposed person rip off his clothes and bathe himself with much soap and water as soon as possible. All his clothes must be cleaned; he must wear only fresh clothing. Some people break out from the smoke of ivy burning miles away. A patient, nine months old, developed a generalized rash when she crawled on the carpet where her father had walked after tramping through the vines. Once the victim has bathed, he is no longer contagious. The serum or ooze from his blisters will not affect another person; only his unwashed clothing will.

Fungus infections (mycotic) are usually confined to the skin or hair in children, but some fungi will invade inside the body (actinomycosis, blastomycosis, cryptococcosis, sporotrichosis, histoplasmosis, coccidioidomycosis).

Athlete's foot is a fungus infection, most common in adolescents when it is perhaps related to sweating and insufficient foot hygiene. The webs between the toes become cracked, white, and thickened, and the areas itch and burn. Redness and scaling on the ball of the foot may be related (or may be due to contact with plastic shoe inserts or nylon). Newer antifungal preparations are effective but may cause local irritation. Most victims first try some ointment with undecylenic acid; these are slower, but may irritate less. Tinactin can be purchased over the counter and is cheap and effective. Don't forget to try usnea and aloe vera gel locally. Zinc, vitamin A, and garlic internally should help. Australian tree tea oil is safe and rapidly curative.

Ringworm of the body is called tinea corporis. It is caused by a fungus, is very common in children, and is spread by close contact with animals or humans. It is usually found on the exposed surfaces—face, neck, forearms, and lower legs.

It is round or oval, scaly, and slightly pink with a raised border as it grows peripherally. Tiny vesicles may dot this leading edge. The center may be almost clear once the lesion is well developed. Ointment with undecylenic acid or Tinactin cream or drops is rapidly curative. A stubborn case may require taking griseofulvin orally for ten days.

Ringworm of the scalp, or tinea capitis, is caused by a fungus that invades the hair shaft, producing a brittleness that allows the hair to break, leaving a well-circumscribed area of stubble. Rarely is there any skin inflammation or itch associated with this. Some types produce only a scaly patch; others invade the skin, producing a violently sensitive, swollen sore, or multiple crusts.

The vast majority are spread by human contact; a few cases may be related to animal exposure. The typical area affected is on the back of the head, where contact has been made with infected hairs left on a theater, bus, or school seat by a previously infected child. The condition is rare in adults.

A two-week course of an internal and relatively safe drug is sufficient to stop the fungus growth in the shaft while the hair continues to grow out. It is permissible to allow the child to return to school as long as he is under treatment, and a gob of some type of antifungal ointment is rubbed into the patch of stubble.

Hair loss or **alopecia** is baldness. Total hair loss may follow severe illness like typhoid fever, drug therapy for cancer, severe stress, or poison ingestion. If the metabolic upset is controlled with vitamins, minerals, amino acids, and correction of the acid/base balance, the hair loss can be regained.[329] If the baldness is patchy, ringworm of the scalp must be ruled out. Some hairstyles (pigtails or ponytails) may pull sufficiently on the roots of the hair to separate the shaft. Tight curlers may loosen hairs. Many women notice loss of hair after a pregnancy. This will return after a few weeks. Hypothyroidism will promote hair loss. Alopecia areata is patchy baldness, leaving smooth, denuded skin. No known cause has been found, and hair usually returns eventually. Compulsive hair pulling (trichotillomania) may be mistaken for this condition.

Herpes simplex (see Canker sore, this chapter.)

Impetigo is a skin infection manifested by oozy, crusty sores, usually following a break in the skin from a bite, scrape, burn, or scratched hive. Children usually pick at anything on their skin; this habit, combined with a purulent nasal discharge, is a good way to seed germs into any break in the skin. Germs grow well in the bloody serum and produce more pus, which inhibits growth of the normal skin over the defect. Skin infections in or on the nose and upper lip are especially dangerous because venous drainage ends in the deep veins near the brain (see Cavernous sinus thrombosis, Chapter 6). Streptococcus and staphylococcus are the usual inhabitants of these sores. If they are small and few, they are easily controlled with an antibiotic ointment, rubbed on after a bath, or soaking that removes the scab. If sores are extensive and thought to be streptococcal, an internal antibiotic like penicillin or erythromycin might heal them from inside faster and preclude development of rheumatic fever, scarlatina, or glomerulonephritis.

Itchy anus or **pruritis ani** is usually due to pinworm infestation, but a variety of foods (coffee, tea, cola, beer, chocolate, citrus, peaches, melon, tomatoes, corn, nuts, and milk) may all cause this. Some scented and/or colored toilet papers will cause a contact rash with an accompanying itch. (Wiping the anal area with poison oak leaves after a bowel movement in the woods seems too obvious to mention.) Bubble bath usually causes a generalized body rash but may be accentuated about the anus. A hard, dry bowel movement may cause a fissure with an associated itch, which is self-perpetuating as the scratching will keep the crack open. Even softening the stools will not allow the fissure to heal promptly.

Keratosis pilaris (sandpaper skin) is a common condition that makes the outer sides of upper arms and thighs feel like a nutmeg grater. Papules develop at the hair follicles. There are no symptoms except embarrassment. In the summer when the sun stimulates the skin to peel off, the lesions disappear. If it represents a subclinical case of vitamin A deficiency, twenty thousand units a day for ten days should eliminate the roughness. Keratolytic agents are helpful.

Lice infestation (pediculosis) is a parasitic disease, usually of the scalp (less commonly of the body or pubic area). The louse must feed daily on the blood of the scalp, setting up an unignorable itch. The broken skin frequently gets infected. Baby lice become glued to the hair shaft (three millimeters from the scalp) as tiny grayish blobs. Some hair shampoos leave residual bits on the shafts that may be confused with the nits of the lice. Rule: If there is no itch, there are no lice.

Antilouse shampoos (Kwell) or permethrin (Nix) are very effective; all family members should be suspected (and inspected). Heavy lice infestation may be associated with mysterious blue spots (tache bleue) on the body.

Molluscum contagiosum is a benign virus infection that produces several papules with a waxy appearance scattered over the body. The center usually has a slight indentation. They cause no symptoms. The usual therapy is for the parent to take a tweezers to them and pull them off, maybe one a day. Cantharone applied topically will peel off the surface layer also.

Psoriasis is a chronic, hereditary skin condition formerly thought to afflict only adults. The indolent, scaly, well-circumscribed patches on the scalp, back, front of knees, and back of elbows usually seen in adults may be mistaken for chronic eczema, dandruff, or seborrhea. Some children will develop a sudden, papular rash that becomes scaly in two weeks and then clears, only to recur with the typical silver scales. Sometimes the nails become pitted and deformed, reminiscent of a fungus invasion. Newer treatments continue to be tried, but there is nothing standard. It makes no sense, but five hundred milligrams of vitamin C every two hours has been known to stop the progress of psoriasis. "Fumaric acid (Psorex) is effective. Topical vitamin D from a compounding pharmacy will help."[330]

Scabies, or seven-year itch, is due to the burrowing into the skin by a mite. The mother mite lays her eggs in these tunnels. A sensitivity develops, followed by a constant, intense itch. These linear, pink areas are most likely to be found in the warm places of the body: webs of fingers, inner side of wrists, groin, folds in front of armpits, and the penis. Scrapings will reveal the mites and eggs. Treatment offers relief in a day or two; a lotion with benzyl benzoate applied after a hot bath will quiet this infestation. Repetition may be necessary. Impetigo is a common secondary infection.

Warts are a virus infection that probably hits 50 percent of children. This papillomavirus causes common skin warts found usually on the hands; they are not due to dirt or handling frogs. They do come from other warty people and will grow if the skin has been abraded. They may persist for months and years and then regress spontaneously. They are innocuous but persistent, and challenge the dermatologist who has tried salicylic acid, surgery, liquid nitrogen treatment, hypnosis, and even X ray. Recurrences are common. When they disappear, we assume the patient has developed a wart immunity. Cantharone is a vesicant and will speed their disappearance. It is an ether extract of ground-up June bugs that, when touched to the top of the wart, produces a vesiculation (blistering) that is often sufficient to separate the growth from the underlying uninvolved dermis. This treatment is safe, leaves no scar, and its application is painless to the apprehensive child—bloodless surgery at its best. From C. L. Entner, M.D., Dunkirk, Indiana, "Methionine, one gram four times daily for one to two months, never fails to get rid of warts. Recently in a boy with numerous warts on his face and hands, the warts all disappeared after two weeks on methionine." Ordinary warts on fingers respond to garlic rubs and nightly moisturizing with castor oil (externally, that is). Thuja oil topically helps. Homeopathic thuja, causticum, and nitric acid will aid in their removal.

Plantar warts are ordinary warts partially covered by the thick skin on the plantar surface of the foot. They feel as if one is walking on a stone. The skin beneath the wart is stimulated to produce more protective skin, and thus the problem is perpetuated. Scraping, picking, and clipping have no effect, as the wart root must be removed. Surgery, X ray, and electrocautery all have their supporters. Salicylic acid or cantharone might encourage their departure. Massive does of vitamin A (two hundred thousand units a day for five days) have made warts disappear for some. Dr. Steven Davis tells us that colloidal silver drops placed directly on these stubborn warts twice daily will make them disappear.[331]

Heat kills the virus. The warts are trimmed to stop the pressure. Then soak the entire foot in water heated to 118 to 120 degrees F.—which is as hot as a person can tolerate—for fifteen minutes daily for two weeks. Use a cooking thermometer. If the warts do not go away after two weeks, the temperature of the water needs to be rechecked.[332]

CHAPTER 14

Points to Ponder

WHAT SORT OF PARENT ARE YOU?

The following is from the Auckland, Australia, *Hyperactivity Association Newsletter* of February 1988:

If you ask questions, you're pushy,

If you don't, you're disinterested,

If you're firm, then you are aggressive,

If you're easygoing, then you're weak,

If you discipline your child, you're hard,

If you don't, then you can't cope,

If you want services for your child, you're demanding,

If you complain about services, you're unreasonable,

If you don't, then you're uncaring,

If you're sad, you must be depressed,

If you're happy, you're too emotional,

If you don't cry, then you are unfeeling.

But the bottom line: You are normal.

"Children are never good at listening to their elders, but they never fail to imitate them."—James Baldwin.

ATHLETICS

Athletics includes any organized program to improve physical fitness, either as a team effort or by individual activity. Competition is the usual motivating force. Suitable sports for children who have not reached maturity are running, swimming, and non-contact games.

The child's body type might be the best criterion for the choice of the sport:

All sizes: soccer, wrestling, because contestants are matched for weight
Small, thin, wiry: track, baseball, gymnastics, tennis
Long, thin ectomorph: sprinting, cross-country running, basketball
Heavy endomorph with weak ligaments: swimming, bowling, billiards

Orthopedic surgeons see so many injuries that they suggest that no contact sports be allowed at least until the child is fully grown with fused epiphyses (after the cartilage between the shaft and the growing ends of bones is completely calcified). Sports-minded children will not heed this warning, of course. If supplied with proper equipment and opportunity at school, however, the young athlete may find her real place in a life in which academic or hobby interests play only minor roles.

Dr. Larry Webster tells us of the dangers of contact sports in the preadolescent: "Contact sports can predispose a child to spinal subluxation; increased symptoms; and in the long run, changes in the normal curvature of the cervical spine. Children should not participate in contact sports."[333] His reasons: lack of total ossification of the skull and cervical spine, lack of development of muscles and cartilage, and lack of physical coordination.

Athletes should be taking enzymes to help them heal if an injury occurs. "Proteolytic enzymes will (1) speed up the inflammatory process and bring it to a conclusion; (2) help clean up the waste products in the area; (3) decrease pain and swelling; (4) dissolve any small blood clots floating nearby; (5) improve the supply of nutrients to the tissue, improving circulation; and (6) aid in easing blood flow."[334]

Exercise improves one's attitude because of the increased oxygen to the brain and the released endorphins. Most children seek the amount of exercise that their bodies should have; unless, of course, they are sick, anemic, eating junk, lacking play area, scared of a big dog nearby, or allowed to watch television all the time.

To Do for the Child Athlete: Get a checkup for anemia and infection. Stop all junk and sugary nothings. Serve nourishing foods, the rawer the better, every two to three hours to keep the blood sugar at an even, opera-tive level. Add one thousand milligrams of vitamin C and a B complex with fifty milligrams of each of the Bs daily. Rotate the foods so that one food, especially milk, is not served more frequently than every four days.

We don't need our children to be Olympic stars. We just want them to be in good enough health to get the most out of their potential. They have to feel good to do a few pushups or swim a lap or two. Start with a walk around the block. It is best if the whole family participates. Jogging is vestibular stimulation which we now know helps academic processes.

DEATH

Death of a sibling, parent, grandparent, or loved one should be faced with open, honest evidence of grief. A child should be allowed to witness appro-priate adult emotion; she needs to work out her mourning of the loss just as her parents do. She must share in sadness just as she does in joy and anger. There is no better way to learn about love and emotion than in the security of a sharing family.

A last private view of the body of a close person may not be so traumatic to the child as an adult might imagine. If done, appropriate consideration of the child's age should be made (under six seems a little young). In any event, he will fare best if he can face the situation with a compassionate adult. The parents must accept the fact of the death before the child is able to do so.

Sudden infant death syndrome (SIDS), or crib death, strikes two out of every one thousand babies at age two to six months, and accounts for almost 40 percent of the total infant mortality. It is a shock to the parents, who thought they were doing a good job. When the baby is found dead in his crib in the morning, the distraught parents can only blame themselves. Post-mortem examination can find no reason for the death, which is frustrating to the pathologist. Overwhelming milk allergy, sudden pneumonia, septicemia, intracranial bleeding, low gamma globulin, calcium metabolism derange-ment, and a narrowed passageway at the back of the nose all have been pro-posed as causes, but repeated post-mortem examinations show no consistent pattern. Recently more complete examination of the cervical spinal cord has revealed epidural hemorrhage near and on the part of the cord that is respon-sible for respiratory function in some of these babies. In the last two decades research "literature has suggested a disorder of the central respiratory control mechanism in the brain stem as the site of this respiratory dysfunction."[335]

These authors postulate a lack of maturational development in this area of the brain stem, possibly due to some trauma or oxygen deprivation. There is a change in the sleep-wake cycle of infants at this critical few weeks to four months. If the infant does not progress through this period, or is subjected to apnea (near-miss) spells, he could be more vulnerable to a minor stressor, such as having a cold, sleeping prone and breathing some toxin from the mattress cover, or getting hit with a vaccine.

"It is postulated that human development progresses through stages with a critical period at two to four months. Immaturity of the brainstem and cervical cord is characterized, histologically, by the presence of reticular dendritic spines on the neurons as well as a proliferation of astrocytes and glial cells. Any process, whether genetic, biochemical, biomechanical, or traumatic, that alters normal development of the respiratory control centers related to spinal constriction and compression following birth trauma may be contributary to sudden infant death syndrome."[336]

Medical researcher Joseph G. Hattersley of Olympia, Washington, has searched the literature and finds good evidence that heart attacks may be the cause of SIDS, just as sudden death in adults is often from a heart attack. SIDS is virtually unknown in third-world societies living on traditional diets. He has found that vitamin C and vitamin B_6 are protective against the toxic homocysteine that comes from a high animal protein diet. Cow milk contains several times more methionine than human milk. Methionine is the source of homocysteine, which generates oxysterols (the source of the fatty material in the blood vessels). Thorough post-mortem examination may reveal that fatty infiltration of coronary arteries is significant in SIDS babies.[337]

Leslie N. Johnston, D.V.M., has another suggestion: "There is evidence to indicate that SIDS is related to high levels of iron in these babies."[338] A family member may have hemochromatosis.

A definite connection exists between the immunization shots (especially the DPTs) given to babies in those first few months of life and SIDS. Although the timing of the two is not consistent—some babies die in the first few days after the shots, while others fall apart two months afterward. Beginning on the first day after these shots, periods of irregular breathing and spells of apnea have been documented.[339] These pathological episodes, which can lead to fatal cessation of breathing, may continue for some weeks after the shot. Since the age of vulnerability to SIDS is from two to four months of age, it makes sense to postpone the shots—if one elects to have them done—until after that time.

There is an increased incidence of SIDS in babies who sleep on their stomachs. Fire retardants in the mattress cover contain phosphorus or an arsenic-based chemical. The warm, moist air from the baby in the prone position could turn the chemicals into lethal phosphine or arsine gases.[340] The high incidence of SIDS that exists in New Zealand may be related to the selenium deficient soil there.[341] "Many of these infants stopped having apnea when they received thiamine in sufficient amounts," states Derrick Lonsdale.

Babies who died from unknown causes showed a positive correlation between the number of amalgam fillings of their mother and the amount of mercury found in the babies' brain tissue.[342] Research has shown that vitamins C and B_6 can also be protective from this needless death.

DISCIPLINE

Discipline is a necessary part of social living. We have to follow some rules. We have to teach the growing child that we must have respect for others. The Golden Rule and the Ten Commandments are helpful reminders of the wherewithal of living together. Most of us can remember that we were spanked as children for some transgression, and most of us parents have found the need to "discipline" our children occasionally. But I try to dispell the belief that corporal punishment is a necessary part of childrearing. Here are some thoughts about spanking from the Maine Child Abuse and Neglect Council: "Spanking teaches children they don't have control over their behavior, that they need to rely on others for control, that violence is a way to solve problems, that it is okay to hit someone you love, that they seek revenge, and it does not teach them appropriate behavior."

Other methods of control and encouragement of compliance are more effective and reliable.

Time out! If your four-year-old has been a nonconforming pest all day, a period of isolation in his room (without toys) might break the cycle of mounting anger. "Stay there five minutes until you feel better; I'll call you when it's time." Then if he deliberately defies you, making him sit in the time-out chair for a longer period tells him that you love him but not his behavior. Does he have hypoglycemia, and is operating on his animal brain? He must be fed some wholesome food every three hours so he will not become a Jekyll-and-Hyde person.

Praise must balance blame, although the balance is often precarious.

If a child seems to need severe and constant discipline, then a search for heavy-metal toxicity, hypoglycemia, food sensitivities, worms, and anemia would be appropriate before psychological counseling is sought.

GENITAL MANIPULATION
Also referred to as masturbation

The penis, highly sensitive to touch, readily becomes erect with slight stimulation, or occasionally when the bladder is full. A male "discovers" his penis at about one year of age when he can see over his protuberant abdomen. It frequently itches because of diaper irritation or food allergy (to orange juice especially). He fools with it and finds the sensation pleasurable, so he continues. If his parents indicate disgust, his interest may be encouraged. Studied indifference should be the parents' attitude when confronted with genital play.

Many obese boys accumulate a pad of fat over the pubic bone that allows the penis almost to disappear. It will become a normal-looking appendage after maturity. (I wonder about a mother who said to me, pointing at her son's penis, "That's the strangest looking penis I've ever seen.")

The three- to six-year-old boy or girl will often rub his or her genitalia against a pillow, mattress, or furniture; the concerned parent should be reassured that it is part of the child's exploratory attempts in his or her learning about body function. Overconcern about the activity will encourage its continuation, as the child thinks, "Hey, I'm really onto something." Frequently an itch will develop from bedwetting or drinking citrus, tomato, or chocolate; the child scratches the genitalia and finds more than local relief. It feels good, so he continues even when he switches to apple juice. With a reasonable child a parent might be able to teach discretion ("it's a private activity"), but threats of "I'll cut it off," "you'll go crazy," or "the boogie man will get you" serve to make adolescent guilt about masturbation more overwhelming.

INTELLIGENCE QUOTIENT

The IQ is the value determined by dividing the mental age by the chronological age and multiplying by one hundred. Roughly speaking, if a ten year-old child scores at the eight-year-old level on an intelligence test, his IQ score is 8 over 10 times 100, or 80. After much testing and refining, intelligence tests are now perfected to the extent that the usual white North American child can be evaluated for his ability to get along in school. A psychologist once said that the intelligence test measures whatever the intelligence test is supposed to measure.

OBESITY

Until recently, doctors were trained to accept a certain weight as ideal for each height, but the rule now is: if someone looks fat, he *is* fat. The most acceptable cause of pure obesity is a genetic proclivity enhanced by psychological and nutritional factors. When the psychiatrists could not slim down the hefties, the guilt was laid on us pediatricians. We ignored the fact that bottle-fed babies are more likely to become obese; it is easy to overfeed with the bottle. We were also the ones who had started the baby (at six weeks of age) on rice cereal and applesauce. We doctors lit up the pleasure center in the baby's thalamus when we pushed the sugary goodies in these innocent little brains, and they became locked into the concept that sugar equals love. Or was it that the mother was always feeding him and smiling at him so he ate when she was nearby? Mea and mother's culpa!

Research has helped discover several reasons for obesity. (1) Genetic: These people have a large intestinal capacity, and the increased surface area of the gut lining enhances the absorption of every last calorie consumed. Endomorphs have an increased number of fat storage cells under their skin, as if nature expects them to store more. (2) The satiety center in the thalamus may have a higher than normal threshold, so the eater gets a delayed message about the level of glucose in the blood. People who eat large meals are more likely to secrete more insulin, which will cause hunger pangs in a couple of hours. (3) Learned behavior: They eat when frustrated or depressed. (4) Low blood sugar triggers the foraging center of the brain: "Eat!" (5) Food sensitivities make the blood sugar bounce around, and the victim craves the very food that caused the rise and fall in the first place. If you love something, it is bad for you! Dr. Marshall Mandell feels that food addictions are the prime cause of obesity; the person is allergic and addicted.[343] (6) Boredom and stress. (7) Not enough exercise, like sitting in front of TV eating chips. Exercise will increase the basal metabolic rate for fifteen hours, has an appetite suppressing effect; increases the self-image; and reduces feelings of tension, anxiety, and depression. Walking only thirty minutes a day without changing their diet, participants were able to lose weight. (8) Some people, genetically susceptible to gain weight, are consuming more calories than their metabolism needs because they are looking for the vitamins and minerals their bodies cannot get from nutrient-poor foods. (9) Something like 80 percent of us in the United States are alkaline, which leads to weight gain. When the metabolism arrives at homeostasis by correcting the acid/base balance and ingesting the optimal nutrients, the weight can be lost more easily. (10) Infections increase in the obese; the mother is anxious for the child to eat and create health. (11) The baby cannot distinguish the hunger drive from other drives; there is usually a history of frequent formula changes and feeding problems during infancy in those destined to become heavy as adults. As grown-ups they are unable to ascertain their gastric filling volumes. (12) People who eat less than three times a day are more likely to gain weight. People who eat small amounts frequently are more likely to maintain their weight, or lose it.

When all else fails, try the Smith Twelve-Mono-Meals-A-Day-Diet. Nibble. Graze. It might be just the ticket: It provides twelve meals a day spaced about an hour or so apart, and each feeding has about fifty to one hundred fifty calories, depending upon the age of the child or adult. It will eliminate obesity, hypoglycemia, some allergies, and some absorption problems. It will not stress the pancreas. Nibbling is the way to go. Research indicates that most humans do better eating somewhat continuously throughout their waking hours. One is more likely to become obese if one eats twenty-four hundred calories at one sitting. During the twenty-three-hour fast between that enormous meal and the next, that person will lose more muscle tissue than fat. Muscle activity is the fat-burning mechanism, so with less muscle it becomes harder to burn the fat. It is also important to eat but one food at each of those twelve feedings. Just a baked potato, then an hour or so later a cup or two of broccoli. After a while, about two ounces of poached fish. Multifoods at one sitting confuses the digestive enzymes. The food will be more thoroughly digested and your friends and family will notice you have less flatus. (Cough and the world coughs with you. Pass wind and you stand alone.)

The doctor is highly frustrated dealing with the obese, as their understanding of the condition is low, their satisfaction is minimal, and the treatment is uncertain. Energy requirements vary widely among individuals of the same age. Some grow fat on less; some stay lean on more than daily allowances. How can one prescribe a diet or caloric intake with nothing to base the diet upon? Why the concern? Statistics indicate a greater incidence and a higher morbidity and mortality of many chronic disorders in the obese: diabetes, arthritis, heart disease, gout, hypertension, kidney disease, hernia, colitis, and cancer.[344] Life expectancy is fifteen years less than that of normal age peers. Forty percent of us have some genetic trait that makes us susceptible to any or all of those conditions mentioned above.[345] You should hear surgeons groan when they must tunnel through four inches of fat to locate a diseased gall bladder. Obesity may also contribute to sterility.

What to Do If Fat Runs in the Family

If both parents are fat, there is an 80 percent chance of the children being overweight. If both parents are thin (ectomorphs), there is only a 7 percent chance. A parent can teach some preventive techniques of eating to her growing, cute but plump child. Like a balloon that is easier to blow up the second time, the body finds it easier to gain weight than to lose. Prophylactic underfeeding of desserts plus overexercising seems to be the only reasonable answer. No matter what the basis is for the extra lard, reduced caloric intake and increased calorie use will facilitate weight loss. But these people love to eat and hate to exercise. It has been shown that if these genetic types (endomorphs) are on a restricted diet early in life, they will not develop so many adipocytes (fat cells) and are less heavy as adults. The enzymes that split fat may decline in response to persistent overtaxation; the victim will acquire fat even on a very low calorie diet. Obese people have a decreased level of adenosine triphosphatae, the enzyme that pumps sodium and potassium across the cell membranes. This transport system uses a lot of energy. Adele Davis felt that lecithin helps the body burn fats. Linoleic acid, B_6, choline, inositol, l-carnitine, chromium, CoQ10, and magnesium are essential for reducing.

Hypothyroidism is rarely encountered in children, although some will respond to thyroid extract. Many of us have seen children become fat after a tonsillectomy or a serious infection (pneumonia, meningitis). I wonder if the severe infection or the anesthesia knocked out the thalamic calorie-control center, or the stressor exhausted some enzyme system.

If family fat runs thick, the baby's oral needs must be satisfied with large volumes of calorie-poor milk (2 percent) and a pacifier. Candy must not be used as a bribe, as it seems to promote eating as an answer to all frustration. One hundred percent fruit drinks, fruits, vegetables, and protein should be established as a *family* habit. Vegan vegetarians are rarely fat. Exercise must be promoted.

Eating the protein of the meal first stimulates the production of cholecystokinin, which stimulates the vagus nerve, which, in turn, tells the hypothalamus to stop eating so much so fast. Meat or protein first, then grains, legumes, and then vegetables. Eat the salad at the end of the meal and call it dessert. Chewing the vegetables thirty times or until the foods are a soup in the mouth (Fletcherization) before swallowing will help you digest the foods better and cut down on gas formation. When foods are digested properly, they will not cause allergic reactions. Digestive enzymes will help here. Rotate foods; try not to eat the same foods every day. Obesity is a flag to tell the bearer that the lifestyle has allowed a genetic trait to appear.

A heavy six- to twelve-year-old has about a 90 percent chance of being an overweight adult. Children with the genetic trait need support, not sabotage. Fat children do well at summer camps or in group therapy, where their food hangups can be bared. Bickering and needling seem only to push the lonely, fat one into quiet, sullen, oral solitude. With diet changes and a *family* exercise program, the heavy child should gain but a few pounds a year, not twelve. He/she then can grow *into* the weight.

Remember the words of Fibber McGee: "More people die from a fork in the mouth than a knife in the back."

SELF-ESTEEM

Self-esteem is the opinion one has of oneself. Self-devaluation is common in our country and in the civilizations that use guilt as a motivating force to control selfish drives. Everyone should be provided with a little of this sense of right and wrong, but if it is overdone, severe depression and suicide may be the result. Low self-esteem occurs when a child is allowed to get away with antisocial behavior.

Parental attitudes that lead to this frustrating, self-destroying devaluation are:

1. Constant harsh discipline for everything the child does (spilling milk, stumbling, soiling himself). Punishment for behavior the child cannot control is one of the most destructive things parents can do. The impulsive, hyperactive child is especially vulnerable because she seems accident-prone. She becomes especially depressed at about twelve years of age when she realizes she cannot control herself without a pill; she hates herself at a time when even *normal* children are struggling with a self-concept.

2. Perfectionistic parents never seem quite satisfied with the child's performance.

3. Overconcern about health may suggest to the child that he is not strong enough to perform.

4. Rejection by parents will be incorporated in the child; he will treat himself the same way.

5. Extremely moralistic, religious, family attitudes may become a way of life for the child who is overwhelmed with guilt for every odd thought he may have. It is hoped he may rebel somehow.

6. Adolescent girls, given the culture of female inferiority, are often lacking in self-esteem.

A child needs to develop skills in which he knows he is achieving something positive; he knows the difference when a parent says, "That's wonderful!" and it really isn't.

Frequently a therapist will suggest, as part of therapy, that a parent spend more time alone with a child—really listening, not lecturing or moralizing. One effective way to do this is to plan an outing to a museum or a surprise meal in a restaurant. No strings attached. No suggestions are to be made that the child must be good or behave. The implication the child should receive is that he is an important person to the parent.

Some guidelines for the development of a reasonably normal human with a good self-image:

1. Do not expect too much or too little from a child. Each develops at a different rate. Letting the child decide about weaning and bowel training seems permissive, but is less frustrating and precludes some childhood anger and aggression.

2. Do not punish thoughts and feelings, but antisocial behavior or aggressive acts are to be limited.

3. Conditioning by a system of rewards for good behavior and ignoring some bad behavior is more suitable in "shaping" a child's behavior than strictly punishment for bad behavior. Consistency is an obvious ingredient.

4. Do nothing to devaluate a child's self-image. Wanting a child before she arrives and loving her once she gets here is the basis of human relations.

5. Do not usurp the child's right of personal responsibility. The child's homework may suffer if he watches too much television; he must answer to the teacher for his deficiency. Parents should provide some general rules of eating and bedtime, but the child should have the option of what he will do with his uncommitted hours.

The student who is doing poorly knows it; there is no conspiracy to keep him from finding out. Failure breeds failure. Before a degrading self-image becomes irreversible, the child's sense of worth must be retrieved with encouragement; a new environment; social engineering; or if he is neurologically handicapped, medication and/or placement in a small ungraded class so that some success will brighten his day (home schooling?). Once labeled a failure, the tendency is to accept the label.

If the parents have been successful, the child will grow into an adult who is able to control his impulses but not be inhibited.

SEX EDUCATION

Sex education is the process of providing information and passing on attitudes to children that allow them to function as reasonably non-neurotic adults: Content with the sex assigned to them by their genes. Organ names are learned from playmates, parents, and sex hygiene courses. That part of sex education is basically anatomical. Many learn the mechanics from animals. Feelings, sex drives, and acceptance of maleness or femaleness are largely determined by the tone of the child's early home environment. Sexual feelings, like jealousy, go underground and emerge as feelings of restlessness, romance, nameless longing. Young adolescent girls often have no idea that the clothes fashion dictates they wear are sexually provocative, so they get labeled as "teases." Sexual feelings may emerge as "love," when it is really hormones driving them into something from which they have no clear escape. Girls may not be aware of these sexual feelings until they become aroused. Just saying "no" may be too late. Young adolescents may not take any sex education from their parents seriously, as they often cannot believe that their parents "did it," or know anything about sex.

The jurisdictional dispute over who teaches what is the basis for the concern of parents about sex education courses in the schools. Some parents feel that they should be the ones to instill a healthy attitude toward sex—in their own time and in the comfortable, natural setting of the home. Sex educators cite case after case involving otherwise intelligent young people who have fallen into sexual problems because of naiveté or simply a lack of accurate information. They feel that if the preadolescent is given sexual facts in the objective classroom by a skilled teacher, he/she will be armed with enough common sense to make the "right decision" when hormones urge novel adventures.

("I couldn't be pregnant; we were standing up." "He said he just got another girl pregnant. He's sterile for nine months, isn't he?" "He said he was giving me artificial respiration, and now I find I am to have his child.")

Many well-meaning parents feel that if the subject is not discussed, the adolescent will not think about it, and he or she can be kept nearly virginal until safely placed in the marriage bed. The rising rates of venereal disease, unwed and teen mothers, and pregnant brides suggests that this attitude is not working. Religious teaching and threats of punishment or banishment have not served to stem the rate of sexual activity. Sex drives seem to overwhelm cerebral control in the most intelligent, moral young people. Desire is almost unavoidable if they are healthy and normal and together for more than twenty-five minutes. Mother Nature wants the human race to go on. Sometimes all parents can do is to interrupt any couple every twenty minutes.

CHAPTER 15

Emergencies, Accidents, Poisonings, and First Aid

Accidents are the major cause of death and deformity from childhood through adolescence, now that infections are under better control. Most are preventable. Each age has its favorite: the one- to four-year-old is more susceptible to poisonings, burns, aspiration (breathing poisonous fumes or inhaling foreign objects), and falls. The adolescent is more likely to be hurt in motor vehicle accidents, shot by an "unloaded" gun, or drown.

Car accidents kill more than fifty thousand people a year; the number with permanent scarring or disfigurement is several times that. We live in a sleep-deprived culture. Most of these accidents happen on Friday night and Monday morning. The safest time to travel is Sunday noon. Booze + no sleep = tragedy. Better highways and safer cars will improve the statistics, but fewer drunks on the road might cut the toll in half.

As soon as a infant starts to cruise around the house, his gregariousness will get him into trouble. The toddler should be protected from his own curiosity. What seems an obvious "no-no" to us is an attractive adventure to him. They use their mouths like we use our eyes.

Throw old medicines away. Boric acid is no longer considered a worthwhile medicine and is a poison. Baby aspirin is rarely used for children now. All purses should be up on a shelf or out of sight. Gasoline, kerosene, paint thinner, furniture polish, and other indigestibles should be stored in their own containers—not in pop bottles—and out of reach. Lead paint should not be used. Laundry products have to be stored out of reach. Have syrup of ipecac on hand to induce vomiting when necessary. Protective play areas, indoors and out, should seal the toddler away from cars, steps, and sudden voids. Special car seats and seat belt use are the law. In an automobile collision, a child's light body frequently ricochets through the interior of the car like a Ping-Pong ball.

Some families are more accident-prone than others. The awkward, the hyperactive, and the brain-damaged child are more likely to fall, stumble, blunder through a glass door, or impulsively pull hot soup off the stove; they are neurologically disorganized, and therapy will help.

You are supposed to teach your child the dangers of the world, but don't overdo your admonishments ("Don't stick beans up your nose") lest they act as inducements to experiment.

The wise parent might get down on his/her hands and knees at the level of the accident-prone one- to three-year-old child and scoot around the floor. See what attractive, low-down nuisances there are in the house, such as detergents under the sink, bottles of kerosene and gasoline, or various sharp objects. Make sure your baby cannot climb onto high furniture or cabinets. Remove doors from unused refrigerators, and have suitable locks or combinations on the medicine closet. Electric wall sockets should be covered. Always, always disconnect appliances from the wall socket; terrible mouth burns result when a toddler puts the "hot" end of an appliance cord in his mouth.

Abrasion is the loss of the superficial skin layers due to friction (e.g., skinned knee or elbow after a fall on a cement sidewalk). It appears as a raw area with oozing of serum and blood.

Cleansing with water is essential. Several quarts of lukewarm water should be poured over the raw area despite the child's objections. Soap is not essential and may even irritate. A special effort should be made to remove dirt, grime, and sand, as foreign objects preclude healing. Bits of asphalt may have to be teased (or scrubbed) out; if allowed to remain, they will be incorporated in the new skin and produce a dark cast in the area, like a tattoo.

The area is patted dry and a large, thick, dry, sterile, nonadherent dressing is placed over the wound to prevent bacteria from being introduced, but also to permit some aeration of the raw surface. The chief function of the dressing is to allow the area to rest so healing can proceed. Some bandages are nonsticking but still porous. Do not use an antibiotic ointment like Neosporin, as the ointments may macerate the wound and interfere with healing; there is also a risk of sensitizing the skin to these medicines. Saint-John's-wort or calendula in ointments will promote healing. Dana Ullman, a homeopathic educator, suggests the gel form because it stays on the skin longer. This initial dressing must be kept dry for about four to six days, at which time it may be changed. If a nonadherent dressing is used, it will not have to be soaked off. If the abrasion is not covered with new skin, another dressing is reapplied.

Do not use waxed paper or plastic over a burn or abrasion. It may be easier to remove, but the occlusive dressing, serum, and blood provide an ideal culture medium for bacterial growth. Do not use iodine, alcohol, mercury tinctures, and such; these irritate more than help. If after two or three days no signs of healing are present or if the area becomes more tender, more red, and a yellow or green exudate appears, medical attention is necessary. A hot pack would help to localize the infection. Lack of attention may lead to impetigo and absorption of toxins.

Ankle is subject to many stresses (see Ankle strain, Chapter 8). If bones are out of alignment—subluxation—a chiropractor would be the one to reset them, and weight bearing may be allowed almost immediately.

A few important basic rules for sprains: Rest, do not let the ankle bear weight, apply ice for eight to twelve hours, and elevate it for the first day. The brave adolescent who plays ball on an injured ankle, so he won't be a quitter or sissy, may wreck his future athletic career. If, on the third day, cautious weight bearing (with the ankle supported with tape or elastic bandage) is painful, the foot should not be used. Mother Nature is telling the victim that healing has not yet taken place. Proteolytic enzymes by mouth are important for healing; they will speed the recovery.[346]

Artificial respiration is the mechanical or manual art of breathing for a victim who has ceased breathing due to drowning, heart attack, electrical shock, or injury.

An airway must be cleared from mouth to lungs by removing any water, food, or vomitus from the victim's mouth, pulling the tongue forward, and arching the head backward. The Heimlich maneuver should be the first consideration to remove what material may be in the lungs, windpipe, or throat.

When air is blown in with mouth-to-mouth contact maintained (and the victim's nose pinched), the ribs or chest wall should move, showing that air is getting to the lungs. This is repeated fifteen to twenty times a minute. If the heart is beating, the circulating blood will pick up oxygen from the lungs and deliver this important nutrient to the brain, which cannot function for long without oxygen.

With a baby or small child, gentle manual pressure can be applied to the chest wall to simulate breathing movements. In any case, the victim needs oxygen, and immediate help should be obtained.

The Red Cross has pamphlets and courses to show us what to do.

Baseball finger is a common chip fracture sustained when a ball hits the end of an outstretched finger. The tendon, tightly attached to the bone, pulls off a small fragment of bone at that point. Swelling, pain, and bruising are noted immediately. Splinting with the joint in the neutral position for three or four weeks is the usual requirement for normal healing.

Battered child is the name given to a child who has been physically beaten. Multiple bruises, burns, black eyes, fractured skull, and broken arms, legs, and ribs appear repeatedly. The location and appearance of the injuries belie the history given by the parents: "He fell down the stairs," "He rolled off the table," "He fell out of bed." X rays reveal new and healing fractures at sites rarely hurt when a toddler falls or bumps himself.

It is small consolation to know that throughout history, children have been killed, mutilated, or beaten by their parents and that these parents are usually sick, drunk, high, or psychotic. It seems odd that a legal, socially acceptable way for parents to transfer their unwanted children to childless couples has not yet been developed in our country.

Most normal parents become exasperated, frustrated, and occasionally screaming mad because of their children's behavior. Most will—if normal—admit, with some guilt feelings, that "I could wring his neck." But normal parents don't when not drinking. Most children sense this ambivalent love-hate feeling and display just enough endearing traits to balance the aggravating ones.

Court action can be brought against parents, and their children taken from them when medical evidence indicates a child has been battered. Placing a child back in this harsh environment only puts him at risk for another physical attack, which might end fatally. If battering is suspected, it must be reported.

Batteries contain mercury. The dry cell used for flashlights has an insignificant amount of mercury, but the small mercury cell battery used for transistor radios and hearing aids has a lethal dose. If a child swallows the latter, he may be in danger if the casing is broken. These batteries will occasionally explode, so they should never be discarded in a stove or fireplace; in addition to the explosion, there is the danger of mercury fumes.

Bites. Animal bites range from the barely noted blue bruises of the tooth marks of the playful family dog, to flesh ripped off by the savage bear. Most are harmless puncture wounds and contiguous abrasions, which require only regular cleansing plus a tetanus booster (usually if it has been more than five years since the last booster), but some bites will raise the fear of the dreaded rabies (see Rabies, Chapter 6).

Animal bites are usually less likely to cause a skin infection than human bites, simply because animal teeth, spaced farther apart, do not harbor as much bacteria. If a bite becomes infected, it becomes red, swollen, tender, and exudes some purulent material. (For treatment see Abscess, Chapter 8.)

Most doctors feel more secure giving the tetanus shot if it is a puncture wound. A tear, scratch, or abrasion would be less likely to need protection from tetanus. If the doctor can be reassured that the patient has had three or four tetanus shots and the most recent one was five years before, he can safely omit it. Most booster shots can be given within a day or two of the bite. However, each wound must be evaluated individually by the treating physician.

For cuts, stings and bites, the Bach flower remedy, Rescue Remedy (see page 147), will relieve the anxiety.

*Insects—chiggers, bedbugs, mosquitoes—*produce very irritating local reactions in susceptible people. The bite itself is usually very pruritic to children, who will scratch the top layer of skin off and introduce an infection. The location of the itchy papules is usually where clothing ends— ankles, neck, wrists, belt line. The usual fleabite lesions are frequently lined up in a triad with one fourth inch separating spaces, as if to represent breakfast, lunch, and dinner for the biter. The bitee may overreact with a large, hivelike wheal due to an allergic histamine release. Some have been able to prevent the bite by the oral intake of vitamin B_1 (thiamine) or brewer's yeast tablets every four hours. This gets to the skin and so nauseates the insect that it moves on. Obviously perfumed soaps and hair sprays will attract the bugs.

Bee stings in this country cause more deaths than snakebites. People can be severely allergic to bee venom, and for some reason, adolescent males react more severely than anyone else. Homeopathic remedies like apis or ledum should be given immediately after the bite of any stinging insect. This sometimes reduces the swelling, itching, and pain that develop anywhere from a few hours to a whole day later. But the person who has a violent reaction such as generalized *hives,* swelling in the throat, or fainting requires an epinephrine injection and/or oxygen from a doctor. If a person has had such a generalized reaction, he should get immunizing shots to protect himself.

An emergency kit should be carried by those who have had a generalized reaction. It includes a tourniquet, antihistamine, and a disposable syringe and needle, with epinephrine.

If available, I have heard that fresh cow manure packed on the throbbing, stinging red skin will stop the problem in seconds. Better use the apis.

Scorpion bite usually causes only a local pain and swelling, but some scorpion poisons have an affinity for the nervous system, causing a motor paralysis and convulsions. As death may occur in young children, a specific antivenin should be given. Intravenous vitamin C in large doses will safely detoxify the poison.

Snakebites are common. The garter snakes, or those without fangs (they have even teeth), are harmless; no treatment is necessary. The poisonous ones, rattlesnakes, copperheads, and coral snakes, cause about fifteen deaths per year in the United States out of about six thousand reported bites. Early spring is the most lethal time, because the poison sacs are full of venom after the winter hibernation.

Identifying the snake is important for diagnosis and treatment. The paired fang punctures in the skin give away the rattlesnakes and copperhead varieties, but the coral snake may give but a slight wound. The latter snake, however, can be identified by the black snout and adjacent red and yellow stripes. ("Red next to yellow, kill the fellow; red next to black, venom lack.") The colorful, innocuous king snake has a red snout, and the red and black areas are adjacent.

Symptoms usually occur within a few minutes of the bite. A burning pain and local swelling soon involve the whole limb. Hemorrhages occur. Vomiting of blood, shock, and respiratory paralysis suggest a fatal outcome. A hemorrhagic toxin and a neurotoxin are found in snake venom.

The victim must be *carried* to the hospital, as activity speeds the venom spread. A tourniquet should be applied only snugly—not with enough pressure to occlude arterial flow. Ice may be helpful. Cutting open the skin at the fang-hole sites and sucking out some of the venom is helpful if there is considerable swelling. Some advocate surgical excision of the whole area (two-inch plug) if it can be done within two hours.

The preceding measures should be taken, but one must not delay getting the patient to a facility where antivenin therapy is available. The safest therapy is intravenous vitamin C at the one hundred *gram* level, to drip in slowly over a couple of hours.

Spider bites are painful but rarely fatal. The **black widow** spider's venom produces immediate local pain, weakness, and severe muscle and abdominal cramps. The venom is more dangerous than a rattlesnake's, but the amount is less. Specific antivenin and calcium given intravenously will slow down the action. The **brown recluse** spider produces an ugly sore that takes weeks to heal. Early surgical removal of the bite area would speed healing.

Tarantula bites are painful, and produce local redness and swelling. Generalized reactions have not been reported.

Tick bite paralysis is due to the injection of the saliva of the wood tick. If a person in tick country develops muscle weakness, he should be inspected thoroughly for a tick. Rapid recovery of muscle function usually follows its removal.

Lyme disease is now the most common tick-borne disease, and occurs in each state. The ticks that carry the infection are small and hard to see (the size of the head of a pin).

The Rocky Mountain wood tick may carry **spotted fever.** Travelers in tick country should protect themselves with high boots and adequate clothing that has been treated with repellents (benzyl benzoate). They should inspect themselves thoroughly twice a day for ticks, especially in the groin, armpits, nape of neck, and scalp. Trying to asphyxiate the tick by coating it with ointment, fingernail polish, alcohol, or a burning match are all useless. Use tweezers, grab the tick as close to the skin as possible, and apply steady pressure, pulling the tick parallel to the skin. It is best to remove the tick in toto, as infection may follow retention of parts. Some protection of local skin at the bite site and of the tick remover must be afforded as the tick feces may carry infection.

Black eye (see Palpebral hematoma, this section).

Broken bones are often quite obvious when they occur in an arm or leg, but hairline fractures may only cause some pain and slight swelling. They all need professional care. The patient should be transported with suitable splinting to a hospital or doctor's office. The obvious bone deformities should be splinted without any attempt to manipulate them: "Splint them where they lie." If a fracture is suspected, careful X rays should be taken because of the need for proper positioning of the bones while healing. Perhaps the most effective "splinting" method that can be done at home is to use a rolled-up newspaper, blanket, or even a pillow to softly support the break. Careful splinting prevents a simple fracture from becoming compound—that is, having the bone end push through the skin. This latter condition may result in infection, which complicates healing.

Burns should be treated immediately, even before the doctor is summoned, by immersing the affected part in cold water. If it is a hand or a foot, a bucket of cold water will do. If the extremity is kept immersed from one to four hours, the cool water may keep a first-degree burn from becoming a second, or a second from becoming a third. If the burned area is on the torso, a wet pack can be used. Make sure the cold water reaches the skin. This usually soothes the pain and somehow interferes with the formation of poison or toxin produced by burned tissue. A sterile dry dressing is next applied. Never use butter, lard, grease, or ointments on a burn—only the cleansing water or the sterile dressing. With large burns requiring hospital attention, a clean sheet is best to wrap up the burn during transport. Any gunk on the skin must be cleaned off, which adds further trauma.

For first- or second-degree burns: myrrh or goldenseal powder, comfrey leaf poultice, marshmallow herbal compresses, calendula tincture or cream, aloe vera, lavender oil, yarrow tincture, Saint-John's-wort oil, tea tree oil; internally, use vitamins C, E, and A, along with zinc.

Chemical burns must be washed with running water immediately. This diluting and neutralizing effect must be continued for at least thirty minutes. Neutralizing an acid with an alkali (or alkali with an acid) may cause further injury from the heat of the chemical reaction, and the delay caused by looking for the suitable antidote allows for continued tissue destruction. Flood it with water!

Carbon monoxide (CO) is a poisonous gas formed by the incomplete burning of carbon, commonly found in auto exhaust. It is invisible and odorless, so the victim is unaware of the effects until headache, dizziness, muscle weakness, and vomiting appear, which may lead to coma and even death. Carbon monoxide competes with oxygen in the blood's red cells, and thus the body cells become starved for oxygen. Treatment is removal from the gas and inhalation of oxygen. It takes about thirty minutes of inhaling pure oxygen to reverse the effects of CO inhalation.

Cardiac massage is the emergency effort to compress the pulseless heart so as to eject blood into the aorta. In the infant, intermittent finger pressure on the lower third of the sternum at the rate of 100 per minute may keep the circulation going until the heart begins its automatic beat. In the older child, both hands (the heel of one hand on top of the other) are required to press on the breastbone at the rate of 60 to 80 times per minute.

Clavicles, or collarbones, are located between the shoulder and the top of the breastbone. They are the easiest bones to break and the easiest to heal with little orthopedic assistance. The bone may be broken during the birth of a large baby through a small or contracted pelvis. This injury usually results from a fall in which the patient strikes his shoulder. The collarbone cracks or splinters, and the bone ends override. The victim may have few symptoms except a tender discolored knob at the site for a few days. Healing takes place with no residual deformity. The callus of hard calcium may be detectable a few days after the injury and remain for four to eight weeks.

Cuts are tears in the skin, most frequent in the two-year-old child who stumbles, falls, and opens a gash on his forehead or chin. The opening gapes apart due to the elastic nature of the skin; blood flows freely and often alarmingly. Head lacerations bleed especially vigorously because of the abundant blood supply, but for the same reason they heal rapidly.

Basic steps are to clean the area with running water and apply a compression dressing to squash the blood vessels flat, thus controlling the bleeding. The next step is to determine whether the cut needs to be sutured. Surgeons like to suture things, so they will if you ask them; but doctors are finding that many cuts can be efficiently pulled together by taping, as cuts on the head heal rapidly. Besides, taping can be done with less physical and emotional trauma for the young child. Usually head cuts heal in three days; on the body the tape has to hold the wound together for a week. In any event, some decision has to be made before six or eight hours have elapsed. If the wound is left open after that time, infection can set in, and sometimes the wound *has* to be left open—which can mean scarring. A tetanus booster for this type of injury is not necessary, as it is not a puncture wound. When bleeding occurs, do not panic. Clean the wound; control bleeding with pressure and not a tourniquet; and make arrangements for medical help, whether it is suturing or taping.

Genital lacerations in the female usually result from sitting down suddenly on the edge of a box, a chair, or bike bar. Contusions, abrasions, and cuts may all be present. Suturing may be indicated if a large gap is present, although these tissues fall together and heal easily. If penetration is suspected (picket fence injury or sexual abuse), a urologist may have to evaluate the integrity of the urethra.

Salty urine passing over the open sore is painful. A protective gob of an ointment may ease the passage. Urination while sitting in a warm bath will be more comfortable.

Drowning is death from asphyxia due to laryngeal spasm and/or water in the lungs and/or ventricular fibrillation. Once the near-drowned victim has been brought to shore, no time should be wasted with postural drainage. The Heimlich maneuver is the first priority to clear the passageways of water. Heimlich himself says that drowning victims can aspirate as much as one and a half quarts of water. Every effort should be made to get oxygen to the brain. If the pupils are dilated and fixed, death probably has already occurred. If the patient is pulseless, cardiac massage is to be carried out simultaneously with mouth-to-mouth breathing.

Elbow (see Subluxation of the Radial head, this chapter).

Electric shock effects are related to the current flowing through the body rather than the voltage. Alternating current is more dangerous than direct current of the same voltage. Death is assumed to be from ventricular fibrillation or respiratory paralysis (see Artificial respiration, this chapter). Electrical burns are treated as in Burns, this chapter.

Epistaxis is a nosebleed. It is sometimes difficult to stop. Nosebleeds are common in children during cold, dry weather, during the hot summer, or after slight trauma. Old tricks like placing a cold knife on the back of the neck or putting ice on the lip or gums are of doubtful value. Almost all nosebleeds originate from eroded capillaries on the first one inch of the nasal septum. Pressure must be applied *there* to flatten the capillaries. Make a tampon by wetting a piece of tissue or part of a cotton ball; it should be big enough just to slide into the nostril. Sometimes a lubricant will help; some favor putting a few drops of a nose-drop solution on the surface of the wad to act as a vasoconstrictor. Push this into the nose and then pinch the wings of the nose together snugly for ten to fifteen minutes. This should stop the bleeding. The patient should not lie down, but bend forward so one can tell if the bleeding has been stopped with the pressure. If blood is still dripping, increase the pressure. Leave the tampon in place for another ten minutes and then s-l-o-w-l-y withdraw it. This should leave a clear, open passageway free of clot. If a clot is allowed to form in the nose, it dries, cracks, and opens the vessels again. Some lubricant should be applied daily to the raw area for a week until healing is complete. If hemorrhage is frequent, cauterizing with a silver nitrate stick may help. Bioflavonoids and vitamin C orally may increase capillary integrity. Nosebleeds that occur without trauma suggest a milk sensitivity.

Eye injuries. Traumatic abrasions to sclera usually leave a bright red area. Patching the eye after a suitable antibiotic ointment is applied is usually all that is necessary. The ophthalmologist or optometrist should be consulted to rule out corneal injury.

Foreign bodies in the eye are potentially dangerous because of the possibility of corneal scarring. Not all serious wounds are painful. If the object is not obviously or easily removed, bringing immediate relief, a doctor should be consulted.

Acids, sprays, or chemicals that get into the eye should be flushed out immediately with lukewarm tap water; don't bother to sterilize it. The dilution of the poison is essential. The longer the flushing can be continued, the better; ten to twenty minutes is ideal. The problem is the overwhelming eyelid spasm that occurs with eye injuries. Two people may be necessary—one to pry open the lid and the other to run the water. Then call the doctor.

Foreign objects such as sand and cinders in the eye should be washed out. Continued irritation suggests an object stuck on the inside of the upper lid. The lid can be everted by having the patient look down; the upper lashes are grasped, and using a thin stick, roll the margin of the lid back over it, exposing the tarsal plate. The cinder can be teased off with a bit of cotton. Penetrating eyeball injuries (BB shot) must be treated by an ophthalmologist.

Blows about the eye usually cause only palpebral hematomata (black eyes). If double vision occurs, an orbital blowout fracture may have occurred. Surgery is indicated.

Fainting spells (syncope). Very young children faint because of organic problems—anemia, disease, epilepsy, or breath holding. The adolescent is more likely to faint from hysteria, low blood sugar, or hyperventilation. Repressed anger can make one faint.

Fainting spells are fairly common in some children with an unstable neurovascular system. Fright, pain, or deep breathing will allow the blood vessels in the abdomen to dilate, effectively reducing the blood and oxygen supply to the brain. Lying down, crying, straining (tightening the abdominal muscles), and bending over are all effective in restoring cerebral circulation. The child who cries when stuck for a blood sample, or when given a shot, will rarely faint. On the other hand, the stoical child who sits quietly during the procedure may turn pale and keel over on the floor two minutes later. Some people are susceptible and faint on suggestion, or while watching operations, or standing motionless after a full meal.

If no reasonable stimulus can be blamed for the episode, the victim should at least be checked for anemia. If fainting occurs on an empty stomach, a fasting blood sugar might be obtained. An electroencephalogram should be considered next if attacks are periodic and without an inciting event. Postural hypotension and hyperventilation must be ruled out. Weak adrenal glands from stressors may cause one to faint. Pantothenic acid and vitamin C will be helpful in that case.

I used to feel faint while singing lustily in Sunday school, wearing a tight collar, after pancakes with syrup for breakfast. It happened again during surgery demonstrations in medical school.

Fishhook, when stuck in the skin, must be pushed through until the barb is exposed. This is then cut off and the remainder is pulled back through from whence it came.

Foreign bodies

Foreign body in the nose is frequently found in an allergic child with an itchy nose; he has been warned not to pick his nose. He cannot ignore the sensation, so he gets around the admonishment by shoving something handy into his nose. Beans, beads, candy, nuts, thumbtacks, bits of paper, pills, and buttons have all been used. The child refuses to admit his act or has forgotten it. After a few days an infection occurs, and a foul-smelling (fetid), bloody, purulent discharge occurs from the involved nostril (usually only one).

The messy glob can defy extraction. An old doctor in the South suggested "blowing" the child's nose for him. Have the child lie down on his back, cover his nose with a tissue, occluding the uninvolved nostril, then with close mouth-to mouth contact, blow sharply and vigorously. The air column turns about the palate and pushes out the mess into the tissue—hopefully. Tweezers might next be tried. If unsuccessful, the ear, nose, and throat doctor should be called. Anesthesia may be necessary. Some allergy control would be advisable to prevent a recurrence.

Larynx. Foreign bodies may be trapped on or between the cords because of the narrow, slitlike opening. The usual story: A two-year-old with a peanut, diced carrot, plastic toy, marble, nails, screws, buttons, or coin in his mouth suddenly laughs or inhales. He is overcome with coughing, gasping, barking, or voice loss. He turns red and frantically clutches his throat and/or mouth. (Croup or barking in the middle of the night would suggest a virus, as a foreign body lodged in the larynx would not allow the child to fall asleep.) He may cough the object up, or it may remain stuck and have to be removed after direct observation with the laryngoscope, or it may move down into a bronchial tube and cause wheezing and/or bronchial-tube obstruction. The Heimlich maneuver must be tried immediately.

It is amazing how a child may cough and choke on a bit of bone or shell, seem to rid himself of the object, but retain it in the laryngeal area with a minimum of symptoms. If the object is not too large or obstructive, it may be forgotten, and symptoms of cough and stridor (noisy inhaling) may reappear days or weeks later. The foreign object will be revealed after antibiotics have failed to cure the symptoms and an X ray is taken. When the object (a nickel, for instance) is shown to the mother, she may remember: "Oh, yes, I recall now he *did* have a coughing spell for a while, but I thought he coughed it out."

X rays may miss it if it is not opaque. Direct viewing is the only way to solve the mystery of a vocal change that cannot be explained by a virus.

Bronchus. A foreign object will wedge itself and defy efforts of coughing and gravity to dislodge it.

The story is similar to the above scenario, but ends up with: "He cried, inhaled, coughed, and turned blue. He's comfortable now, but he has a wheeze." The location of the object will determine the symptoms and signs. If no air is moving in or out of the right side of the chest, the obstruction is in the right main-stem bronchus. Once the object gets to the bronchial tree, the Heimlich maneuver is not as useful. X rays determine the position accurately if the object is radiopaque. Bronchoscopy is the usual method of discovery and removal.

Prevention is obviously the best cure. Dolls and toys should not have detachable buttons. Candy should not contain nuts; a no-candy rule is even better. Safety pins should always be kept closed and out of reach. Stop the habit of carrying objects—including cigarettes—in your mouth; imitative children don't know the dangers.

Swallowed foreign object. If a child has swallowed a foreign object, it is worth remembering that the narrowest passage is between the mouth and the stomach: the esophagus. It is the tube most likely to be involved for infants who swallow almost anything they can put in their mouths. Fortunately, buttons, marbles, small toys, beads, bits of bone, and coins are easily passed. If the parent is positive that the object was swallowed, if there are no symptoms, and if the child can swallow some food without immediate regurgitation, the object probably has reached the stomach.

If the swallowed object has arrived in the stomach, it will usually make the remaining journey without incident. Straining the stools may be rewarding if parents are that curious, or if the object is valuable enough to warrant it; most parents do nothing unless symptoms of abdominal distress are noted. If the child suddenly refuses food, or chokes or vomits at mealtime, an object in the esophagus should be considered.

X rays will demonstrate its position if it is radiopaque. A bit of barium-soaked cotton in some food would lodge on a nonopaque object (X ray would pass through plastic or leather) and reveal the level of obstruction.

I observed a six-year-old girl who was able to swallow a quarter with some tears and substernal chest pain. Eating was normal for a day or so until she began to have some nausea and upper-right abdominal pain. An X ray revealed the coin stuck at the pylorus (exit from the stomach). A day or two of atropine relaxed the muscles there, and the quarter passed on.

Pins, needles, sharp bones, and small open safety pins may drop straight into the stomach from the mouth, but be unable to make the turns in the small bowel. Stomach pain, tenderness, and fever suggest impingement and penetration through the wall. Surgery is indicated. The paucity of complications suggest that the bowel wall recoils from the sharp point as the object tumbles on down (like a worm retracting from a sharp stick). Occasionally a foreign object will get hung up at the anal sphincter, and sometimes has to be teased out with a lubricated finger. Pennies and dimes seem to travel through easily. A nickel possibly could get hung up, and a quarter almost always does. (If coins are swallowed, watch the stools for any change.)

Corrosive esophagitis is an obviously sore, raw, bleeding esophagus following the ingestion of chemicals that eat away the lining. Lye and acids, especially drain cleaners and electric-dishwasher detergents, will burn the gullet. Before the doctor is called, the caretaker must pour as much water as possible down the child's throat. A quart is ideal. No effort is made to neutralize the chemical; just dilute it with water as fast as possible.

It heals, of course, but scar tissue about the esophagus will frequently constrict and cause narrowing or obstruction to the passage of food. If no opening is present, the surgeon may be able to fashion a functioning gullet from a loop of intestine, thus connecting the throat with the stomach.

Foreign body in the ear. Children, especially boys, seem to have a rule that goes, "If you have a hole in your body, put something in it." Almost daily doctors are pulling bits of paper, foil, pencil, erasers, crayon, or beads out of some two- to-six-year-old's ear canal. Moreover, children who do this have forgotten when, and are reluctant to tell why, they put the object in there. It suggests, however, that something brought their attention to the hole: The canal itched because of an allergy, fungus infection, or middle-ear infection (otitis media); or fluid accumulation (serous otitis media) gave a sensation of fullness, deafness, or pressure that required some form of probing investigation. Small objects may be teased or washed out; large impacted objects may require anesthesia in a small child, since the wall of the canal is tender. Bugs, beetles, earwigs, flies, and bees may be subdued with oil, alcohol, or whiskey and then removed. Vegetable matter (seeds, stems) should not be washed with water; the material swells up and may become impacted.

Frenulum is a bridge of tissue extending from the center of the upper gum to the upper lip. Dr. Thom suggests that this membrane may be thick enough to separate the upper incisors if it attaches between the teeth.

Many two-year-old children fall on their faces and tear this membrane, because the lip is pulled sharply to the side. Vigorous bleeding will follow as this tissue contains a big vein. Direct pressure against the lip from the outside will occlude this vessel flat on the gum and stop the leak.

Frostbite is the formation of ice crystals in the skin cells and blood vessels due to exposure to low temperature. Redness, then pallor, occurs. Immediate immersion in hot water (103 to 105 degrees F.) is the best treatment. (Comfortably hot bath water is 95 to 97 degrees F.) Twenty minutes are usually required to pink up the nail beds. The more rapid the rewarming, the better the results. The ice must be melted, and oxygen must reenter the tissues. The frozen tissues must *not* be rubbed; they are already damaged enough.

Head injuries usually cause some concussion. Concussion is a swelling of the brain, the symptoms of which are headache, drowsiness, and vomiting. The skull may or *may not* be cracked; X rays of the skull are not as important as the symptoms. Skull fracture may go undetected since an X ray is not taken every time a child falls down the steps and bumps his head. The pupils may or may not be dilated, constricted, or unequal. Concussion in most cases lasts six to ten hours, after which the victim's symptoms improve. If after twelve to twenty-four hours the headache, drowsiness, and vomiting become worse, then bleeding into or over the surface of the brain must be considered. It is probably better to allow him to sleep, but to arouse him every thirty minutes to evaluate his level of consciousness.

Intervention is dictated by the persistence and/or severity of the symptoms. Each of the following should be tested periodically, maybe every hour or two: (1) response to pain (none, withdrawal, or retaliation); (2) response to verbal contact (none, nonspecific, or inappropriate); (3) amnesia (last remembered event—with time, if events closer to the injury are remembered, the patient is improving); (4) recent memory (if events following the injury are remembered and recall of random digits is correct, the patient is recovering), because with brain damage, the ability to recall events is one of the first functions to go. If personality changes occur postrecovery, neurological rehabilitation will help restore normal function.

At least one hospital, Hennepin County Medical Center (Minneapolis, Minnesota), has been having success using a hyperbaric chamber that can administer concentrated oxygen under greater than atomspheric pressure. "This therapy can decrease tissue distortion, relieve strain on the injured blood vessels, and diffuse oxygen to the areas of the brain where cells may be dying."[347]

Emergency room doctors use the following mnemonic device to help them arrive at a diagnosis for anyone who is unconscious: AEIOUTIPPS

Acidosis or Alcohol	Epilepsy	Insulin
Opiates	Uremia	Trauma
Infection	Psychogenic	Poisoning
Shock		

Heat stroke. An average, active person *must* produce and evaporate over a pint of sweat an hour to keep body temperature down. If the day is humid or the person is fully clothed, the sweat is not vaporized. Heat stroke is the result of increasing heat production (exercise) and decreasing heat loss (high environmental temperature and humidity, plus insulating clothing). If an athlete is exercising in high temperature and humidity, the competition between the skin and muscles for blood creates a demand on the cardiovascular system. If the sweat losses constitute only 2 percent of body weight, circulation is compromised. Treatment must be provided with adequate water and salt replacement, or the afflicted one may collapse (see Athletics, Chapter 14).

Hematemesis is vomiting of blood. It usually follows swallowing of blood from a bloody nose. Nursing infants sucking from a cracked nipple may swallow enough blood to cause vomiting. It may be caused by a foreign object down the gullet, a stomach or duodenal ulcer may be bleeding, or the child may have consumed corrosive poisons, iron tablets, or aspirin.

Hernia, incarcerated, is a hernia that is stuck, usually in the inguinal canal. Most babies notice no symptoms unless the hernia gets stuck and cannot be reduced. These hernias must be surgically repaired, regardless of the paucity of symptoms, as trusses are worthless and an occasional hernia becomes stuck or incarcerated, requiring an emergency operation. In the latter case the lump would be hard and tender, and the infant would be screaming with pain and perhaps vomiting. Surgery is always indicated, whether for a ten-day-old baby or a hundred-year-old man.

Mouth puncture wounds usually gush with blood immediately, but are treated symptomatically unless bleeding does not subside to a slight ooze in thirty minutes.

On the third day a white clot is seen at the site; this is not pus but a normal clot with the red cells washed away.

Nosebleed (see Epistaxis, above).

Nose injury is common after falling facedown or not catching a ball. It is actually difficult to break a small child's nose because of the large amount of cartilage that constitutes his nasal structure. If the nose has been struck and bleeds from the inside, it implies that the cartilage or bone has broken through the mucous membranes. Whether the bones are still in good alignment is difficult to tell. X rays may be necessary to determine this. In general, if the tip of the nose is centered between the pupils of the eyes when the patient is evaluated from the front view, then his nose may not be broken. Also, if the bridge of the nose is not depressed, it may not be broken. However, many septal injuries cause a collection of blood on one side. This interferes with healing; one side of the nose may grow faster than the other, or destruction of the septum may lead to a saddle nose. The patient may develop a deviated septum later in life, even though he might not have actually broken his nose.

If there is doubt whether the nose is broken, careful X rays will determine if bone (but not cartilage) segments are out of place. In the first three or four days, these bones can be moved back to the proper position for healing. Otherwise—if they heal in incorrect positions—remedial surgery will be necessary later in life.

Palpebral hematoma is blood that has leaked out of the capillaries into the eyelids (black eyes). If a blow on the forehead or on the eyebrows is severe enough to break the vessels under the skin, the free blood will migrate down to the loosely attached eyelids, which become blue and distended. Ice and compression (or raw beefsteak from the refrigerator) at the time of injury may reduce some of the lid swelling that appears the next day. Once the swelling and blood are present, moist heat compresses or hot packs will increase the blood flow through the lids and allow the old dead blood to be absorbed more quickly. As the blood disintegrates, it becomes green, then yellow. Usually three weeks are required for the tissues to return to normal. Leeches are sometimes still used to suck the dead blood out of the eyelid, but every once in a while they will transmit the hepatitis virus from one person to another. Vitamin C and proteolytic enzymes (protein digesting) are the therapy now. Homeopathics that help: arnica, ledum, symphytum.

Poisons require an immediate call to the doctor or your local poison control center. Have the numbers handy. Doctors are called at least daily about a toddler getting into something that was left about: detergents, polish, lye, and solvents that were stored under the sink or in a handy cupboard. Forty percent of poison cases occur in the kitchen. The two- to four-year-old is likely to get into the unlocked medicine cabinet or mother's purse. Seventy percent of poison cases involve substances that are visible to the child.

Swallowed poisons do not remain in the stomach long, so it is wise to get the child to vomit immediately, unless the substance is a strong acid, alkali, or petroleum product (gasoline, lighter fluid, furniture polish). Every home with small children should have a bottle of syrup of ipecac handy. *Vomiting may be dangerous if kerosene or petroleum distillates have been ingested.* Three teaspoons of this syrup of ipecac should be given while you are placing the call to your doctor—and the local poison control center. Make the child drink six ounces of water. Vomiting should occur in about fifteen to thirty minutes. (You might want the child to sit outside in the garden or at the curb for the expected explosion.) Vomiting empties the stomach more efficiently than lavage (passing a stomach tube, injecting water, and aspirating the stomach contents until the return is clear). Emptying the stomach *as soon as possible* after poison ingestion may be lifesaving. The empty bottle or list of ingredients *must* be brought along to the doctor's office or emergency room.

Activated charcoal will absorb large amounts of some drugs (a teaspoonful in a glass of water). A mixture of milk and egg white will subdue toxic effects of metals. Strong tea counteracts some alkaloids.

Boric acid is a chemical formerly used for eye care and as a diaper-rinse. Tears are about as effective as boric acid for eyes; if an infection exists, more efficient antibiotic solutions or ointments are available. Boric acid is actually a lethal substance and should not be in the house; it serves no purpose medically.

Contraceptives, oral, are frequently left at the bedside for the mother's convenience. No harm comes to the child by an occasional dose; it just throws the mother's schedule off a little. The child's stomach probably should be emptied if he takes more than five or ten pills.

Crayons usually contain harmless vegetable dyes (supposed to be marked with AP, CP or CS 130–146). Some have aniline dyes, but the small amount incorporated in the wax of the crayon is not sufficient to cause harm.

Detergents are not soaps; their action in cleaning is to lower the surface tension of water and emulsify the dirt. The phosphates they contain and the alkalinity of the solution may cause esophageal burning if swallowed, but rarely as severe as with alkalis. Stomach pain, diarrhea, and distention usually respond to milk and fluids. Electric-dishwasher detergents are very toxic and may cause a corrosion of the esophagus.

Lead poisoning is not uncommon in children (one child in six) living in old, crowded, paint-peeling ghetto areas. Old paint on the crib and walls is the most common source, but it may come from lead pipes, lead in fruit sprays, lead in toys, or lead in the air—if storage batteries are burned.

If the daily lead intake is greater than the body's ability to excrete it or deposit it in the bones, signs of poisoning develop slowly. Irritability, headache, stomachache, anemia, and pallor are signs of many diseases, but when confusion, poor coordination, weakness—all signs of brain involvement—progress to convulsions and coma, lead poisoning should be considered.

The first step in diagnosing lead poisoning is to think of it. Many a "peculiar" child, written off as a neurotic, has later been found to have lead in his brain and bones. A pale child with headaches who eats dirt or plaster should have urine and hair tests for lead, a blood test for anemia (lead causes stippling in the red cells), and X rays for lead lines in the bones. Spinal fluid is under extra pressure because of the swollen brain. Urinalysis shows albumin and blood.

The treatment is the removal of environmental lead so that it cannot get to the patient, plus the mobilization of lead from the tissues and its excretion. Some chemicals are capable of forming nontoxic compounds with lead, which are then safely eliminated in the urine.

Even with careful removal of lead from the body, the brain may be irreversibly damaged. Mental retardation is the most common residual defect.

Mercury poisoning is usually due to the inadvertent ingestion of bichloride of mercury. Intestinal hemorrhages and profuse diarrhea may cause shock, coma, and death. If the patient survives this, he may succumb because of the kidney damage due to uremia. The sooner he vomits after ingestion, the better the chance of recovery. Ipecac would be helpful, followed by lavage of the stomach with milk. Frequent injections of BAL (British Anti-Lewisite) may detoxify the chemical. Acrodynia is not seen anymore, since it is not used in teething powders, but it can be found in calomel, mercury ointments, and paint. The pure metal quicksilver, in toys and thermometers, could be converted by stomach acid to the dangerous salt form. It is known that the mercury in the silver/mercury amalgam fillings can leech out and damage the kidneys, the brain, and the liver. Tuna fish from some areas have been found to be contaminated with mercury salts. A Texas family was poisoned when they ate a pig that had eaten mercury-treated grain that was intended for use as seed.

Nutmeg may cause excitement or delirium followed by collapse and coma. Syrup of ipecac early is standard.

Opiates (*e.g., morphine*) cause drowsiness, coma, and pinpoint pupils. Respiratory depression—two to four breaths a minute—might require a respirator.

Pencil lead is not lead, but graphite, and has no toxic effect. If some graphite is left under the skin after a puncture with a pencil, it might leave a tattoo.

Phenols (creosote, carbolic acid, Lysol) cause rapid respiratory failure. Lavage is done with olive oil, as these chemicals are soluble in it.

Phenolphthalein is widely used in candy-flavored cathartics (like Ex-Lax). Violent cramps and severe diarrhea occur minutes or hours after ingestion. If emesis does not occur immediately and symptoms have already begun—because the child let no one know what he did—paregoric is the proper antidote. Rash, high fever, dehydration, and kidney and liver damage might ensue.

Phosphorus is found in rodent poisons, fertilizers, and fireworks. (The phosphorus in present-day matchheads is red phosphorus and nontoxic.) Rapid onset of intestinal symptoms is followed by coma, liver injury, jaundice, and hemorrhages. Syrup of ipecac should be given and followed by lavage.

Phosphate esters (chlorothion, malathion, parathion) may be inhaled, ingested, or absorbed through the skin. A metabolite of these highly toxic substances inhibits the action of cholinesterase, which metabolizes acetylcholine. Functions of the body dependent upon the latter chemical for action are overstimulated: cramps, diarrhea, cough, increased sweating, pinpoint pupils, and slow heart rate follow. Atropine is the antidote.

Plant foods and fertilizers are usually safe to ingest, but some contain nitrates. Bacteria in the intestine may convert these to nitrites, which may cause methemoglobinemia.

Polishes and waxes for furniture and floor are basically **hydrocarbons.** They are dangerous if swallowed.

Salicylates (aspirin, some liniments) are the common poisons. One grain of aspirin per ten pounds of body weight is the usual therapeutic dose; but one grain per pound may cause ringing in the ears and stomach distress in some people. These symptoms should be cause for administering syrup of ipecac, even as long as two to four hours after ingestion, as some is usually still in the stomach.

Hyperventilation (air hunger) is the first clue. The body compensates for the acidosis by exhaling carbon dioxide (an acid). This respiratory alkalosis urges the kidneys to secrete base alkaline substances, and metabolic acidosis occurs. Intravenous fluids, with monitoring of the salicylate blood level and pH (acidity), becomes complicated.

Shampoos and hair-care preparations are usually safe unless large amounts are consumed.

Talc is dangerous when inhaled as it produces a violent (depending on amount) pulmonary reaction that is almost impossible to treat. Do not allow a cloud of this silicate to settle down on the baby. Sprinkle a little in your hand and transfer this to his skin. Cornstarch might be better.

Warfarin is a rat poison that interferes with blood coagulation. The effect is slow but may last several days. Hemorrhages occur from nose, mouth, and intestines. Blood transfusions and vitamin K are necessary.

Poisonous plants are ubiquitous. *It would be best to induce vomiting after the ingestion of any unknown substance.* Syrup of ipecac should be in your home. Where specific treatment is not given, the doctor should be called.

House plants: castor bean, dumbcane, elephant's ear, calla lily, mistletoe, philodendron, racunculus, caladium, poinsettia, lantana.

Vegetables: mango skin, potato (green tubers and new sprouts), rhubarb leaves.

Garden plants: bleeding heart foliage, buttercup, foxglove leaves (digitalis); crocus, daffodil, narcissus, and jonquil bulbs; daphne, deadly nightshade, Christmas rose, hemlock (Socrates died from this), hydrangea, iris root, jasmine, jimson weed, larkspur, delphinium, lily of the valley, monkshood, morning glory seeds, mountain laurel, oleander, pokeweed root, rhododendron, star of Bethlehem, sweet pea seeds, wisteria, yew.

Shrubs and trees: black locust, box, cherry (entire plant except fruit), elderberry (entire plant except berries), holly berries, horse chestnuts, oak leaves and acorns, privet leaves and berries.

Mushroom poisoning is caused by muscarine, which produces abdominal cramps, perspiration, convulsions, coma, and death. Atropine counteracts this chemical, and large doses may have to be given frequently until the chemical is metabolized.

I know people who pick their own mushrooms in the woods. If they are unsure of a mushroom's toxic effect, they will have one small slice of one. If no symptoms occur within the hour, they assume that they are of a non-poisonous variety and include them in the dinner. A dangerous practice— buy your mushrooms from your friendly, reliable grocer.

Puncture wounds require no more than gentle washing with running water to flush out superficial dirt. Vigorous scrubbing with soap and brush, or use of alcohol or medicines, will only cause further damage to injured skin. A tetanus booster should be administered within the next forty-eight hours if there has been no booster within five years, and the puncture was from a dirty nail or some outside object. Stab wounds with the kitchen knife are usually fairly sterile and need no more than a bandage. Puncture wounds of the foot require special handling by a surgeon. Because of the anatomy of the foot and the fact that bits of shoe, sock, sand, and dirt have been pushed into deep, inaccessible regions, many surgeons now feel obliged to remove a small cone of tissue including the puncture tract to prevent infection.

Radiation by X rays is essential in making diagnosis of many body ills, but it must be remembered that X rays are destructive. Excessive X ray radiation is more harmful to growing tissues and cells than to adult organs, because of the higher rate of cell division in the younger age groups.

The government has set guidelines for radiation exposure for atomic-energy workers, with the recommendation that the general population receive much less. Cosmic rays and certain trace radioactive elements bombard us all the time. Diagnostic X rays may increase the amount of radiation to a person comparable to the increase a person would receive if he moved to the mountains (more cosmic rays). X rays are to be respected and avoided unless a diagnosis cannot be made without them.

Some statistics suggest a higher-than-normal rate of thyroid cancer in those who were X rayed for thymus enlargement as infants. Some feel that, if a pregnant woman receives X rays, her baby has a greater chance of developing leukemia. Those receiving X ray therapy for acne may develop a skin cancer in later life. It still happens.

The radiologists are aware of these hazards, and procedures and equipment are now designed to reduce excessive exposure. X rays, however, are less injurious than the fluoroscope. A dentist who X-rays teeth too frequently (once a year is plenty) or a doctor who X-rays every bruise should be censured.

Rib fracture is common after a direct blow to the chest (falls on objects, car accidents). X rays are usually not indicated in the simple cases. Although taping the chest has long been the standard treatment, a few patients have developed pneumonia because of inadequate aeration of lungs. Rest and analgesics (codeine) are now advised. An elastic bandage could be used for broken ribs that lie below the lungs.

Sex abuse happens to about one out of four girls. It took me years to figure out what some young girls age three to ten years were trying to tell me during office visits. It was nothing verbal, but looking back, they were really shouting at me. These girls would scream and stiffen when I would try to bend them at the waist to take a peek at their perineal areas as part of the exam. It finally dawned on me that they had been sexually molested and this stranger (me) was going to do it again! How stupid and naive of me not to understand this normal response of a child trying to protect herself.

Pedophilia is sexual abuse in which children are the preferred sex object. The motivation behind this despicable act seems to be related to power and opportunity, more than sexual excitement itself. It was once thought that these adult perpetrators had been sexually molested as children and they now have to "pay someone back." This is more wishful thinking than fact. It turns out that only about a quarter of child molesters were molested themselves. This is the same statistic in the general population. (Females are more likely to be abused as children, but they are less likely to become sex offenders as adults.) The molested child should have therapy from a psychologist.

This is a frightening, anger-provoking, hysteria-producing situation for all concerned. The police should be notified. The child should be examined. Most children with supportive therapy and counseling survive these perverse acts with a minimum of physical and psychic trauma. Children may be frightened by the hysteria of the adults. However, they usually know that something is wrong, especially if the perpetrator says, "Don't tell anyone or I will punish you!" Treatment of the child should be determined by how the child perceives the situation. Betsy McAlister Groves, director of Child Witness to Violence Project, reminds us, "Children need permission to talk about the scary things in their lives. Adults not talking about it doesn't make it go away." Follow-up studies on girls who have been molested as children reveal a mixture: Some carry all sorts of sexual attitude distortions and frigidity, and others may seem relatively free of psychic trauma or show surprisingly little distortion of their psychosexual development.

We pediatricians, parents, teachers, and grandparents should be able to read the faces of children and intuit that something is amiss. Look for love, fear, disgust, sadness (we are supposed to say, "You look sad"; it might bring out a response), anger, boredom, pain, cheerfulness. We are our brothers', sisters', and our children's keepers.

Shock is the condition of low blood pressure sufficient to prevent oxygenation of body tissues, notably the brain. Calling 911 seems wise. Syncope (fainting) would be a mild form of shock, but easily treated by the recumbent position. Prolonged vomiting and diarrhea will eventually deplete the blood necessary to maintain adequate volume. Septicemia and anaphylaxis will cause a circulatory collapse. One must evaluate if: (1) the airway is open; (2) the victim is breathing; (3) the carotid pulse in the neck is palpable; and (4) there is severe bleeding.

The patient is to be kept flat. Control of bleeding by pressure is safer than a tourniquet. Comfort is provided, but extra warmth is not indicated. Reassurance is important. Intravenous therapy is indicated.

Subconjunctival hemorrhage shows as a bright red spot of blood against the white of the sclera. A baby may nick his eye with his fingernail when he is waving his arms about, signaling to be fed. It may appear after a bout of coughing and is not uncommon with whooping cough. It does no damage to vision, but inspection of the cornea would be advisable if the bleeding is a result of trauma.

The red turns to blue, then green, then yellow as the blood pigment is metabolized and absorbed in about two weeks' time.

Subluxation of the radial head is a partial dislocation of the head of the radius bone at the elbow. Often mistaken for a sprained wrist, this occurs almost exclusively in the under-four-year-old. The cause is a tug on the hand when the child's arm is straight. (The child is lifted by his hands; the mother is walking with the child's hand in hers, the child stops suddenly, and the mother pulls the child forward; or a friendly adult swings the child about in a circle; or the infant in the playpen doesn't let go of the playpen railing when he sits down suddenly.) The end of the radius bone at the elbow is pulled down and forward from its usual position at the joint. The sudden pain makes the child scream and hold his arm uselessly at his side. The whole arm seems to hurt from wrist to shoulder, but elbow bending elicits the most pain.

Pressure applied against the radius at the elbow simultaneous with forceful elbow bending will usually drop the bone back into its normal position with a "pop" and cause immediate restoration of function and loss of pain.

Some children are prone to this, but growth reduces the proclivity. Children should be lifted by the rib cage under their arms.

Doctors like this treatable problem because the results are so immediate and gratifying.

Subungual hematoma is a blob of blood under a finger- or toenail, usually following a hammer blow (to the fingernail instead of the nail in the board), or the dropping of a stone on a shoeless toe. If there is no escape for the blood, the pressure builds up and creates severe pain. If the affected part can be held high up above the heart, pain will subside. Heating the end of an opened paper clip until red-hot and carefully piercing a hole in the nail (only the nail, not the skin beneath) will allow the trapped blood to escape, and the pain will stop. Hypericum for pain is almost immediately helpful. A new nail usually grows out within six months.

Sunburn can be treated like burns, if one can get the ice on the struggling victim. Usually the treatment is delayed beyond the time of benefit. Cool, wet tea bags will soothe burned skin. Aloe vera juice, gel, or cream will soothe and heal. Calendula and stinging nettle speed the healing. Vinegar rinses and tomato juice have their advocates. When the blisters break, treat as an abrasion.

Tongue bites or trauma from sticks or toys shoved in the mouth are common. Bleeding is brisk and alarming at first, but because of the good blood supply, these wounds heal rapidly. A tetanus booster is appropriate if the foreign object has been on the ground. Surgery is rarely needed; a widely gaping wound will heal spontaneously in a week with no care. The scarring is minimal. Suturing may be necessary for a wide wound from which bleeding has not slowed to an ooze by an hour or so. (See Mouth puncture wounds, this section.) Saliva takes care of the problem. Pain may be assuaged with local anesthetic troches, something with a "-caine" drug in it.

Primary tooth injury occurs in about 25 percent of children, usually just before two years of age.

Displaced baby teeth following injury rarely cause defects of the underlying permanent teeth, but X rays are suggested. If repositioning and splinting by the dentist is necessary, this should be done as soon as possible. The gray-blue discoloration of injured teeth is due to bleeding; follow-up study of these teeth is important. A dead tooth should be treated or extracted.

Intrusions (teeth pushed into the gums) are seldom a threat to the permanent teeth. The displaced teeth, if pulp is not exposed, are allowed to reerupt, but abscess formation could require extraction.

Some drifting of teeth is expected after tooth loss, but space-saving appliances are usually not necessary for the upper front deciduous teeth as normal growth forces of the face allow adequate room for permanent teeth in this area.

Tooth avulsion (knocked out with root) of a permanent incisor is a dental emergency. A study indicated that if the tooth is reimplanted and splinted within thirty minutes, replantation will be successful in most cases. If the out-of-socket time was more than two hours, success was near zero percent. Root canal therapy is usually necessary afterward.

Conversion Table

Apothecary	Metric
1 grain	60 milligrams or 0.06 grams
5 grains	300 milligrams or 0.3 grams
60 grains (1 dram)	4 grams
1 ounce	30 grams
1 pound (16 ounces)	454 grams
10 pounds	4.8 kilograms
1 minim (1 drop)	0.06 milliliters
60 minims (one teaspoon)	4 milliliters
1 fluid ounce	30 milliliters
16 fluid ounces (I pint)	473 milliliters
32 fluid ounces (1 quart)	946 milliliters

(These equivalents are approximate. To be strictly accurate, 1000 milliliters or one liter is equal to 1.0567 quarts.)

APPENDIX B

Sources of Information

Alternative Medicine Digest, 5009 Pacific Highway East, #6, Fife, WA 98424.

Alternative Medicine Yellow Pages, Future Medicine Publishing, Puyallup, WA. A resource tool for those interested in contacting alternative health care practitioners. Contains names, addresses, and telephone numbers.

American Academy of Environmental Medicine, P.O. Box 16106, Denver, CO 80216; 303/622-9755. Treats people with allergens, sensitivities, adverse reactions to chemicals and pollutants.

American Association of Acupuncture and Oriental Medicine, 4101 Lake Boone Trail, #201, Raleigh, NC; 919/787-5181. A trade organization of acupuncturists who can provide the names and locations of local members.

American Association of Naturopathic Physicians, 2366 Eastlake Ave, Suite 322, Seattle, WA 98102; 206/323-7610. Provides names and addresses of NDs.

American Chiropractic Association, 1701 Claredon Blvd., Arlington, VA 22209; 703/276-8800

American Massage Therapy Association, 820 Davis St., Suite 100, Evanston, IL 60201; 312/761-2682. Provides information on bodywork and massage.

American Preventive Medical Association, 459 Walker Road, Great Falls, VA 22066; 1/800/230-2762.

Citizens for Health, Tacoma, WA; 1/800/357-2211. This is a health action group. They have contracted with the Alternative Health Group of Thousand Oaks, California, to provide a comprehensive health plan covering alternative therapies for Citizens for Health members available in all fifty states.

Health Alert is published monthly for $78 per year by Dr. Bruce West, 1000 8th St., #101, Monterey, CA 93940.

Health News Naturally is published quarterly by Keats Publishing, 27 Pine St., New Canaan, CT 06840. They publish many books on health topics.

Indoor Air Pollution, An Introduction for Health Professionals, Indoor Air Quality Information Clearinghouse (a service of the EPA), P.O. Box 37133, Washington, DC 20013-7133. Twenty-seven page booklet, with references. Free.

International Chiropractors Association, 1110 North Glebe Rd, Ste 1000, Arlington, VA 22201; 703/528-5000

International College of Applied Kinesiology, P.O. Box 905, Lawrence, KS 66044-0905; 913/542-1801. Applied kinesiology involves testing various muscle and nerve reflexes to determine the strength or weakness of organ systems. They will supply information.

Let's Live, 320 No. Larchmont Blvd., Los Angeles, CA 90004.

Maharishi Ayur-Veda Medical Center, P.O. Box 282, Fairfield, IA 52556; 1/800/843-8322.
An ancient system of medicine from India. Treatment uses diet, exercise, herbal medicine, and meditation.

National Center for Homeopathy, 801 North Fairfax, Ste 306, Alexandria, VA 22314. 703/548-7790.

NF Formulas, Inc., 9775 SW Commerce Circle, #C5, Wilsonville, OR 97070; 800/547-4891.
Provides vitamin, mineral, botanical, homeopathic, and glandular products. You may call and get the name of a health-care provider in your area who could order products for you.

Organic Network, 12100 Lima Center Rd., Clinton, MI 49236-9618; 517/456-4288.Provides information on suppliers of organic foods.

Total Health, 165 North, 100 East, #2, St. George, UT 84770.

Townsend Letter for Doctors and Patients, 911 Tyler St., Port Townsend, WA 98368-6541; 360/385-6021.

Vegetarian Resource Group, P.O. Box 1463, Baltimore, MD; 21203. 410/366-8343.

Well Mind Association, 4649 Sunnyside North, Seattle, WA; 206/547-6167.

Wolf's Digest of Alternative Medicine: A Plain English Resource on the Science of Health, P.O. Box 2049, Sequim, WA 98382-2049; 1/800/683-7014. A source of information on alternative health.

Your Health, newsletter of the International Academy of Nutrition and Preventive Medicine, P.O. Box 18433, Asheville, NC 28814; 704/258-3243.

Introduction

New England School of Homeopathy, 115 Elm St., Suite 210, Enfield, CT 06082.

Chapter I

American College of Nurse-Midwives, 1522 K St. NW, Washington, DC 20005; 202/347-5445.

Informed Birth and Parenting, P.O. Box 3675, Ann Arbor, MI 48106; 313/662-6857.

International Childbirth Education Assoc., P.O. Box 20048, Minneapolis, MN 55420; 612/854-8660.

Midwives Alliance of North America (MANA), P.O. Box 1121, Bristol, VA 24203; 615/764-5561.

National Association of Childbirth Assistants, 219 Meridan Avenue, San Jose, CA 95126; 409/225-9167.

Preconception Care Foundation, Inc., 5724 Clymer Road, Quakertown, PA 18951.

Chapter II

Breastfeeding Mother Support

International Lactation Consultant Association (ILCA), 200 North Michigan Ave, Chicago, IL 60601.

La Leche League International (LLLI), 1400 North Meacham Rd., Schaumburg, IL 60173-4840.

Breast Pumps, Hospital

Ameda/Egnell Corp., 755 Industrial Dr., Cary, IL 60013; 800/323-8750.

Medela, Inc., P.O. Box 660, McHenry, IL 60051-0660; 800/435-8316.

Purified Lanolin

Lansinoh, Lansinoh Lab., 1670 Oak Ridge Turnpike, Oak Ridge, TN, 800/292-4794.

Pure Lan, Medela, Inc.

Feeding Tube Devices

Lact-Aid, P.O. Box 1066, Athens, TN 37303; 615/744-9090.

Supplemental Nursing System, Medela, Inc.

Circumcision Information Resources

AARP Grandparent Information Center, 601 E. St NW, Washington, DC.

Birth with Dignity, Ted Pong, Box 321, Freeland, WA 98249.

Circumcision Resource Center, Moshe Rothenberg, 715 Ocean Parkway, Brooklyn, NY 11230. Ron Goldman, Box 232, Boston, MA 02133.

ETHIC (End the Horror of Infant Circumcision), Bettie Malofie, Box 10, Group 546, RR5, Winnipeg, MB R2C 2Z2, Canada.

Intact Network Newsletter, Ken Derifield, P.O. Box 82, Wahpeton, ND 58074.

National Organization of Circumcision Information Resource Centers (NOCIRC), P.O. Box 2512, San Anselmo, CA 94979-2512. Dr. George Williams, P.O. Box 248, Menai, NSW 2234, Australia.

National Organization to Halt the Abuse and Routine Mutilation of Males (NOHARMM), Tim Hammond, founder, P.O. Box 460795, San Francisco, CA 94146-0795. Jerry Warner, Southern Editor, 10010 Karen Dr, Baton Rouge, LA 70815; 504/272-2794.

Nurses for the Rights of the Child, Mary Conant, R.N., Betty Katz Sperlich, R.N., founders, 369 Montezuma, #354, Santa Fe, NM 87501.

Peaceful Beginnings, Rosemary Romberg, 13020 Homestead Ct., Anchorage, AK 99416-2633.

RECAP, Dr. Wayne Giffiths, 3205 Northwood Dr., Ste. 209, Concord, CA 94520. Assists men with foreskin reconstruction.

ROCKING (Raising Our Children's Kids: An Intergenerational Network of Grandparenting) links custodial grandparents with support groups. P.O. Box 96, Niles, MI 49120; 608/238-8751.

Chapter V

American Sleep Disorder Institute, 1610 14 St. NW, Ste. 300, Rochester, MN 55901; 507/287-6006.

Chapter VII

Aspartame Consumer Safety Network, P.O. Box 780634, Dallas, TX 75378; 214/352-4268.

Chronic Fatigue Association, P.O. Box 220398, Charlotte, NC 28222; 1/800/442-3437. Nation's largest and most active charitable organization dedicated to conquering Chronic Fatigue Syndrome.

Dissatisfied Parents Together, 128 Branch Road, Vienna, VA 22180; 703/938-DPT3.

Foundation for Toxic Free Dentistry, P.O. Box 608010, Orlando, FL 32860-8010; 407/299-4149. A nonprofit group that educates and refers.

Health Alternatives and Vaccine Awareness Committee, (HAVAC) Has information to help parents decide to vaccinate or not. P.O. Box 881, Trabuco Canyon, CA 92678; 714/589-0932.

International Vaccination Newsletter, Kris Gaublomme, Krekenstraat 4, 3600 Genk, Belgium. This is done in English. He compiles information from around the world.

Mothering Magazine, P.O. Box 346, New York, NY 10023; 212/870-5117.

National Center for Homeopathy, 1500 Massachusetts Ave, NW, Suite 42, Washington, DC 20050, 202/223-6182.

New Atlantean Press, large selection of vaccination material. Call for catalog. P.O. Box 9638, Sante Fe, NM 87504; 505/983-1856.

National Vaccine Information Center/Dissatified Parents Together (NVIC/DPT). 512 W. Maple Ave, #206, Vienna, VA 22180; 1/800/909 SHOT (7468).

Physicians Committee for Responsible Medicine, P.O. Box 6322, Washington, DC 20015.

Physicians for Social Responsibility, 1101 14th St., NW, #700, Washington, DC 20005; 202/898-0150. They have publications about the following: *Preventing Exposure to Hazardous Pesticides; Children and Pesticides; Environmental Pollutants and Reproductive Health; Nuclear Weapons Cleanup; Tap Water Blues; Putting the Lid on Dioxins; Human Health and the Environment.*

Chapters VIII and IX

Children and Adults with Attention Deficit Disorders, 499 NW 70 Ave., #1010, Plantation, FL 800/233-4050.

Citizens Commission on Human Rights, 6362 Hollywood Blvd, Suite B, Los Angeles, CA 90028; 800/869-2247. Investigating and exposing psychiatric violations of human rights since 1969. They seek alternative methods of controlling hyperactive behavior other than with drugs.

Developmental Delay Registry, a not-for-profit organization promoting healthy options for children with developmental delays. Patricia Lemer, MEd, 7801 Norfolk Ave, Suite #102, Bethesda, MD 20814; 301/652-2263.

FairTest, 342 Broadway, Cambridge, MA 02139. They have a bibliography on testing in the public schools that covers all the different problems with testing.

Hypoglycemia Association, 18008 New Hampshire Ave., Box 165, Ashton, MD 20861-0165.

National Center for Learning Disabilities, Inc., 381 Park Ave So., #1420, New York, NY 10016; 212/545-7510.

Northwest Neurodevelopmental Training Center, 152 Arthur St., Woodburn, OR; 503/981-0635. Florence Scott, R.N., Director.

Orton Dyslexia Society (National), 724 York Rd., Baltimore, MD 21204.

Carl Pfeiffer Treatment Center, 1804 Centre Point Frive, Suite 102, Naperville, IL 60567; 708/505-0300. The center investigates and treats children and adults who have chemical problems due to vitamin and mineral deficiencies and heavy-metal toxicities.

Shedd Kentucky Assoc., 200 High Rise Dr., Louisville, KY 40213.

Unschoolers Network, 2 Smith St., Farmingdale, NJ 07727. Gives help and encouragement for home schooler setup and curriculum.

Chapter X

Autism Research Institute, 4182 Adams Avenue, San Diego, CA 92116; 619/281-7165. Dr. Bernard Rimland has a list of doctors around the country who might be helpful if you suspect your child might have some of the symptoms of autism. He can provide his book, Bernard Rimland, *Infantile Autism*, 1964.

Chapter XII

Cyclic Vomiting Syndrome Association, 13180 Caroline Court, Elm Grove, WI 53122; 414/784-6842. An information and support center for children who have periodic bouts of vomiting who remain normal between bouts.

Reliable Laboratories

Bionostics, Inc, 170 W. Roosevelt Road, West Chicago, IL 60185; 708/231-3649. They specialize in the interpretations of amino acid analysis. The amino acids should be analyzed if routine treatment for the following conditions have failed: chronic fatigue, headaches, bowel irregularity, intolerances to foods and chemicals, frequent infections, learning disabilities, malnutrition, and neurological disorders.

Doctor's Data, P.O. Box 111, West Chicago, IL 60185; 1/800/323-2784. Doctor-referred testing for hair minerals and urine and blood amino acids.

Great Smokies Diagnostic Laboratory, 18 A Regent Park Blvd, Asheville, NC 1/800/522-4762. Specialists in testing for parasites in stool, bacterial overgrowth of the small intestine; comprehensive digestive stool analysis, liver detoxification profile, intestinal permeability, lactose intolerance, and oxidative stress.

Klaire Laboratories, 1573 West Seminole, San Marcos, CA 92069; 619/744-9680.

Lendon H. Smith, M.D., *Feed Your Body Right,* M. Evans and Company, Inc., New York, NY 10017, 1994. I have worked with John Kitkoski, who put the Life Balances Program together (503/221-1779). With his help I wrote the book. The program removes the guesswork from supplementation. By a combination of the standard blood test (24 chemical screen, complete blood count), and a complete history of diseases and lifestyle, the methodology can produce for the participant a comprehensive, scientifically oriented program of what supplements would be most appropriate for a person's health. The blood analysis is run through the computer and the results are charted according to the deviation from the mean.

The main ingredients of the program are (1) electrolytes to be taken with milk or juice, (2) twenty bottles of vitamins and minerals that one takes depending upon the subjective response from smelling the contents, and (3) six dropper bottles of minerals that may be needed for those with nutrient deficiencies. The program is compatible with other modalities of therapy including chiropractic, naturopathy, homeopathy, psychology, massage, and whatever. It will allow these other methods to produce results more surely and more rapidly.

Bibliography

Appleton, Nancy, *Lick the Sugar Habit,* Avery Publishing, Garden City Park, NY, 1996.

Baumel, Syd, *Dealing with Depression Naturally,* Keats Publishing Co., New Canaan, CT, 1995.

Bellak, Leopold, *Psychiatric Aspects of MBD in Adults,* Grune and Stratton, 1979.

Brewer, Thomas H., M.D., *Metabolic Toxemia of Late Pregnancy,* Charles Thomas, 1966.

Brewer, Thomas and Gail, *What Every Pregnant Woman Should Know,* Viking Press, 1985.

Buttram, Harold, M.D., and John Chris Hoffman, *Vaccinations and Immune Malfunctions,* Humanitarian Publishing Company, Quakertown, PA, 1982.

Coulter, H., Vaccination: *Social Violence and Criminality,* Koren Pub., Philadelphia, PA, 1993.

Crook, Billy, M.D., *The Yeast Connection and the Woman,* Professional Books, Box 3246, Jackson, TN, 1995.

Dennison, Paul, Ph.D., and Gail Dennison, *Brain Gym: Simple Activities for Whole Brain Learning.*

Elam, Dan, *Building Better Babies,* Celestial Arts, Millbrae, CA, 1980.

Feingold, Benjamin, M.D., *Why Your Child is Hyperactive,* Random House, New York, 1975.

Gilgoff, A., *Home Birth,* Coward, McCann, Geoghegan, Inc., 1978.

Gold, Svea, *When Children Invite Child Abuse,* Fern Ridge Press, Eugene, OR, 1986.

Herron, Timothy, *Doctors' Protocol Journal: Everyone's Guide to Natural Health,* Arroyo Sayo Publishing Co., Greenfield, CA, 1995. Contains a complete list of diseases and their natural remedies.

Hoffer, A., M.D., Ph.D., and M. Walker, D.P.M., *Putting It All Together: The New Orthomolecular Nutrition,* Keats Publishing, New Canaan, CT, 1996.

Kalokerinos, Archie, *Every Second Child,* Keats Publishing, New Canaan, CT, 1981.

Klaus, Marshall and Phyllis, *The Amazing Newborn,* Addison Wesley Publishers, Reading, MA, 1985.

Lappé, Frances Moore, *Diet for a Small Planet,* Ballantine Books, New York, 1971.

Leboyer, Frederick, *Birth Without Violence,* Alfred Knopf, New York, 1984.

Levinson, Harold, M.D., *Smart, But Feeling Dumb,* Warner Books, New York, 1984.

May, J., M.D., *A Physician Looks at Psychiatry,* 1958.

Mendelsohn, Robert, M.D., *How to Raise a Healthy Child in Spite of Your Doctor,* Contemporary Books, Chicago, IL, 1984.

Millichap, Gordon, M.D., *Is Our Drinking Water Safe to Drink?*, PNB Publishers, P.O. Box 11391, Chicago, IL, 60611.

Moss, Hilde, M.D., *The Complete Handbook of Children's Reading Disorders,* Human Sciences Press, New York, 1982. (In paperback at the Riggs Institute, Beaverton, OR.)

Noble, E., *Childbirth with Insight,* Houghton Mifflin, Co., Boston, MA, 1983.

Powers, Michael, *Children with Autism: A Parents' Guide,* 1987.

Rapp, Doris, M.D., *The Impossible Child,* Life Sciences Press, Tacoma, WA, 1986.

Rogers, Sherry, M.D., *Wellness Against All Odds,* Prestige Publishing Company, Syracuse, NY, 1995.

Scheibner, Viera, Ph.D., *Vaccination: The Medical Assault on the Immune System,* Koren Publ, Philadelphia, PA.

Shanklin and J. Hodin, *Maternal Nutrition and Child Health,* CC Thomas, Springfield, IL, 1978.

Tew, M., *Safer Childbirth?* Chapman and Hall, London, 1990.

Thomas, Evan, M.D., *Brain Injured Children,* Charles Thomas, 1989.

Yudkin, John A., *Sweet and Dangerous,* Peter H. Wyden, 1972.

Notes

1. E. Cheraskin, M.D., D.M.D., William Ringsdorf, D.M.D., and J.W. Clark, D.M.D., *Diet and Disease* (New Canaan, Conn., Keats Publishing, 1968), 80.
2. J. J. Rommer, *Sterility, Its Causes and Its Treatment* (Springfield, Ill., Charles C. Thomas Publisher, 1952), 54–55.
3. Margaret and Arthur Wynn, *The Case for Preconception Care of Men and Women* (AB Bicester, England, Academic Publishers, 1991). Jonathan Maberly, M.D., is quoted in this book.
4. Y. Kumamoto, et al, "Clinical Efficacy of Mecobalamin in Treatment of Oligozoospermia," *Acta Urol Jpn* 34, (1988): 1109–1132.
5. C. G. Fraga, et al, "Ascorbic Acid Protects Against Endogenous Oxidative DNA Damage in Human Sperm," *Proceedings of the National Academy of Sciences*, 88 (1991): 11003–11006.
6. Fred Shull, M.D., Bellingham, Wash., letter to the *Townsend Letter for Doctors and Patients*, (March 1989).
7. M. F. Goldberg, M.D. *Journal of the American Medical Association* 242 (Nov. 1979): 2292–2294.
8. Dr. Zsolt Harsanyi and Richard Hutton, *Genetic Prophecy: Beyond the Double Helix* (New York: Rawson-Wade Publishers, 1981).
9. "Government Sets Folate Standard to Prevent Birth Defects," *Nutrition Week* 22(37) (Sept. 25, 1992): 2–3.
10. R. L. Goldenberg, et al, "Serum Folate and Fetal Growth Retardation," *Journal of Obstetrics & Gynecology*, 79 (5.1) (1992): 719–722.
11. W. Smithells, *Lancet* (May 7, 1983).
12. M. Renine, et al, "Maternal Hyperhomocysteinemia: A Risk Factor for Neural-Tube Defect?" *Metabolism* 43 (1994) 1475–1480.
13. M. Tolarova, M.D., *Lancet* (July 24, 1982).
14. Cheraskin, et al, *Diet and Disease* 122.
15. Sylvia Guendelman, "Mexican Women in the United States," *Lancet* 344 (Aug. 6, 1994) 352.
16. C. Klein, et al, "Does Episiotomy Prevent Perineal Trauma?" *Online Journal of Current Clinical Trials*, no. 10 (July 1, 1992).
17. *Lancet* (Oct. 9, 1993).

18. *Canadian Medical Association Journal* (Nov. 15, 1993).
19. National Research Council, *Pesticides in the Diet of Infants and Children* (Washington, D.C.: National Academy Press, 1990).
20. "Quantum Sufficient," *American Family Physician* 43 (5) (1991): 1499.
21. J. B. Sibbison, "USA, Lead in Soil" *Lancet* 339 (1992): 921–922.
22. J. H. Graziano, and C. Blum, "Lead Exposure from Lead Crystal," *Lancet* 337 (1991): 141–142.
23. F. L. Lorscheider and M. L. Vimy, "Mercury Exposure from Interior Latex Paint," *New England Journal of Medicine,* 324 (1991): 851–852.
24. Richard Naeye, M.D., *Medical World News* (Jan. 5, 1981): 37-38.
25. R. B. Hakim and J. M. Tielsch, "Maternal Cigarette Smoking During Pregnancy," *Arch Ophthal,* 110 (1992): 1459–1462.
26. D. L. Olds, "Intellectual Impairment in Children of Women Who Smoke Cigarettes During Pregnancy," *Pediatrics* 93 (1994): 221–227.
27. T. O. Scholl, et al, "Low Zinc Intake During Pregnancy," *American Journal Epidem.* 137 (10) (1993): 1115–1124.
28. K. Kisters, et al, "Copper and Zinc Plasma Levels, and Intracellular Magnesium Concentrations in Pregnancy and Preeclampsia," *Trace Elements in Medicine* 10 (1993): 158–162.
29. *American Journal of Clinical Nutrition* (Apr, 1980): 811–815.
30. Weston Price, D.D.S., *Nutrition and Physical Degeneration* (New Canaan, Conn.: Keats Publishing, 1989).
31. Francis Pottenger, M.D., *Pottenger's Cats* (San Diego, Calif.: Price-Pottenger Nutrition Foundation, 1983).
32. Ray Peat, Ph.D., Eugene, Oregon, personal communication.
33. Katharina Dalton, MRCGP, "Prenatal Progesterone and Educational Attainment," *British Journal of Psychiatry* 129 (1976): 438-442.
34. Michael Crawford and David Marsh, *The Driving Force—Food, Evolution, and the Future* (New York: Harper & Row, 1989).
35. Cheraskin, et al, *Diet and Disease,* 176.
36. Norbert Freinkel, M.D., Northwestern Medical School.
37. Thomas Brewer, M.D., *Medical Tribune* (Aug. 2, 1972).
38. E. B. Dawson and R. Kelly, "Calcium, Magnesium, and Lead Relationships in Pre-eclampsia," *American Journal of Clinical Nutrition,* 51 (1990): 512.
39. Myron Winick, M.D., *Curr Presc* (July 1976).
40. D. Suharno, et al, "Supplementation with Vitamin A and Iron for Nutritional Anemia in Pregnant Women in West Java, Indonesia," *Lancet* 342 (1993): 1325–1328.
41. Michael Klaper, M.D., "Pregnancy, Children and the Vegan Diet," *Total Health* (June 1990).
42. Nikki Goldbeck, *As You Eat So Your Baby Grows* (Woodstock, N.Y.: Ceres Press, 1982).
43. Carolyn Dean, M.D., *Carolyn Dean's Complementary Natural Prescriptions for Common Ailments* (New Canaan, Conn.: Keats Publishing, 1994).
44. Victoria Arcadi, D.C., "How Do You Treat Hyperemesis Gravidarum?" *Dynamic Chiropractic* (March 29, 1991).
45. W. N. Spellacy, et al, *American Journal of Obstetrics and Gynecology,* 127 (1977): 599.
46. Roger Williams, Ph.D., *Journal of Applied Nutrition* 38 no.112 (1986).
47. Abram Hoffer, Ph.D., M.D., from a symposium on nutrition, 1988.
48. E. M. Martin, "Report on the Clinical Use of Bone Meal," *Canadian Medical Association Journal* 50 (1944): 562.
49. L. Spatling and G. Spatling, *British Journal of Obstetrics and Gynecology* 95 (1988): 120–125.
50. L. J. Taper, Ph.D., *American Journal of Clinical Nutrition* (June 1985).
51. Lendon Smith, M.D. *Clinical Guide to the Use of Vitamin C* (Tacoma, Wash.: Life Sciences Press, 1988).
52. William Connor, M.D., *World Review of Nutrition & Dietetics* 66 (1991): 118–132.
53. Leo Stern, M.D. *Pediatric News* (February 1981).
54. Carl Jones, *Mind Over Labor,* Assoc of Childbirth Companions, Florida (1990).
55. Scalzo, Richard, N.D. *Naturopathic Handbook of Herbal Formulas* (Durango, Colo.: Kivaki Press, 1994).

56. Timothy Herron, BGG, *Doctors' Protocol Journal* (Greenfield, Calif.: Arroyo Sayo Publishing Co., 1995).
57. *Gray's Anatomy,* 36th British edition.
58. Joan Fallon, D.C., "Chiropractic and Pregnancy," *ICA International Rev. of Chiro.* (Nov–Dec, 1990).
59. Michael Genco, D.C., "Will Chiropractic Make a Pregnancy Easier?," *Total Health* (Feb. 1992).
60. Steven Davis, D., Anderson, Calif., personal communication, 1995.
61. A. Gilgoff, *Home Birth* (New York: Coward, McCann, & Geoghegan, 1978).
62. Robert S. Mendelsohn, M.D., *Confessions of a Medical Heretic* (Chicago: Contemporary Books, 1979).
63. Marshall Klaus, John Kennell, and Phyllis Klaus, *Mothering the Mother* (Addison-Wesley Publishers, 1993).
64. Associated Press, "CDC Says Too Many Cesarean Sections Performed" *Argus Leader,* Sioux Falls, April 4, 1993.
65. Carolyn DeMarco, M.D., *Health Naturally* (April–May 1995).
66. M. Gabay, and S. M. Wolfe, *Unnecessary Cesarean Sections* (Washington, D.C.: Public Citizen, 1994).
67. Information from the ICEA, International Childbirth Education Association, P.O. Box 20048, Minneapolis, Minn., 55420 (1991).
68. Bruce West, D.C., *Natural Fitness Newsletter,* 9 issue 2, P.O. Box 222797, Carmel, Calif. 93922.
69. J. Kennell, et al, "Continuous Emotional Support During Labour in a U.S. Hospital," *Journal of the American Medical Association* 265 (1991): 2197–2201
70. Shari Roan, "The Fourth Trimester," *Women's Health Letter* (Sept. 1994).
71. Newborn Rights Society, Box 48, St Peters, Penn. 19470.
72. Svea Gold, *When Children Invite Child Abuse* (Eugene, Oreg:, Fern Ridge Press, 1986).
73. T. Berry Brazelton, M.D., pediatrician. (Lecture in Portland, Oreg., 1990).
74. Peter Fysh, D.C., "The Newborn Infant," *Dynamic Chiropractic* (Feb. 28, 1992).
75. Abraham Towbin, M.D., "Spinal Injury Related to the Syndrome of Sudden Infant Death in Infants," *American Journal of Clinical Pathology,* 49 no.4 (Apr. 1968): 562-567.
76. Marc Gottlieb, "Neglected Spinal Cord, Brain Stem, and Musculoskeletal Injuries Stemming from Birth Trauma," *J Manip & Physiol Therap,* 16 no. 8 (Oct. 1993).
77. Sally Goddard, N.D.T., *Reflexes: The Basis of Education,* Institute for Neuro-Physiological Psychology, Chester, England, paper presented in Mar. 1994.
78. Ibid.
79. K. E. Paige, "The Ritual of Circumcision," *Human Nature* (May 1978): 40–48.
80. P. C. Remondino, *History of Circumcision from Earliest Times to the Present* (Philadelphia: Davis, 1891). (Republished New York: AMS Press, 1974): 161–182.
81. Bigelow, *The Joy of Uncircumcising* (Aptos, Calif.: Hourglass Publ., 1992).
82. Hammond, *Awakenings: A Preliminary Poll of Circumcised Men,* National Organization to Halt the Abuse and Routine Mutilation of Males (NOHARMM), P.O. Box 460795, San Francisco, Calif., 94146; 415/826-9351 (1994): 64–100.
83. National Organization of Circumcision Information Resource Centers (NOCIRC), P.O. Box 2512, San Anselmo, Calif., 94979–2512; 415/488-9883.
84. Circumcision Information Network, *The Guardian Angell,* 4 no. 5 (13 June 1995), 3865 Duncan Place, Palo Alto, Calif., 94306.
85. NOHARMM.
86. Marilyn Milos, R.N., "Circumcision: Male–Effects upon Human Sexuality," *Human Sexuality: An Encyclopedia* (Garland Press, N.Y.: 1994): 119–121.
87. American Academy of Pediatrics, *1994 Red Book: Report of the Committee on Infectious Diseases,* 23rd edition (Elk Grove Village, Ill.: AAP, 1994).
88. Rachelle Fishman, H.B., Perinatal Medicine Conference, *Lancet* 344 (August 27, 1994): 605.
89. Maxine McMullen, R.N., D.C., "Handicapped Infants and Chiropractic Care," *ICA International Rev of Chiro* (July–Aug. 1990).
90. John Unruh, Ph.D., *Down Syndrome: Successful Parenting of Children with Down Syndrome* (Eugene, Oreg.: Fern Ridge Press, 1994).

91. Karen Gromada, R.N., *Mothering Multiples,* La Leche League International, 1981.
92. Victoria Arcadi, D.C., *Birth Induced TMJ Dysfunction: The Most Common Cause of Breastfeeding Difficulties* (read before the Second Annual Pediatric Conference, Palm Springs, Calif., Oct. 1993).
93. Judy Torgus, La Leche League.
94. Elizabeth Baldwin, Miami attorney and a member of the legal advisory council of the La Leche League International.
95. "Personal View" (letter to editor), *British Medical Journal,* 298 (1989): 1461.
96. Sheila Kitzinger, *The Experience of Breastfeeding* (New York: Penguin Books, 1979).
97. Ruth Lawrence, M.D., *Breastfeeding; A Guide for the Medical Profession* (St. Louis: Mosby, 1994).
98. A. Ironside, "A Survey of Infantile Gastroenteritis," *British Medical Journal 3* (1970): 20.
99. A. Cunningham, "Morbidity in Breastfed and Artificially Fed Infants," *Journal of Pediatrics* 90 (1977): 726.
100. La Leche League, 1400 North Meacham Rd., P.O. Box 4079, Schaumburg, Ill., 60168; 708/519-7730.
101. Jean Liedloff, *The Continuum Concept* (New York: Warner Books, 1979).
102. Urs A. Hunziker, M.D. and Ronald G. Barr, M.D.C.M., "Increased Carrying Reduces Infant Crying." *Pediatrics,* 77 no. 5 (May 1986).
103. Ashley Montagu, *Touching* (New York: Harper & Row, 1971).
104. James W. Prescott, Ph.D., "Alienation of Affection," *M.O.M.* newsletter (Winter 1986).
105. Tiffany M. Field, Ph.D., et al, "Tactile/Kinesthetic Stimulation Effects on Preterm Infants," *Pediatrics,* 77 no.5 (May 1986).
106. J. Biedermann, "Kinesmatic Imbalances Due to Suboccipital Strain in Newborns," *Journal Manual Med.,* 6 (1992): 151-156.
107. Victoria Arcadi, D.C., *Dynamic Chiropractic* (Feb 1, 1991).
108. Steven Davis, D.C., personal communication.
109. *Journal of the American Medical Association* (Mar 8, 1995).
110. E. Cheraskin, et al, *Diet and Disease:* 168.
111. Beatrice Trum Hunter, "Shortchanging Infants with Shortcomings of Infant Feeding Formulas," *Natural Food and Farming* (Nov–Dec 1992).
112. Clara M. Davis, M.D., "Self-selection of Diet by Newly Weaned Infants," *American J Dis Childr,* 36 (1928): 651–679.
113. Smith, Lendon, M.D., *Feed Your Body Right* (New York: M. Evans, 1994).
114. Steven Davis, D.C., Anderson, Calif., personal communication, 1995.
115. Jennifer Jacobs, M.D., "Homeopathic Treatment of Diarrhea in Children," *Pediatrics* 93 (May 1994): 719–725.
116. Custy F. Fernnandez, Ph.D., et al, "Control of Diarrhea by Lactobacilli," *Journal of Applied Nutrition* 40 no. 1 (1988).
117. Corey Resnick, N.D., "Plant Enzymes," *Townsend Letter for Doctors and Patients* (Aug–Sept, 1993).
118. Elaine Gottschall, *Breaking the Vicious Cycle, and Intestinal Health Through Diet* (Ontario, Canada: Kirkton Press, 1994).
119. "The Etiology and Implications of Lactose Intolerance," *Nutrition Reviews,* 31 no. 6 (June 1973).
120. Harold Simpson, *Acres, USA* (Sept. 1994). He is in the Christian Legal Education Assoc., 4842 North Magnolia, Chicago, Ill., 60640.
121. Udo Erasmus, Ph.D., *Fats That Heal; Fats That Kill* (Burnaby, B.C., Canada: Alive Books, 1993).
122. E. Cheraskin, et al, *Diet and Disease,* 329.
123. Vegetarian Information Service, P.O. Box 5888, Bethesda, Md., 20814.
124. Ronald A. Newcomb, *The Healthkeepers Journal* (May 1995).
125. Lendon Smith, *Feed Your Body Right.*
126. E. Cheraskin, *Diet and Disease.*
127. Sally Rockwell, Ph.D., Seattle, Wash., personal communication.

128. Leslie N. Johnston, D.V.M., "Stopping Crib Death," *Townsend Letter for Doctors and Patients* (Apr 1995).
129. Earl Mindell, Pharm.B., *Earl Mindell's Vitamin Bible* (New York: Rawson-Wade Publishers, 1979).
130. Gordon Pederson, Ph.D., personal communication.
131. Harlan Wright, D.O., "Vitamin A Supplementation," *Journal of Applied Nutrition*, 47 nos.1 and 2 (1995).
132. Abram Hoffer, M.D., Ph.D., personal communication.
133. Joseph Hattersley, "Vitamin B$_6$: The Overlooked Key to Preventing Heart Attacks," *Journal of Applied Nutrition* 47 nos.1 and 2 (1995).
134. Roger Williams, Ph.D., discoverer of pantothenic acid.
135. Dr. Jack Redman, Albuquerque, N.M., personal communication.
136. Emanuel Cheraskin, D.D.S., M.D., *Vitamin C: Who Needs It?* (Birmingham, Ala.: Arlington Press, 1993).
137. Dr. E. Baumgartner, Los Angeles Veterans Hospital, Calif.
138. Dr. Edward Howell, *Enzyme Nutrition* (Wayne, N.J.: Avery Publishing Group, 1985).
139. Herbert Boynton, researcher with Jay Patrick of Alacer Company, lecture in 1991.
140. Anthony Cichoke, D.C., *Enzymes and Enzyme Therapy* (New Canaan, Conn.: Keats Publishing, 1994).
141. Michael Jacobson, *What Are We Feeding Our Kids?* (Workman Publishing, 1993).
142. University of Southern Calif., School of Medicine, *Cancer Causes and Control* (June 1994).
143. Lendon Smith, M.D., *Feed Your Body Right*.
144. Walter L. Voegtlin, M.D., *The Stone Age Diet* (New York: Vantage Press, 1975).
145. Sally Goddard, *Reflexes, The Basis of Education*.
146. Burton White, *The First Three Years of Life* (Englewood Cliffs, N.J.: Prentice Hall, 1985).
147. Ibid.
148. Maxine McMullen, D.C., *Physical Stresses of Childhood* (paper presented at the Palmer Chiropractic University, Davenport, Iowa, 1992).
149. Florence Scott, R.N. *The Brain: Fact, Function, Fantasy* (Woodburn, Oregon: Northwest Neurodevelopmental Training Center, 1995).
150. Svea Gold, *When Children Invite Child Abuse*.
151. Richard K. Bernstein, *Diabetes: The Glucograf Method for Normalizing Blood Sugar* (New York: St. Martin's Press, 1984).
152. Lendon Smith, M.D., *Feed Your Body Right*.
153. Richard Hopping, O.D., The Better Vision Institute of Rosslyn, Va. (800/424-8422).
154. Parents Active for Vision Education (PAVE), 9620 Chesapeake Dr., No. 105, San Diego, Calif., 92123.
155. Dr. William Ludham (ten-year study), Dr. Francis Young (study on monkeys, and the Burroughs, Alaska, study).
156. H. Labbok, and G. E. Hendershot, "Does Breastfeeding Protect Against Malocclusion?" *American Journal of Preventive Medicine*, 3 (1987): 227-232.
157. Svea Gold, *When Children Invite Child Abuse*.
158. David Couch, D.C., Orlando, Fla., personal communication.
159. Svea Gold, personal communication.
160. American Academy of Pediatrics, *Your Child's Growth: Developmental Milestones*, AAP Dept. of Publications, 141 Northwest Point Blvd., Elk Grove Village, Ill. 60009-0927.
161. Hal Huggins, D.D.S., Colo., personal communication.
162. Norman Cousins, *Anatomy of an Illness* (New York: Bantam Books, 1983).
163. Melinda Beck, Ph.D., *Journal of Med Virol* 43 (1994): 66–70.
164. Steven Davis, D.C., personal communication.
165. Harris Coulter, Ph.D., *Homeopathic Science and Modern Medicine* (Berkeley, Calif.: North Atlantic Books, 1980).
166. Michael Castleman, "Echinacea," *Your Health* magazine (New Canaan, Conn.: Keats Publishing, Dec. 3, 1991).
167. Daniel B. Mowrey, Ph.D., *Echinacea* (New Canaan, Conn.: Keats Publishing, 1995).

168. Michael Schmidt, D.C., Lendon Smith, M.D., Keith Sehnert, M.D., *Beyond Antibiotics* (Berkeley, Calif.: New Atlantic Books, 1992).
169. Dick Thom, N.D., D.D.S., personal communication.
170. Procyanidol, product name; company is NaturalCeuticals; 800/488-2840.
171. R. Farwell, et al, "Phenobarbital for Febrile Seizures," *New England Journal of Medicine,* 322 (1990) 364–369.
172. Carolyn Dean, M.D., *Complementary Natural Prescriptions for Common Ailments* (New Canaan, Conn.: Keats Publishing, 1994).
173. Peter N. Fysh, D.C., "Upper Respiratory Infections in Children," *ICA Internat. Rev. Chiro* (Mar.–Apr. 1990).
174. Dick Thom, N.D., D.D.S., personal communication.
175. Steven Davis, D.C., personal communication.
176. Zhang and Jong-Yen Hsu, *AIDS and Chinese Medicine* (New Canaan, Conn.: Keats Publishing, 1995).
177. C. Jarvis, M.D., *Folk Medicine* (New York: Fawcett Publishing, 1985).
178. Marc Lappé, M.D., professor at the University of Illinois.
179. Stephen L. Reisman, M.D., *Townsend Letter for Doctors and Patients,* letters to the editor (Feb.–Mar. 1995).
180. Dr. Walter Gilbert, Harvard professor quoted in *Newsweek.*
181. Anthony Cichoke, D.C., *Enzymes and Enzyme Therapy.*
182. Michael Schmidt, D.C., *Children's Ear Infections* (Berkeley, Calif.: North Atlantic Books, 1992).
183. Drs. Marcus and Bertil Diamant, "Abuse and Timing of Use of Antibiotics in Acute Otitis Media," *Arch Otolaryng* 100 (Sept. 1974): 226–232.
184. Cantekin, et al, "Antibiotic Treatment of Ear Infections," *Journal of the American Medical Association* 266 (Dec. 1991): 3309.
185. Backon, "Prolonged Breast Feeding as a Prophylaxis for Recurrent Otitis Media," *Medical Hypothesis* 13 (1984): 161.
186. M. Nsouli, M.D., et al, "Role of Food Allergy in Serous Otitis Media," *Annal Allergy* 73 (Sept. 1994): 215–219.
187. Patricia S. Lemer, M.Ed., N.C.C., Executive Director, *Newsletter of the Developmental Delay Registry,* 7801 Norfolk Ave, No. 102, Bethesda, Md. 20814.
188. Randi J. Hagerman, M.D., and Alice R. Falkenstein, Report from the Department of Pediatrics (University of Colorado Health Science Center, Denver, Colo.)
189. William Crook, M.D., *The Yeast Connection* (Jackson, Tenn.: Professional Books, 1989).
190. Dr. H. J. Roberts, *Aspartame: Is It Safe?* (Philadelphia: Charles Press, 1989).
191. Dr. H. J. Roberts, "Aspartame-Associated Epilepsy," *Clinical Research* 36 (1988): 349A.
192. Dr. H. J. Roberts, *Townsend Letter for Doctors and Patients,* letters to the editor (Aug.–Sept. 1995).
193. Croft Woodruff, *Townsend Newsletter for Doctors and Patients,* February/March, 1995.
194. National Research Council, *Health Effects of Ingested Fluoride* (Aug. 17, 1993): 30.
195. National Research Council, *Fluorides* (Washington, D.C.: National Academy of Sciences, 1971), 66.
196. National Academy of Sciences, *Fluoride* 23 (1990): 55–67.
197. National Research Council, *Health Effects of Ingested Fluoride* (1993): 37.
198. *Journal of the American Medical Association,* 264 (1990): 500–502; *Journal of the American Medical Association,* 266 (1991): 513; *Journal of the American Medical Association,* 268 (1992): 746–748; *Journal of the American Medical Association,* 273 (1995): 775–776.
199. George W. Heard, "Man vs. Toothache," letter to C. A. Barden (June 12, 1956).
200. *New York State Dental Journal,* 36 (1970) 15–19; *Australian Dental Journal* 15 (1970): 126–132.
201. New York State Bureau of Dental Health and the U.S. Public Health Service.
202. John Yiamouyiannis, Ph.D., *Fluoride: The Aging Factor* (Delaware, Ohio: Health Action Press, 1993).
203. Richard G. Foulkes, "Celebration or Shame? Fifty Years of Fluoridation," *Townsend Letter for Doctors and Patients* (Nov. 1995).

204. Dr. Randall Neustaedter, *The Immunization Decision* (Berkeley, Calif.: North Atlantic Books, 1990).

205. *American Academy of Pediatrics, 1994 Red Book.*

206. Robert Mendelsohn, *Confessions of a Medical Heretic,* 143.

207. C. C. C. Christie, et al, "The 1993 Epidemic of Pertussis in Cincinnati," *New England Journal of Medicine* 331 (1994): 16–21.

208. Ian Sinclair, *Health: The Only Immunity* (Ryde, New South Wales, Australia: Ian Sinclair, Publisher, 1995).

209. Archie Kalokerinos, M.D., *Every Second Child* (New Canaan, Conn.: Keats Publishing, 1981).

210. Viera Scheibner, Ph.D., *Vaccination* (Maryborough, Australia: Australian Print Group, 1993).

211. Randall Neustaedter, *The Immunization Decision.*

212. American Academy of Pediatrics, *1994 Red Book.*

213. M. J. Marsh and I. A. Murdoch, "Acute Epiglottitis after Hib Vaccination," *Lancet* 344 (1994).

214. T. Osterholm, "Lack of Efficacy of Haemophilus b Vaccine in Minnesota," *Journal of the American Medical Association* 260 (1988): 1423–1428.

215. J. B. Milstien, et al, "Adverse Reactions Following Haemophilus influenzae type b Vaccine," *Pediatrics* 80 (1987): 270–274.

216. Moskowitz, "The Case Against Immunizations," *Journal of American Institutional Homeopathy* 76 (1983): 7–25.

217. L. Levy, "The Future of Measles in Highly Immunized Populations," *American Journal of Epidemiology* 120 no. 1 (July 1984): 39–48.

218. *The Vaccine Reaction,* newsletter by the National Vaccine Information Center, Vienna, Va., Barbara Loe Fisher, editor.

219. R. Neustaedter, *The Immunization Decision.*

220. Harold Buttram, M.D., and John Chriss Hoffman, *Vaccinations and Immune Malfunction* (Quakertown, Penn.:Humanitarian Publishing Co, 1982).

221. M. Eibl, et al, "Abnormal T-lymphocyte Subpopulations in Healthy Subjects after Tetanus Booster Immunization," *New England Journal of Medicine* 310 (3) (Jan. 19, 1984): 198–199.

222. National Institute of Health, *News from National Institute of Allergy and Infectious Disease* (Feb. 5, 1993).

223. Cindy Goldenberg, "The Goldenberg Family," *Belonging Magazine* (Caremark, Therapeutic Services Division, Redlands, Calif., 1995).

224. M. R. Odent, E. E. Culpin, and T. Kimmel, "Pertussis Vaccination and Asthma: Is There a Link?" Primal Health Research Centre, London, *Journal of the American Medical Association* 272 (8)(1994): 592–593.

225. Harold L. Coulter, Ph.D., *Vaccination, Social Violence, and Criminality* (Berkeley, Calif.: North Atlantic Books, 1990).

226. Harry Clarke, "Join the Army; Join the Jabbed," *International Vaccination Newsletter* (Belgium, 1995).

227. Bruce West, D.C., *Health Alert Newsletter* 12 no. 9.

228. Author unknown, "Long-Term Effects of Exposure to Low Doses of Lead in Childhood," *New England Journal of Medicine* (Jan. 1990).

229. Physicians for Social Responsibility, 1101 Fourteenth Street NW, Suite 700, Washington D.C. (1995).

230. Physicians for Social Responsibility, *Pesticides and Children* (1995).

231. H. L. Needleman, M.D., and Philip Landrigan, M.D., *Raising Children Toxic Free* (New York: Farrar, Straus, and Giroux, 1994).

232. National Research Council and National Academy of Sciences, *Pesticides in Diets of Infants and Children* (Washington, D.C.: National Academy Press, 1993); 800/624-6242.

233. Syd Baumel, *Dealing with Depression Naturally* (New Canaan, Conn.: Keats Publishing, 1995).

234. Kathleen Rodgers, Ph.D., and Dolph Ellefson, "Mechanism of the Modulation of Murine Peritoneal Cell Function," *Agents Action* 35 (1992): 57–63.

235. Ibid.

236. Acres, USA, P.O. Box 8800, Metairie, La 70011-8800.

237. J. Gordon Millichap, M.D., *Is Our Water Safe To Drink?* (Chicago: PNB Publishers, 1995).

238. *NOHA News,* Nutrition for Optimal Health Association newsletter (Winnetka, Ill.: Summer 1995).

239. NaturalCeuticals, Inc; product name: Procyanidol; 800/488-2840.

240. *Bio-Probe Newsletter,* 5508 Edgewater Dr., Orlando, Fla. (Sept 1995).

241. Ibid.

242. S. Soderstom, et al, "The Effect of Mercury Vapour on Cholinergic Neurons in the Fetal Brain," *Brain Res Dev Brain Res,* 85 (1) (Mar. 1995): 96–108.

243. G. Drasch, et al, "Mercury Burden of Human Fetal and Infant Tissues," *European Journal of Pediatrics* 153 (8) (1994): 607–610.

244. Christer Malmstrom, D.D.S., et al, "Amalgam-derived Mercury in Feces," conference on Trace Elements in Health and Disease, Stockholm, May 25–29, 1992.

245. P. Hultman, et al, "Adverse Immunological Effects and Autoimmunity Induced by Dental Amalgam and Alloy in Mice," *FASEB J,* 8 (1994): 1183–1190.

246. David W. Eggleston, D.D.S., "Effect of Dental Amalgam and Nickel Alloys on T-lymphocytes," *Journal of Prosthetic Dentistry* (1992): 617.

247. Anne Summers, et al, *APUA Newsletter* (Fall 1991).

248. Robert Mendelsohn, *Confessions of a Medical Heretic,* 58.

249. Florence Scott, R.N., Director, Northwest Neurodevelopmental Training Center, 152 Arthur St., Woodburn, Oreg., 97071, personal communication.

250. Svea Gold, personal communication.

251. S. A. Raver, "The Effects of Vestibular Stimulation on Retarded Toddlers," *Child Study Journal* 10 (1980): 77–86.

252. Svea Gold, personal communication.

253. Jeffery S. Bland, Ph.D., "A Functional Approach to Mental Illness," *Townsend Letter for Doctors and Patients* (Dec. 1994).

254. Korsak and Sato, "Effects of Chronic Organophosphate Pesticide Exposure on the Central Nervous System," *Clinical Toxicology* 11 no. 1 (1977): 83–95.

255. Savage, et al, "Chronic Neurological Sequelae of Acute Organophosphate Pesticide Poisoning," *Arch of Environ Health* 43 no.1 (1988): 38–45.

256. Neal Barnard, M.D., *Eat Right, Live Longer* (New York: Harmony Books, 1995).

257. Earl Mindell, R.Ph., Ph.D., *Live Longer and Feel Better with Vitamins and Minerals* (New Canaan, Conn.: Keats Publishing, 1994).

258. Karin Nelson, et al, "Drugs May Help Curb Some Cases of Cerebral Palsy," *Pediatrics* (Feb. 9, 1995).

259. Thomas Armstrong, Ph.D., *The Myth of the A.D.D. Child* (New York: Dutton, 1995).

260. Svea Gold, personal communication.

261. Randi Hagerman, M.D., and Alice R. Falkenstein, M.A., M.S.W., "An Association Between Recurrent Otitis Media in Infancy and Later Hyperactivity," *Clinical Pediatrics* 26 no.5 (May 1987).

262. Carolyn Dean, M.D., *Homeopathic Remedies for Children's Common Ailments* (New Canaan, Conn.: Keats Publishing, 1994).

263. The Developmental Delay Registry, Silver Springs, Md., newsletter (Feb. 1996).

264. P. N. F. Faulkner, B.D., B.Sc., *The Detection of Neurophysiological Factors in Children with Reading Problems,* monograph, 23 Poplars Rd., Buckingham, England.

265. Viola Frymann, D.O., "Learning Difficulties of Children Viewed in the Light of the Osteopathic Concept," *JAOA,* 76 (Sept. 1976).

266. Svea Gold, *When Children Invite Child Abuse.*

267. Lendon Smith, M.D., *Hyper Kids: A Workbook for Parents and Teachers* (Santa Monica, Calif.: Shaw/Spelling Books, 1990).

268. David Benton and Gwilym Roberts, "The Effect of Vitamin and Mineral Supplementation on Intelligence of a Sample of Schoolchildren," *Lancet* (Jan. 23, 1988).

269. John Upledger, D.O., O.M.M., *Your Inner Physician and You* (Berkeley, Calif.: North Atlantic Books 1991).

270. R. W. Thatcher, *Archives of Environmental Health* 37 no. 3.
271. Moon, et al, *Journal of Learning Disabilities* 18, no.4 (1985).
272. Airey, *Environmental Health Perspectives* 51 (1983): 303–316.
273. Sally Goddard, *Reflexes: The Basics of Education.*
274. Lendon Smith M.D., *Feed Your Body Right.*
275. Richard Konkol, M.D., *Pediatric Medicine* (Baltimore: Williams and Wilkins Co., 1994).
276. Natelson, et al, *Clinical Chemistry* 25 (6) (1979): 889–897.
277. E. W. J. Mackay and H. J. Barbash, *Ment Sci,* 72 (1931): 83–85.
278. Carl Pfeiffer, M.D., Ph.D., *Mental and Elemental Nutrients* (New Canaan, Conn.: Keats Publishing): 278.
279. *Bull. Environ. Contain Toxicol,* 26 (4) (1981): 400–471.
280. Charlie Foundation, 1223 Wilshire Blvd., Santa Monica, Calif.
281. Roberto Ruggiero, *The Do's and Don'ts of Low Blood Sugar* (Hollywood, Fla.: Lifetime Books, 1993).
282. Jane Brody, "Kids Really Do Get a Sugar Buzz," *Seattle Post-Intelligencer* (Mar. 15, 1995).
283. Jean Callahan, *New Age Journal* (May–June 1994).
284. Donald E. Greydanus, M.D., and Helen D. Pratt, Ph.D., *Emotional and Behavioral Disorders of Adolescence,* Adolescent Health Update, Amer Acad Peds, 8: no. 1, September 1995.
285. Greg Jantz, Ph.D., *Hope, Help, and Healing for Eating Disorders* (Wheaton, Ill.: Harold Shaw Publishers, 1995).
286. Janet Aiken, Ph.D., *Your Health,* newsletter of the International Academy of Nutrition and Preventive Medicine, 1994.
287. Francis Pottenger, *Pottenger's Cats.*
288. Pamela Taulbee, "Solving the Mystery of Anxiety," *Science News* (July 16, 1983): 45.
289. Dr. Herbert Benon, "Stress: Can We Cope," *Time* (June 6, 1983): 48.
290. Melvyn Werbach, M.D., *Nutritional Influences on Mental Illness* (Tarzana, Calif.: Third Line Press, 1991).
291. Carolyn Dean, M.D., *Homeopathic Remedies.*
292. Lendon H. Smith, M.D., *Feed Your Body Right.*
293. Dr. William Shaw, American Autism Society annual conference, July 1995.
294. Dick Thom, N.D., D.D.S., personal communication.
295. J. Greenberg, "Suicide Linked to Brain Chemical Deficit," *Science News,* Washington, D.C. (May 29, 1982): 355.
296. Author unknown, "Therapy for Depression," *Communication in Psychopharmacology* 2 no. 4 (1978).
297. Author unkown, "Treatment of Depression," *Modern Pharmacology-Toxicology* (1978).
298. Alan Gelenberg, M.D., "Tyrosine in Depression," *Lancet* (Aug. 1980): 364.
299. M. W. Carney,et al, "Red Cell Folate Concentrations in Psychiatric Patients," *Journal of Affective Disorders* 19 (3) (July 1990): 217-223.
300. Dr. Thomas Stone, personal communication.
301. G. Harrer, and H. Sommer, "Treatment of Mild/Moderate Depressions with Hypericum," *Phytomedicine* 1 (1994): 3–8.
302. Rudolf Wiley, Ph.D., *BioBalancing* (Tacoma, Wash: Life Sciences Press, 1988).
303. William Rea, M.D., "Sensitivities: The Twentieth Century Disease," *Total Health* (Dec. 1986).
304. *Bio-Probe* newsletter (May 1994).
305. Gruskay, *Clinical Pediatrics* 21 (Aug 1982): 486
306. Yaychuk-Arabei, Ph.D., "Enjoying Summer–Allergy-Free," *Health Naturally Magazine* (June–July 1995).
307. Harold E. Bertram, M.D., "Children and Toxic Chemicals," *Townsend Letter for Doctors and Patients* (Apr. 1993).
308. Robert Phalem, *Profiles in Environmental Health* 1 (Nov.–Dec. 1989).
309. *Archives of Pediatric and Adolescent Medicine* (July 1995).
310. H. S. Kaufman and O. L. Frick, "Prevention of Asthma," *Clinical Allerg,* 11 (1981): 549.
311. Alan R. Gaby, M.D., *Magnesium and B$_6$: The Natural Healer* (New Canaan, Conn.: Keats Publishing, 1993).

312. Melvyn R. Werbach, M.D., "Bronchial Asthma," *Townsend Letter for Doctors and Patients* (Aug.–Sept. 1993).
313. G. E. Hatch, "Asthma, Inhaled Oxidants, and Dietary Antioxidants," *American Journal of Clinical Nutrition* 61 suppl. (1995): 625S–630S.
314. R. E. Kaufman, "Effect of Vitamin B_{12} in Asthma," *Annals Allergy* 9 (1951): 517.
315. Bernard S. Zussman, M.D., *Health Beat* (Mar.–Apr. 1992).
316. Maesimund Panos, M.D., and Jane Heimlich, *Homeopathic Medicine at Home* (Los Angeles, Calif.: J. P. Tarcher, 1980).
317. William C. Deamer, M.D., "Recurrent Abdominal Pain," *CMD* (Feb. 1973).
318. Dick Thom, D.D.S., N.D., *Surviving the Nineties; Coping with Food Intolerances* (Portland, Oregon: Better Impressions Publisher, 1991).
319. Elaine Gottschall, B.A., M.Sc., "Digestion and Schizophrenia," *Nutrition and Mental Health* newsletter of the Canadian Schizophrenia Foundation (Summer 1994).
320. Sherry A. Rogers, M.D., "The Leaky Gut Syndrome," *Townsend Letter for Doctors and Patients* (Feb.–Mar. 1995).
321. Sherry A. Rogers, M.D., *Wellness Against All Odds* (Syracuse, N.Y.: Prestige Publishing, 1995).
322. Anthony Cichoke, D.C., *Enzymes and Enzyme Therapy.*
323. J. Egger, et al, "Is Migraine a Food Allergy?" *Lancet* (1983): 865–869.
324. *Postgraduate Medicine,* 75 no. 4 (1984): 221.
325. Dick Thom, N.D., D.D.S., personal communication.
326. Steven Davis, D.C., personal communication.
327. Troussier, et al, "Back Pain in School Children," *Scandinavian Journal of Rehabilitative Medicine* 26 (1994): 143–146
328. Steven Davis, D.C., personal communication.
329. Lendon Smith, M.D., *Feed Your Body Right.*
330. Dick Thom, N.D., D.D.S., personal communication.
331. Steven Davis, D.C., personal communication.
332. Arthur Ennis, M.D., *Modern Medicine* (Feb. 1976).
333. Larry L. Webster, D.C., "Children and Contact Sports," *ICA International Rev. of Chiro* (Mar.–Apr. 1990).
334. Anthony Cichoke, D.C., *Enzymes and Enzyme Therapy.*
335. Nobuhisa Baba, M.D., et al, "Possible Role of the Brain Stem in Sudden Infant Death Syndrome," *Journal of the American Medical Association,* 249 no. 20 (May 27, 1983): 2789.
336. Brad D. Banks, B.H.K., et al, "Sudden Infant Death Syndrome: A Literature Review with Chiropractic Implications," *J Manip & Physiol Therap* 10 no. 5 (Oct. 1987): 246–252.
337. M. M. Suzman, et al, "Long-Term Mortality of Cardiovascular Diseases in Middle-aged Men," *Journal of the American Medical Association* 266 (1973): 1225-1229.
338. Leslie N. Johnston, D.V.M., "SIDS and Iron Overload," *Townsend Letter for Doctors and Patients* (July 1994).
339. Viera Scheibner, Ph.D., *Vaccination.*
340. N. Toblitz, "A Possible Explanation for Sudden Infant Death Syndrome," *Our Toxic Times,* University of Oregon (Jan. 1995).
341. Derrick Lonsdale, M.D. (Stopping Crib Death,) letters to the editor, *Townsend Letter for Doctors and Patients* (Feb.–Mar. 1995).
342. G. Drasch, et al, "Mercury Burden of Human Fetal and Infant Tissues," *Pediatrics* 153 (8) (Aug. 1994): 607-610.
343. Marshall Mandell, M.D., *Five-Day Allergy Relief System* (New York: Pocket Books, 1979).
344. E. Cheraskin, *Diet and Disease,* 332.
345. E. Cheraskin, *Diet and Disease,* 315.
346. Anthony Cichoke, D.C., *Enzymes and Enzyme Therapy.*
347. Hennepin County Medical Center newsletter, Minneapolis, Minn., Spring 1995.

Index

abdominal pain. *See* pain, abdominal
abrasions, 334–335
   See also cuts
abscesses, 312
absence seizures (petit mal), 256
accident proneness, 132–133
accidents, 333–334
   See also drowning *and* first aid
acid/base balance, 177–178
acne, 312–314
ADD (attention deficit disorder), 27, 243–249
adenoidectomy, 219–220
adopted babies, breast-feeding, 47–48
   See also newborns
aggressive reactions, 263
alcohol, during pregnancy, 8
alcoholism, toddlers and, 131
allergies, 56–57, 154, 277–296
   antibodies and, 294
   antigens and, 294
   arthritis, allergic, 309
   asthma, 281–286
   atopy and, 294
   behavior problems and, 291
   cold hives, 290
   crying babies and, 56–57
   definition of, 277–278
   delayed hypersensitivity and, 294
   desensitization and, 294
   eczema, 65, 286–289
   fevers and, 154

allergies (continued):
   food allergies, 290–294
   gastrointestinal allergies, 292–293
   geography tongue and, 294
   hay fever (allergic rhinitis), 289
   hives or welts, 289–290
   hypersensitivity and, 295
   leaky gut syndrome, 295–296
   overview of, 277–281
   solar hives, 290
   tension-fatigue syndrome, 291–292
   See also skin diseases
alopecia, 318
amalgam fillings, 216–218, 325, 352
amino acids, 86–87
ammoniacal diaper, 314
anal fissure, 56
anal ring, 35
anemia, 65, 66
ankle injuries, 309, 335
anorexia nervosa, 80–81, 131, 264–265
antibiotics
   during pregnancy, 6
   fevers, infections and, 153, 178–179, 183
   parasites and, 273
antibodies, 294
antigens, 294
antioxidants, 216
anus, itchy, 318–319
anxiety, 130, 265–268
aphthous ulcers, 315

377